E

OAXACA

FIRST EDITION

Oaxaca

Great Destinations Mexico

Paige R. Penland

The Countryman Press
Woodstock, Vermont

ISBN 978-1-58157-102-8

Cover photo by the author
Interior photographs by the author unless otherwise specified
Maps by Moore Creative Designs, © The Countryman Press
Book design by Bodenweber Design
Composition by PerfecType, Nashville, TN

Published by The Countryman Press, P.O. Box 748, Woodstock, VT 05091
Distributed by W. W. Norton & Company, Inc., 500 Fifth Avenue, New York, NY 10110
Printed in the United States of America

10 9 8 7 6 5 4 3 2 1

GREAT DESTINATIONS TRAVEL GUIDEBOOK SERIES

Recommended by *National Geographic Traveler* and *Travel + Leisure* magazines

A crisp and critical approach, for travelers who want to live like locals.
—*USA Today*

Great Destinations™ guidebooks are known for their comprehensive, critical coverage of regions of extraordinary cultural interest and natural beauty. Each title in this series is continuously updated with each printing to ensure accurate and timely information. All the books contain more than one hundred photographs and maps.

Current titles available:

THE ADIRONDACK BOOK

THE ALASKA PANHANDLE

ATLANTA

AUSTIN, SAN ANTONIO & THE TEXAS HILL COUNTRY

BALTIMORE, ANNAPOLIS & THE CHESAPEAKE BAY

THE BERKSHIRE BOOK

BIG SUR, MONTEREY BAY
  & GOLD COAST WINE COUNTRY

CAPE CANAVERAL, COCOA BEACH
& FLORIDA'S SPACE COAST

THE CHARLESTON, SAVANNAH
  & COASTAL ISLANDS BOOK

THE COAST OF MAINE BOOK

COLORADO'S CLASSIC MOUNTAIN TOWNS

COSTA RICA

DOMINICAN REPUBLIC

THE ERIE CANAL

THE FINGER LAKES BOOK

THE FOUR CORNERS REGION

GALVESTON, SOUTH PADRE ISLAND
  & THE TEXAS GULF COAST

GLACIER NATIONAL PARK & THE CANADIAN ROCKIES

GUATEMALA

THE HAMPTONS BOOK

HAWAII'S BIG ISLAND

HONOLULU & OAHU

THE JERSEY SHORE: ATLANTIC CITY TO CAPE MAY

KAUAI

LAKE TAHOE & RENO

LAS VEGAS

LOS CABOS & BAJA CALIFORNIA SUR

MAUI

MEMPHIS AND THE DELTA BLUES TRAIL

MEXICO CITY, PUEBLA & CUERNAVACA

MICHIGAN'S UPPER PENINSULA

MONTREAL & QUEBEC CITY

THE NANTUCKET BOOK

THE NAPA & SONOMA BOOK

NORTH CAROLINA'S OUTER BANKS
  & THE CRYSTAL COAST

NOVA SCOTIA & PRINCE EDWARD ISLAND

OAXACA

OREGON WINE COUNTRY

PALM BEACH, FORT LAUDERDALE, MIAMI
  & THE FLORIDA KEYS

PALM SPRINGS & DESERT RESORTS

PHILADELPHIA, BRANDYWINE VALLEY
  & BUCKS COUNTY

PHOENIX, SCOTTSDALE, SEDONA
  & CENTRAL ARIZONA

PLAYA DEL CARMEN, TULUM & THE RIVIERA MAYA

SALT LAKE CITY, PARK CITY, PROVO
  & UTAH'S HIGH COUNTRY RESORTS

SAN DIEGO & TIJUANA

SAN JUAN, VIEQUES & CULEBRA

SAN MIGUEL DE ALLENDE & GUANAJUATO

THE SANTA FE & TAOS BOOK

SANTA BARBARA AND CALIFORNIA'S CENTRAL COAST

THE SARASOTA, SANIBEL ISLAND & NAPLES BOOK

THE SEATTLE & VANCOUVER BOOK

THE SHENANDOAH VALLEY BOOK

TOURING EAST COAST WINE COUNTRY

TUCSON

VIRGINIA BEACH, RICHMOND
  & TIDEWATER VIRGINIA

WASHINGTON, D.C., AND NORTHERN VIRGINIA

YELLOWSTONE & GRAND TETON NATIONAL PARKS
  & JACKSON HOLE

YOSEMITE & THE SOUTHERN SIERRA NEVADA

The authors in this series are professional travel writers who have lived for many years in the regions they describe. Honest and painstakingly critical, full of information only a local can provide, Great Destinations guidebooks give you all the practical knowledge you need to enjoy the best of each region.

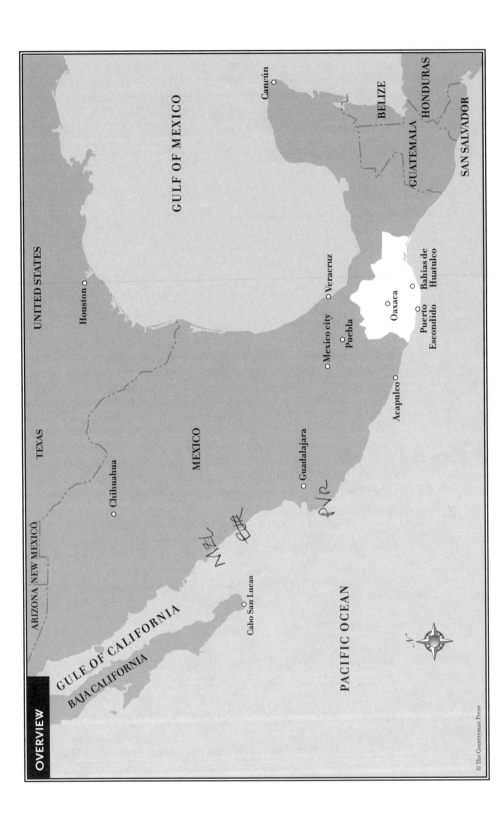

OVERVIEW

UNITED STATES

ARIZONA NEW MEXICO

TEXAS

GULF OF MEXICO

Houston

Chihuahua

Cancún

BELIZE

GUATEMALA

HONDURAS

SAN SALVADOR

Veracruz

Mexico city

Puebla

Oaxaca

Bahias de
Huatulco

Puerto
Escondido

Acapulco

MEXICO

Guadalajara

GULF OF CALIFORNIA

BAJA CALIFORNIA

Cabo San Lucas

PACIFIC OCEAN

© The Countryman Press

Contents

ACKNOWLEDGMENTS

First, and as always, this book would not have been possible without the support of my family, in particular my mom/agent, Wanda Olson, and my sister Beth Penland, who contributed the María Sabina and mole sidebars, and who seriously helped with editing—you two are the best. Thanks also to Kim Grant, Lisa Sacks, Kermit Hummel, Lucia Huntington, and everyone at Countryman Press; quite literally, this book wouldn't have been possible without you. And a heartfelt thanks goes out to everyone in Oaxaca who gave me a hand along the way, including (but by no means limited to) Armando, Ann, the Huatulco Tourism Office, the Association of Hotels and Motels in Oaxaca City, Jasibe, María, Ramon, Ricardo, Rick and Janet, and Saúl—*muchisimas gracias*. And a great big thanks to Maggie Gould, wherever you are, for convincing me to eat those *chapulines* when we were here the first time . . . when was that? In 1993? Which I assume means that I'll see you on the Zócalo one of these days.

Monte Alban 124

Introduction

Three sun-drenched valleys, stretched long and languid through the pine-forested mountains in fields of maize, *maguey,* and marigolds, converge upon an ancient city hewn of pale green *cantera* stone. This is Ciudad Oaxaca, the Antequera Verde, a luminous oasis of art, music, culture, and cuisine rising to intricately carved towers erected centuries ago by Spaniards who called themselves *conquistadors.*

But the tales this land has to tell stretch back centuries beyond, into the fierce polychrome deserts of the Mixteca, cloud-forested peaks of La Cañada, humid rainforests of the Papaloapan, and to the sapphire-blue Pacific, edged in endless sandy beaches and rocky, protected bays. From these myriad landscapes rise stone buildings all but lost to time—pyramids, ball courts, marketplaces, and palaces—massive cities bearing enigmatic testament to the genius of their builders. And their descendants remain, still speaking the hushed tongues of those forgotten architects: Zapotec, Mixtec, and many more. Through the centuries they have retained their rituals and arts, their political structures and commitment to community, all that brought a people to greatness in millennia past—and present. It was Oaxaca's pure Zapotec son Benito Juárez who as president delivered Mexico from dictatorship and occupation into this independent future.

And it is beautiful here, in the green and gold cradle of these great civilizations and modern wonders, where ritual and craft remain intimately connected. The delicate embroidery of a gauzy hand-woven *huipil,* or the raised ceramic relief on a pit-fired bowl; all are intricately interwoven with the insights and awareness of artisans caught between these different worlds.

So take a seat on the Zócalo, the paved central plaza at the heart of it all, and contemplate for a moment where your personal journey through these lands might take you. Drink in the colors of the indigenous costumes and crafts, the grace of the cathedral and its attendant architectural marvels, the complex flavors of your rich *mole negro,* carefully conjured from dozens of different ingredients, lovingly prepared over days or weeks.

What was it, exactly, that brought you here, to this wondrous place in the sun? Do you remember? A desire to dive into the brilliant blue waters of a palm-fringed artesian well? Or climb the massive staircase into the infinite heavens arcing over the pyramids of Monte Albán? Perhaps slide through the Mexican Pipeline at Playa Zicatela, one of the world's best beach breaks; or belly up to the bar in Bahías de Huatulco, Oaxaca's ecologically sound answer to Acapulco? Or was it something deeper?

Some say that this land called to them, across the desert and the sea; they could not resist. Many come, and many stay, relaxing into the embrace of a city that loves its cosmopolitan, international swirl. They are woven, with magic, into its fabric, intricate and intimate, rich as fresh-ground chocolate and light as a dancer's lace-trimmed skirt.

THE WAY THIS BOOK WORKS

Organization

This book covers the entire State of Oaxaca, at 95,364 square kilometers (36,820 square miles), about the same size as Portugal or the U.S. state of Indiana. It is located in tropical Southern Mexico, and bordered by the states of Guerrero (home to Acapulco) to the west; Puebla and Veracruz to the north; Chiapas to the west; and the Pacific Ocean to the south.

Oaxaca City is both the state capital and its cultural, economic, and transportation hub, conveniently located at the center of the state. The **Central Valleys**, a fertile triad of valleys extending north, east, and southwest of the city, are home to the region's most impressive archaeological sites, churches, and handicrafts villages, most within an hour of the capital.

Stretching some 600 sunny kilometers (375 scenic miles) along Oaxaca's southern shore is the **Pacific Coast**, usually divided into three culturally distinct areas. Clockwise from the eastern border, the Isthmus of Tehuantepec is home to the fascinating indigenous cities of Tehuantepec and Juchitán, as well as the important port city of Salina Cruz. *La Costa,* sometimes called the "Oaxacan Riviera" by tourism professionals, stretches between the state's three major resort areas—Huatulco, the Puerto Ángel beaches, and Puerto Escondido, all offering an abundance of hotels, restaurants, tours, and activities. To the west, the Mixtec Coast and its fascinating cultural mix is centered on Pinotepa Nacional, not particularly well developed for tourism.

The cloud forests, deserts, pine-covered mountains, and rainforested lowlands of **Northern Oaxaca** are also often divided into smaller areas. The Mixteca stretches, arid and awe-inspiring, to the northwest; cloud-forested La Cañada is draped across the high mountains directly north of Oaxaca City; followed by the rolling, humid tropical lowlands of the Papaloapan River Valley, and the chilly pine mountains of the Sierra Juárez.

The **History** and **Culture** chapters aim to introduce you to the many wonders of Oaxaca, setting the stage for your destination. The **Cuisine** and **Shopping** chapters let you explore those favorite Oaxacan pastimes in detail. The **Transportation** and **Planning** chapters contain the nitty-gritty you need to polish a smooth vacation.

Indices at the back of the book provide easy access to information. The first, a standard index, lists entries and subjects in alphabetical order. Next, hotels, B&Bs, and ecotourism projects are categorized by price. Restaurants are indexed twice: once by price, once by type of cuisine.

Favorites

In addition to listing the finest hotels, B&Bs, and ecotourism projects, as well as the best restaurants and attractions, I've added a ✪ symbol next to places that are personal favorites.

Price Codes

Rather than give specific prices, this guide rates dining and lodging options within a range.

Cost of lodging is based on an average per-room, double-occupancy during peak season (July; November through mid-January), not including the mandatory 18 percent tax, which may be waived for cash payment. Rates are often reduced during low season (June, August through September), and can double during the Christmas and New Year's holidays, Día de los Muertos (October 20 to November 5), and particularly for the beaches, Semana Santa (the week before Easter). Make reservations in advance during holiday periods.

Meal prices are based on the cost of a dinner entrée with a nonalcoholic beverage, not including the usually voluntary (but check your receipt) 10–15 percent gratuity that should be added unless service is atrocious. The coding "B, L, C, D" refers to U.S.-style meals (breakfast, lunch, dinner), as well as the typical Mexican multi-course *comida*, traditionally the biggest meal of the day, served in lieu of lunch from about 2 AM to 6 PM and often a much better value than other meals. Prices are calculated at 10 pesos to the dollar.

	Lodging	Dining
Inexpensive ($)	Up to US$50	Up to US$5
Moderate ($$)	US$50 to US$100	US$5 to US$10
Expensive ($$$)	US$100 to US$200	$10 to $20
Very Expensive ($$$$)	US$200 and up	US$20 or more

Country and Area Codes

Mexico's country code is 52, and is followed by a three-digit area code and seven-digit phone number. Oaxaca State uses several area codes, including: Oaxaca City and the Central Valleys (951); Huatulco (958); Puerto Escondido (954); Huajuapan (953); and Tuxtepec (287).

History

Oaxaca has cradled one of the world's richest histories. The region's oldest continuously inhabited village, Teotitlán del Valle, was founded about the same time (8,000 years ago) as Eurasia's oldest permanent city: Jarmo, Iraq. Oaxaca's first major city-state, El Mogote, was building temples and trading throughout Mesoamerica at about the same time that Athens, Greece, was coming to power.

Oaxaca's Zapotec Indians developed the hemisphere's first true writing around 700 B.C., before the Romans founded their Republic and near the time Japan's first emperor was ascending to power. These Zapotecs leveled entire mountaintops for massive, planned cities such as Monte Albán—complete with sewage systems, sports stadiums, and earthquake-resistant architecture—about 300 years before the Chinese started on the Great Wall.

As Europe plunged into the Dark Ages, the Zapotec Empire was undergoing a technological "great leap forward," with improved tools and firing techniques. Ceramic pieces from this time depict nobility with distinctively slanted eyes, suggesting that Asian fleets might have landed in Oaxaca, bringing technical innovation with them.

Zapotec power began to fade with the arrival of the Mixtecs, just as the Moors began their conquest of the Iberian Peninsula. The Caliphate of Córdoba, Spain, was founded in 756 A.D.—almost exactly the time that Monte Albán was mysteriously abandoned.

New powers rose to the north of both cities. In Spain, Christian forces mounted a military resistance in the 900s, defeating the Muslims at the battle of Las Navas de Tolosa in 1212. A century earlier, in 1111, the Aztec tribe had abandoned their mysterious homeland of Aztlán (probably in the U.S. Southwest); some years later they founded their majestic new capital, Tenochtitlán, in the Mexican basin.

Both the Spanish Christians and Aztec Empire would continue to combine their respective military dominance and religious fervor to consolidate power. In Spain, it was called the Inquisition, and more than 250,000 people were killed, many burned alive in public, for worshipping the wrong God. In Mesoamerica, they called it the Triple Alliance, and cities that resisted, such as Yuhuitlán, Oaxaca, would watch helplessly as thousands of civilians were marched to the capital and publicly sacrificed for the crowds.

In 1450, the Aztec military arrived in Oaxaca, and though both the Zapotecs and Mixtecs resisted, only the Costa Mixteca would remain free. In 1486 the Aztecs set up a permanent garrison, Huaxyácac, on El Fortín above Oaxaca City, assuming absolute control. A world away, in Medellín, Spain, an infant boy, Hernán Cortés, was learning to crawl.

The 1492 "discovery" of the New World by explorer Christopher Columbus would bring these two worlds together.

Descend into the cool, dark tombs beneath Zaachila Archaeological Park, where frescos echo the dreams you may have had after snorkeling the Costa Mixteca.

In 1511, Cortés arrived in the Americas to seek his fortune. By 1519, he had begun his march on Tenochtitlán, presided over by Emperor Moctezuma. Through superior technology, sheer bravado, and allies among the Empire's unhappy and oppressed subjects (including the Zapotecs and Mixtecs of Oaxaca), Cortés conquered the Aztec Empire. He was awarded much of Oaxaca's heart, and the title "Marqués del Valle."

ARCHAEOLOGICAL OAXACA

There are at least 7,000 known archaeological sites in Oaxaca State, a handful of them easily accessible to visitors. Museums large and small hold priceless treasures found while excavating great cities, or plowing fields and paving roads.

Though both the Mixtecs and Zapotecs kept careful historical records in painted *codices,* or folding books with 50 or more pages, most were destroyed during the Spanish Occupation. Spain's own chroniclers, such as Toribio Motolinia (who wrote about Mitla in 1533), recorded observations of the indigenous Oaxacan lifestyle, while the crown's archaeologists, such as Guillermo Dupaix (1750–1817), were among the first to survey major sites. Mexican archaeologist Alfonso Caso (1896–1970), however, who uncovered Monte Albán's gold-laden Tomb Seven, discovered much of what we know about Oaxaca's unusual history.

NATURAL HISTORY

Oaxaca is the most geographically, ecologically, and linguistically varied region in Mexico. The state has a dozen different ecosystems ranging from arid desert and cloud forest to tropical lowland and coastal plain, at elevations from sea level to more than 3750 meters

Online Resources

Oaxaca is one of the most researched and documented spots on earth; this is just the tip of the iceberg.

Ancient Scripts (www.ancientscripts.com/ma_ws.html) Mesoamerican languages, including numbers and calendar dates, are explained.

Arqueología Mexicana (www.arqueomex.com) Beautiful, bimonthly, full-color archaeology magazine has English-language articles in pdf form; click under "Articulos en Linea." You can collect back issues at gift shops at Monte Albán and Santo Domingo.

Colonial Mexico (www.colonial-mexico.com) Author Richard D. Perry's Web site has photos and English-language articles about Colonial sites and discoveries, mostly in Southern Mexico.

Hernán Cortés Page (www.motecuhzoma.de/start-es.html) Everything you always wanted to know about the Marqués del Valle, in Spanish and German.

Mexican History.org (www.mexicanhistory.org) English-language articles and photos on Mexican history, including Oaxacan subjects such as the Zapotecs and Benito Juárez.

National Institute of Anthropology and History (www.inah.gob.mx) Spanish-language information about the archaeological sites, churches, and museums of Mexico.

(12,300 feet). Early populations were separated by broad rivers and deep canyons, isolating pockets of culture where art, music, and myth could thrive.

The diversity of climates was a boon to the hunter-gatherers who first made semipermanent camp in the frost-free flood plains of the Central Valley. The mountains were riddled with caves as well, used for shelter, burials, and even painting by this artsy Paleolithic crowd.

The most famous of these include Ejutla Cave, south of Ocotlán, with several tombs; Blade Cave, in the cloud forest of Huautla, with scores of obsidian and chert tools; and nearby Tenango Cave, with ornate ceramics and gold jewelry. But the most valuable treasure was discovered in a cave close to Mitla, Guilá Naquitz: domesticated gourds and three charred ears of *teosinte*, the probable ancestor of corn, dating to 5400 B.C., centuries before any other examples of Mexican cuisine's most important ingredient.

SOCIAL HISTORY

The Original Oaxaqueños

The first Oaxacans arrived around 12,000 years ago, hunting with fluted stone points similar to those found in Clovis, New Mexico. Though almost all of Oaxaca's indigenous groups know the story of their arrival, the Zapotecs tell no such tale. They emerged directly from the caves and trees, and call themselves Be'ena'a, "People of the Place."

These early Oaxacans, wherever they originated, developed tongs for harvesting cactus, traps for small animals, and stone grinders to remove the hard outer shell of *teosinte*. By 4500 B.C., they had cultivated the Central Valleys with amaranth, avocado, black beans, cacao, tomatoes, chiles, and *maguey*, a type of agave that the Spanish would turn into mezcal, but then more important as a source of sugar and protein, as well as needle and thread.

Huaxyácac (acacia) trees, like this beauty at the Jardín Etnóbotanico, were once so highly valued for their edible seeds and other assets that they inspired the name of many places, including Oaxaca.

As agricultural families began out-producing hunter-gatherers, farmers erected thatched-roof adobe shelters and began living in communities of three to 10 extended families, with loose patriarchal governments. As these villages grew, people began wearing fiber loincloths and skirts, elaborate jewelry and hairstyles, and sandals. They traded with Veracruz, Teotihuacán, and even Guatemala; they created ceremonies to mark the harvest, family events, and even death, placing a green stone in the mouths of loved ones. Around 1500 B.C., Oaxaca's first city-state, with pyramids, emerged: El Mogote, or "Hill of Trees."

Rise of El Mogote and the Great Trading Routes

Agriculture meant more free time, and more specialization within society. A ruling class developed, perhaps concurrently with a religious elite, which managed community resources. The market economy focused on El Mogote, hosting traders from all over Oaxaca and Mesoamerica.

Little is known about this era. Though there were at least a dozen distinct groups inhabiting Oaxaca, only the Zapotecs and Mixtecs became powerbrokers and dominant cultures in the state. Both peoples adopted expansionist attitudes, becoming great builders. The Zapotecs had a firm grasp of math, astronomy, and architecture, and built irrigation channels in their fields. They maintained communications and trade with the three major cities of the Mixteca: Cerro de las Minas, Cerro Pachón, and Tequixtepec, all of which had writing, pyramids, and social stratification. The major populations on the coast, including Tututepec, Pochutla, and Huatulco, were still small fishing villages at this time, but there was clearly trade with the rest of the state.

The Olmecs (1400–400 B.C.) were an important presence in Oaxaca by 1100 B.C., apparently importing the region's jewelry, textiles, and ceramics from El Mogote to the rest of their empire. In return, they introduced Oaxaca to corn tortillas and ceramic *comales,* among other new trade items.

Around 500 B.C., an ambitious group of city planners and architects, apparently exiled from El Mogote after a political coup, arrived atop a hill. The hill overlooked the axis of Oaxaca's three great Central Valleys, and had easy access to spring water and raw materials including timber, chert, clay, and limestone for preparing corn. The newcomers leveled the mountaintop and built earthquake-resistant stone foundations, then erected precisely aligned temples, ball courts, pyramids, and observatories in harmony with the seasons and stars.

Monte Albán Period

From 500 B.C. to around 750 A.D., Monte Albán was Oaxaca's political, economic, and cultural center, with a massive stone market, huge *cantera* pyramids, and an expansive central plaza that hosted Zapotecs and their guests from all over the Americas. The ball court was one of Oaxaca's finest, inspiring the construction of dozens of others all over the state.

The city eventually spanned 7 square kilometers (3 square miles), with some 25,000 inhabitants. Though political tension existed with other ethnic groups, the region was better known for its artisanship than military might. Oaxacan ceramics, *codices*, paintings, carvings, copper axes, woven cotton cloth, and cast-gold jewelry became popular all over Mesoamerica.

As their cultural influence grew, the Zapotecs discarded Olmec religious symbols—bats, snakes, alligators, and jaguars, often depicted as partially human—and created their own iconography: conch shells, flowers, birds, stars, planets, insects, and skulls.

Monte Albán, the ancient capital of the Zapotec Empire, remains architecturally impressive more than two millennia later.

By 200 A.D., smaller cities were springing up in the Central Valleys, including Yagül, Zaachila, and Dainzú. But when Monte Albán was abandoned, around 750 A.D., the political landscape changed. The valley towns seemed to thrive, merely switching allegiances to the Mixtec capital of Mitla. But in the mountains of the Mixteca Alta, things were thrown into chaos.

Only after Emperor Eight Deer Jaguar Claw consolidated the Alta, Baja, and Coastal Mixteca in the War of the Heavens would peace reign again over the Mixtec homeland. The situation would remain relatively stable for centuries—until 1458, when the Aztec armies arrived.

Despite local resistance, the Aztecs soon controlled the Mixteca and Central Valleys, and by the 1480s they had established a permanent garrison atop Huaxyácac Hill, across from Monte Albán. From this privileged position, they controlled local trade routes and populations, oppressively. Their presence was reviled, and when word came that a new and exotic military force had arrived to fight the Aztec occupiers, Zapotec leaders sent a delegation to seek an alliance with the new force.

Cortés accepted. On November 25, 1521, the Spanish arrived in the Central Valleys, and took control of the area.

Spanish Occupation

Enjoying his accolades after defeating Moctezuma, the last emperor of the Aztec Empire, Cortés retired to Oaxaca's Central Valleys, accompanied by the Spanish military and a contingent of Catholic priests from the Dominican Order—the same order that had spawned Grand Inquisitor Tomás de Torquemada, the great villain of the Spanish Inquisition.

The Dominicans would often entirely dismantle ancient pyramids to build their enormous churches. Sometimes, however, they cut a few corners.

In their centuries of war against the Muslims and Jews, the Spanish had learned that killing men changes little if their sacred texts survive. Oaxaqueños, like most Mesoamericans, carefully kept elaborate *codices,* maintained by special scribes. Though these were more history books than religious works, the Spanish methodically collected and burned all they could find. Only eight from Oaxaca, known as the Mixtec Codices, survived.

The Spanish kept obsessive records of indigenous life, however, and detailed maps called *lienzos,* which are invaluable to today's archaeologists. They also introduced novel concepts that rocked the very foundation of indigenous society, such as private land ownership, sexual sin, and a fear of bathing. Though much of Mexico suffered under Spanish rule, the Zapotecs and Mixtecs, thanks to their early alliance, enjoyed a bit more autonomy and equality (and cleanliness) within the new empire.

According to Spanish chroniclers, these early years went well, and locals apparently appreciated the wealth of new agricultural techniques and crops, particularly wheat; domesticated animals including horses, burros, chickens, and sheep; and improved technology such as aqueducts, floor looms, and high-fired ceramics. Roads were improved for horse-drawn wagons, while ports in Huatulco and Salina Cruz opened up trade with far-off lands such as Peru and the Philippines. But there is mention of a 1546 rebellion, suggesting that at least some of the atrocities committed elsewhere in New Spain took place here, as well.

By the 1580s, smallpox had reached Oaxaca, halving the native population, leaving fields fallow, and stopping construction on many of the Dominican churches. By this time, the Spanish were completely dependent on native labor, and they began working the surviving Indians overtime. It did little good, as earthquakes shattered every church they attempted to erect.

Thus was pioneered a new form of architecture, called "Oaxaca baroque" or "earthquake baroque," which combined the flexible, mortar-free construction and thick walls used by Zapotec engineers with the ornate stone and stucco ornamentation favored in Spain. Finally, rising from its own ruins, Santo Domingo de Oaxaca, the Dominicans' mother church and a symbol of Christian Oaxaca, was consecrated in 1666.

By this time, New Spain had legally recognized different racial "classes" of people. Spaniards, born in Spain, and Criollos, Mexicans of pure Spanish blood, had full civil rights. Mestizos, with mixed Spanish and indigenous blood, were allowed to hold many jobs by the late 1700s. Native peoples, however, were barred from most careers, and often worked for subsistence wages on huge Spanish-owned haciendas. Combined with an economic collapse caused by the wars in Europe, this inequality began to foment resistance to Spanish domination in almost every sector.

Independence

On September 15, 1810, Oaxacans answered the "Grito de Hidalgo," the call for independence sounded by renegade Catholic priest Miguel Hidalgo. The first wave of fighting was unsuccessful, but Oaxaca would rise again in 1821, with General Antonio de León of Huajuapan declaring Oaxaca independent on July 29, a month before the rest of Mexico. As his troops marched into a newly liberated Oaxaca City, the earth moved. This quake, according to legend, cast the huge, carved Spanish coat of arms above the Jesuit college onto the plaza, shattering it forever.

Mexican monarchists, landowners, and Vatican officials did not want a democracy, however. In a coup against pro-democracy forces, they crowned young Agustín de Iturbide

Juárez, the hemisphere's first modern indigenous head of state, and Oaxaca's favorite son, has had his accomplishments celebrated by artists in every medium.

"Emperor" of Mexico in 1822. His main achievement was shutting down the Mexican Congress and arming Central American monarchists, fomenting bloody civil wars that would drag on for decades. Iturbide was ousted in November 1823, and executed by firing squad the following year.

Though the Mexican Republic was beset on all sides by traitors, Oaxaca's commitment to democratic revolution, combined with its relative isolation, helped it achieve quiet victories. In 1827, Oaxaca's first secular university, the State Institute of Arts and Sciences, opened its doors to students of all races. In 1834, a young Zapotec, Benito Juárez, graduated as its first lawyer.

That same year, Santa Anna, a dictator who was president in name only, abolished slavery throughout the country. This incensed the U.S. citizens, most of them pro-slavery Southerners, who had settled, with Mexico's blessing, the border state of Texas. These slave owners famously mounted an impassioned but doomed defense of their rights at the Alamo. Not one survived Santa Anna's swift counterattack.

Juárez was elected governor of Oaxaca in 1847, and used his position to oppose Santa Anna's dictatorship. He and several other leaders drafted the Plan of Ayutla, which called for Santa Anna's removal and the formation of a constitutional assembly. Several years of war and political maneuvering followed, and in 1861 free elections brought Juárez to power as president of Mexico, and Americas' first indigenous head of state since the European conquest.

Reform

Juárez inherited a divided nation, bankrupted by war and corruption. The "War of Reform" had raged for three years, and Juárez's victory ushered in a period called the *Reforma*, realizing separation of church and state, recognizing civil marriages, granting voting rights to non-landowners, and most controversially, nationalizing church properties. Previous administrations had borrowed heavily from Europe to finance their wars, and Juárez had hoped to raise money from the sale of church property to help repay those debts. But it wasn't nearly enough.

Juárez called for a two-year moratorium on foreign debt repayment. This irritated the European powers, strapped for cash, as well as the Vatican, which had lost its gold-encrusted churches and seen its religious orders basically cast into the street. They began working with French and Spanish leaders to overthrow Juárez and install as king a member of the Hapsburgs, a German family to whom European superstition accorded a "divine right of rule," granted by God.

In 1861, some 9,000 troops from Spain, France, and Britain landed in Veracruz, over-threw the democratically elected government, and installed a 32-year-old Austrian prince, Maximilian Hapsburg-Lorraine, as emperor of Mexico. As the foreign militaries closed in, Congress granted Juárez an emergency extension of his presidential term until new elections could be held, then disbanded.

Though Maximilian honored most of the reform laws, liberals still resisted his monarchy, most famously at the 1862 Battle of Puebla, a victory celebrated on May 5, Cinco de Mayo. The U.S., nervous about a new European base on its border, began arming and funding Juárez, as well as his ally from the Oaxacan Sierra Norte, Porfirio Díaz. In 1867, they were victorious, and Juárez was re-elected. On his order, Maximilian was executed by firing squad.

In 1872 Juárez died of a heart attack while working at his desk. His memory was toasted across throughout the world, and his name immortalized in the city of Oaxaca de Juárez, the Sierra Juárez mountains where he was born, Mexico City's international airport, and many other places. His most famous quote is emblazoned on murals, buildings, and across Cerro Fortín: "Among individuals, as among nations, respect for the rights of others is peace."

Revolution

After a brief period of peace and democracy, another Oaxaqueño, of mixed Japanese-Mixtec heritage, took the national stage. General Porfirio Díaz was a liberal hero who would become Mexico's most powerful dictator. His "Order and Progress" reign (1867–1911) benefitted Oaxaca enormously, with new roads, rail lines, and the modernized port of Salina Cruz. Oaxaca City became a showcase for his dramatic architectural commissions, such as the stunning Teatro Macedonio Alcalá.

Díaz invested heavily in silver mines and oil fields, and these began to refill Mexico's treasury and rebuild its demoralized military. He also controlled the press, fixed elections, and used his power to undermine his rivals. His reform laws concentrated all titled land in the hands of 2 percent of Mexicans (and several wealthy foreigners), who grew export crops such as coffee on their huge haciendas. The population grumbled, but did not revolt until 1910, when a global economic downturn left children starving while surrounded by fertile soil and plentiful water.

A wealthy landowner, Francisco Madero, decided to challenge Díaz in the 1910 elections. Díaz had him jailed, and was then "re-elected" almost unanimously. Madero, exiled to the U.S., began calling for revolution. The nation answered.

Oaxaca rallied around Emiliano Zapata, while the northern resistance was led by Pancho

Though protests are now peaceful, would-be revolutionaries still keep the graffiti cleaners gainfully employed.

Villa. Díaz abdicated almost immediately, and went into exile in Paris. Madero took over briefly, but was betrayed by Victoriano Huerta, who declared himself president and set up a brief but brutal military dictatorship. Oaxaca, unimpressed, declared itself the Sovereign State of Oaxaca, without ties to the historic villain. It would join the newly formed United States of Mexico only in 1919, after Huerta was unceremoniously deposed.

Modern Oaxaca

Oaxaca remained somewhat isolated, despite its new road and rail connections, until the early 1950s. German immigrants who had begun arriving after the revolution, establishing vast coffee plantations in the Sierra Sur, began modernizing roads between Oaxaca City and the Coast, and developed both Puerto Ángel and Puerto Escondido to ship the "golden bean."

In the 1950s, the Panamerican Highway was built, slicing through the Sierra Madre and bringing visitors from Mexico City and Puebla. Soon, a small regional airport just south of Oaxaca City, served by Mexicana Airlines, began targeting U.S. and Canadian travelers flush with post-World War II wealth.

By the 1960s, Oaxaca had become a favorite stop on the "Gringo Trail," and adventurous hippies discovered two Oaxacan traditions they shared with the world: hallucinogenic mushrooms from the northern cloud forests of Huautla, and the *serape*, a type of wool cape, from Teotitlán.

As tourism and the handicrafts market grew, many Oaxacans abandoned agriculture, once the basis of the region's economy, and turned to handicrafts such as *tapetes* (wool rugs), *alebrijes* (colorful carved animals), and other handicrafts that tourists loved. Today, tourism is Oaxaca's most important industry. In 1987, Oaxaca City and Monte Albán were declared humanity's cultural heritage sites by UNESCO. In 1994, Oaxaca City and the Central Valleys were declared priority tourism development zones by the federal government. Right now, the Pacific resort town of Huatulco is receiving a billion-dollar makeover. Your vacation is serious business.

Though the benefits of tourism are obvious—thriving crafts and cultural traditions, increased protection of wilderness areas, and more hard currency in general—the Teachers' Insurrection of 2006 (see the Oaxaca City chapter) that basically closed the city for nine months showed how fickle that industry can be.

But the tourists are returning, spurred, perhaps, by the global economic crisis that makes Oaxaca, a relatively inexpensive destination quite close to the United States, more attractive than a European vacation. Their presence is appreciated, in many ways.

2

CULTURE AND LANGUAGE

Oaxaca's rich history and diverse populations have combined to create a cultural wealth that is its most alluring attraction. History and myth have poured from the mountains into the fertile Central Valleys, cults of beauty and death in vivid marigold tones, blooming across the rich and varied terrain.

The Ministry of Tourism likes to play with the number seven, perhaps for luck. But it is too modest. Only seven moles? There are dozens, like Huajuapan's savory *mole de calderas*, made with the hindquarters of goats, or the light, herb-scented *mole verde* of the northern regions, made with completely different ingredients than the *mole verde* of Oaxaca City.

And only seven lands, represented by the Fountain of the Seven Regions in Colonia Reforma? If only the cultural geographers had it as easy as the sculptor; Oaxaca is home to at least 12 geographical regions, 17 recognized languages, and any number of cultures caught in between. Heck, there are more than seven major dances, themselves with roots in three different continents, specific just to the region around Pinotepa Nacional.

Small communities with closets full of quality artifacts have opened fascinating museos comunitarios *all over the state, including Huamelulpan's excellent Hitalu.*

PEOPLE

Today, 17 distinct languages (Spanish and 16 indigenous tongues) are spoken in Oaxaca. Oaxaca's populations is one of the most heavily indigenous in the Americas, with some 40 percent of its people claiming pure native blood, compared to around 15 percent for Mexico as a whole, or 2 percent in Canada and the United States.

The Spanish occupation was closely followed by the introduction of African culture through the slave trade. Today's "African Oaxacan" population, perhaps descended from survivors of nearby shipwrecks, is concentrated on the Mixtec Coast, around the city of Pinotepa Nacional, and retains many of the dances, dishes, and other customs of Africa. The indigenous, European, and African populations form what some people call the "beautiful golden braid" of Mexican Culture.

Many indigenous areas exercise some legal autonomy, and still use an ancient system of government. To oversimplify, a council of elders, generally men older than 30 who have proven themselves assets to the community, guide largely communal societies using discussion and consensus. There are many variations and exceptions to this description, and women play an important role, traditionally directing economic activity. All these towns participate normally in state and federal elections.

Pueblo governments also often employ the "Sistema de Cargos," which obligates men (and sometimes women) to perform community service each month. Often the docents at community museums and managers of indigenous ecotourism projects are completing their monthly requirement.

Oaxaca's largest indigenous groups are the **Zapotecs**, numbering some 347,000 people, and **Mixtecs**, with 241,000. Both their languages spring from the same root tongue,

The poor of the Northern mountains build log and mud-daub houses that may closely resemble those built in the once-thickly forested Central Valleys during the time of Monte Albán.

present more than 6,000 years ago in Oaxaca. By 1500 B.C., the language had split into more than a dozen dialects, including these.

The two dominant empires of Oaxaca's past, the Mixtecs and Zapotecs remain the most powerful indigenous groups in the state. But there are many others. For a complete overview, visit Oaxaca's Tourist Guide (www.oaxaca-travel.com/guide/indigenous). Note that most common names are Nahuatl translations; the name each group calls itself is included in italics.

Amuzgos (20,000; Southwest Oaxaca) Stretching into neighboring Guerrero State, the Amuzgos call themselves *Tzjon non* (People of Textiles).

Chatinos (40,000; Southwest Oaxaca) Perhaps predating even the Zapotecs, the *Kitse cha'tnio* (Work of Words) is a historically militarized group who were subjugated by the Mixtecs just prior to the Aztec occupation.

Chinantecos (104,000; Papaloapan) Stretched from Valle Nacional to Tuxtepec and into Veracruz state, the *Dsa jmii* (Plains People) fended off the Zapotecs and Mixtecs, finally falling to the Aztecs around 1500 A.D. The group operates four wonderful ecotourism projects, including a community museum near Valle Nacional.

Chochos (Mixteca Alta) Another member of the Oto-Manguean group, the *Runiza ngiigua* (Those Who Speak the Language) were fierce enemies of the Mixtecs, and joined forced with the Aztecs against them.

Chontales (4,600; Southern Oaxaca) The *Slijuala xanuc* (People of the Mountains) speak a language similar to that of many New Mexico Pueblo Indians. Late arrivals to the region, they settled here in 1374. While the Zapotecs eventually subjugated them, the Spanish never did.

Cuicatecos (12,000; Northwest Oaxaca) Descendants of the Toltecs, this group settled what is now the Tehuacán-Cuicatlán Biosphere Reserve.

Huaves (14,000; Isthmus of Tehuantepec) Believed to have arrived here by sea from Nicaragua or Peru, the *Mero ikooc* (True Us) now occupy the pretty lagoons southeast of Tehuantepec.

Ixcatecos (Northern Oaxaca) This tiny group has scratched a living out of the arid region around Santa María de Ixcatlán for centuries, largely unmolested thanks to their undesirable real estate.

Mazatecos (174,000; La Cañada and Papaloapan) The *Ha shuta enima* (People of Custom) arrived about 800 years ago, and are perhaps best known for shaman María Sabina and the psychoactive mushrooms she used in traditional healing ceremonies.

Mixes (105,000; Northeastern Oaxaca) The *Ayuuk* (The People) are historically insular and combative, and were never conquered by the Zapotecs, Aztecs, or Spanish. Today, almost 40,000 Mixes still speak no Spanish.

Popolocas (4,000; scattered) Because their language was so different from Nahuatl, the Aztecs called them "Barbarians." Their real name is *Homshuk* (God of Corn).

Tacuates (Mixtec Coast) A small band centered in neighboring Guerrero State with few municipalities in Oaxaca.

Triquis (15,000; Western Highlands) This small population has a huge presence in Oaxaca City, where their distinctive red-striped wool *huipiles* and other weavings are favorites of tourists and Oaxaqueños alike. Repeatedly defeated by other indigenous groups, as well as the Spanish, the Triquis basically packed up and moved to the distant and frigid Sierra Madre Mountains. There they live in peace and poverty, making beautiful weavings and hoping to avoid further problems from troublesome empires.

Though some Oaxaqueños don't want their photo taken, others, like these cute kids on Isla Soyaltepec, are happy to ham it up for the camera.

Zoques (10,000; Eastern Oaxaca) Concentrated in the state of Chiapas, the *O'deput* (People of Language) also have a small population in Oaxaca, where they live among the Mixes.

DANCE

One of Oaxaca's oldest and most important forms of cultural expression is dance, most famously celebrated during the *Guelaguetza*, or "The Offering." Also called "Mondays on the Hill," the celebration takes place on the first two Mondays following July 16 (unless it's July 18, the day Benito Juárez died, in which case celebrations begin July 25).

Today one of Oaxaca's most important attractions, it originally honored the Zapotec Goddess of Corn. The modern extravaganza (with tickets, tourists, and an 11,000-seat stadium) began in 1932 as part of the city's 400th anniversary.

Some dances now regularly performed were almost lost, such as certain *sones,* very traditional, flirtatious, and mestizo dances, often with risqué lyrics; *jarabes,* romantic dances often involving mariachis; and *chilenas,* a romantic comedy of a dance that originated in South America, probably brought here by Chilean sailors stopping over in Huatulco.

Oaxaca City and Central Valleys

The fertile Central Valleys, cradle of Oaxacan civilization, gave rise to a great variety of dance. The *Chinas Oaxaqueñas* bring their flowered baskets for a dance that represents a day at the market, while dancers from Ejutla de Crespo show women how to win a man's love.

Perhaps the most famous of the Central Valleys' dances celebrates the conquistador Hernán Cortés and his victory over Emperor Moctezuma and the Aztecs. The *Danza de la Pluma* is easily recognized by the large feathered hat that symbolizes Moctezuma's crown. The *Chareos* dance represents the battle between the Spanish and Muslims, led by St. James (*Santiago*), dressed in feathered headdresses, drums, and flutes.

Pacific Coast

Oaxaca's coastline is divided into three main regions, each telling its story with specific costumes and music.

The **Isthmus of Tehuantepec** is known for its lush embroidered dance costumes, with beautiful flowers inspired by shawls that arrived with Chinese railroad workers. The glittering gold jewelry and flowers are accented with starched lace petticoats and veil in pure Colonial Spanish style. Istmeños call their fiestas *velas,* and their music has a distinct marimba feel. Dances include *La Mareña* from Santa Maria Huazolotitlán, depicting the collection of sea turtle eggs from the shore. (This is not to be confused with the African Oaxacan *Turtle Dance,* which makes fun of Spanish slave owners.)

The **Central Coast** was influenced by the Spanish ports of call, bringing Turks, Filipinos, Peruvians, British pirates, and later Germans and international tourists, to its shores. The costumes are Spanish in silhouette, with full skirts and cinched waists. Dances include *El Zipolite* (The Buzzard), *Perro* (Dog), and *El Borracho* (The Drunk). In the *Chilena,* or Chilean, two couples dance with handkerchiefs above their heads while the guitarist and singer tell jokes.

The **Mixtec Coast** is most interesting to the African Oaxacan people, whose African rhythms still permeate the dance. The *Petate Bull Dance*, with Colonial costumes and blue-eyed masks, commemorates a Spanish rancher who once owned the entire Mixtec Coast. The *Tiger Dance* tells the story of ranchers whose cows were stolen by a magic tiger. The *Devil's Dance* is a physical request to the African deity Ruja asking for deliverance from slavery; it is traditionally performed on All Saints Day. The *Old Badger Dance* is performed during Lent, with barefoot men and women in traditional Mixtec garb depicting the Passion of Christ.

Northern Oaxaca

Subdivided for centuries into six culturally, linguistically, and ecologically distinct areas, Northern Oaxaca offers many unique dances.

The traditional **Mixteca** dances include the *Dance of los Tejorones* (or Dance of los Chililos), depicting the hunting and killing of a jaguar; the *Jarabe Mixteca,* a local version of a popular romantic dance, often set to mariachi music with Spanish and Moorish influences; the *Jarabe de la Botella,* with its white gowns, seems influenced by North Africans. *The Masked Dance* is actually a parody of French dancers and their garish uniforms during the attempted occupation of the 1860s.

Perhaps the most famous cultural expression of the region, however, is the song "Canción Mixteca," composed by José López Alavés during the Mexican Revolution. It remains quietly relevant to the thousands of Mixtecas who make their danger-filled way to the U.S. to work illegally: "How far I am from the land/Where I was born/Like a leaf in the wind/I would like to cry/I would like to die/Oh, land of the sun, oh, to see you/Now so far away."

The northern highlands of **La Cañada** and Huautla de Jiménez are known for their beribboned costumes with embroidered flowers, black veils, and a "suave, mystical dance" for the Goddess of Corn. The **Sierra Juárez** offers a simple dance with costumes of white *huipiles* and red belts that may indicate Peruvian influences.

The region's most famous dance comes from Tuxtepec and the hills of the **Papaloapan**, the *Flor de Piña,* or Pineapple Flower dance. With ribbons woven through the thin, bright regional *traje,* the women celebrate a good pineapple harvest and then, in the spirit of the Guelaguetza, "offer" the fruit to the crowd. Careful!

FESTIVALS AND HOLIDAYS

Each region's most popular festivals and events are listed at the end of the appropriate chapter, but that's just the beginning. Every town is dedicated to a particular Catholic saint, whose feast day is celebrated with a week-long party, huge markets, fireworks, special Masses, processions, and lots of mezcal.

Some festivals are celebrated throughout the state, including *Día de los Muertos,* the Day of the Dead, from October 31 through November 2. Oaxaca City and the surrounding towns are best for international visitors, with tours to the *panteones* (cemeteries) where families commune with loved ones in all-night vigils. Every town has similar celebrations, and most accommodate visits to the beautifully decorated cemeteries. The Guelaguetza is most famously celebrated in Oaxaca City each July, but there are smaller dance festivals throughout the state.

Mexico has several public holidays, when state offices and many businesses are closed or keep shorter hours.

On the way to the altar on Día de los Muertos.

New Year's Day	January 1
Constitution Day	February 4
Fat Tuesday	March or April (day before Lent begins)
Good Friday	March or April
Labor Day	May 1
Anniversary of the Battle of Puebla	May 5
Independence Day	September 16
Día de la Raza (Columbus Day)	October 12
Día de los Muertos	November 2
Revolution Day	November 20
Feast Day of Virgin of Guadalupe	December 12
Christmas	December 25

PLACE NAMES

Oaxaca's cities and towns have several names, the most common usually from the Aztec language, Nahuatl. However, the old Mixtec and Zapotec names are still often used; community museums, for example, may use the older name.

The Spanish conquerors usually added the name of a patron saint before town names, for instance, San Juán Coixtlahuaca, an ancient city with a new (well, 500-year-old) church dedicated to Saint John. Some suffixes, such as Teotitlán del Valle (Teotitlán of the Valley), are geographical.

After independence, the Mexican government added other, generally political, appellations to already complicated names. The Heroica Ciudad de Tlaxiaco celebrates the city's heroism during the French invasion, while Oaxaca de Juárez is named for the former president.

Put it all together and you get tongue twisters like Patriótica Villa de San Miguel Soyaltepec, which locals still call by its Mazatec name of Naxhingee, "ragged hill," or by its new name, Isla Soyaltepec, dubbed after the Miguel Alemán Dam flooded the lowlands around the hill.

SPECTATOR SPORTS

There are several city parks where you can find pickup games of *futbol* (soccer), baseball, and other sports.

Beisball

Catch the minor-league **Guerreros de Oaxaca** (www.guerrerosdeoaxaca.com.mx) baseball team at the Eduardo Vasconcelos Stadium (Avenida Heroes de Chapultepec, three blocks east of the Autobuses del Oriente) from March to September. For more information, check the National Beisbal League (www.natbeisbol.com) Web site.

Mixtec Ball

Aficionados claim this is a direct descendant of the ancient ballgame played at the huge stone stadiums scattered around Oaxaca's major archaeological sites. The game, played irregularly throughout the state, is similar to tennis, using special gloves to hit a 5–10 kilo-gram rubber ball, similar to those popularized by the Olmec Empire back in 1000 B.C.

LANGUAGE

The official language of Mexico, and Oaxaca State, is Spanish, but 16 other indigenous tongues are used, and in many places Spanish is barely spoken. Visitors who speak it less than fluently may appreciate the simplified Spanish employed in the region.

Adventurous English speakers headed to the hinterlands, particularly the Mixteca, may be surprised. In most of Latin America, English is spoken primarily by wealthy, urban Latinos with a private education. In Oaxaca, where rural peasants often work several years in the U.S., you may be welcomed to the smallest, most isolated community in English. I spent an afternoon in Santa María Yucuhiti, more than an hour from the nearest paved road, commiserating with a Mixtec woman who had worked four years in North Carolina about Oaxaca's tragic lack of quality biscuits and gravy. Regardless, I recommend that non-Spanish speakers bring a Spanish phrasebook and perhaps a Spanish-English dictionary. Or consider classes at one of Oaxaca's excellent Spanish schools. Prices vary, but run about US$15 per hour for private lessons, US$150 for 20 hours of group instruction.

Weekly rates usually include activities, such as dance and cooking classes, volunteer opportunities, and day trips. Most schools arrange homestays or good rates at local hotels. The **Spanish School Association of Oaxaca** (www.aseseo.com.mx) links to the city's longest-standing schools. Freelance Spanish teachers may offer better rates, and leave fly-ers on bulletin boards all over town. These are just a few of the Spanish schools available:

Academia Vinigúlaza (951-513-2763; www.vinigulaza.com; Abasolo 503, Centro; credit cards accepted) The school offers classes for kids, fully furnished apartments for students, and a second "campus" at a beachfront villa in Puerto Escondido.

Amigos del Sol (951-133-6052; www.oaxacanews.com/amigosdelsol.htm; Calzada San Felipe del Agua 322) Convenient from Colonia Reforma or San Felipe del Agua hotels, the school provides transport from Oaxaca Centro.

Becari Language School (951-514-6076, www.becari.com.mx; Bravo 210, Centro) Becari is accredited by U.S. high schools.

Instituto de Comunicación y Cultura (ICC; 951-516-3443; www.iccoax.com; Alcalá 307, Centro) The institute offers several different classes, and organizes cooking, weaving and other workshops, as well as volunteer opportunities.

Instituto Cultural Oaxaca (951-515-3404; www.icomexico.com; Juárez 909, corner of Chapultepec) The grand grounds and gardens of an atmospheric 19th century estate, as well as a very professional staff, make this a winner. It arranges homestays and hotels, but only accepts cash and PayPal.

Oaxaca Spanish Magic (951-516-7316; www.oaxacaspanishmagic.com; Berriozábal 200) The classes have experienced teachers and interesting activities.

Solexico (951-516-5680; www.solexico.com; Absolo 217, Centro) This large operation with cute Colonial classrooms offers courses geared to professionals, such as teachers and medical personnel.

Xcanda (951-515-9899; www.xcandaspanishschool.com; Hidalgo 104, Jalatlaco) On one of the quiet cobbled streets of this residential neighborhood a 10-minute walk from the center, this school also offers flexible hours and a month-long course in English as a second language.

3

CITY OF OAXACA
(CIUDAD DE OAXACA)

Cultural Treasure

Oaxaca's wonders are manifold, as richly textured as a cathedral façade, as simple as a smile. From the endless fiestas that fill the streets with fireworks, song, and dance, to the tempting aromas that drift with love from ancient abodes of adobe and stone, it sometimes seems that even the smallest gestures are made in conscious homage to humanity's infinitely creative soul.

But where to begin unraveling the mysteries of this most magnificent tapestry, Oaxaca, woven from so many centuries, cultures, and stories? How to caress the fabric of this ephemeral swirl of light and color and sound?

The Fountain of the Seven Regions in Colonia Reforma uses Guelegüetza motif to symbolize the major cultures of Oaxaca.

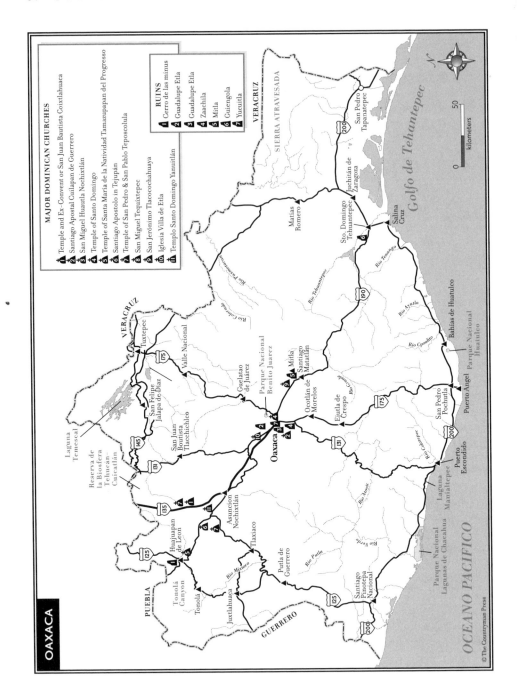

OAXACA

MAJOR DOMINICAN CHURCHES

1. Temple and Ex-Convent or San Juan Bautista Coixtlahuaca
2. Santiago Apostal Cuilapan de Guerrero
3. San Miguel Huautla Nochixtlán
4. Temple of Santo Domingo
5. Temple of Santa María de la Natividad Tamazulapan del Progresso
6. Santiago Apostolo in Teyupán
7. Temple of San Pedro & San Pablo Teposcolula
8. San Miguel Tequixtepec
9. San Jerónimo Tlacochahuaya
10. Iglesia Villa de Etla
11. Templo Santo Domingo Yanuitlán

RUINS
1. Cerro de las minus
2. Guadalupe Etla
3. Guadalupe Etla
4. Zaachila
5. Mitla
6. Guiengola
7. Yucuitla

© The Countryman Press

CITY OF OAXACA

To Hwy 131,190
Villa de Etla (18km/11mi)
Noxchitlán (69km/43 mi)
Mexico City (450 km/279 mi)

N

0   400m

CERRO
FORTIN

STAIRS TO
EL FORTIN

OAXACA CENTRO

RIO ATOYAC

AV. MEXICAPAN

PERIFERICO

To San Felipe
del Agua

AV. SAN FELIPE DEL AGUA

NARANJOS

H. ESCUELA NAVAL MILITAR

COLONIA
REFORMA

H. COLEGIC MILITAR

BELISARIO DOMINGUEZ

COLONIA
XOCHIMILCO

CALZ. HEROES DE CHAPTEPEC

To Hwy 190;
Mitla (46km/29mi)
Tehuanttepec
(250km/155mi)

BARRIO
JALATLACO

150

CALZ. EDUARDO VASCONCELOS

AV. JUAREZ

AV. MORELOS
AV. INDEPENDENCIA
AV. HILDALGO

BUSTAMANTE

AV. GUERRERO

PERIFERICO

PERIFERICO

To Hwy 175; Ocotlán
(25km/16m).
Puerto Angel (250km/155m)

KEY

🏛 Museum
† Church
🏪 Market

© The Countryman Press

1 Museo y Antigua Estación
  del Farrocarril 🏛
2 Second-Class Bus Station
3 Mercado Abastos 🏪
4 Mercado de Artesanías 🏪
5 Nuestra Señora de la Defensa †
6 Nuestra Señora de Consolación †
7 Iglesia Trinidad de las Huertas †
8 Ex-Convento de Siete Principes, † 🏛
  Casa de la Cultura Oaxaca

9 Iglesia la Merced †
10 Mercado la Merced †
11 Nuestra Señora de las Nieves †
12 San Matías Jalatlaco †
13 La Curtiduria, Espacio de Arte 🏛
   Contemporáneo
14 El Patrocino †
15 First-Class Bus Station
16 Parque de Beisbol Eduardo
   Vasconcelos
17 Fuente de las Siete Regiones

18 Oaxaca State Tourism Office
19 Santo Tomás Xochimilco †
20 Conzatti Park
21 Parque El Llano
22 The Zócalo
23 Panteón San Miguel
24 Iglesia Guadalupe †
25 Auditorio Güelaguetza
26 Centro Cultural Santo Domingo 🏛

There is no blueprint for beauty, of course, but consider making your way, on that first overwhelming day, into the heart of the ancient stone city, that tangled warren of handicrafts and gossip that is the city market. Dozens of *fondas*, or tiny restaurants, in Mercado 20 de Noviembre await your arrival with a handmade ceramic bowl of foaming hot chocolate, freshly ground with cinnamon, almonds, and vanilla, and hand-patted into delicious pure endorphins. It is served with *pan de yema*, a bread that requires literally hours of kneading before it's baked to airy perfection. Come October, this same delight is given a small sweet face and called *pan de muerte*, "bread of the dead," used to adorn the marigold altars of sugar skulls and candles honoring those who have passed beyond the veil.

That veil seems thinner in this remarkable place, never more so than during Día de los Muertos, when prayers and magic flow through the ancient streets, monumental churches, and into the broad stone expanse of the Zócalo, or central plaza. But as you sip your chocolate, pay attention to every splash of color, every carefully embroidered pattern, decorating the crowds crushing by.

Humor, for a moment, the women and children pressing their handmade wares into your hands; there will be plenty of time to wave them away later in your journey. Look closely at their simple crafts; these are not the famed *alebrijes*, colorful carved wooden animals, or stunning *tapetes*, beautifully woven wool rugs, or the elegant fine art for which Oaxaca is famed. These are small things, carved wooden bookmarks painted with birds, simple paintings, gauzy *huipiles*, nothing special. And yet, they are. In even these modest creations, can't you sense the spark of the infinite creative? That is the engine upon which all Oaxaca turns.

Something sweet for your family's Día de los Muertos *altar.*

Online Resources

All About Oaxaca (www.allaboutoaxaca.com) This friendly, down-to-earth site offers comprehensive listings and straightforward reviews.

Aquí Oaxaca (www.aquioaxaca.com) A Spanish-language site with cultural articles and excellent photo essays.

An Expatriate Life (www.realoaxaca.com) Writer Stan Gotlieb and photographer Diana Ricci chronicle the expat lifestyle and offer a reasonably priced newsletter.

Gobierno del Estado de Oaxaca (www.oaxaca.gob.mx) and **Oaxaca Municipal Government** (www.oaxacainfo.gob.mx) The official state and city sites offer hard information in Spanish.

Go-Oaxaca (www.go-oaxaca.com) Go-Oaxaca is an informative site with articles, links, an events calendar, and a small classifieds section.

El Jogorio Cultural (www.eljolgoriocultural.net) This Spanish-language entertainment 'zine has an events calendar.

Oaxaca Magazine (www.oaxaca.magazzine.net) The online edition of glossy tourist 'zine has photos, links, and editions for Huatulco, Veracruz, and Puebla.

✪**OaxacaOaxaca.com** (www.oaxacaoaxaca.com) This top-notch site promoting four five-star hotels provides a wealth of information for everyone, including restaurant reviews, artisan listings, and more.

Oaxaca Profundo (www.oaxacaprofundo.com.mx) The online version of the Spanish-language glossy magazine probes Oaxaca's cultural attractions.

Oaxaca Times (www.oaxacatimes.com) A free, fabulous, English-language monthly that publishes online restaurant and events reviews, articles, and a solid classified section.

✪**Oaxaca's Tourist Guide** (www.oaxaca-travel.com) This well-designed site offers excellent historical and cultural information, articles and travelogues, and great suggestions for little-visited rural towns and eco-attractions.

✪**Planeta** (www.planeta.com) This amazing, sprawling "global journal of practical ecotourism" covers community- and eco-conscious travel worldwide, but is based in Oaxaca. The site offers an eclectic collection of articles, reviews, maps, videos, photo essays, links, even a Oaxaca Wiki, which, sadly, is not called Oaxacapedia.

Revista Mujeres (www.revista-mujeres.com) A saucy Spanish-language women's magazine that covers Oaxaca's lipstick feminist scene.

As you make your way out of the *mercado,* pay attention to the ancient but unbent old woman selling something small and red. You may not be quite ready for this bit of magic, not yet, not your first day. These are *chapulines,* grasshoppers stewed in chile and lime, beloved by children and possessed of a most remarkable enchantment. Eat just one, they say, and you will one day be borne back to this fair city on their whirring gossamer wings.

But that can wait. Now it is time to emerge into the sunshine and begin your exploration anew. Grab a palm-thatched hat from one of the vendors; it may be the best 20 pesos you spend all day. And enjoy.

Safety

Oaxaca is very safe for tourists, and has suffered little of the drug-related violence plaguing other parts of Mexico. The city is patrolled by heavily armed police, a remnant of the 2006 teachers' union protests, but this seems to be primarily a show of force to deter potential troublemakers. (Freedom of speech and peaceful protest are tolerated, however; there were several festive demonstrations while I was in town.) The very visible police presence deters criminals as well.

Regardless, use common sense. As in any tourist town, visitors are targeted for non-violent theft. Pickpockets frequent festivals, markets, and evenings on the Zócalo. Carry bags in front of you and stay alert. Leave flashy clothes and jewelry at home, and whenever possible, leave money cards, passports, and other important documents in the hotel safe. At bars, never accept drinks that could have been drugged.

There are occasional armed muggings along the beautiful walk to El Fortín; go with a friend, preferably early in the day, and take only what you'd cheerfully hand over at knife-point. The Zócalo attracts all sorts of beggars, including children; the Charity Guide (www .charity-charities.org/Mexico-charities/Oaxaca.html) lists other options for donating money and time. Scam artists also abound, latching onto to unwary tourists with tales of indigenous spirituality, impoverished circumstances, and/or undying love; keep a smile on your face and a hand on your wallet when dealing with these guys.

The Teachers' Insurrection of 2006

Every May for a quarter century, the Oaxaca teachers' union has mounted a protest. With marches, chants, and signs, they demand equal education in tiny indigenous pueblos, as well as a pay hike for themselves. Peaceful, political, and like everything Oaxaqueño, colorful, it had become a tradition.

Until 2006, when things changed.

Attendance had swollen as Mexico's increasing oil revenues failed to translate into any benefit for the people. Ulises Ruiz, the unpopular governor accused of fixing the 2004 elections, became a lightning rod for insulting chants and clever signs. Unwisely, he struck back, sending thousands of police to break up the protests. This backfired, dramatically.

Area activists formed a new coalition: APPO, the Popular Assembly of the People of Oaxaca. On June 17, they set up camp in the center of the Zócalo (and in front of Ruiz's home) and began filming—and uploading—video of police brutalizing protesters. They also blocked the roads, graffitied the graceful old buildings, took over the university radio stations, and in July, blockaded the Guelaguetza, one of Oaxaca's most popular festivals. "Tourists go home!" read one scrawl across the ancient *cantera*. "In Oaxaca, we are not capitalists."

Though a "People's Guelaguetza" did go on, filling the torn and tattered streets with music and dance, the tourists did go elsewhere. (As did Ruiz, who went into hiding at a five-star Mexico City hotel, on the taxpayer's peso.) The city fell into chaos, its main industry (tourism) gone, armed gangs "patrolling" the streets, and tear gas filling the air. It seemed a violent stalemate, until October 29, just before the Day of the Dead.

Instead of marigolds and sugar skulls, it was teargas and bullets: Police attacked an APPO barricade (claiming protesters had fired first) and killed three people, including IndyMedia journalist Bradley Will.

Mexican president Vicente Fox, who apparently had been waiting for the situation to cool on its own, had to act. Some 4,000 federal troops rolled into the city in an unprecedented show of force, systematically dismantling barricades, reopening schools, and pressuring protesters to go back to work. It was not over, however. Bombs exploded in Mexico City; the APPO condemned teachers who returned to their posts. And on November 25, it mounted a massive protest into the heart of the federally held city center.

Tear gas, as usual, poisoned the air; rubber bullets, as usual, flew. But this time the protesters were ready for battle, and began hurling Molotov cocktails into cars and buildings, filling the night with explosions and acrid smoke. Fox finally authorized soldiers to make arrests. Within 48 hours, hundreds were jailed, their barricades torn down, their radio stations returned to regular programming. It was over.

APPO, though it has abandoned violence, continues to hold peaceful protests; more than likely, you'll see a demonstration while you're here. Colorful banners, live music, and impassioned speeches—it's more Mahatma Gandhi than Che Guevara these days. Meanwhile, heavily armed police still cruise the streets, with parades and other shows of force, in their own successful bid for nonviolence. And the peace has held.

Mementos of 2006: spray paint, a punk rock Emiliano Zapata T-shirt, and the Sacred Virgin of the Barricades.

GETTING AROUND

Though the city of Oaxaca sprawls into the surrounding valley, most attractions, hotels, and other tourist services are in the old Colonial city center, or *Centro,* radiating about eight blocks in all directions from the Zócalo. This is an eminently walkable district, though cabs are everywhere. Maps, labeled with museums and churches, are available all over town if you want to leave this book in the room.

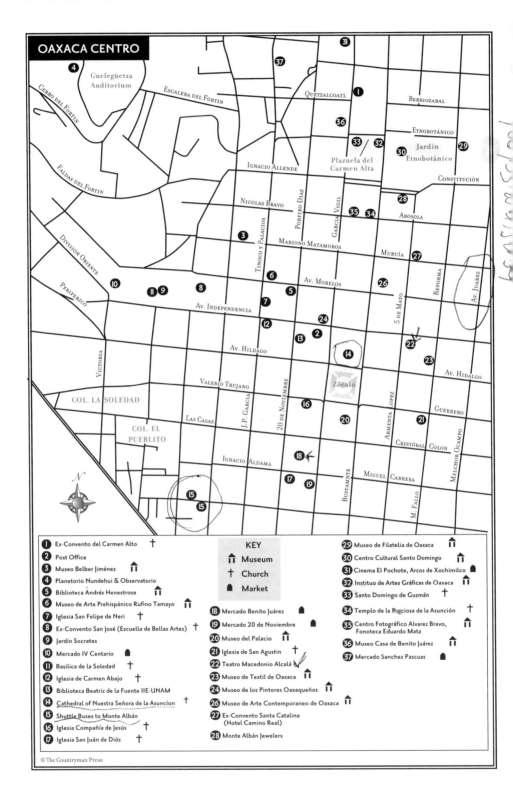

OAXACA CENTRO

Guelegüetza Auditorium

KEY

🏛 Museum
† Church
🏪 Market

1 Ex-Convento del Carmen Alto †
2 Post Office
3 Museo Belber Jiménez 🏛
4 Planetorio Nundehui & Observatorio
5 Biblioteca Andrés Henestrosa
6 Museo de Arte Prehispánico Rufino Tamayo 🏛
7 Iglesia San Felipe de Neri †
8 Ex-Convento San José (Escuela de Bellas Artes) †
9 Jardín Socrates
10 Mercado IV Centario 🏪
11 Basilica de la Soledad †
12 Iglesia de Carmen Abajo †
13 Biblioteca Beatriz de la Fuente IIE-UNAM
14 Cathedral of Nuestra Señora de la Asunción †
15 Shuttle Buses to Monte Albán
16 Iglesia Compañía de Jesús †
17 Iglesia San Juán de Diós †

18 Mercado Benito Juárez 🏪
19 Mercado 20 de Noviembre 🏪
20 Museo del Palacio 🏛
21 Iglesia de San Agustín †
22 Teatro Macedonio Alcalá
23 Museo de Textil de Oaxaca 🏛
24 Museo de los Pintores Oaxaqueños 🏛
26 Museo de Arte Contemporaneo de Oaxaca 🏛
27 Ex-Convento Santa Catalina (Hotel Camino Real)
28 Monte Albán Jewelers

29 Museo de Filatelia de Oaxaca 🏛
30 Centro Cultural Santo Domingo 🏛
31 Cinema El Pochote, Arcos de Xochimilco 🏪
32 Instituo de Artes Gráficas de Oaxaca 🏛
33 Santo Domingo de Guzmán †
34 Templo de la Preciosa de la Asunción †
35 Centro Fotográfico Alvarez Bravo, Fonoteca Eduardo Mata 🏛
36 Museo Casa de Benito Juárez 🏛
37 Mercado Sanchez Pascuas 🏪

Addresses are numbered in blocks of 100, beginning at the crossroads of Avenida Independencia and Avenida Alcalá (which becomes Valdivieso south of Independencia). Thus, 302 Macedo Alcalá is three blocks north of Avenida Independencia. All north-south streets change their name when crossing Independencia, as do most east-west streets crossing Alcalá (with the exception of major thoroughfares such as Independencia, Morelos, and Hidalgo), so there's little chance for confusion with addresses. Regardless, most addresses are given with the nearest cross street, cathedral, or plaza; if you're still confused, simply ask a local to point out a destination on your map.

Note that in the surrounding neighborhoods, such as Jaelitza and Reforma (both *barrio* and *colonia* can be roughly translated as "neighborhood") there may be duplicate street names; for instance, Avenida Cinco de Mayo, Jaelitza, is several blocks east of Avenida Cinco de Mayo, Centro.

Many streets are one-way (noted on most maps) and heavily trafficked, making driving and parking in town a bit of a hassle; if you rent a car, have the staff give you explicit directions out of the city, and/or plan your route before driving away. Many hotels have parking lots, some do not; *estaciomientos publicos* (public parking lots) are common, and run about US$10 per 24-hour day.

Local buses run to other important neighborhoods for tourists, including Colonia Reforma and San Felipe del Agua. Though they depart Abastos Centro, the second-class bus station, in the southeast quadrant of the city, they may pass close to your hotel, so ask. The first-class bus station, Calzado Niños de Chapultepec 1036, is just north of Parque El Llano. For more information about buses and destinations to the rest of the state, check the Transportation chapter.

Just beyond the tourist claptrap, the real Oaxaca goes about its day-to-day business.

LODGING

Perhaps Oaxaca's accommodations are best known for their Spanish Colonial grace, ancient arcades of centuries-old *cantera* surrounding flowering central courtyards. Such hotels are common in every price range, from humble US$10 dorm rooms to the five-star luxury of fabulous El Camino Real. No matter the cost, room size, shape, and lighting will vary widely in real Colonials. Ask to see a few rooms if the first one doesn't appeal.

Most of the top-tier and mid-range hotels are located within a few blocks of the Zócalo and Santo Domingo, making this very strollable city even more inviting. Note that hotels close to the Zócalo can get noisy during fiestas (which is to say, most nights). Light sleepers can request interior rooms, or stay a few blocks from the action.

There are several great mid-range hotels in the quiet, cobblestoned neighborhood of Jalatlaco, a 10-minute walk from the city center. North of town, and best reached by very convenient public bus or taxi, the residential neighborhoods of professional Colonia Reforma and posh San Felipe de Agua offer several more intriguing options. There are dozens of budget hotels scattered throughout the bustling, southwestern quadrant of the city center, between Mercados 20 de Noviembre and Abastos.

Oaxaca has well over 200 hotels offering more than 6,000 rooms, far more than can be listed here. I've included my favorites, but also check:

Oaxaca Bed & Breakfast Association (www.oaxacabedandbreakfast.org) Listings, English-language descriptions with photos, and links to 17 great B&Bs.

Hostel Planet (www.hostelplanet.com) The site describes more than a dozen Oaxaca hostels.

✪ **Hoteles de Oaxaca** (www.hotelesdeoaxaca.com) This excellent Spanish-language site is easy for anyone to navigate, with lots of photos. It has great statewide listings, and a great searchable selection for Oaxaca City.

Hotels in Oaxaca (www.hotelsinoaxaca.com) This English-language site offers listings and contact information.

Oaxaca Hoteles y Moteles (www.oaxacahotelesymoteles.com.mx) This Spanish-language site lists more than 100 hotels, searchable by cost and quality, from one to five stars.

Lodging Price Code

Cost of lodging is based on an average per-room, double-occupancy during peak season (November through mid-January), not including the mandatory 18 percent tax, which may be waived for cash payment. Rates are often reduced during low season (June and August through September), and can double during the Christmas–New Year's holidays, Guelaguetza (all of July), Día de los Muertos (October 31–November 2), and Semana Santa (the week before Easter), when the best hotels are booked weeks and months out. Costs are calculated at 10 pesos to the U.S. dollar.

Inexpensive	Up to US$50
Moderate	US$50 to US$100
Expensive	US$100 to US$150
Very Expensive	More than US$150

Hotels

✪ El Camino Real Oaxaca

Hotel Director: Omar Gil Celis
951-501-6100
1-800-722-6466 United States and Canada
www.camino-real-oaxaca.com,
www.caminoreal.com.mx/oaxaca
oaxaca@caminoreal.com.mx
Cinco de Mayo 300
Price: Very Expensive
Credit Cards: Yes
Handicapped Access: Challenging
Special features: Inhabits the 16th-century
former convent of Santa Catalina.

Ciudad Oaxaca's most famous and beautiful hotel lies behind high *cantera* walls originally built to cloister nuns dedicated to Santa Catalina. Though the exquisite masterpiece of baroque architecture has seen plenty of action over the years—since nationalization under President Juárez in 1859, it has served as a prison, police precinct, art school, night school, Masonic lodge, and cinema—thanks to the National Institute of Anthropology and History and the El Camino Real luxury hotel chain, it is also a masterpiece of preservation.

To stay here is to sleep in the heart of the Antequera, where archways painted with faded floral frescos are still illuminated with candles, following massive stone arcades and tunnels leading through the maze of courtyards and gardens. Wander and you will find several good restaurants; cozy Las Novicias bar, with its low leather chairs and ancient library; a small heated swimming pool; and graceful Los Lavaderos, a stone pavilion covering cool deep basins of fresh water, where the sisters once washed their clothes. Today it is more often filled with flowers, the perfect backdrop for wedding portraits.

There are five classes of room, all with royal purple color schemes, dark wood king-sized beds fitted with luxury bedding, and beautifully tiled bathrooms furnished with all the fine personal care products

The ancient archways and enchanting gardens of 1576 Santa Catalina Convent, today the luxurious Hotel Camino Real, surround this beautiful laundry, which is often filled with flowers.

and fluffy bathrobes you expect, as well as authentic touches such as hand-blown water glasses (you can drink the water). But bear in mind that El Camino Real has been prohibited, by federal law, from fully updating the almost five-century-old building. Thus, the less expensive rooms have windows opening onto the streets (go for a quieter "garden room"), while the naked stone walls, even in the spacious suites with archways, columns, and niches filled with well-lit religious art, might seem a bit cavernous.

But these are trifles, and this is history. Even if you don't splash out for a stay behind these storied walls, it's well worth a visit. Bilingual tours begin every evening at 5 PM, the perfect time for photos, or (better), book the Friday evening Guelaguetza performance and buffet dinner at the acoustically impressive *capilla* (chapel). The Desayuno Oaxaqueño (Oaxacan Breakfast; 951-501-6100; 7 AM–noon daily), is a rather epic breakfast event in the same astounding stone setting.

✪ Casa Antigua

Manager: Virginia Castillo
951-501-1240
www.hotelcasaantigua.com
reservaciones@hotelcasaantigua.com
Cinco de Mayo 206, Centro
Price: Expensive to Very Expensive
Credit Cards: Yes
Handicapped Access: Yes
Special features: Wonderful rooftop *terraza*.

This gleaming, five-star gem is a tranquil escape at the city center, boasting 15 elegantly whitewashed rooms, resplendent with marble floors, elegant wood furnishings, and high Colonial ceilings supported by thick *vegas*. Only two rooms have excellent balconies overlooking the bustle below, but interior rooms are much quieter, with plenty of light thanks to the central courtyard.

Oaxaca is one city where a hotel with a rooftop terraza, *such as this spectacular spot atop Hotel Casa Antigua, may be worth a few extra dollars.*

Amenities are pure luxury, right down to the fluffy bathrobes; some rooms have deep marble bathtubs, and all have wide-screen televisions; the master suite has two, and a Jacuzzi. All include the amenities you'd expect at these prices, plus the rooftop *terraza*, with a covered lounge where you can relax and read while watching the shadows shift across the city and mountains. Order up from the pleasant courtyard **restaurant** ($$$; B, L, C, D) and bar, serving international and Oaxacan cuisine.

Casa Cid de León

General Manager: Leticia Cid de León
951-514-1893
www.casaciddeleon.com
letyricardez@casaciddeleon.com
Avenida Morelos 602, Centro
Price: Very Expensive
Credit Cards: Yes
Handicapped Access: None

This old family mansion, tucked into a narrow adobe with a less than grand lobby, offers four of the largest suites in the city, all outfitted to five-star specifications. Each is individually decorated, with hand-carved furnishings, velvet sofas, religious statues, original modern art, original archways, wrought-iron accents, glazed ceramic tile, even private gardens and patios. They are at once romantic and homey, evoking Oaxaca's patrician past while offering modern amenities including air conditioning, WiFi, Jacuzzis, gas fireplaces, and wide-screen televisions.

Families could book the two-story Mio Cid, the largest suite, once shared by the four Cid de León sons, with two floors sleeping five comfortably. The best suite, however, is the Bella Época, with three delightful balconies.

The décor—think display cases filled with candles, dolls, stuffed animals, angels, and other tchotchkes—may be a bit frilly for some. But everyone enjoys a big

Oaxacan breakfast served on the rooftop *terraza*.

Casa Conzatti Hotel

Manager: Guadalupe Acevedo
951-513-8500; 800-717-9974
www.oaxacalive.com/conzatti
hconzatti@prodigy.net.com
Gómez Farias 218
Price: Expensive
Credit Cards: Yes
Handicapped Access: Yes

Quiet Conzatti Park, a few blocks north of all the downtown bustle, fronts this large, 41-room hotel once owned by Don Cassiano Conzatti Bartolame, director of the Jardín Botánico. Standard rooms are quite standard, immaculate and cheerfully decorated, with Oaxacan details (textiles, artwork) and all the modern amenities, such as WiFi, air conditioning, cable TV, telephones, safe, and room service. Suites are larger (but without separate rooms) and offer more artsy extras and small Jacuzzi tubs. Staff is exceptionally helpful. A solid choice.

✪ Casa de los Abuelos

Owner: Rosa Luis
951-516-1982
www.lacasa-de-rosita.com
lacasadelosabuelos@hotmail.com
Reforma 410, Centro
Price: Moderate
Credit Cards: Cash only
Handicapped Access: None
Special Features: Weekly and monthly rates; children younger than 12 not allowed.

A dream come true for DIY travelers, this spot offers six spacious, wonderful, a bit rough-around-the-edges apartments built in the early 1700s to house Dominican priests. Each faces a cool stone patio, its shady lounge areas framed in flowering vines.

Each gently settling adobe apartment has two floors, with an upstairs master bedroom; the old staircase may not appeal to the mobility-impaired. Each is unique, eclectically decorated with an innate sense of style: tempting sofas, groovy lamps, thick rugs, and almost-antiques imbuing everything with that "cool professor" kind of vibe. Most have tiled full kitchens, complete with hand-made glass and ceramic tableware, all come with cable TV, WiFi, and other modern amenities.

Casa de los Frailes

Manager: Jorge Alberto Meixueiro Flores
951-514-1151
413-303-0488 U.S. and Canada
www.casadelosfrailes.com
casadelosfrailes@yahoo.com.mx
Constitución 203, Centro
Price: Moderate to Expensive
Credit Cards: Yes
Handicapped Access: Yes

This newish, impeccably detailed boutique hotel is polished and pretty, with bright modern rooms bedecked with fresh flowers (and plenty of silk ones), as well as all sorts of local *artesanías* including *tapetes* on the floor, hand-woven spreads on the wonderful king-sized beds with antique headboards, even *lata* (beaten tin) Kleenex-box covers in the fully outfitted luxury bathrooms, with great showers; suites even have big bathtubs.

The hotel offers two rates, the *Plan Americano*, with breakfast on the rooftop terrace and WiFi access; and the *Plan Europeo*, for the room only. All rooms include coffee service, satellite TV, and air conditioning, while larger suites include a microwave, minifridge, phone, and private patio.

The same owners operate the small **Hospederia La Reja** (951-514-5939; www.hospederialareja.com.mx; Abasolo 103, Centro; credit cards accepted; $$), right next to Santo Domingo Church, just seven rooms with WiFi and cable TV surrounding a cute little courtyard, decorated with a

modern and rather minimalist take on the whole Spanish Colonial theme. Breakfast is included.

Casa de Sierra Azul

Manager: Maria Luisa Calvo
951-514-7171
www.hotelcasadesierrazul.com.mx
sierrazu@prodigy.net.mx
Hidalgo 1002
Price: Expensive
Credit Cards: Yes
Handicapped Access: None

Architecture buffs will appreciate this beautifully maintained 19th-century mansion near the Zócalo, featuring 15 rooms surrounding a fine arcaded patio centered on a burbling fountain. All the rooms are different shapes and sizes, some of them enormous and others smallish, all with high ceilings and thick adobe walls. It's worth seeing a few rooms before choosing, as some have columns, air-conditioning, and/or Jacuzzis; unfortunately, at least a couple of them also had some mold. All are outfitted for four-star billing, with cable TV, phone, luxury personal products, hairdryers, WiFi, nice lighting, and original art.

Casa de Siete Balcones

Manager: Lizbeth A. Sierra
951-516-0133; 951-516-1952
www.casadesietebalcones.com
contacto@casadesietebalcones.com
Morelos 800, Centro
Price: Expensive to Very Expensive
Credit Cards: Yes
Handicapped Access: None

This 200-year-old Spanish Colonial stunner offers only seven flawless rooms, each of them as spacious and elegant as this former *cafetalera* mansion was meant to be. (Check out the coffee-themed ceramic floor tiles.)

High ceilings and a pale palette seem to amplify the sunshine streaming in from the skylights, and through the tropical hardwood-framed doors opening onto any of the hotel's seven balconies. Antique hardwood and wrought-iron furnishings, and brand-new beds outfitted with top-quality mattresses and bedding, work together for an easy elegance atop the cool ceramic floors. Each of the rooms is unique, and two can be connected for families. The enormous junior suite is certainly honeymoon-worthy. A continental breakfast is included, as is valet parking.

Casa Pereyra

Owner: Rosaelena Castro Pereyra, Manager: Patricia Coronado
951-516-0248
877-568-0457 U.S. and Canada
www.casapereyra.com.mx
casapereyra@yahoo.com.mx
Independencia 304, Centro
Price: Moderate
Credit Cards: Yes
Handicapped Access: None

This sweet spot is close to Basílica Soledad, a few blocks from the busy Centro, which can be nice. The cozy eight-room adobe, more than two centuries old, has been immaculately maintained with warm color schemes, a tidy courtyard garden, and lovely rooms, some of them oddly shaped, others with two floors or even small interior balconies overlooking the covered courtyard. The suite has its own private garden, complete with table and chairs. Studios come with full kitchens, while *sencillo*, or simple, rooms only have microwaves. Soft lighting, great tiled bathrooms, a small library, and good service make this a great choice.

La Catrina de Acalá

Owner: Rolando Rojas
951-516-0519, 915-514-5304
www.casacatrina.com.mx
ventas@casacatarina.com.mx

García Vigil 703
Price: Moderate to Expensive
Credit Cards: Yes
Handicapped Access: None

Designed by owner, artist, and architect Rolando Rojas, this striking choice offers six spacious, modern rooms within an exceptional Colonial structure. All the rooms are different (though most are decorated with Rojas's paintings), and each is coordinated to the color for which it is named and furnished. For instance, the Red Room master suite is romantic, with a Jacuzzi, private terrace, and king-sized bed. The expansive Green Room opens onto the gardens. All are outfitted with cable TV, air conditioning, safety box, minibar, and other amenities.

One of the best of these is the onsite ✪ **restaurant** (951-514-5704; B, C, D; closed Sun.; $$–$$$) in a fabulous formal courtyard, always artfully decorated. Waitstaff in traditional costumes deliver upscale international dishes, such as eggs Benedict and big salads, and very traditional Oaxacan cuisine, such as deer seasoned with local herbs and served with mole and corn. Rates include breakfast.

Fiesta Inn

Manager: Carlos Ortiz López
951-501-6000; 1-800-504-5000
www.fiestainn.com
Avenida Universidad 140, across from Plaza del Sol
Price: Expensive
Credit Cards: Yes
Handicapped Access: Yes
Special features: Close to the airport and mall.

Part of Mexico's best business-class chain, the ultra-modern, five-star Fiesta Inn is flawless and efficient, from the crisply uniformed greeter and friendly, multilingual check-in right down to the corporate-perfect rooms.

Each is basically identical, all totally outfitted with ergonomic desks, high-speed Internet, international phone, and deluxe, king-sized beds draped with bedding of extravagant thread count, facing the huge wide-screen television with endless English-language options. There's even a tiny balcony overlooking the huge courtyard pool. No, it's not authentic or Colonial, at all, and moreover you're a solid 20 minutes south of downtown by bus or taxi. But sometimes, that's exactly what you want.

✪ Hostal Casa del Sótano

Manager: Rosalba Hernandez
951-516-2494
www.oaxaca-mio.com/casadelsotano.htm
hotel_casa_sotano@hotmail.com
Tinoco and Palacios 414
Price: Moderate
Credit Cards: Yes
Handicapped Access: None

The original stone construction of the old Sótano family mansion makes a striking first impression. Accented with a burnt golden adobe construction and polished wood *vegas* supported by dozens of columns, many of the 23 rooms sport tiny balconies.

And what a view: the iconic façade of Santo Domingo. If you can't see it from your room, take it in from the third-floor *terraza* restaurant, where you can enjoy a continental breakfast.

The drawback? Rooms are small, though the high ceilings, thoughtful layout, and ample storage make navigating the space easier. Furnishings fit the space (i.e., double beds, not king-sized) and are lovely and hand-carved. All the rooms are well equipped with WiFi, cable TV, and fans, and, of course, those cute little balconies welcoming the breeze. An excellent mid-range choice.

Hostal los Pilares

Managers: Javier Jímenez and Rodrigo Rivas Palacio
951-518-7000, 518-6999
www.lospilareshostal.com
reservaciones@lospilareshostal.com
Curtidurias 721-A, Barrio Jalatlaco
Price: Expensive
Credit Cards: Yes
Handicapped Access: None
Special features: Rooftop *terraza* restaurant.

This quiet, personalized luxury hotel hidden away in Barrio Jalatlaco offers small but lovingly detailed rooms, with frilly vines painted on the archways and gold ribbons wrapped around the bathrobes. It's a bit precious, but does include all the world-class extras: air conditioning, Sky TV, telephones, WiFi, and a well-stocked minibar, as well as elegantly rustic furnishings, top-tier bedding, and hand-tiled bathrooms. Enjoy your complimentary breakfast either in the traditional courtyard patio-bar, or upstairs on the exceptional rooftop *terraza*, with views of Santo Domingo and the surrounding mountains. Huge ceramic urns bloom with flowering vines and other exotic plants around a small Jacuzzi under the stars, while a popular **restaurant** ($$–$$$; B, L, C, D) serves Oaxacan classics with a transcendent view; consider just stopping by for coffee.

Hotel Cazomalli

Owner: Francisco Perez
951-513-3513
www.hotelcazomalli.com
cazomalli@infosel.net.mx
El Salto 104, corner of Aldama
Price: Moderate
Credit Cards: Yes
Handicapped Access: None

Well away from the crowds in the city center, Barrio Jalatlaco's cobbled streets are just steps from festive Parque El Llano and a 10-minute walk to the Zócalo. There are a handful of great hotels in the area, including this family owned inn with cozy, cheerfully decorated rooms and sunny rooftop terrace overlooking San Matías Church. The rooms, with vaulted brick ceilings, colorful hand-carved furnishings, WiFi, cable TV, and other amenities, surround an informal covered central courtyard; the rooftop terrace is also a real winner. It's a good deal, particularly the "suites," actually family rooms with three or four beds. The owners also rent two homes.

Hotel de la Parra Oaxaca

Manager: Marla Patricia Cruz
951-514-1900
www.hoteldelaparra.com
frontdesk@hoteldelparra.com
Guerrero 117, Centro
Price: Expensive to Very Expensive
Credit Cards: Yes
Handicapped Access: No

Behind the high walls of these old Spanish cities are private courtyards and gardens with trickling fountains, where local nobility have maneuvered Oaxaca's intertwining social circles for centuries. Welcome to the de la Parra, a five-star boutique hotel set amid a truly grand *cantera* and adobe construction. English-speaking staff in sharp traditional garb welcome you to the first courtyard, where trellises covered with flowering vines and palm trees shade a very private pool. A second, even quieter, courtyard is just beyond, a boon so close to the Zócalo.

Both gardens are surrounded with whitewashed rooms, their size amplified by pale ceramic tile floors and light colored bedding and rugs, some Oaxacan and others Persian. This lightness is offset by wrought-iron light fixtures and elegant, dark-wood furnishings, such as heavy floor-length mirrors and hand-carved cupboards camouflaging huge televisions and minibars. It's definitely worth the extra US$25 to upgrade to a junior or master suite, which are much more spacious; some have Jacuzzis and/or secluded terraces.

✪ Hotel Hacienda and Spa Los Laureles

General Manager: Peter Kaiser
951-501-5300
www.hotelhaciendaloslaureles.com
bookings@hotelhaciendaloslaureles.com
Hidalgo 21, San Felipe del Agua
Price: Very Expensive
Credit Cards: Yes
Handicapped Access: Yes
Special features: Small spa and brilliant restaurant amid gorgeous gardens.

The 23 quietly opulent rooms and suites of this excellent boutique hotel surround some of the city's loveliest gardens: endless uncut bouquets of flowers, tropical plants, and shady trees that accent an expanse of lawn seemingly designed for a picture-perfect wedding. This is one of Oaxaca's finest hotels, a former hacienda that has been impeccably remodeled with world-class comfort in mind. In the upscale neighborhood of San Felipe del Agua, it's a short cab or bus ride from the Zócalo, but a world away from the hustle and bustle.

There are several types of room, and you are welcomed to each with papery amethyst bougainvillea flowers spelling *"bienvenido"* across the large, luxuriously outfitted beds. Even the least expensive standards are spacious and serenely furnished with polished wood, fine art, and soft-colored rugs and tapestries. Tall Colonial-style windows pour golden light across the interior, while lovely bathrooms are outfitted with robes, fluffy towels, and Pecksniff's Mood Therapy personal products. Spring for a more spacious superior or suite, and enjoy Persian rugs, Mexican ceramics, fruit baskets, sitting areas with antique furniture, bathtubs, and perhaps even tiny balconies. All come with cable television, air conditioning, minibars, WiFi, and all the other modern amenities you might desire.

Also onsite is the Petit Spa, offering several different massages, hydrotherapy treatments, facials, and exfoliations using natural products; there's even a *temazcal*. Or just enjoy the small pool next door. The superb onsite restaurant **Los Cypreses** (B, L, C, D; $$$$) is a local landmark, attracting Oaxacan society's "ladies who lunch" and businesspeople buttering each other up with upscale Oaxacan food, international haute cuisine, and the outstanding wine list. Everything goes upscale at dinner, when candles and stars illuminate the glass-enclosed patio overlooking the garden. Chef Horacio Reyes offers cooking classes onsite. All sorts of packages, including meals, transportation, or even weddings are available.

Hotel Los Olivos and Spa

Owner: Roberto Estrada
951-514-1946, 1-800-202-0739
www.losolivosspa.com.mx
oli1@losolivosspa.com.mx
Calzada Madero 1254, Colonia Exmarquezado
Price: Moderate

Credit Cards: Yes
Handicapped Access: Yes
Special Features: Full-service holistic spa, lap pool, yoga classes, vegetarian restaurant.

Sprawling 70-room, adobe hotel on the outskirts of downtown, convenient to Monte Albán and the Mixteca, dates from the late 1920s. Once quite the glamorous spot, it boasts a roster of photos of Mexican movie stars from the black-and-white film era, as well as writers, artists, and other luminaries. Though well maintained, this Southwest-revival-style beauty was long ago eclipsed by more fabulous hotels downtown.

Thus, the hotel has remade itself into something of a health retreat, with all the perks: an almost Olympic-sized swimming pool, jogging track, beautiful gardens fully equipped for wheelchairs. To this they've added one of Oaxaca's best spas, with standard facial and massage services, plus doz-

Oaxacan cuisine has gone upscale, and it's worth splashing out at one of the city's fine dining restaurants, such as Los Cypreses, at Hacienda Los Laureles in San Felipe.

For over a thousand years, Mesoamericans have enjoyed the temazcal, *a type of sauna that includes a fresh herbal massage.*

ens of holistic wellness treatments, such as hydrotherapy, yoga, and chakra alignment. There's even a 60-person *temazcal* (and a smaller one, too). A healthy vegetarian breakfast is included, courtesy of restaurant **Verde Aceituna** ($; B, L, C), worth the trek for vegetarians for its excellent *comida*.

Rooms are spacious with rather retro furnishings and color schemes that reinforce that Route 66 feel. Older rooms are nicer, with Mexican Art Deco extras such as great tile floors and frescoed ceilings. Those closest to the office have WiFi. It's a US$2 cab ride or 20-minute walk to the Zócalo, and there's convenient bus service.

Hotel Marqués del Valle

Manager: Alfonso Rule Doorman
951-514-0688; 800-849-9936 Mexico
www.hotelmarquesdelvalle.com.mx
hamarques@prodigy.net
Portal de Claveria, Zócalo
Price: Moderate to Expensive
Credit Cards: Yes

Handicapped Access: Yes
Special features: Balcony rooms overlooking the Zócalo.

Location, location, location: Sure, the venerable Marqués del Valle, the Zócalo's grand dame for more than 60 years, may charge a tiny bit more than other hotels for its large, marble-floored rooms with attractive wood furnishings, locally made bedspreads, cable TV, and phone (the lobby has WiFi). And, yes, it can get noisy on fiesta nights, when the *castillo de fuego* fireworks displays go off pretty much right outside your room. But that is exactly why you're staying here, so why not reserve one of the balcony rooms and get ready to party. Service is great, and they really do take care of the gracefully aging rooms, so enjoy yourself.

Also right on the Zócalo is much more basic, cavernous, 300-year-old **Hotel Monte Albán** (951-516-2777; travelbymexico.com/oaxaca/montealban; Alameda de León 1, Zócalo; credit cards accepted; $$), with authentic (perhaps too authentic for some) Colonial-style rooms that come with cable TV, air conditioning, creaky beds, and theoretically 24-hour hot water.

✪ Posada Casa Oaxaca

Owners: Antonio and Alejandro Ruiz
Telephone: 951-514-4173
www.casaoaxaca.com.mx
reservaciones@casaoaxaca.com.mx
García Vigil 407
Price: Very Expensive
Credit Cards: Yes
Handicapped Access: Challenging
Special Features: One of Oaxaca's best restaurants onsite.

Hidden behind high walls is this white-washed Colonial boutique hotel, with just a handful of sophisticated rooms surrounding an elegant stone courtyard with a pool, *temazcal,* and fine-dining restaurant. The setting is almost Zen, with a rather minimalist take on five-star Colonial luxury. Rooms are relaxed and polished, with heavy antique wood furnishings that accent the authentic window and door frames, rescued from another era.

King-sized beds are new, however, as are the other comfortable furnishings that seem designed to soothe. Built-in partial walls offer some privacy and another intriguing design element. All rooms come with WiFi, satellite TV, and other conveniences. Suites are even larger; the excellent upstairs suite has two separate bedrooms.

Of course, they offer tours, medical recommendations, child care, and other services, but this is a particularly good choice for foodies. Everyone's favorite amenity is a complimentary, cooked-to-order breakfast by chef Alejandro Ruiz, generally recognized as one of Oaxaca's (i.e., the world's) best chefs. Ask about cooking classes and market tours. With a day's notice, he'll prepare almost anything for you.

Bed & Breakfasts

Oaxaca is just a B&B kind of town, with several beautiful and artsy options for every budget. These are a few of my favorites, but be sure to check the **Oaxaca Bed & Breakfast Association** (www.oaxaca bedandbreakfast.org) for more options, many with just one or two rooms.

Casa Colonial

Owner: Jane Robison
951-516-5280
www.casa-colonial.com
reservations@casa-colonial.com
Calle Miguel Negrete 105
Price: Moderate to Expensive
Credit Cards: Yes
Handicapped Access: No

A bit off the beaten track, this brightly painted Colonial mansion is a great choice for garden lovers, with meandering pathways through the intense tropical foliage leading to secret spots to relax on small patios or strategically hung hammocks. Nine rooms are arranged around this sweet-smelling centerpiece, all lovingly maintained with big windows, pretty décor, and outstanding bathrooms.

Rooms have individual entrances, and children and pets are accepted. A full Oaxacan breakfast with all the trimmings is served in the expansive dining room, and you can make reservations for *comida* or dinner as well.

✪ Casa de las Bugambilias

Manager: Aurora Cabrera
951-516-1165; 866-829-6778 USA & Canada
www.lasbugambilias.com
bugambilias@lasbugambilias.com
Reforma 402, between Abasolo and Constitución
Price: Moderate
Credit Cards: Yes
Handicapped Access: Yes

Special features: Cooking school and outstanding onsite restaurant.

Delightfully offbeat B&B displays its festive art collection throughout the old Cabrera family home, a more modern structure with big windows, sliding French doors, modern fixtures, and wonderful flower-strewn courtyards. The owners (who speak fluent English) have refreshed the house with eclectic antiques, ranging from 17th-century Spanish imports and early hand-carved Oaxacan armoires and desks to a jumble of more recent styles expertly mixed and matched throughout the premises. Intermingled are exquisite examples of local *artesanías,* not your ordinary selection of *alejibres,* and contemporary art from the region's best painters.

All the rooms are unique, but all include comfortable beds and deluxe bedding, natural Oaxacan personal care products, fresh flowers, WiFi, and free or inexpensive international calls. Some have private terraces and/or wheelchair access, but only the Girasol Suite (the only room where children are accepted) has a private television, as well as two separate bedrooms, air conditioning, and a refrigerator. There's a TV in one of the lounge areas for everyone else. Breakfast is legendary, as is the adjacent restaurant, ✪ **La Olla** (B, L, C, D; $–$$$). The owners will also arrange all sorts of tours, teach you how to create the perfect mole at their highly rated cooking school, or arrange a *temazcal* for couples and small groups.

They also manage two other B&Bs. **Casa de los Milagros** (951-501-2262; casadelos-milagros.com; info@casadelosmilagros .com; Matamoros 500-C, corner of Crespo, Centro; MC, V; $$$) is a thoughtfully decorated, modern home with three white-washed rooms surrounding a brick court-yard; one has a private patio with waterfall. **La Casa de los Sabores** (951-516-5704; www.mexonline.com/sabores.htm; Libres

205, Centro; MC, V; $$) is a more traditional Colonial hotel that offers package deals with the cooking school.

✪ La Casa de Mis Recuerdos
Owner: William Frederick
951-515-8483
877-234-4706 U.S. and Canada
www.misrecuerdos.net
misrecue@hotmail.com
Pino Suárez 508, Centro
Price: Moderate to Expensive
Credit Cards: Yes
Handicapped Access: None
Special features: Cooking school and market tours.

This absolutely flawless B&B set in a fine old Colonial offers an authentic Oaxacan experience. Nine rooms, all with different shapes, sizes, and décor, are furnished with beautiful antiques and Colonial art, fine local furniture, and fabulous handicrafts. Many are painted in relaxed colors, with arches, columns, and perhaps private porches or patios. Some rooms are rather small, such as Alondra, which has a tiny but exquisitely tiled bath. Though none of the rooms has television, three do have air conditioning.

The spectacularly tiled kitchen serves full Oaxaca breakfasts on the bougainvillea-draped patio and is also home to **Cocina de Nora**, offering cooking classes and market tours, including tours to the surrounding crafts villages of the Central Valleys. Details are at **Alma de Mi Tierra Tours** (www .almademitierra.net).

Casa de Mis Recuerdos also manages apartments and two B&Bs without permanent onsite staff, though they do cook breakfast for you; details are on the Web site. **Estancia de Valencia** ($$–$$$), about three blocks away, is a contemporary three-bedroom home with a small courtyard and fountain, sunny communal areas, and lots of wrought iron. Mission Revival-style

Encanto Jalatlaco ($$-$$$), a bit further from the city center, has rooms with private patios, gardens, and/or balconies.

Hotel Las Mariposas
Owner: Teresa Villareal
951-515-5854
619-793-5121 U.S. and Canada
www.lasmariposas.com.mx
Pino Suárez 517
Price: Moderate
Credit Cards: Yes
Handicapped Access: None

Great value B&B offers a sprawl of 20 good-sized accommodations, many with full kitchens. Rooms are comfortable, with small but beautifully tiled hot-water bathrooms, new beds, WiFi, and useful furniture, but are by no means plush; there's no air conditioning, and only broadcast television. The high ceilings and large windows of the older, Colonial part of the complex make these rooms seem even larger and more atmospheric, with colorful paint schemes, exposed adobe brick, and eclectic furnishings. Newer rooms may be quieter and more comfortable, but perhaps a bit sterile and small.

And you just can't beat those endless gardens and pretty patios that are basically a maze of tropical trees and flowering vines, with hammocks, fountains, and sitting areas. The full breakfast comes with organic coffee, and purified water is available throughout the day. It's popular with the flashpacker set, so be sure to make reservations, particularly during fiestas.

Oaxaca Bed & Breakfast Ollin
Owners: Jon McKinley and Judith Reyes Lopez
951-514-9126, 619-787-5141 in the U.S.
www.oaxacabedandbreakfast.com
reservations@oaxacabedandbreakfast.com
Quintana Roo 213
Price: Moderate

Credit Cards: Yes
Handicapped Access: Challenging

Perfect for folks who love B&Bs but also appreciate privacy, this nice spot offers several rooms arranged like a hotel, around a cheerful little pool, with private entrances onto the flowering patio. The rooms, while quite modern, are decorated with Oaxacan touches, such as handcrafted bedspreads and rugs, curtains, furniture, and art. The bathrooms are beautifully tiled, and the main building has a homey, wood-paneled breakfast room. The owners can arrange guides, tours, and almost anything else.

Other Hotels
La Casa de Adobe (951-520-0536; www.lacasadeadobe.com; Avenida de las Etnias; credit cards accepted; $$$$) Warmly furnished "small luxury suites" surround Casa de Adobe's pleasant grounds with fountains and a pool, making it a good choice for families. There's an onsite restaurant and bar serving traditional Oaxacan food.

✪ **Casa los Cantaros** (Christina Palacios Castillo; 951-513-9297; www.hotelcasaloscantaros.com; Porfirio Díaz 127; credit cards accepted; $$-$$$) This beautiful, new four-star just opened, allowing guests to enjoy eight classy boutique rooms with antique and handmade wood and wrought-iron furnishing accessorized with classic B&B style. WiFi, cable TV, coffee machine, and hair dryer are all included; the two suites are larger, with two separate bedrooms. Breakfast, served in the gorgeous little gardens, costs extra, however.

COLONIA REFORMA
This modern neighborhood almost exactly between San Felipe and El Centro (and on the same bus route) has great restaurants and cafés, cute shops, and lots of Oaxacans . . . trying to escape the tourists.

Hostal las Cúpulas (951-520-1116; www.oaxaca-mio.com/lascupulas.htm; Calle

Oaxaca on a Budget

Seasoned budget travelers will have no problem finding cheap lodging. Penny pinchers can check out **Couchsurfing** (www.couchsurfing.com) and **Hostel Planet** (www.hostelplanet.com), while Spanish schools can help even non-students arrange homestays, a great deal on room and board. There are dozens of budget hotels, with rooms from US$10–25 double, in the busy southwest quadrant of the city, roughly between Mercado 20 de Noviembre and Abastos Centro. These vary widely in quality; look at a few before committing. I visited perhaps 40 budget hotels, not even half of what's available. Here are a few of my favorites.

✪**Casa Arnel** (951-515-2856; www.casaarnel.com.mx; Aldama 404, Jalatlaco; cash only; $–$$) This truly wonderful spot in Barrio Jalatlaco offers 20 rooms of all shapes and sizes around outstanding gardens with rock walls, parrots, and even a Zapotec-style lending library. Immaculate rooms have hard beds, stylish furniture, and original art, some with shared bath. The staff arranges all the tours and offers inexpensive cooking classes.

Casa Azucenas (951-514-7918, 800-717-2540 Mexico, 1-800-882-6089 U.S. and Canada; www .hotelazucenas.com; Aranda 203, before Union; credit cards accepted; $–$$) About a block north of the Basílica de la Soledad, this classic Colonial is popular with volunteer groups and NGOs. Ten thoughtfully refurbished rooms, some with balconies and others with no windows at all, all have pretty furnishings, WiFi, and tiny televisions by request. A big buffet breakfast (US$4.40) is available on the sunny, flower-filled rooftop terrace.

✪**Hotel Florida** (951-516-5911; Aldama 417; cash only; $) Of all the budget hotels in Oaxaca, this is my top pick. Large, clean rooms are impeccably attended and have good beds, hot water, fans, a small courtyard, and a third-floor terrace with views over the street scene and El Fortín. It's not Colonial, and there's no WiFi, but the owners are real sweethearts and have a small store with a fruit stand right off the lobby. Convenient.

Hotel Posada del Tía (951-514-1963; Cinco de Mayo 108; credit cards accepted; $) Classic colonial mansion surrounding a relaxed patio offers simple, spotless rooms with high ceilings and tiled private baths, as well as WiFi, fans, televisions, mismatched but functional furnishings, and comfortable beds. Seven of the posada's 15 rooms sleep up to five, with two floors connected by a metal spiral staircase.

The Oaxaca Learning Center (951-515-0122, skype: garytitus; www.tolc.org.mx; Murguia 703, Centro; $) This cheerful, comfortable, and basic B&B with two nicely decorated, fan-cooled rooms benefits the Learning Center, a non-profit that provides free tutoring to area teens. For details on how you can help, check out the Web site.

✪**Posada Catarina** (951-516-4270; www.travelbymexico.com/oaxa/posadacatarina; Aldama 325, Centro; credit cards accepted; $–$$) This well-run, immaculate family hotel three blocks from the plaza offers 30 clean, modern rooms scattered around several shady courtyards and hidden gardens. Rustic furnishings, WiFi, telephones, small cable TVs, and a few rooms with air conditioning make this a wonderful choice.

Posada del Centro (951-516-1874; www.mexonline.com/posada.htm; Independencia 403; credit cards accepted; $–$$) A charming, sprawling, colorfully restored (by owner Doris Josefina Acevedo) spot with patios, potted plants, fountains, and places to relax, it has different-sized and -decorated rooms outfitted with WiFi, local TV, and *artesanías*. Six rooms have shared bath, even less expensive.

Iturbide 213-A; credit cards accepted; $$$$) Tiny boutique hotel one block off Hidalgo offers nine pretty rooms, of different shapes and sizes, on three floors. A member of the Raintree Vacation Club, Las Cúpulas offers a lot of luxury in a small (perhaps claustrophobic) package, with all the five-star amenities and lovely décor, plus a rooftop terrace with wonderful views.

Hotel Angel Inn (951-133-6128, 133 6129; www.hotelangelinn.com.mx; Hidalgo 204; credit cards accepted; $$–$$$) You can't miss this brightly painted, very family friendly hotel, with 32 colorful, modern rooms surrounding a narrow central courtyard. It's landscaped with delightful flowers, merry-go-round horses, and a small pool with a shallow kiddie section. Children love the bright décor (antique pedal cars, anyone?) and have their own menu of familiar foods at the reasonably priced second-floor **El Retablo Restaurant** (B, L, C, D; $$), with a full bar and lots of old movie posters. There are two suites with Jacuzzi tubs.

San Felipe del Agua

Oaxaca's poshest suburb boasts a city park with waterfalls and great birding, quiet streets to stroll, a crumbling Spanish aqueduct, and a handful of excellent hotels, including Hacienda Los Laureles, covered earlier. There aren't really any restaurants or shops within an easy walk, but that's part of the appeal. It's a US$5 cab ride to the Zócalo, and convenient public buses (US

50¢) run every 10 minutes straight into the city center.

Suites Regente (951-132-4257; Porfiro Díaz 101; credit cards accepted; $$$) An excellent deal for families or groups, Regente offers eight big, business-style and beautiful suites with wood floors, new furniture, glass-brick bathrooms, and balconies. Each has two bedrooms (one with an excellent full-size bed, the other with two twins, both with cable televisions), a huge living room, full kitchen with microwave and coffee maker, and WiFi.

Vacation Rentals

There are hundreds of vacation rentals available in Oaxaca City, but not many local Web sites covering them. Check the **Oaxaca Times** (www.oaxacatimes.com/html/classifieds.html) and **Craigslist Oaxaca** (www.oaxaca.en.craigslist.com.mx) for other listings.

J&S Real Estate (951-221-1251; jassibeoax .googlepages.com; jassibeoax@gmail.com; Calzada de la Republica 717) Owner Jassibe Moon offers apartments and rooms in private houses.

MEXonline (www.mexonline.com/oaxaca/oaxaca-lodgings.htm) Dozens of hotel, B&B, vacation rental, and apartment listings

VRBO (www.vrbo.com) The vacation rental giant has some Oaxaca listings.

RESTAURANTS AND FOOD PURVEYORS

Oaxaca's cuisine is the city's pride and joy, and this is one of the world's premier foodie destinations. From the famed moles and richly spiced hot chocolate known throughout the world to more unusual ingredients that you'll be hard pressed to find back home, such as squash blossoms, *escamole* (ant caviar), and *huitlacoche* (corn fungus), there is no end to its variety.

There are hundreds of restaurants in and around town, many of them listed by **CANIRAC** (Oaxacan Restaurant Association; caniracoaxaca.com.mx), with entries that can be sorted by children's menu *(menu para niños),* delivery service *(entrega a domicilio),* and liquor license *(servicio de bar).*

As in most of Mexico, *comida* (literally, "food") is the major meal, usually served between 2 PM and 6 PM. Most restaurants offer a set *menú* (a menu is usually called a *carta*), a prix-fixe meal with four or more courses, generally a soup or salad followed by a pasta, main dish, and dessert, served with a fruit drink. This is usually the best deal of the day.

Some guidebooks will warn you away from the many street vendors and market stalls selling delicious, authentic, and inexpensive Oaxacan food, from *elotes* (corn on the cob served with mayonnaise, chile, and/or lime) to *tamales,* but this isn't one of them. Stands and markets in Oaxaca City cater to international tourists, and food is usually prepared using purified water in clean kitchens, with standards equal to or higher than many full-service restaurants (where the kitchen is hidden from view). Of course, use your best judgment when selecting a stand or stall, choosing a spot that looks clean, preferably packed with local clientele. Outside the city center, however, be more selective.

Choose your tasajo, *and watch as it's grilled to perfection while you choose the sides. Grilled* nopales *(cactus paddles), perhaps?*

Restaurants and Food Purveyors Price Code

The following prices are based on the cost of a dinner entrée with a non-alcoholic beverage, not including the usually voluntary (but check your receipt) 10–15 percent gratuity that should probably be added. The coding "B, L, C, D" refers to U.S.-style meals (breakfast, lunch, dinner), as well as the typical Mexican *comida,* traditionally the biggest meal of the day, served in lieu of lunch from about 2 PM to 6 PM. Prices are calculated at 10 pesos to the dollar.

Inexpensive:	Up to US$5
Moderate:	US$5 to US$10
Expensive:	US$10 to US$20
Very Expensive:	US$20 or more

Restaurants

1254 Marco Polo

951-513-4308
Pino Suárez 806, Llano Park
Closed: Tues.
Price: Moderate to Expensive
Credit Cards: Yes
Cuisine: Seafood
Serving: B, L, C, D
Reservations: Yes

Whether for a reasonably priced *comida* or romantic seafood dinner, take a seat in this lush, shady patio, right off Parque El Llano. Hung over? Begin with the *vuelve a la vida* (return to life), a spicy ceviche marinated in a light tomato, lime, cilantro, and onion broth, also purported to have aphrodisiac qualities. Or go for the *chilpachole,* a soup made with roasted shrimp, peppers, onions, and tomatoes. The main course could include a special chile relleno, stuffed with seafood, or the *huauchinango a la Verona,* red snapper baked in a wood-fired oven with corn, peppers, and cheese. There's a good wine list and several desserts, perfect for a fine evening out.

There are two choices of *comida,* a less expensive option without seafood, and a pricier version with two seafood courses and a glass of white wine. Light eaters can opt for fish tacos or shrimp *tlayudas,* and big breakfasts are also served. There's another branch in the city center, at Cinco de Mayo 103, with smaller, less atmospheric seating on two floors; go upstairs for a quieter meal overlooking the busy street below.

El Bicho Pobre

951-513-4636
Calzada de la Republica 600, Jalatlaco
Price: Moderate
Credit Cards: Cash only
Cuisine: Oaxacan
Serving: B, L, C, D
Reservations: No

Busy, no-frills, diner-style eatery serves solid Oaxacan cuisine at good prices in an old Spanish Colonial mansion. Grab a heavy wooden table draped with a cheerful hand-woven green *tela* and take your pick from the traditional and inexpensive eats: *molletes, tlayudas,* omelets, *chilaquiles,* beef tongue in salsa . . . the list goes on. It's all authentic, all delicious, and at breakfast, it all comes with a bottomless cup of coffee.

✪ La Biznaga

951-516-1800
García Vigil 512
Closed: Sun.
Price: $54–100
Credit Cards: Yes
Cuisine: Mexican fusion

Serving: L, C, D
Reservations: For dinner

A relaxed and airy option just perfect for *comida,* a drink, or one of the best dinners in town, La Biznaga inhabits a spacious open-air patio with a retractable roof and jazz in the background. Big blackboard menus offer any number of Latin fusion interpretations of Oaxacan classics, such as a delicious mole made with *guayaba,* chicken in a tangy *jamaica* (hibiscus) or blackberry sauce, and much, much more, all courtesy of chef Rodrigo López.

Big salads get special raves, with intriguing combinations such as the *Tehuana de Berros,* with pear, pistachios and Roquefort cheese. Food is made fresh to order, so come expecting a leisurely meal; two nice *artesanías* shops onsite will keep kids and other impatient sorts busy. Portions are huge and the menu of mezcals impressive; try the Chichicapa, or any of more than a dozen others, or a recommended margarita.

Casa del Tio Güero
951-516-9584
García Vigil 715, at Cosijope
Price: Inexpensive
Credit Cards: Cash only
Cuisine: Oaxacan, vegetarian
Serving: B, L, C, D
Reservations: No

Inhabiting the high-ceilinged former home of Dominican monks, the old *cantera* walls decorated with *hojalata* and traditional masks, this inexpensive eatery serves traditional Oaxacan food, including many vegetarian options, at excellent prices. Big salads, mushroom and squash blossom *tlayudas,* and *pollo a la jamaica* (chicken in hibiscus sauce) are all popular, but the signature dish is the vegetarian *chiles rellenos,* poblano chiles stuffed with soy meat,

Hungry? Why not head to your local market for a tasty tlayuda, *hot off the* comal *and topped with squash blossoms.*

mushrooms, dried fruit, and almonds, garnished with pomegranate seeds. Though the friendly main dining room is a fine place to eat, an upstairs terrace provides a more romantic ambience. The owners also offer cooking classes.

✪ Casa Oaxaca

951-516-8889, 951-502-6017
www.casa-oaxaca.com
oaxacacafe@hotmail.com
Constitución 104-A; García Vigil 407
Closed: Sun.
Price: Very Expensive
Credit Cards: Yes
Cuisine: Gourmet Oaxacan
Serving: D
Reservations: Highly recommended

When you're ready to propose, Oaxaca's favorite fine dining restaurant has two impeccable locations, both enjoying raves from all quarters for its innovative Mexican cuisine. The García Vigil branch, within the high walls of Posada Casa Oaxaca, its beautiful boutique hotel, is more intimate. But I preferred the more popular satellite branch, across from Santo Domingo, with a classy, whitewashed "nuevo Oaxaqueño" style that rather fits the cuisine.

Chef Alejandro Ruiz specializes in creative Mexican, with specialties such as *manchamateles* mole ("stains the table-cloth" mole, so be careful) served over pork; tacos with *chapulines,* and splendid fish dishes hailing from the Isthmus, such as the shrimp-stuffed sea bass. Some items seem to be pure invention, for instance, the squash blossoms stuffed with cheese and honey. All sorts of tapas and a full bar can help prime your appetite. Ruiz can prepare almost anything, however; simply make your request one day in advance, so he can purchase the ingredients.

El Che

951-514-2122
Cinco de Mayo 413
Price: Expensive to Very Expensive
Credit Cards: Yes
Cuisine: Steak, Argentine
Serving: D
Reservations: Yes

This trendy steakhouse close to Santo Domingo church has a beautiful dining room with huge windows onto all the late-evening action. And that's when you should arrive, after 9:30 PM or so, when (in true Argentine style) things really get started. The specialty is Argentine cuts of steak, and there's an excellent wine list. Or just have an entrée or two, perhaps those fabulous empanadas, with the fine vintage of your choice. This is a see-and-be-seen scene, so dress to impress, and enjoy the pampering.

✪ Escapularío

951-516-4687
García Vigil 617
Price: Inexpensive to Moderate
Credit Cards: Cash only
Cuisine: Oaxacan
Serving: B, L, C, D
Reservations: No

The simple second-story restaurant in a slightly frayed old Colonial offers awesome views over the city and churches, and seriously traditional Oaxacan cuisine. The specialty of the house, served on handmade ceramic plates, is chicken breast swimming in either salsa Oaxaca, made with *chapulines* (crickets), or even more unusual salsa *chicatanas,* made with a local and very large ant. On the side, have one of their many traditional aguas, including *chía,* a nutritious seed, *pepino,* or cucumber, and *horchata* made with amaranth rather than rice. Breakfast is also recommended, and not quite as traditional; try the eggs with nopales. *Comida* is a great value.

La Hierba Santa

951-516-3543
lahierbasanta@gmail.com
Matamoros 101, Centro
Closed: Sun.
Price: Moderate to Expensive
Credit Cards: Yes
Cuisine: Oaxacan
Serving: C, D
Reservations: Yes

A laid-back place with chunky wooden furniture, flattering lighting, and good music, this is a relaxed spot to enjoy excellent, upscale "Oaxacan fusion" cuisine. The ingredients are traditional, the preparations less so. Start with warm rolls and the house pesto and an upscale version of *sopa de elote* (corn soup), with poblano chiles and calabaza flowers. Then, perhaps, shrimp sautéed with lime, or the house specialty, red snapper wrapped in the herb from which the restaurant takes its name, a broad leaf with tender checkerboard veins and a slight hint of anise, and steamed. There's a solid wine and liquor selection.

✪ La Olla

951-516-1165
www.laolla.com.mx
Reforma 402, between Abasolo and Constitución
Closed: Sun.
Price: Moderate
Credit Cards: Yes
Cuisine: Oaxacan
Serving: B, L, C, D
Reservations: Yes

Everyone loves La Olla for its uncompromising excellence and moderate prices, making it one of the most popular spots in the city. It specializes in well-prepared local favorites, such as delicious moles served with freshly made *queso fresco,* or agua and pasilla chiles stuffed with chicken and vegetables. But specialties from around the state, such as the *huachinango* in *hierba santa,* red

snapper steamed wrapped with the broad-leafed, anise-tasting herb, are also on offer.

Los Pacos

951-516-1704
www.lospacos.com.mx
Absolo 121, Centro
Price: Moderate to Expensive
Credit Cards: Yes
Cuisine: Oaxacan
Serving: B, L, C, D
Reservations: Yes

"Paquitos," as locals affectionately refer to this neighborhood landmark, is probably best known for its faithful production of all seven moles, served on different days of the week. Though the food is excellent and traditional, with outstanding and rather upscale takes on *enmolladas, chilaquiles, brochetas de tasajo,* and other Oaxacan classics, this is also a top spot to meet friends for a drink and *botanas* before heading out on the town.

There's another branch in Colonia Reforma (951-515-3573; Belisario Domínguez 108-1), but it doesn't have quite the same cache with *fiesteros* (party people).

Las Quince Letras

951-514-3769
Absolo 300, between Juárez and Pino Suarez
Closed: Sun.
Price: Moderate
Credit Cards: Cash only
Cuisine: Oaxacan
Serving: B, L, C, D
Reservations: No

This friendly and atmospheric typical restaurant offers all your Oaxacan (and Sonoran) favorites with attentive service and a little more flair than the average eatery. Feast in the cozy, colorful front dining room with views onto the street, or the more soothing back patio, on favorites such as the *rollo de tasajo especial,* Oaxaca's distinctively seasoned, thinly cut steak, served with *chapulines, epazote,* and soft cheese; or go for pre-Columbian flavor with the *sopa Oaxaqueña,* a black-bean soup seasoned with indigenous herbs such as *hierba conejo.*

Though the international crowd is catered to with big salads and pastas, go for the excellent five-course menú, or the *botana Oaxaqueña* sample platter.

Restaurant Catedral

951-516-3285
www.restaurantecatedral.com.mx
García Vigil 105
Price: Moderate to Expensive
Credit Cards: Yes
Cuisine: Oaxacan, buffet
Serving: B, L, C, D
Reservations: For groups

A local institution, this rather elegant bar and restaurant surrounding a quiet patio and fountain (or try the dining room, perfect for huge parties) serves perfectly acceptable Oaxacan classics, such as the *sopa catedral,* a creamy cheese soup with pumpkin, squash blossoms, and corn; cheese-stuffed plantain medallions; and the perennial favorite, whole roasted suckling pig. But the reason to come is the surreal Sunday buffet (8 AM–2 PM), an entire room full of Oaxacan, Mexican, and international favorites and an almost hallucinogenic choice of desserts. Don't hurt yourself.

Restaurante los Danzantes

951-501-1184
www.losdanzantes.com
Alcalá 403-404
Price: Moderate to Expensive
Credit Cards: Yes
Cuisine: Contemporary Oaxacan
Serving: C, D
Reservations: Yes

Even locals who don't "do" touristy restaurants on Alcalá grudgingly admit their love for Los Danzantes, a class act with one of the most beautiful dining rooms in town. Pieces commissioned from Oaxaca's up-and-coming artists welcome guests into the beautifully lit, adobe-walled inner sanctum, classic and yet absolutely modern.

And that's the vision for the food, which combines classic Oaxacan ingredients with creative recipes, such as the zucchini flowers stuffed with cheese and avocado leaves, chayote coulis, or the *huitlacoche* (corn fungus) ravioli in a light squash blossom sauce. The black mole crème brulee is a dessert you'll find nowhere else. Match it all with your choice from one of the state's best wine lists, or perhaps something from their house mezcal distillery, in Matatlán. Though most items are on the pricey side, it offers one of the best *comidas* in town for US$8.

Temple Restaurant and Bar

951-516-8676
www.temple.com.mx
García Vigil 409-A
Price: Expensive
Credit Cards: Yes
Cuisine: Contemporary Latin fusion
Serving: D
Reservations: Yes

Sophisticated and innovative, this beautiful restaurant is a local favorite for its excellent service and unusual menu. Chef José Antonio Cuéllar mixes local and international ingredients and techniques to create winning dishes such as raviolis stuffed with traditional Oaxacan picadillo in a salmon pesto sauce, or spring rolls stuffed with fried squash blossoms. The tapas menu, and very full bar, are probably bigger attractions, as is the live jazz on Wednesday, Friday, and Saturday at 9 PM. Not that anyone shows up that early; the hip crowd meanders in around 10:30 or so.

La Toscana

951-513-8742
latoscana@hotmail.com
Cinco de Mayo 614, corner of Alianza, Jalatlaco
Credit Cards: Yes
Cuisine: Italian
Serving: C, D
Reservations: Yes

An elegant option offering fine Italian cuisine served inside a whitewashed Colonial mansion in the quiet cobblestoned neighborhood of Jalatlaco. The dining room is beautiful, anchored by an ancient well that today is used as a gorgeous central water feature, reverberating with live cello music on weekends. Try the salmon Toscana, with a slightly sweet sauce made of raisins over spinach, or the coconut shrimp, served here with a sauce of pureed pasilla chile, ginger, and pineapple. Pastas are made fresh; try yours with the duck in pesto. There's an excellent wine list and full bar.

Trastévere

951-512-925
Díaz Quintas 117, corner of Maza, Centro
Closed: 6 PM Sun.
Price: Expensive to Very Expensive
Credit Cards: Yes
Serving: L, D
Reservation: No

When you've reached mole saturation, come to Trastévere for upscale Italian food courtesy of chef Mario Saggessi, formerly employed by the Vatican. Different home-made pastas come topped, for example, *con gamberi e fungi,* with mushrooms imported from Italy, or *primavera,* made with locally produced vegetables and shrimp. Veal, aged steak, chicken, and other dishes are faithfully prepared by Italian methods, paired with something exquisite from the extensive wine and liquor list. Finish off with *zuccotto,* a pastry stuffed with fruit and sweet cheese, or anything else off their extensive dessert menu,

Service is formal and outstanding; the dining room contemporary and sleek, with elegant marble floors, dark wood tables, modern art and red accents quite different from the usual upscale Oaxacan eatery.

Zandunga

951-516-2265
García Vigil and Jesús Carranza, Centro
Closed: Sun.
Price: Moderate to Expensive
Credit Cards: No
Cuisine: Istmeño
Serving: C, D
Reservations: Yes

The Isthmus of Tehuantepec, on the Pacific Coast at the far southeast corner of the state, is home to some of the best traditional cuisine in Mexico. Seafood is, of course, the specialty, and here it's served, perfectly cooked, spiced, and shredded with salsa and *totopos,* crunchy corn chips unique to the Isthmus, the moment you sit down.

The classic Istmeño dish is the *garnacha,* a thick fried tortilla topped with meat, *queso fresco,* salsa, and pickled cabbage. Then take your pick. The slightly sweet tamales of Tehuantepec, stuffed with meat and dried fruit? Or the *estofada,* chicken stewed with fruits and vegetables? Be sure to save room for the spiced hot chocolate, a bit different then you'll find elsewhere.

Can't get enough Istmeño cuisine? Also try **Yu Ne Nisa** (Amapolas 1425, Reforma), well known for its dried shrimp mole.

Food Purveyors

Asian

Casablanca (951-513-4617; Circuito 113-A, la Cascada, Reforma; L, C, D; $$$; credit cards accepted) The best Chinese food in town.

Coppel Hidalgo Department store } + Av de Independara Zocalo

Super Oriental y Cafetéria Nagomi (951-121-3514; Hidalgo 1208 between Delgado and Xtcotenéatl) This Japanese grocery store also offers *comida*.

Sushi Express Kin Su (951-515-0075; Naranjos 100, corner of Las Rosas, Reforma; credit cards accepted) Also delivers.

Sushi Itto (951-514-0522; www.sushi-itto.com; Juárez 114, Centro) The international chain serves acceptable sushi and other Japanese dishes.

Bakeries
Most bakeries produce traditional Mexican pastries, perhaps lighter, dryer, and crustier than you're used to. At many markets, you'll also find called *pan de yema*, or a

slightly sweet egg bread with swirls of cinnamon.

CentroBamby Pan (951-516-2510; García Vigil 205, right off Zócalo) Very typical, very good, *very* cheap: Grab a round metal tray and set of pincers, then carbo load. They'll tally everything at the counter, then hand you your bill; pay at the *caja*, or cashier.

La Carmelita (951-513-0240; 803 Libres, Centro) On the border of Barrio Jalatlaco, this fine bakery specializes in pastries and fine cakes, but also sells breads, sandwiches, and other goodies.

Pan & Co. (951-501-1672; Allende 113, corner of García Vigil; open 9 AM–8:30 PM Mon.–Sat.) European-style (focaccia, baguettes, rye, and much more) loaves made with only natural ingredients. Pan

---

Dining on the Zócalo

At the heart of the city (and perhaps the universe) is the Zócalo, always alive with music, art, color, and of course, flavor. The arcaded portals that surround the pale green expanse of stone and life shelter at least a dozen restaurants and coffee shops, all with bistro seating and the best views in town. Pick a place. All are excellent, offering Oaxacan favorites, international options, fine wine, and rich coffee to the endless parade of tourists and locals, lovers and fighters, vendors and seekers who make the rounds. All take credit cards and most include a tip right on the bill. Here are a few favorites.

El Asador Vasco (951-514-4755; www.asadorvasco.com; Portal de Flores N0.10-A; B, C, D; $$$) Popular, award-winning restaurant, which claims to be one of Oaxaca's first, offers delicate Spanish Basque cuisine as well as robust Oaxacan favorites.

Casa de la Abuela (951-516-3544; casadelaabuela2002@yahoo.com; Hidalgo 616, second story; C, D; $$–$$$) The airy second-story dining room lined with beautiful Mexican ceramics and huge French windows offers awesome views (you must have a meal, not just drinks) and excellent traditional cuisine, including *caldillo de nopales* (cactus soup), signature squash blossom *tlayudas*, and real *café de olla*, coffee prepared in a caldron.

Como Agua pa' Chocolate (951-516-2917; www.comoaguapachocolate.com; Hidalgo 612; B, L, C, D; $$–$$$) This frilly, feminine café inspired by the eponymous book (quotes from which are featured on the walls) offers great Mexican dishes adapted from the novel. There are plenty of vegetarian and flashy international (think flambés) options.

Terranova (951-516-4752; www.terranova-oaxaca.com.mx; Portal Benito Juárez 116; B, L, C, D; $$–$$$) Well loved for its excellent Oaxacan cuisine, Terranova is often described as the best on the Zócalo.

Street performers and their fans relax on the pedestrian walkways and plazas of downtown Oaxaca.

& Co. also sells natural yogurts, cheeses, pestos, and more. There's another branch in Reforma (Belisario Domínguez 612).

Pandería Fidel (20 Noviembre 211; 9 AM–9:30 PM Mon.–Sat.) This inexpensive, Mexican-style bakery sells only whole wheat breads, sweet and savory, plus vegetarian burgers and sandwiches. There's another outlet in Colonia Reforma.

La Pasión (951-513-8100; Amapolas 1519, Colonia Reforma; closed Mon.) An excellent excuse to make the trip north to Reforma, this outstanding bakery offers European-style breads and pastries, sinful chocolates, and a variety of imported teas.

Cafés

Oaxaca is a coffee lover's dream, with scores of cafés featuring organic beans, contemporary art, good food, outdoor seating, live music, and more. Traditionalists may want to try *café a la olla*, made by boiling grounds with cinnamon and

sugar. Non-traditionalists may prefer the ✪ **Italian Coffee Company** (www.italian coffee.com), which is neither Italian nor American, but actually a huge Puebla-based chain and Starbucks clone *par excellence*. True to form, there are a dozen outlets in town, including one right on the Zócalo. **Arabia Café** (Reforma 117, Conzatti Park; closed Sun.) A cool, unpretentious café with groovy '70s architectural details, great salads, and lots of magazines to peruse.

Café–Bakery La Visconia (951-516-2677; Independencia 907) Serving piping hot coffee and cookies by the pound since 1947, this relaxed, plant-filled, attitude-free café retains old Oaxaca's casual cool.

✪ **Café Brújula** (951-516-7255; García Vigil 409-D; B, L, D; closed 3 PM Sun.; $) The cozy, cool café's tattooed and pierced staff offer espresso beverages, WiFi, homemade pastries, contemporary art, and "bagel tapas," plus mostly vegetarian salads and sandwiches.

Café del Teatro Macedonio Alcalá
(951-516-8292; Independencia and Armenta
y López; B, L, C, D; $$) The century-old
Porfirista theater offers coffee, a full bar,
free WiFi, light meals, and live jazz Thursday
through Sunday in extravagant environs.

Café La Antigua (951-516-5726; www
.cafelaantigua.com.mx; Reforma 401; B, L,
C, D; $$; closed Sun.) The flagship store
for Antigua Pluma organic coffee has great
people-watching, big breakfasts, and local
chocolate.

Café Royal (951-572-5754; García Vigil
403; $$) This elegantly rustic French
café run by a former Four Seasons chef,
Bordeaux native Cristophe Tessier, serves
creative crepes and other French clas-
sics such as *pollo* cordon bleu and *res*
Bourgogne, as well as salads, sandwiches,
coffee beverages and martinis in quaint
Colonial surroundings, with plenty of *New
Yorkers* and *Paris Matches* to flip through.

Ice Cream
Oaxaca has its own unique ice cream,
called *nieve* (literally, snow), sold at *nev-
erías* all over town, as either a light ice
milk *(con leche)* or sherbet *(con agua)*.
Popsicles, called *paletas*, are also avail-
able everywhere; look for **Popeye's** stores.
A bewildering array of flavors awaits the
gourmand, from pedestrian chocolate
and *fresas* (strawberry) to unusual flavors
such as *leche quemado* (burnt milk, like
toasted caramel), *beso de angel* (fruit and
nuts), mezcal, *tamarindo con chile* (spicy
and tangy), *elote* (corn), *tuna* (prickly-pear
fruit), and more.

Gelato (Portal de Clavera, Valdivieso, and
Hidalgo; open 11 AM–10 PM) Right off the
Zócalo, the tiny store owned by a half-Ital-
ian, half-Mexican sweetheart offers at least
18 flavors of gelato (two sugar-free) daily.

✪ **Jardín Sócrates** (Independencia and
Galeana) On the plaza just west of Basílica

Soledad, this is *the* place for *nieves,* with
a dozen vendors offering bistro seating.
There, beneath festively striped umbrel-
las, half a dozen *neverias* offer fancy fluted
glasses piled high with your new favorite
flavors.

Nieves Chagüita (951-516-1350; Mercado
Benito Juárez 27; $) Thirty-five flavors of
excellent *nieves* and sorbets.

Pizza
Casa de Maria Lombardo (951-516-1714;
Absolo 304; C, D; $$) Big salads, well-
prepared pastas, baguettes, and live music
Thursday through Saturday.

Pizza La Rustica (951-518-7696; Murgia
101, corner of Alcalá; C, D; $$) This local
chain uses natural ingredients for a huge
menu of pizzas, pastas and other Italian
and Oaxacan dishes. Try the house "Pizza
Rústica," with *flor de calabaza* and chile
pobalano, or one of the big salads served
in hand-carved wooden bowls. There are
other locations in Centro (951-516-7500;
Alcalá 804) and Colonia Reforma (951-515-
3518; Belisario Dominguez 405). All three
deliver.

El Sagrario (951-514-0303; www.sagrario
.com.mx; Valdivieso 120, Centro; $$) A
sleek, cool restaurant and bar with *cantera*
columns and popular dance floor, Sagrario
specializes in pizza and pasta, but also
serves well-prepared Oaxacan classics.
Delivers.

Vieja Lira (951-516-1122; Pino Suárez 100;
C, D; closed Tues.; $$–$$$) This delightful,
upscale Italian restaurant is known for its
excellent thin-crust pizza, but also offers
lovely Italian-style salads and antipasti,
as well as fresh-baked breads served with
locally inspired salsas. Don't skip dessert;
the panna cotta is recommended.

Specialty Foods and Delis
Many ingredients in Oaxacan cuisine simply

can't be found elsewhere, so stock up before heading home. You should check what foods can and can't cross the border, but customs officers generally seem more likely to let commercially packaged moles and chocolates through than unpackaged versions.

Chocolate y Mole La Soledad (951-516-3807; www.chocolatedeoaxaca.com.mx; Mina 212) There are several outlets for this popular brand of mole and chocolate, open 365 days with loads of free samples.

Mayordomo (951-516-0246; Mina and 20 de Noviembre) Major chocolate producer with stores all over town offers free tastings of half a dozen varieties. Get pre-prepared mixes or have them custom grind a blend for you.

✪ **Xiguela** (951-521-2425; Hidalgo 104-C, Jalatlaco; B, L, C; closed Sun.) This great natural grocer sells organic, community-conscious regional specialties and international brands, including Yu Vila artisanal chocolate, made by a women's collective, and ✪ **Naom Quie** (951-520-1142; Juquila) organic coffee. An onsite cafeteria specializes in fresh, healthy, Oaxacan food, with lots of vegetarian options but plenty of organic, free-range meat on the menu.

Yasín (corner of Allende and García Vigil, Centro) A gourmet deli with lots of locally produced moles, marmalades, chocolate, vanilla, fresh cheeses, and meats, and more, all made with 100 percent natural ingredients.

Liquor Stores
In addition to the many, many mezcal sellers clinging to the sides of Mercado 20 Noviembre, there are a few places where you can find a little something special.

La Cava Los Danzantes (951-515-2335; jorge@losdanzantes.com; Gómez Farias 218, Parque Conzatti) The store has an excellent wine selection, most from Mexico but also

Spain, France, Italy, Chile and elsewhere, as well as lots of upscale mezcals.

Prissa Gourmet (951-513-1763; www.prissa.com.mx; Porfiro Díaz 155-A, Reforma) In addition to wines and liquors from all over the world, Prissa sells Italian and Spanish meats, French cheeses, and other delicacies.

Fast Food
Real, U.S.-style fast food is hard to find in town, but get your junk-food fix in and around the mall, south of town.

La Antequera (951-518-5309; Porfiro Díaz, Reforma; C, D; $) Antequera has great tacos Árabes and other allegedly Middle Eastern food, and it delivers.

La Gran Torta (951-501-0100; Porfirio Díaz 208, Centro; C, D; closed Tues.; $) Since the

It's worth working your way past Mercado 20 de Noviembre on busy Calle Mina, lined with chocolate molinas (grinders), just for the smell.

1950s, "The Big Sandwich" has specialized in crusty *bonillo* rolls piled high with barbecued meats, local cheeses, rich local avocados and much more. *Pozole,* a hominy stew served with lime, shredded chicken, onions and fresh herbs, is another winner.

Itanoní: Flowering of Corn (951-513-9223; Belisario Domínguez 513, Reforma; B, L, C; $) Doña Leyva believes that the key to Oaxaqueña life and culture is corn, and serves only the flavorful, locally raised variety here in several dishes, including the best tortillas you will ever enjoy.

Mall Plaza del Valle (Avenida Universidad) McDonalds, Subway, KFC, Pizza Hut, and much, much more.

Tacos Alvaro (951-516-7482; Porfirio Díaz 617, corner of Quetzalcoatl; C, D; closed Sun.; $) A popular spot for quality tacos, it specializes in *al pastor,* and also does a great *pozole;* open till 1:30 AM.

Vegetarian
Vegetarians will be happy here in Oaxaca.

❂ **100% Natural** (951-132-4343; www .100natural.com; Dr. Liceaga 115, Parque El Llano; MC, V; $$; B, C, L, D) In a cool white marble dining room in a sleek, remodeled Colonial palace, with views to Parque el Llano's monuments and skateboarders, 100% Natural offers a huge juice menu (aloe vera, noni, bee pollen, soy, beet, etc.) and inventive international food options such as hummus pitas stuffed with grilled vegetables and goat cheese. But it excels with Oaxacan specialties done meat-free. Try the whole-wheat *molletes,* soy fajitas, and variety of enchiladas and omelets.

Flor de Loto (951-514-3944; Morelos 509; open 10 AM–10 PM; L, C, D; $) This classic backpacker hangout has been dishing up vegetarian (and regular) versions of Oaxacan and international cuisine for 20 years. The *comida,* which always includes vegetarian choices, is a good deal.

Manantial (951-514-5602; Tinoco y Palacios 303, corner of Matamoros, Centro; MC, V; B, L, C, D; $$) The regular menu always offers excellent meat-free Oaxacan dishes, and the outstanding ❂ **Saturday Brunch** (2 PM–6 PM) is a buffet featuring all of them, plus meatier options to keep everyone happy.

Naturel (951-132-7798; Netzahualcóyotl 312, Reforma; B, L, C, D; $–$$) Soothingly designed health food restaurant with open-air seating and some meat dishes offers carefully prepared cuisine designed to fight obesity, diabetes, hypertension, and other ailments.

Trigo y Miel (951-516-2369; J.P. García 207, Centro; B, L, C, D; $) Cheap, tasty, and convenient, this spot's healthy veggie burgers, whole-wheat pizza by the slice, and inexpensive *comida* are the best meatless deal in town.

❂ **Verde Aceituna** (951-514-1946; www .losolivosspa.com.mx; Calzada Madero 1254, Colonia Exmarquezado; B, L, C; $) At Hotel Los Olivos, on the edge of downtown, this small vegetarian restaurant serves a spectacular US$5 *comida* at 2 PM daily.

Grocery Stores
The markets are really the best place to get anything, particularly the shops in Mercado 20 de Noviembre. See Markets and Malls, later in this chapter, for more information.

Piticó (Reforma 703; open 7 AM–9 PM) The biggest grocery store close to the center is next to Conzatti Park, and has a small produce section and bakery.

Soriana Mega Grocery (123 Madera) Just west of Soledad Church, this large, modern grocery store is the city center's best.

Soriana Plaza del Valle (150 Universidad) The largest mega-grocer in the state is at the mall (buses run regularly, or get a cab for about US$4) just west of town.

CULTURE

With a rich history stretching back through centuries, endless decades dedicated to exploring humanity's creative potential—cuisine, art, architecture, dance, and so many other endeavors—it is no wonder that Oaxaca is considered one of Mexico's most rewarding cultural destinations.

Architecture

One thing indigenous Oaxaqueños and Spanish conquistadors had in common (other than a mutual enemy, the Aztecs) was their appreciation of the plaza, a public space where the entire community, regardless of race or class, could relax, meet friends, have a drink, see a live performance, flirt, and simply enjoy life and love. As throughout Mexico, Oaxaca's central plaza is called the Zócalo, in deference to Mexico City's central square.

From its founding in the late 1520s, the Spanish elite in Oaxaca were intent on building a monumental capital that could compete with the beautiful stone Zapotec and Mixtec cities that surrounded them. Though earthquakes leveled their original efforts, by the late 1600s, flush with wealth from the growing textile and *cochineal* (carmine dye) trade, Catholic

Santo Domingo from Cerro El Fortín, from which an occupying Aztec garrison kept watch for only three decades.

powerbrokers including the Dominican order and Bishop Angel Maldonado, and patrons including Manuel Fiallo, were finally sending their own stone spires toward the heavens.

Many of the high stone walls, massive churches, and old adobes of the city center date from this era, as do the old **aqueduct** running from San Felipe del Agua to the Oaxaca City Center, still visible on the main road between them, and the "**Arches of Xochimilco.**" Other edifices, once taken down by the rumbling earth, are newer, such as the massive arcades of the **Palacio del Gobierno**, last rebuilt in 1884.

In the Zócalo's center is an early 20th-century **gazebo bandstand**, with a domed metal roof and Victorian gingerbread trim in classic Porfirian style. This is one of the many buildings constructed during the dictatorship of Porfirio Díaz, a Oaxaqueño whose ambitious modernization program inspired many of the federalist buildings along Independencia, as well as the **Bishop's Palace** (today Hotel Monte Albán) and the magnificent 1909 **Teatro Macedonio Alcalá**.

Alcalá, also the pedestrian walkway connecting the Zócalo and Santo Domingo, is lined with Colonial mansions such as **La Casa de Cortés** (Macedonio Alcalá 202), today the Museum of Contemporary Art, but probably never home to the eponymous conquistador. One block over, on Calle Cinco de Mayo, are ornately carved mansions dating to the same period, including 1624 **La Casa Bohorquez**, across from the Camino Real, and 18th-century **Casa Magro**, now the School of Architecture, where Oaxaca's future is being planned.

Churches

Oaxaca is home to one of Mexico's most important collection of Spanish Colonial religious art and architecture, rivaling that of even Mexico City or Puebla, with 29 monumental Catholic churches, 16 of them constructed by the Dominican Order.

Oaxaca baroque, sometimes referred to as "earthquake baroque," features huge, thick, buttressed walls with room for *cantera* blocks to shift during tremors, and ornate *retablo*-style façades, with "boxes" of elaborately carved saints and scenes within heavily ornamented frames, separated by Renaissance and baroque adornment such as columns, cherubs, and especially stylized vines and flowers.

In 1859, in one of his most controversial acts as president, Benito Juárez nationalized the churches. Many became military garrisons in the war against the French, and priceless art and artifacts were destroyed. The Vatican has slowly but surely re-acquired and redecorated most of them, and today they are a wonderful way to wile away your time.

That said, it's easy to get church fatigue, particularly if you plan to follow the Dominican Route (see the Northern Oaxaca chapter). Serious church lovers will want to pick up a copy of *Exploring Colonial Oaxaca* by Richard D. Perry, or book a tour with Linda Martin (ridgecliff@hotmail.com; see Tours, later). Everyone else can plan to take in a handful as part of their regular itinerary, and leave the rest to chance. Photographers should note that Dominican churches always face west.

One of the loveliest churches is the **ex-Convento of Santa Catalina**, now the five-star hotel, El Camino Real; see Hotels, earlier.

✪ Santo Domingo de Oaxaca
Plaza del Rosario, corner of Alacalá and Allende

This is one of the finest churches in the hemisphere and most beautiful buildings in Mexico, home to Oaxaca's best museum, its vast Jardín Etnobótanico (see Parks and

Gardens, below), and an interior of such extraordinary ornamentation that it will leave even devout atheists in awe.

When the Dominicans arrived in 1529, they quickly erected an adobe Iglesia San Pablo; it was promptly destroyed by earthquakes. Subsequent efforts were similarly smashed by acts of God. Finally, after incorporating huge walls and flexible, mortar-free joints, the current creation was completed in 1666, and has not been destroyed since.

The *retablo* façade marks the beginning of Oaxacan baroque style, with Renaissance elements such as stucco cherubim and vines. Ornate "boxes," with carved friezes and elaborate frames, make this style recognizably Oaxacan. But the real sensory tsunami comes as you walk through the doors.

An elaborate, gold-leafed grapevine traces the lineage of Don Felix de Gúzman, a 23.5-karat gold swirl of saints, virgins, martyrs, and kings that surround statues of the first six Dominican friars to enter the city. The new Rosary Chapel, completed in 1731, was modeled after the Rosary Chapel in Puebla, and features some of the finest paintings in the church. Almost half were painted by one artist, a mestizo from the tiny town of Tlalixtac, Miguel Cabrera (1695–1768).

This is one place where it's worthwhile to ask the services of one of the many freelance English-speaking guides who hang around the church.

Basílica de la Soledad

Avenida Independencia 107, corner of Victoria, Centro

The arrival of the Patroness of Oaxaca, the Virgin of Solitude, depicting a distraught Mary after the death of her son, is a miraculous tale. A heavily laden burro of mysterious origin simply appeared outside town in 1534, then fell to the ground, spilling its load next to a rock still preserved onsite: the beautifully carved Virgin. Her chapel was built right here.

Detail from Basilica la Soledad's awe-inspiring retablo-style façade.

Historical facts seem to differ a bit; there was evidently an adobe shrine to the Virgin of Solitude atop El Fortín as early as 1532, though the statuette, which seems to have been carved in Guatemala or the Philippines, must be from a later date. The rock may have even been moved here in 1617, perhaps from the original mountaintop shrine.

But miracles are miracles, and this remarkable church is certainly one of them, the very epitome of Oaxacan earthquake-baroque style. The *retablo* façade, completed in 1719 and imitated ever since, is unusual in that it faces east. Take photos in the morning, when shadows cross each of the distinctive boxes, delineated by columns, San Pedro, San Pablo, Santa Rosa de Lima, and the Virgin herself, with a skull that seems somehow syncretized with older Zapotec customs.

The ornamented interior, second only to Santo Domingo, has one of the region's oldest and most ornamented *retablos* (altar pieces), focused on the diminutive Virgin. Her original crown, made of pure gold, and her robes, richly embroidered with pearls and precious gems, were stolen several years ago; the reproductions are still quite valuable. Her feast day, December 18, is a time of pilgrimage, when the massive Plaza de la Danza and Jardín Sócrates are packed with penitents from all over the state.

Carmen Alto
Carranza and García Vigil

The Catholic Church has for centuries allowed the "syncretization" of Christianity with older, more stubborn religions; even Easter and Christmas fall suspiciously close to pagan European holidays. In Oaxaca City, the most important deity was Centéotle, the Goddess of Corn, and her temple hosted the region's most important festival, "The Offering" atop the hill—in Zapotec, the Guelaguetza.

The Spanish dismantled and rebuilt the temple, dedicated it to "Our Lady of Perpetual Help," and rebranded the hilltop dance extravaganza as the Feast Day of Saint Carmen. The enormous complex and its expansive plazas are impressive, and part of the original aqueduct to San Felipe del Agua is visible by the south gate. Smaller **Carmen Abajo** (Tinoco y Palacios 620), a sister church, administered to the Franciscan sect's indigenous nuns.

Cathedral of Nuestra Señora de la Asuncion
Alameda de León, corner of Independencia and García Vigil

At the heart of all Oaxaca, rising above the Zócalo's vendors and cafés, is this beautiful cathedral. An adobe church sat upon this spot as early as 1535, but repeated earthquakes and fires destroyed most of the original edifice; only the cross hanging inside is original. Part of the original Cross of Huatulco (see Churches in the Pacific Oaxaca chapter) is also here.

The current incarnation, designed by architect Miguel de Sanabria with thick, squat walls able to sway with the rumbling earth, was completed between 1733 and 1752. The towers, however, are a bit newer; Sanabria's were knocked down in a 1931 earthquake.

Compañia de Jesús
Trujano and Cabrera

The Jesuits arrived to Oaxaca late in the game, 1576, and promptly constructed this graceful but simple church, which differs from the Dominican temples by virtue of its rather Byzantine accents and east-facing façade. It was most recently rebuilt 1760, around the

The ethereal Virgin of Nieves casts a shadow trinity at La Compañia de Jesús.

original Churrigueresque *retablo,* just before the Jesuits were expelled from Mexico. Today, the church is lovely if a bit watermarked, with an old mural in the chapel dedicated to the Virgin of Guadalupe that translates into 13 native dialects the question, "Am I not here for you, I who am your mother?"

La Merced
Doblado, between Independencia and Hidalgo

This simple church dedicated to the Virgin of Mercy was founded as a college in the late 1660s, and has one of the most ornate interiors in the city. The shady front plaza, a popular place for schoolchildren, fills up on August 31 for the Blessing of the Animals, when people dress up their pets to present to smiling priests.

Las Nieves
Reforma and Morelos

Built by the Jesuits (thus it faces east; take photos in the morning), Las Nieves was the first seminary school in Oaxaca. Originally built in 1579 and repeatedly destroyed by earthquakes, it was most recently rebuilt in the late 1770s with a clean, classic take on Oaxaca baroque style. The excellent collection of *retablos* inside is also worth a look, as are the dragonfly tiles. Interestingly, Reforma—a street name unsubtly celebrating the nationalization of the churches—was originally Calle Las Nieves, perhaps indicating that this church was a particular focus of Juárez' distaste.

Preciosa Sangre de Cristo
Alcalá, corner of Abasolo

A simple stone façade and whitewashed barrel vault nave mark the spot of one of Oaxaca's first churches, on the site of the first city cemetery. The Temple of the Sacred Blood of Christ, erected in 1689 and declared a parish in 1893, is best known for its ornate *portada,* or entryway, and an oil painting of the Holy Trinity from the 1700s.

San Agustín
Guerrero and Armento y López

Though the Augustinian Order's mother church in Oaxaca was most recently rebuilt in 1732, the façade, by architect Tomás de Saguenay, is still much as it was when unveiled in 1696. Earthquakes have taken their toll on Oaxaca's widest church, as the "framed" stone portrait of San Agustín on the façade has been covered with fine netting to keep shards of stone from falling onto the plaza below.

San Felipe Neri
Independencia and Tinoco y Palacios

Most famous as the site of the wedding of Benito Juárez and Margarita Maza (and, perhaps coincidentally, one of the churches spared the worst of the 1859 Reform Law), this 1644 beauty also has a landmark Oaxacan baroque façade and magnificent Churrigueresque *retablos* inside. The art collection is outstanding, from 18th-century oils to Art Deco angels.

San Francisco
Bustamante and Armenta y López

Famed architect Felipe de Ureña, whose work in Puebla and Mexico City ranks among the finest in the hemisphere, came to Oaxaca toward the end of his career. Though he planned serious renovations of several churches, the only plan completed, in the 1760s, was a special project for the Franciscan Order. Though the Order never had a real presence in Oaxaca, this church served as a way station to its stronghold in the Philippines. Ureña eschewed the boxy Oaxacan style for his signature, soaring, and much more delicate lines, hewn from smooth gray limestone instead of *cantera* tuff.

San José
Morelos and Union, across from Soledad

Founded by Jesuits in 1595, and rebuilt in 1728 after several earthquakes, this former convent once housed Franciscan nuns from Spanish families. They called themselves the *Capuchinas de Arriba* to differentiate themselves from the indigenous nuns at Las Siete Principes, the *Capuchinas de Abajo*. Today, the classic Colonial courtyard and its delicate arcade are the province of the School of Fine Arts, covered with creative graffiti and hosting cutting-edge exhibitions, punk rock shows, and other events.

San Juan de Dios
Aldama and 20 de Noviembre

Right by the market, this has been a consecrated spot since 1521, when Oaxaca's first Christian church, of adobe and thatch, was erected right here. The current version was

The impressive interior of Templo San José's arcade, built in 1744 and now inhabited by an art school, still offers inspiration.

built in 1867, and is most famous for the amazing, if age-obscured, 17th-century oil paintings by Urbana Olivera depicting the Cross of Huatulco, the baptism of King Cosijoeza,
the Revolution of the Martires de Cojones, and other events in Oaxaca's early history. The
church's old plaza, which predates even the Zócalo, is now Benito Juárez Market.

San Matías Jalatlaco
Aldama and Hidalgo, Jalatlaco

The recently restored church dating to the 1600s presides over this hip, artsy, cobblestoned neighborhood in the northeast quadrant of the city. Unusual for its geometric
friezes and beautiful spiral design on the towerless side, it is best known for its 19th-
century pipe organ, also recently restored.

Siete Principes
Gonzalez-Ortega 403, corner of Colón

Today the festive Casa de la Cultura, with art exhibits and events, this small 1770 church
represents the furthest reaches of the original Oaxaca aqueduct, the ancient edge of town.
Long recognized as a little-sung beauty, this pretty *cantera* temple may also have been
designed by Felipe de Ureña, but no one knows for sure.

Trinidad de las Huertas Church
La Noria, corner of Santos Degollado

Modest (by Oaxacan standards), this whitewashed adobe church, Trinity of the Vegetable
Gardens, is appropriately trimmed in green. It was built in the late 1600s on what was

*Where there's a culture, there's an equal and awesome counterculture, here displayed as guerrilla artwork on
a cobblestone Jalatlaco side street.*

then the rural outskirts of town, where indigenous "workers" farmed small as they labored for the Spanish. This spot also saw the first celebration of the Night of the Radishes (see Events), a tradition that probably dates to the first chapel built on this spot, about a kilometer southeast of the Zócalo, in the early 1530s.

Museums and Libraries

Oaxaca is a museum lover's dream, but pace yourself. It's easy to go into art and archaeology overload in this town. Note that most museums charge extra to use a camera or video camera, usually about US$3.

Antigua Estación del Ferrocarril

951-516-9388
Old Train Station
Calzada Madero 511, Barrio del Ex-Marquesado
Open: Hours vary
Admission: Free

The museum isn't much—there's a nice display about the history of Mexican trains, as well as a few old tools and other items of interest. Most people visit, however, for two reasons. During the day, it's a great spot for kids, who are catered to with playrooms in three out-of-service train cars stocked with toys and games. There's plenty of room outside for them to wander around. In the evening, this becomes a hot spot for cool, local special events (few tourists make it out this far) featuring live music, performances, and art openings.

The unusually delicate arcade of this 200-year-old former convent, now the Biblioteca Pública Central, is an atmospheric spot to enjoy a movie.

Biblioteca Andrés Henestrosa, Casa de la Ciudad

951-516-9750
Porfirio Díaz 115 corner of Morelos, Centro
Open: 9 AM–8 PM daily
Admission: free

The cool, whitewashed Colonial dates from the late 1700s, and specializes in free exhibits of political, feminist, and other message art. The library focuses on Oaxacan and Mexican history, Latin American literature, and urban planning (including many old photos and drawings of the city), with many tomes dating to the 18th century.

Biblioteca Pública Central

951-516-1835Alcalá 200, Centro
Open: Mon.–Fri. 9 AM–8 PM, Sat. 9 AM–3 PM
Closed: Sun.
Admission: Free

Once a convent for Irish nuns, dating from the early 1800s, the building became the Margarita Maza de Juárez Library in 1985. The unusually delicate courtyard, supported by slender, eight-sided columns, makes an atmospheric spot to see exhibitions from local artists, or watch movies (6 PM Thurs.; US$1).

Centro Fotográfico Manuel Álvarez Bravo and Fonoteca Eduardo Mata
951-516-9800
www.cfmab.blogspot.com; www.fonotecaeduardomata.blogspot.com
M. Bravo 116, corner of García Vigil, Centro
Open: 10 AM–8 PM Wed.–Mon.
Closed: Tues.
Admission: Free

A rotating collection of classic photography and gallery space for contemporary artists showcases all sorts of photography.

La Curtiduría, Espacio de Arte Contemporáneo
951-119-9952
Cinco de Mayo 307, Barrio Jalatlaco
Open: 10 AM–2 PM Mon.–Fri.
Closed: Sat. and Sun.
Admission: Free

Founded in 2006 by artist Demián Flores, "The Tannery" provides a beautiful space for community and environmentally conscious exhibitions, many showcasing local talent, others on loan from Mexico City and other international museums.

Instituto de Artes Gráficas de Oaxaca
951-516-6980
www.biblioiago.blogspot.com
Macedonio Alcalá 507, Centro
Gallery open 9 AM–8 PM Wed.–Mon.; library open 9 AM–8 PM Mon.–Sat.
Admission: Free

Founded by artist and philanthropist Francisco Toledo, this newish museum showcases the work of prominent artists from around the state and nation. The library has one of the best collections of art books in the country.

✪ Museo de Arte Contemporáneo de Oaxaca
951-514-2818
www.museomaco.com
Macedonio Alcalá 202, Centro
Open: 10 AM–8 PM Wed.–Mon.
Closed: Tues.
Admission: US$1, free Sun.

It all depends on the exhibition, of course, but with this, the architecturally dazzling Colonial mansion was one of the best I'd ever seen. "Family Reunion," was the name of the show, and the rambling maze of whitewashed galleries had thousands of photos dating from the 1990s to the 1920s of local families, most of them obviously amateur. This also a great outlet for site-specific artists, who also set up a *trés* modern "haunted house" for Día de los Muertos, with plastic-wrapped trees, floating candles, fog machines, and free beer.

✪ Museo de Arte Prehispánico Rufino Tamayo

951-516-7617
Morelos 503, Centro
Open: 10 AM–2 PM and 4 PM–7 PM Mon., Wed–Sat., 10 AM–3 PM Sun.
Closed: Tues.
Admission: US$2.50

This gem of a museum doesn't just display the same collection of pre-Hispanic artifacts with placards guestimating their dates and uses; in fact, there's not much signage at all. (Though what there is has been conveniently translated into French and English, with placards on the walls of all six salons). Artist Rufino Tamayo, perhaps Oaxaca's most important painter, collected pre-Columbian artifacts not because of their religious, historic, or geographic significance, but for "their beauty, their power, and their originality." The collection is inspiring, as is the location, built in the 1700s as the home of the commissary general who administrated the Oaxacan Inquisition. Don't skip this one.

Museo Belber Jiménez

951-514-5095
www.museobelberjimenez.org
Matamoros 307, corner of Tinoco y Palacios, Centro
Open: 11 AM–2 PM and 5 PM–7:30 PM Mon.–Fri., 10 AM–2 PM Sat.
Closed: Sun.
Admission: Free

This brand-new museum displays the collection of local antiquities dealers Federico y Ellen Belber Jiménez. Exhibits transport you through time using jewelry and textiles, beginning with the Spaniards' introduction of glass beads and religious imagery, including the famous crosses of Villa Hidalgo Yalalag and Tehuantepec's renowned *bejuco* jewelry combining gold coins and filigree. More modern pieces from Mexico's top 20th-century designers are another highlight. There are also rooms full of top-notch Colonial and indigenous ceramics, coconuts carved by prisoners from San Juan de Ulúa, Veracruz, and first-class *serapes* and *huipiles*. Though the museum was free at the time of research, the family plans to start charging around US$3. It's still worth it.

Museo de Filatelia de Oaxaca

951-514-2366
www.mufi.org.mx
Reforma 504
Open: 10 AM–8 PM Tues.–Sun.
Closed: Mon.
Admission: Free

This expansive Colonial mansion houses Mexico's largest public stamp collection, as well as a library with philatelic books from all over the world; a postal museum with old mailboxes, scales, and other postal ephemera, including a portrait of Benito Juárez made entirely of postage stamps; and several rooms featuring rotating shows of stamp-related modern art. At the heart of the museum, in a climate-controlled vault, is a case filled with thousands of amazing stamps (pull the handles hard) printed since the 1830s, as well as several letters from Frida Kahlo. A great museum even for folks not usually interested in stamps.

Museo del Palacio

915-501-1662
Zócalo
mupal.oax@gmail.com
Open: 10 AM–7 PM Tues.–Sun.
Closed: Mon.
Admission: Free

One of Oaxaca's newest museums is housed within one of its oldest and grandest buildings, the magnificently arcaded 1884 Palace of the Government, overlooking the Zócalo. The main reason to visit is the architecture itself, as well as the mural of indigenous culture painted by Arturo García Bustos. Though mostly used for civic events and private parties, there are exhibition rooms off to the side; when I was there, an exhibition by painter Saúl de Anda, "Fiesta de Gallos," portrayed the very traditional sport of cockfighting in an explosion of color and texture.

Museo de los Pintores Oaxaqueños

951-516-5645
Independencia 607
Open: 10 AM–8 PM Mon.–Sat., until 6 PM Sun.
Admission: US$2

Oaxaca has been a center for the fine arts for decades (millennia, really) and this gorgeous space is dedicated to the city's finest painters, photographers, and sculptors. The whitewashed and wood-floored space, gallery after gallery, is an artist's dream, perfect for displaying the vibrant colors for which the city is known. Displays change regularly, but are generally devoted to just one or two artists, with pieces loaned from area collectors.

Museo de Sitio Casa Juárez

951-516-1860
García Vigil 609
Open: 10 AM–7 PM Tues.–Sun.
Admission: US$3.50

This small museum is housed in the family home of Rosendo Pérez Pinacho, whose parents, Italian immigrants, took in young Benito Juárez. Their Zapotec ward would grow up to be a lawyer, and later the president of Mexico and the first modern indigenous head of state in the hemisphere. History buffs may find the handful of rooms with period furnishings and Spanish-language descriptions of Juárez's life interesting, but most folks could give this one a miss. A short documentary (also in Spanish) is on continuous loop, and one room has rotating exhibitions of contemporary art.

Museo de la Soledad

Independencia 107
Open: 8 AM–2 PM and 4 PM–7 PM Fri.–Wed., 10 AM–2 PM Thurs.
Closed: Mon.
Admission: US$1 donation requested

If you've already made it to this wonderful church, why not pop into its cute little museum?
The garden dioramas illustrate the story of the Virgen de la Soledad's arrival to Oaxaca,
while the inside is just packed with Catholic kitsch. Saints, Virgins, a really gory Jesus,
Colonial artwork, religious costumes, traditional indigenous costumes, amazing stained
glass, old bottles, antique jewelry, scores of tin Milagros, really anything that the sweet
old ladies running the place seemed to think was worth remembering about Old Oaxaca.
Standout pieces include the primativist painting showing the virgin's arrival.

Museo Textil de Oaxaca

951-501-1104
www.museotextildeoaxaca.org.mx
Hidalgo 917, corner of Fiallo, Centro
Open: 10 AM–8 PM Wed.–Mon.
Closed: Tues.
Admission: Free

A fantastic museum for getting your bear-
ings before seriously investing in area
textiles, this massive, rotating collection
of hand-woven clothing, rugs, and other
items always displays the best of the art.
The building is outstanding, an old convent, and there are permanent displays of
local costumes and natural dyes. The onsite
library specializes in books about—what
else?—weaving.

*The riches of Monte Albán's Tomb Seven, including
this jade-encrusted skull, are displayed at Santo
Domingo in Oaxaca City.*
Courtesy of www.advantagemexico.com

✪ Museum of the Cultures of Oaxaca

951-516-2991
Ex-Convento Santo Domingo, Macedonio
Alcalá and Adolfo Gurrión
Open: 10 AM–7 PM Tues.–Sun.
Closed: Mon.
Admission: US$4.80
audio guides cost an extra US$4 in Spanish, US$5 in English

The city's most important and impressive museum occupies part of the old Convent of
Santo Domingo, along with the ethnobotanical gardens. The rooms which once housed
Dominican monks now hold exhibits arranged chronologically, beginning with ceramics
and stone tools from several thousand years ago, through the rise of the great Zapotec cities
of El Mogote and Monte Albán.

   The most famous display in the museum comprises the treasures discovered in Tomb

Seven of Monte Albán in 1932, considered the second-richest discovery in archaeological history, after King Tut's tomb in Egypt. The museum goes on to display artifacts from the Spanish conquest, including tools, religious art, and mezcal stills. A fascinating place.

Music and Nightlife

There's always something going on in Oaxaca, and the finest entertainment is absolutely free. Roving *trovadores* (troubadours), mariachi bands, and dance troupes make all the Zócalo a stage, and are out in force for *Noche del Luces* (Night of Lights), on the Saturday evening closest to the 15th of the month. Everyone comes down to the historic center to mingle, try special dishes at area restaurants, visit art openings, and otherwise enjoy themselves.

The **Zócalo** has big-band concerts (often accompanied by older couples, dancing like they mean it) at 6 PM on Monday, Tuesday, Thursday, and Sunday. More *danzón* can be seen on Wednesday at 6:30 PM and Friday at 12:30 PM. The **State Band of Oaxaca** plays at noon on Wednesday and Saturday, while the **State Marimba Band** goes onstage Monday and Saturday at 7 PM.

Jardín Conzatti has live music Saturday starting at around 7 PM, while **Parque El Llano** also stages live entertainment most weekends. **Margaret Barkley's Oaxaca Calendar** (www.oaxacacalendar.com) helps keep track of events.

Bars

Have a seat and order a *chela* (beer), flavored with *suero* (lime juice) or even *michelada* (chile), then relax with a *botana* (free snack) and smile fetchingly. Fact: Your Spanish will improve within just a few drinks.

Bar Fly (www.barfly.com.mx; Constitución 207, Centro; closed Mon.; US$5 cover weekends) This sleek new martini bar serves upscale Oaxaca-Italian fusion cuisine ($$$) alongside a serious martini menu (US$6) in sophisticated environs; live jazz from local songstress Marta Sáenz makes weekends even more romantic.

La Cantina (951-516-8961; 303 Alcalá) This fun restaurant-bar is just slightly cheesy (check out the giant snake), so why not try the *queso fundido* while enjoying live music at 10 PM Monday through Saturday, to fuel up for the dance floor.

Casa de Mezcal (951-516-2191; Flores Magón 209, across from Mercado Benito Juárez) A Oaxaca landmark since 1935, the relaxed bar offers nightly drink specials and Wednesday's "Fiesta del Mezcal," a great time to sample every mezcal known to exist.

La Divina (Adolfo Gurión 103, across from Santo Domingo; open noon–3 AM daily) A basic cement bar with US$1 beers and US$5 cocktails by the liter, La Divina features live music Wednesday through Saturday, and cool movies other nights. There's no cover. Packed with backpackers and the locals who love them.

La Farola (951-516-5352; 20 de Noviembre between Las Casas and Trujano) Swagger through the saloon doors to the oldest bar in town, serving stiff drinks to revolutionaries, luminaries, and regular bums since 1916.

Rosso Appetizer Bar (951-569-1123; Manuel Doblado 108, Centro) Sleek, modern, and ostensibly Asian, with a glowing glass-brick floor, big fish tanks, and sci-fi furnishings, this isn't your typical cantina.

Clubs
This is the reason you packed that sexy outfit, so don't be shy. Dance the night away.

✪ **Candela** (951-514-2010; Murgia 413; open 10 PM–2 AM Thu.–Sat.; US$5 cover) Serious salsa dancers dominate the long courtyard dance floor with precise and passionate moves, which doesn't exactly inspire amateurs to join in. Learn how with free lessons (offered earlier in the evening), or show up by 10 PM to grab a candle-lit table, arranged to enjoy the show. Dress to impress.

La Cucaracha (951-501-1636; Porfiro Díaz 301-A) Choose between a low-lit bar with a long list of cocktails and mezcals and a dance floor with live DJs, and a more relaxed lounge with *trova* (acoustic) performers.

Elefante (20 de Noviembre 110; open 9 PM–4 AM Tues.–Sat.; US$4 cover) A young crowd grooves to Latin and international dance long after the other bars close.

Free Bar (Matamoros 100-C, Centro) No cover, relatively inexpensive drinks (compared to the neighboring clubs), and a small dance floor make this Oaxaca's favorite place for tourists and locals to meet, greet, and try to hook up.

Insomnia (951-514-0999; www.hotellaprovincia.com.mx; Porfiro Díaz 108, Centro) An elegant option atop Hotel La Provincia has lounge-style décor complete with big comfy couches, international DJs, and good food.

✪ **Tentacion** (951-514-9521; Matamoros 101; open 9 PM–2 AM Tues.–Sun.; US$3–5 cover) Oaxaca's best disco gets started around 11 PM, with salsa weekends, hip-hop, cumbia, merengue, reggae, and more. Drinks are pricey, so consider getting started elsewhere.

Guelaguetza Performances
If you couldn't make it to the Guelaguetza dance festival in July, fear not! Several spots offer encore performances throughout the year.

Camino Real Oaxaca (951-501-6100; www.caminoreal.com/oaxaca; Cinco de Mayo 300, Centro; Friday 7 PM; US$31.50) Consider splashing out for this impressive show, in a centuries-old convent designed for acoustic excellence. A buffet dinner is included.

Casa de Cantera (951-514-7585; Murgia 102, Centro; US$13) Performances of folk dancing and live music begin nightly at 8:30 PM, and a traditional three-course Oaxacan menu is available.

Hotel Monte Albán (951-516-2777; Alameda de León 1, on the Zócalo; 8:30 PM daily; US$9) The three-century-old hotel right on the Zócalo offers a more affordable show in their central auditorium, with optional dinner service.

Live Music
Barlequin (951-516-0739; Hidalgo 608) Great sound equipment brings in bands from all over MesoAmerica, including indie, ska, and reggae. There's inexpensive Oaxacan food, a pool table, and a dance floor.

Café Café (Tinoco y Palacios 604) This small café on a Xochimilco side street has outdoor seating and live *trova* (acoustic) performances. A romantic little local hangout.

Café Central (951-501-1337; www.cafecentraloaxaca.blogspot.com; Hidalgo 302, Centro)
A youngish, artsy crowd of writers, artists, and musicians comes for the full bar, low light,
and provocative exhibits. Alternative films show on Wednesday, there's jazz on Thursday,
and live music (sometimes with a cover) Friday and Saturday at 9 PM.

○ **La Nueva Babel** (Porfirio Diaz 224; B, L, C, D) A super groovy spot with upstairs chill-
out spaces where you can recline on piles of pillows and contemplate the very cool artwork.
Offers live music almost nightly at 9:30 PM: jazz, *trova,* blues, funk, European, bohemian,
etc., on the tiny stage, with dancing on the interior patio. Beloved by lefties, lovers, painters, writers, and hipsters.

El Paseo Cantina (951-514-8003; Juárez 605, Centro) This laid-back lounge on Parque El
Llano gets the nod for best free *botanas* (and WiFi, too), and there's usually live music.

Movies
In general, foreign cartoons are dubbed into Spanish, while live-action movies are usually
subtitled. Several spots other than theaters show movies, including **Café Central** (see Live
Music, above) and **Casa de la Cultura Andrés Henestrosa** (free, Sunday at 10 PM).

Biblioteca Pública Central (M. Alcalá 200; 6 PM Thurs.; US$1) Art flicks, classics, or cult
favorites are screened in a lovely colonial courtyard.

Cine Reforma (951-516-5530; Trujano 119, Reforma) Mostly wide-release blockbusters in
air-conditioned comfort.

Mall Plaza del Valle (Avenida Universidad) Grab any bus marked Plaza del Valle to Oaxaca
State's biggest mall, with two air-conditioned, multi-screen, modern cinemas showing
mostly Hollywood blockbusters: **Multimax** (951-514-7881; www.mmcinemas.com) and
Cinépolis (951-506-0885; www.cinepolis.com.mx). Schedules are on their Web sites, and
tickets runs about US$5 for adults, US$3 for children.

El Pochote Cineclub (951-514-1194; www.elpochote.blogspot.com; García Vigil 817,
Centro; by donation) Usually older, artsy, or documentary films are shown among the
arquitos at 6 PM and/or 8 PM almost nightly.

Theater
Teatro Benito Juárez (951-502-5476; www.teatrojuarez.org; Juárez 703, Parque El Llano)
The theater offers a variety of musical and dramatic performances, including many that
showcase folkloric dance. Shows typically go on at 8 PM Thursday through Saturday, with a
Sunday 1 PM matinee.

○ **Teatro Macedonio Alcalá** (951-516-3387; Independencia and Cinco de Mayo, Centro)
The absolutely ravishing Belle Époque theater was recently refurbished for maximum
glitz; Santo Domingo's designers would be so proud. The landmark theater was originally
constructed during the coffee boom years, between 1903 and 1909, and is named for
Macedonio Alcalá, the composer of "Dios nunca muere," one of Oaxaca's favorite tunes
and particularly appropriate for Día de los Muertos. Stucco ribbons and bows, with lots
of gold leaf, intertwine across the rows of private box seats. It's worth the effort to enjoy a
relatively inexpensive performance, often traditional dance, right here.

RECREATION

Though there are certainly escapes within the city, check the Central Valleys chapter for even more adventures, most within an hour of town.

Parks and Gardens

Cerro Fortín

Rising from the center of Oaxaca to a glittering crown of cell phone towers, this escape from the city can be accessed by a seriously steep staircase or private car; taxis run about US$3 from the city center. Named for the Aztec fortress that once stood here, Cerro Fortín is probably best known as home to the **Guelaguetza Stadium**.

Keep climbing, however, and you'll enjoy excellent city views from the **Benito Juárez Monument** and overlook, or even further up from **Planetario Nundehui** (951-514-5379; open 8 AM–6 PM Mon.–Fri.; shows US$2.50 adults, US$1.50 children, with astronomy-themed films for kids). There's an **observatory** nearby, and several picnic tables and jogging trails that seem to stay busy. Note that there have been armed muggings along the staircase up Cerro Fortín; bring a friend and leave valuables at the hotel.

Ciudad de las Canteras

Four kilometers (2 miles) east of Oaxaca Centro on Calzada Chapultepec (Hwy. 190) This unusual park, perhaps best appreciated by families with active young kids, was once the quarry where Oaxaca's pale green *cantera* was originally mined. Today it is a grassy expanse, with a large pond and pleasant waterfall pouring down the jagged quarry. Enjoy the elaborate stone archways, an impressive collection of native plants, and several simple food stands. Also onsite is the 1,200-seat **Teatro Aire Libre Álvaro Carrillo**, which sometimes hosts performances.

✪ Jardín Ethnobotánico de Oaxaca

951-516-5325; 951-516-7915
jetnobot@prodigy.net.mx
Gurrión, adjacent to Templo Santo Domingo
Open: By guided tour only: English 11 AM Tues., Thurs., & Sat.; Spanish 10 AM, noon, 5 PM Mon.–Sat.
Closed: Sun.
Admission: US$10 English (2-hour tour), US$5 Spanish (1-hour tour)

For more insight into the real roots of Oaxaca's remarkable culture, take a tour of these botanical gardens, enclosed within the former convent of Santo Domingo. Here, Dominican friars built an impressive underground cistern, which is still used to water plants through the long dry season. After nationalization, the huge and heavily fortified courtyard was used as a military garrison, and later abandoned.

In 1994, the city announced its plans to transform this sacred ground into a luxury hotel or convention center. Oaxacans rebelled, with live music and marches, and instead secured the park as a modern ark, with 932 species actually growing and a seed bank protecting 7,130 more. A dozen different agaves, an eight-ton cactus, and *teocinte,* corn's ancient ancestor, are just a few of the plants displayed on the creatively landscaped grounds. Mezcal lovers should ask to see the *prim poleo* bush, a local hangover cure.

There's also a library of scientific tomes, while a separate reading library offers dozens of daily newspapers, all in Spanish.

Parque San Felipe del Agua
5 kilometers (3 miles) north of Oaxaca Centro

The mountains above the lovely suburb of San Felipe are protected as part of Benito Juárez National Park, and most tour outfits can arrange guided hikes, particularly for birders. You can easily visit on your own, however. There are well-marked hiking trails, including a steep 10-kilometer (6-mile) round-trip hike to two pretty waterfalls. San Felipe buses drop you off at their turnaround, about three blocks from the entrance of the park. Or take a taxi (US$6) from Oaxaca Centro.

City Parks
In addition to the famed Zócalo, Oaxaca's festive *cantera* heart, there are dozens more plaza and parks in Oaxaca. Here are just a few.

✪ **Parque El Llano** (Juárez and Berriozábal, Centro) On the north end of the city center, this former zoo provides a low-key alternative to the Zócalo, where you can relax and enjoy a *tlayuda* or candied fig on a shady park bench without being hassled by touts. There are a couple of excellent restaurants overlooking the plaza, live music and dance performances most weekends, and skateboarders working the stone central fountains and Benito Juárez throughout the week. You'll also find free WiFi and a traditional Friday food market.

Jardín Conzatti (corner of Reforma and Gomez Farias), a shady little plaza just northwest of El Llano, has a great coffee shop on one corner and a good *tortas* (sandwiches) stand on the other.

Close to Santo Domingo, craftspeople set up with all sorts of artesanías at **Parque Labastida** (Absolo, between Alcalá and Cinco de Mayo). Nearby **Plazuela de Carmen Alto** (just northwest of Santo Domingo) also often has vendors displaying their wares.

Basílica de la Soledad is also flanked by two excellent plazas. On the northeast side is the enormous **Plaza de la Danza**, host to all sorts of performances and what must be the largest Day of the Dead altar in town. As the Virgin's December 18 feast day draws near, vendors and faithful fill the expansive plaza instead. Continue down the stairs to shady ✪ **Jardín Sócrates**, with several stands offering bistro seating and dozens of flavors of *nieve,* Oaxacan ice cream (*con leche*) and sorbet (*con agua*).

Bicycle Tours and Rental
✪ **Bicicletas Pedro Martinez** (951-514-5935; www.bicicletaspedromartinez.com; Aldama 418 Mesón la Brisa, center) This mountain-bike tour operator organizes day trips (4–6 hours) and all-inclusive multi-day tours through some of Oaxaca's most scenic spots, from the Apoala Valley to Puerto Escondido. It also rents bikes and sells gear.

Zona Bici (951-516-0953; boccaletti@prodigy.net.mx; García Vigil 406, Interior 1) The shop offers day and half-day bike tours of the city and valley, and rents bikes.

Dance Classes

Candela (see Clubs, earlier) offers impromptu salsa lessons; get there before 10 PM.

Salsa Artistica (951-514-4410; Colón 302, between Fiallo and Melchor Ocampo) Salsa dance lessons are the specialty here.

Salsa Na'Ma (951-130-3502; Reforma Agraria 225, Centro) Na'Ma offers salsa classes and performances at Salon Melina.

Ecotours

The most accessible opportunities for ecotourism from Oaxaca City are in the Sierra Norte, which has its own section in the Northern Oaxaca chapter. Also check out **Ecoturismo en Oaxaca** (www.ecoturismoenoaxaca.com), a Spanish-language guide to Oaxaca's diverse ecosystems, and the **National Committee for Development in Indigenous Communities** (www.cdi.gob.mx/ecoturismo/oaxaca.html), which has photos and videos of Oaxaca's indigenous ecotourism projects.

Adventours Oaxaca (951-199-7049; oaxacanconnections@hotmail.com; M. Bravo 210-A) Eric Ramirez organizes fully customizable one- to six-day ecotourism trips throughout Oaxaca State.

EcoEscapes Oaxaca (951-513-6422; Libres 604-B; albertozamacona@cten.org) This outfit organizes and guides hiking, mountain biking, and camping trips.

Oaxaca Birding Tours (951-524-4371; roque_antonio740@hotmail.com; Cuauhtémoc 5, Teotitlán del Valle) This group offers birding tours throughout the Central Valleys. The tours include transport from Oaxaca City, and are led by Roque Antonio Santiago.

Rancho Buenavista (951-439-9629, 338-6219-710 Italy; www.ranchobuenavista.com.mx; San Pedro Ixtlahuaca) This ecotourism outfit offers hiking, trekking, mountain biking, kayaking, caving, rock-climbing, and visits to all sorts of rural ecotourism projects including Apoala, the Sierra Norte, and beyond. The actual ranch is just west of town, toward Monte Albán, and offers attractive brick bungalows using solar electricity and a shared kitchen; there's also camping.

Terra Ventura Ecoturismo (951-501-1363; www.tierraventura.com; Abasolo 217) The outfit offers trekking and cultural tours, such as learning to make your own natural medicines.

Trekking in Oaxaca (951-502-0130; www.trekkinginoaxaca.com.mx; Manuel Bravo 210, Centro) Carlos Rivera Bennetts offers fully bilingual ecotours of the Sierra Norte, Mixteca, coastal regions, and other areas.

Golf

Club de Golf Vista Hermosa (951 547-1177; Carretera a San Agustín Etla, 25 minutes north of Oaxaca) The only golf course in the Oaxaca Valley is this pleasant nine-hole course, with tennis courts, hidden away in the hills.

Gyms

Aurobic's Fitness (951-514-2608; Constitución 300, Centro; open 6 AM–10 PM) This good-sized gym has weights and cardio machines, Pilates and aerobics classes, and more. The club offers daily (US$8) and weekly (US$25) memberships.

Calipso Fitness Center (951-516-8000; www.calipso.com.mx; Ignacio Allende 211, Centro; open 6 AM–11 PM Mon.–Fri.; 6 AM–6 PM Sat.) This huge, modern facility claims to be the biggest gym in Southern Mexico; there's another branch in Colonia Reforma (951-515-8918; Heroico Colegio Militar 321).

Horseback Riding

Both **Horseback Mexico** (www.horsebackmexico.com) and **Hidden Trails** (www.hidden trails.com) offer all-inclusive horseback riding tours in Oaxaca.

Hípico La Golondrina Escuela de Equitación (951-512-7570; sisikaa@yahoo.com.mx; Rivera Río Atoyac 800, San Jacinto Amilpas) North of Oaxaca, this horseback riding school can arrange lessons and tours. Contact them in advance.

La Mano Mágica (951-516-4275; www.casasagrada.com; Alcalá 203) Organizes horseback tours in and around Teotitlán.

Other Tours

Air Explora (951-547-1209, 951-129-4116; www.airexplora.com) Learn to paraglide, with or without a motor; certified flyers are offered tours all over the state.

Hang Gliding (951-514-7204; M Bravo 210-D, centro) This outfit offers tandem, free, and powered hang gliding.

Walking Tours of Colonial Churches (ridgecliff@hotmail.com; US$10 donation) Join Linda Martin for her "irreverent" architecture and church tours; groups meet at 10 AM Tuesday and Saturday in front of the Oaxaca Cathedral. Email to schedule other times.

Tennis

Club de Tennis Brenamiel (951-512-6822; Hwy. 190, kilometer 539.5) Just 5 kilometers (3 miles) north of Oaxaca Centro in a scenic setting, the club features nine tennis courts and a swimming pool.

Deportivo Oaxaca (951-517-5271; Carretera al Tule kilometer 6.5) Deportivo offers seven courts, a pool, and a sauna.

Central Valleys Tours

Every hotel and tour operator in town offers a variety of day trips into the Central Valleys, with incredible pre-Columbian ruins, awe-inspiring churches, and fascinating craft towns where you can watch *tapetes* being woven, *alebrijes* carved, and ceramics polished to a luminous black sheen. Oaxaca City-based operators are listed in a special sidebar in the Central Valleys chapter; the Shopping chapter offers a more in-depth discussion of arts and crafts.

Yoga

Instituto de Yoga Patañjali (951-514-1946; Calzada Madero 1254, Ex-Marquezado) Hatha Yoga classes, as well as kickboxing, aerobics, and Tai Chi are on the schedule here.

Prashad Kundalini Yoga (951-216-8604; Naranjos 1101) You can also find reiki and belly dancing here.

Satha Yoga (951-514-9874; Cinco de Mayo 412) Satha holds classes Monday and Wednesday at 6:30 PM.

Spas

Oaxaca's signature spa treatment is the *temazcal,* a type of sweat lodge that became popular about 1,200 years ago. Used for both medical and recreational purposes, these saunas predictably scandalized pious conquistadors, who were uncomfortable even bathing (nudity and vanity—a double sin). After giving the treatment a try, however, the Spanish were won over and *temazcals* remained legal. Today, this relaxing bit of magic and medicine is offered all over town. Treatments vary widely, but generally last about an hour and are guided by a shaman, who uses massage, bouquets of herbs, special oil, and alternating heat and cold to help purify your body and spirit.

Not for you? Most spots also offer more traditional spa treatments.

Namaste (951-516-9645; namasteei@yahoo.com; Constitución 100-3, Centro; open 10 AM–8 PM) Holistic spa offers massages, yoga, meditation, a *temazcal,* and variety of facials and standard spa treatments.

Patio de Luz Schaá Massage (951-514-9874; schaapatiodeluz@yahoo.com.mx; Cinco de Mayo 412) The deep-tissue massages here are recommended by locals.

Petit Spa (951-133-6003; www.hotelhaciendaloslaureles.com; Hidalgo 21, San Felipe del Agua) The elegant little spa at Hacienda Los Laureles (see Hotels, earlier) in San Felipe del Agua also has a *temazcal.*

Curious? Consider taking a market tour, with a guide who'll explain exactly what all these herbs are used for.

Renacer Spa (951-520-1716; www.renacerspa.com.mx; Bajío del Sabino 300, corner of Camino Antiguo a San Felipe) This modern spa offers facials, a full beauty salon, and traditional *temazcal*.

Spacios Spa (951-516-9769; www.losolivosspa.com.mx; Calzada Madero 1254) A natural spa at Hotel Los Olivos surrounds a 60-person *temazcal* with Swedish showers, dozens of massages (including hydromassage), and alternate therapies such as floral therapy, kinesiology, chakra balancing, geotherapy, and more.

Spa San Pablo (951-518-5050; 1a Priv de Independencia 6, Centro) The full-service medical spa offers massages, mani-pedis, facials, Botox, laser treatments, and facial implants.

Vida (951-186-4685; vidaespaciodesanacion@hotmail.com; García Vigil, Plaza las Etnias, Centro) Vida has *temazcal,* massages, facials, and more.

Temazcals

Ceviarem (951-132-4551; cirigojk@hotmail.com; Las Rosas 119, Colonia Reforma) Traditional massage and *temazcal,* for groups and individuals.

Mano Mágica (951-516-4275; www.lamanomagica.com; Alcalá 203) Traditional *temazcals* and a primer on indigenous medicine at this B&B in Teotitlán del Valle.

Pedidgom's (951-117-5493; www.pedigoms.com.mx; Barrio Jalatlaco) Pedidgom's services include transportation to the *temazcal,* in the hills outside El Tule.

Temazcal (951-516-4644; ceciproc@prodigy.net.mx; Callejón del Carmen 108, Centro) This in-town *temazcal* requires reservations.

Temazcal Las Bugambilias (951-516-1165; www.lasbugambilias.com; Reforma 402, Centro) Make reservations through Las Bugambilias B&B for a holistic, detoxifying ritual.

Shopping

For handicrafts and *artesanías,* see the Shopping chapter.

Books and Magazines

✪ **Amate Books** (951-516-6960; www.amatebooks.com; Alcalá 307-2) The best selection of English-language books in the state, and one of the best covering Latin America, period. Read before you leave by ordering from the store's Web site.

Librería de Cristal (951-514-0361; Cinco de Mayo 114, corner of Morelos) The biggest bookstore in Central Oaxaca has thousands of titles, from academic tomes to photo-heavy coffee table books, almost all in Spanish.

Libería Grañén Porrúa (951-516-9901; www.libreriagp.com; Alcalá 104, Centro) A huge, beautiful bookstore, with 99 percent of its titles in Spanish. Its stock includes loads of coffee table books and a great selection of CDs. There's a cute courtyard coffee shop serving an inexpensive *menú,* too.

Morado (951-516-1089; Alcala 100, Centro) This upscale jeans and clothing store also has a great selection of English-language magazines, including fashion, gossip, cars, sports, and other hard-to-find titles.

Markets

✪ **Casa de las Artesanías de Oaxaca** (951 516 5062; infoarte@casadelasartesanias.com. mx; Matamoros 105 at García Vigil) An awesome artists' collective, owned, operated, and staffed by silversmiths, ceramicists, woodcarvers, *latistas* (the folks who make that gorgeous hammered tin), painters, and many more. It showcases some of the city's finest work.

Jardín Labastida (Abasolo, between Alcalá and Cinco de Mayo) Several stands here sell *huipiles, tapetes, alebrijes,* and other traditional *artesanías.*

Mall Plaza del Valle (Avenida Universidad) Just west of Oaxaca City, this is one of the state's biggest malls, with a 15-screen movie theater and several trendy shops, cafés, and fast-food outlets.

✪ **Mercado Abastos** (Periferíco and Prol de Victoria) The biggest, most important market in Oaxaca State sells just about everything you could possibly want or need, cheap. An amazing experience.

Mercado Benito Juárez (Las Casas and 20 Noviembre) This handicraft-packed market just bustles with shopping possibilities, from US$2 woven-palm sombreros to US$200 *tapetes,* or sandals, leather purses, traditional *huipiles,* plastic shopping bags emblazoned with María Sabina smoking a joint . . . seriously, if there is such a thing as a Oaxacan snow globe, this is where you'll find it.

Mercado de la Merced (Democracia) (Morelos and Nicolás el Puerto, Centro) The less-touristed answer to Mercado 20 de Noviembre, with all the produce, meat, breads, and pirated CDs, plus tiny, inexpensive *comedors* surrounding a sunny plaza centered on a flower-filled fountain. Best of all, there are no kids trying to sell you paintings and jewelry.

Mercado IV Centario (Victoria, between Morelos and Independencia) This small market on the west side of Soledad Church has fresh produce, bread, and meats, plus a stairway lined with inexpensive *comedors.*

✪ **Mercado 20 Noviembre** (Calles Mina & 20 Noviembre) The most highly rated place to eat in this book is within the smoky maze of stalls and *comedors* of Mercado 20 Noviembre. The entire Calle Mina side is lined with mole and chocolate factories, while the 20 de Noviembre side is devoted to pottery from Atzompa and San Bartolo Coyotepec.

Mujeres Artesanas de las Regiones de Oaxaca (MARO; Artisan Women from the Regions of Oaxaca; 951-516-0670; mujeres_artesanas@yahoo.com.mx; Cinco de Mayo 204; open 9 AM–8 PM daily) This women's collective allows artisans from all over the state to sell their work directly to the public. The quality varies and crafts are eclectic, ranging from $1 hammered-tin magnets to $300 rugs and weavings, and just about everything (sparkling Virgins of Guadalupe, papier-mâché skeleton puppets, Frida Kahlo dioramas, etc.) in between. The prices and selection are quite good. There's another branch at Santo Domingo Alcalá.

Plaza de las Etnias (García Vigil 304) A festive strip mall offering *huipiles,* rugs, hammered tin, and all the other usual *artesanías,* plus live demonstrations.

Plaza las Vírgenes (Labastida 115, Centro) This pretty plaza tucked away in an old colonial across from Jardín Labastida has several small, top-quality crafts stores.

✪ **El Pochote** (595-952-1506; www.elpochote.blogspot.com; Garcia Vigíl 817; 8 AM–3 PM Fri.–Sat.) In this small organic market "beneath the arches" of Garcia Vigíl, you can find organic fruits, veggies, coffee, and even organic mezcal by **Ricardi** (951-116-1117) and **Real Minero Mezcal** (www.realminero.com.mx). It's worth the walk just for **Alegría de Angeles**, a Korean-Italian bakery serving awesome pizzas, pastries, and Korean-Oaxacan snacks.

Sporting Goods

Jumbo Deportes (951-516-1916; Independencia 506 between JP García and 20 Noviembre) A huge sports store.

Martí (951-501-0921; www.marti.com.mx; Independencia 1005, Centro) This mammoth sports store has everything from kayaks and snorkel gear to running shoes and swimsuits, as well as some camping gear.

EVENTS

There is really no end to the Oaxacan events calendar. These are the highlights, but expect that on any given night, someone will have found an excuse for dancing and fireworks on the Zócalo. The Planning chapter lists national holidays.

January

Three King's Day (January 6) Enjoy your cake, but be aware that a *muñeco,* or plastic baby doll, has been baked inside. Chew carefully. If you find the doll, it's up to you to host the next big party, on February 2.

February

La Candelaria (February 2) Processions celebrate the Blessing of the Infant Jesus, which is also marked with a *mayordomía* (competitive gift giving) in Santa María del Tule.

Lent (40 days prior to Easter) The Catholic celebration of abstinence kicks off 40 days before Easter and includes several ceremonies, including Good Friday's **Procession of Silence**. Penitents in purple-coned hoods silently follow an ancient statue of Jesus doubled over beneath the cross through the streets; that evening, the Virgin of Soledad is carried around the Basílica.

March

Birthday of President Benito Juárez (March 21) The national holiday has special significance here in the influential president's former home.

Semana Santa (March or April) The week before Easter Sunday has several events, culminating on Easter day with the *Danza de la Pluma* at Carmen Alto Church, commemorating Cortés's defeat of the Aztecs.

April

Anniversary of Oaxaca (April 25) In 1532, Spain officially recognized the royal city of Antequera de Oaxaca, which is a fine excuse for a party.

Feast Day of San Felipe (April 29) The upscale suburb of San Felipe del Agua, about 5 kilometers (3 miles) north of Oaxaca Centro, celebrates its civic fiestas.

May

Labor Day (May 1) This national holiday is celebrated with official parades and events, and perhaps protests from local leftists.

Mother's Day (May 10) Hint: It's hard to go wrong with Oaxacan chocolate.

July

Fiesta of the Seven Moles (mid-July) Oaxaca's restaurants and *comedores* prepare their best moles for this feast.

✪ The Guelaguetza (First Monday after July 16) Oaxaca's most important festival was originally a sacred rite, when Zapotecs would meet upon a hill and make an offering (*guelaguetza*) to Centéotle, the Goddess of Corn. Today, festivities begin with processions and Mass at Carmen Alto, but quickly return to their indigenous roots as dancers gather in full traditional regalia at Guelaguetza Stadium. Most events are still free, with dancers showing their stuff at parks and plazas all over town. It's worth getting tickets in advance for main events at the stadium ($40; www.ticketmaster.com.mx); performances such as the pyrotechnics-laden Legend of Donaji are sold out weeks in advance.

August

Blessing of the Animals (August 31) The faithful dress their pets to impress and have them blessed at Iglesia La Merced.

September

Mexican Independence Day (September 16) Parades, fireworks, and drinking begin the day before, building to a drunken cry of "Viva Mexico!" at exactly 11 PM.

Feast Day of the Virgin of Merced (September 24) A market, carnival rides, fireworks, and live entertainment surround the Iglesia de la Merced.

October

Festival de Otoño (Festival of Autumn; mid-October) Five days of music and dance honor native Oaxaca composer and conductor Eduardo Mata. Many events are free, but the finest take place at venues throughout town, including Teatro Macedonio Alcalá and Santo Domingo Church.

Food of the Gods Festival (first week in October) This newish festival has restaurant and market tours and other food-related events.

Día de los Muertos (Day of the Dead; October 31–November 2) Oaxaca's iconic festival is born as October dies and the markets fill with sugar skulls, copal incense, and *cempazuchitl* (marigold) flowers for family altars and graves. Festivities officially begin on October 31, centered on Oaxaca Centro, a less reverent celebration with plenty of Halloween costumes (hey, why not?), as well as live music, performance art, and incredible public altars all over the city. More serious and sacred ceremonies take place on November 1 and 2, when families hold mezcal-soaked vigils for those who have gone beyond. Oaxaca City's Panteon San

The cathedral's massive cantera *façade, glowing with eerie light, has presided over the Day of the Dead for almost five centuries.*

Miguel has activities November 1, while many other towns, including Xoxocotlán, Santa María Atzompa, and Etla, celebrate on November 2. Several operators offer night tours to the cemeteries, well worth the effort.

November

International Book Fair of Oaxaca (www.vivelalectura.com.mx; Jardín El Pañuelito) The annual book fair brings in dealers from all over Latin America to Oaxaca for three weeks, with events, readings, and activities, many geared to children.

International Organ and Early Music Festival (mid-November; www.iohio.org.mx/en/index/htm) Home to some 24 organs built before the 18th century, many recently refurbished and once again in use, Oaxaca invites organists and fans from all over the world for this unique celebration of sacred acoustics, in churches all over the Valleys and Mixteca.

Revolution Day (November 20) National holiday celebrates the 1910 revolution.

December

Feast Day of the Virgin of Guadalupe (December 12) Nationwide celebrations for Mexico's patron saint.

Feast Day of Virgin of Soledad (December 17–18) Oaxaca's patron saint and basílica are surrounded by pilgrims and an outstanding holiday market, waiting for the jewel-bedecked Virgin of Solitude to make her way around the church and city on a carriage filled with flowers.

La Posada (December 16–24) Joseph and Mary wander Oaxaca in search of shelter, and are refused until Christmas Eve.

✪ **Noche de las Rábanos** (December 23) It's difficult to explain the translucent beauty of these large and marvelously detailed sculptures, white flesh gleaming in backlit patterns, offset by a softer glow through the intact pink skin. These aren't your normal, garden-variety radishes; these are huge, inedible things, specifically grown to construct gently undulating cathedrals and street scenes, pyramids and crèches. The sculptures are carved over five days, and assembled at the Zócalo the morning of the 23rd, artists feverishly securing every petal on every rose in Guadalupe's gown with tiny toothpicks. It's something to see. *Totomoxtle,* or corn-husk dolls and sculptures, are also displayed.

Noche Buena (Christmas Eve; December 24) *Calendas* featuring floats and lights make their way through the city, while churches offer especially impressive midnight Masses.

All ages are welcome at Oaxaca's myriad fiestas, including the Day of the Revolution.

4

CENTRAL VALLEYS

The Fertile Cradle of Oaxacan Culture

The Central Valleys, or Valles de Oaxaca, the largest in the Southern Mexican highlands, are not merely a single scenic fold in the earth. These are actually three broad valleys, reaching northwest, south, and east from the natural hub marked by both Oaxaca City, and the ruined Zapotec capital of Monte Albán.

The Valleys are called by ancient names: Tlacolula, "Place of Many Trunks," stretching 50 kilometers (31 miles) east toward the great 1,000-year-old city of Mitla; the vast Zimatlán, "Place of Roots," sometimes called Valle Ocotlán (Place of Pines) for its bustling major city; and Etla Valley, "Where Beans Grow in Abundance" reaching 40 kilometers (25 miles) northwest into the Mixteca homeland.

These names, and many others, seem to describe a lusher place, and indeed, Oaxaca has grown arid over the years. As its population expands, more water is diverted to the cities and farmland lies fallow. But the growing tourist market has allowed local families to invest energy in traditional handicrafts. Today, the famous *tapetes* (wool rugs) of Teotitlán, black pottery of San Bartolo Coyotepec, and colorful *alebrijes* (carved animals) tempt shoppers into the rolling countryside, to meet the artist in his or her humble family workshop, and see for themselves how such beauty is conjured from the Valleys' cultural mélange.

But there are other reasons to head into the Valleys, where hundreds of stone monuments rise in testament to humanity's epic sense of eternity. Since 1500 B.C., when the rulers of San José El Mogote began building massive pyramids and ball courts, it seems each century has inspired its own stone shrines to immortality. From the architects of Monte Albán, who removed an entire mountaintop to build their astronomically aligned city, to the Dominican friars, whose immense stone churches are among the world's most impressive, there is much to admire in this cradle of civilizations.

There are four major "routes" extending outward from Oaxaca, usually explored on day trips. These can be combined with visits to the surrounding mountains of the Sierra Juárez, Mixteca, and Papaloapan (see the Northern Oaxaca chapter), or en route to the beach towns covered in the Pacific Coast chapter. For more information about the handcrafts and artisan towns, check out the Shopping chapter.

MONTE ALBÁN—ZAACHILA ROUTE

A must on any Oaxaca itinerary are the magnificent ruins of ✪ **Monte Albán** (20 kilometers/ 12 miles), their ancient stone walls glowing above Oaxaca City, at their loveliest in the morning and evening.

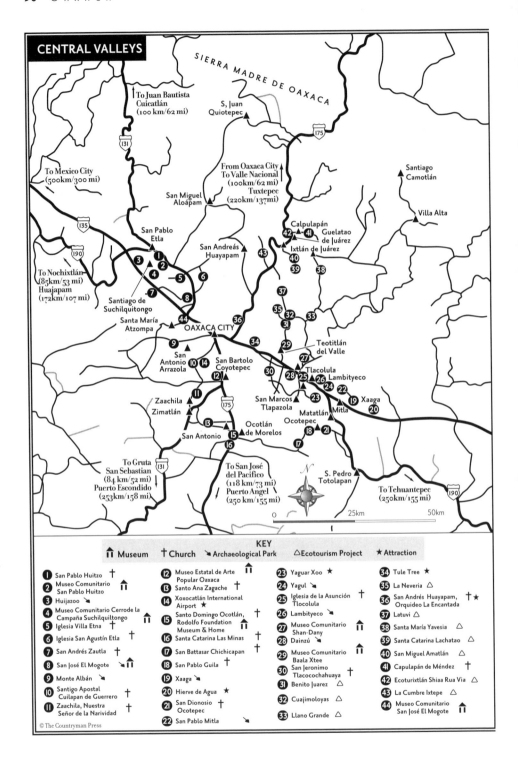

CENTRAL VALLEYS

SIERRA MADRE DE OAXACA

To Juan Bautista
Cuicatlán
(100 km/62 mi)

S, Juan
Quiotepec

To Mexico City
(500km/300 mi)

From Oaxaca City
To Valle Nacional
(100km/62 mi)
Tuxtepec
(220km/137mi)

Santiago
Camotlán

Villa Alta

San Miguel
Aloápam

San Pablo
Etla

Calpulapán
Guelatao
de Juárez

Ixtlán de Juárez

San Andreás
Huayapam

To Nochixtlán
(85km/53 mi)
Huajapam
(172km/107 mi)

Santiago de
Suchilquitongo

Santa María
Atzompa

OAXACA CITY

San
Antonio
Arrazola

San Bartolo
Coyotepec

Teotitlán
del Valle

Tlacolula
Lambityeco

Xaaga

Zaachila
Zimatlán

San Marcos
Tlapazola

Matatlán
Ocotepec

Mitla

San Antonio

Ocotlán
de Morelos

To Gruta
San Sebastian
(84 km/52 mi)
Puerto Escondido
(253km/158 mi)

To San José
del Pacífico
(118 km/73 mi)
Puerto Angel
(250 km/155 mi)

S. Pedro
Totolapan

To Tehuantepec
(250km/155 mi)

0   25km   50km

KEY

🏛 Museum   † Church   ⌇ Archaeological Park   △ Ecotourism Project   ★ Attraction

1 San Pablo Huitzo †
2 Museo Comunitario San Pablo Huitzo 🏛
3 Huijazoo ⌇
4 Museo Comunitario Cerrode la Campaña Suchilquitongo 🏛
5 Iglesia Villa Etna †
6 Iglesia San Agustín Etla †
7 San Andrés Zautla †
8 San José El Mogote ⌇🏛
9 Monte Albán ⌇
10 Santigo Apostal Cuilapan de Guerrero †
11 Zaachila, Nuestra Señor de la Narividad †

12 Museo Estatal de Arte Popular Oaxaca 🏛
13 Santo Ana Zagache †
14 Xoxocatlán International Airport ★
15 Santo Domingo Ocotlán, Rodolfo Foundation Museum & Home 🏛
16 Santa Catarina Las Minas
17 San Battasar Chichicapan
18 San Pablo Guila †
19 Xaaga ⌇
20 Hierve de Agua ★
21 San Dionosio Ocotepec †
22 San Pablo Mitla ⌇

23 Yaguar Xoo ★
24 Yagul ⌇
25 Iglesia de la Asunción Tlocolula †
26 Lambityeco ⌇
27 Museo Comunitario Shan-Dany 🏛
28 Dainzú ⌇
29 Museo Comunitario Baala Xtee 🏛
30 San Jeronimo Tlacocochahuaya †
31 Benito Juarez △
32 Cuajimoloyas △
33 Llano Grande △

34 Tule Tree ★
35 La Neveria △
36 San Andrés Huayapam, Orquideo La Encantada †★
37 Latuvi △
38 Santa María Yavesia △
39 Santa Catarina Lachatao △
40 San Miguel Amatlán △
41 Capulapán de Méndez †
42 Ecoturixtlán Shiaa Rua Via △
43 La Cumbre Ixtepe △
44 Museo Comunitario San José El Mogote 🏛

© The Countryman Press

There are two wonderful crafts villages close to the ruins, the ceramics-producing neighborhood of ✪ **Santa María Atzompa** (8 kilometers/10 miles), well known for its distinctive green ceramic glaze, and the adorable *alebrijes*-carving town of **San Antonio Arrazola** (12 kilometers/7 miles) just beneath the opposite side of Monte Albán. Public buses serve both from Abastos in Oaxaca City. You'll pass through **Xoxocotlán**, known for its mystical Day of the Dead celebrations, on the way.

Santiago Apostal **Cuilapan de Guerrero's** (12 kilometers/7 miles) unfinished, 16th-century cathedral is a symphony in light and shadow that ranks among the Dominicans' finest work. Finally, the ancient Zapotec metropolis of ✪ **Zaachila** (17 kilometers/10 miles) offers a wonderful Thursday market, another lovely church, and best of all, the mostly unexcavated ruins of the city, atop a small hill just behind the cathedral. This route makes a convenient boondoggle en route to Hwy. 131 and Puerto Escondido.

VALLEY OF ETLA

Northwest of Oaxaca City lies the fertile Etla Valley, home to dozens of Zapotec-Mixtec villages, huge Dominican-era churches, and the region's oldest ruins. It is the gateway to the Mixteca region, including the Dominican Route, covered in the Northern Oaxaca chapter.

There are several tiny towns named Etla, with most visitors headed to **Villa de Etla** (19 kilometers/12 miles), home to the Dominicans' final Oaxacan church and festive Wednesday market, and nearby **San Agustín Etla** (16 kilometers/10 miles), with a paper-producing cooperative. Most tours are offered on Wednesday only, and visit the ruins of Oaxaca's first major city, **San José El Mogote** (18 kilometers/11 miles), with a community museum onsite. Archaeology buffs can use buses or private vehicles to continue past the Etlas to ✪ **Suchilquitongo**, which has a top-notch museum and hilltop ruins.

MITLA ROUTE

This popular guided day trip is the best way for visitors to enjoy the region's highlights in a short period of time. Serious shoppers and archaeology buffs may opt for private transport, or use public buses to spend more time in one spot.

San Andrés Huayapan (4 kilometers/2 miles) is almost a suburb, with a couple of good hotels and a botanical garden, at the gateway to Northern Oaxaca on Hwy. 175. Tour buses fly past, instead stopping at the famous **Tule Tree** (13 kilometers/8 miles), the world's widest, dwarfing the neighboring church. The fantastic Dominican church at **Tlacochahuaya** (23 kilometers/14 miles) is angled to catch the setting sun, as are the dramatic ruins of **Dainzú** (24 kilometers/15 miles) and **Lambityeco** (26 kilometers/16 miles).

The famous *tapete*-weaving town of **Teotitlán del Valle** (28 kilometers/17 miles) is on every day-trip itinerary, usually a quick stop for demonstrations, but you could spend all day exploring the different workshops. If you have time, enjoy neighboring **Santa Ana del Valle** (32 kilometers/20 miles), a lesser-known *tapete* town, with a great market and community museum. Tour groups also miss the fascinating ruins of **Yagül** (36 kilometers/22 miles), with their awesome *mirador* and enormous ball court, and the agricultural town of **Tlacolula** (28 kilometers/17 miles). The **Yaguar Xoo** (40 kilometers/24 miles), a small wild animal park, might be fun for families, but everyone will love the fantastic ruins of **Mitla** (47 kilometers/29 miles). A trip to **Hierve el Agua** (72 kilometers/45 miles) is perfect for

The fiercely independent Mixtec capital displays what's called a greca mosaic, repeating geometrical patterns that appear to change with the light.

hikers and nature lovers, while the distilleries of **Matatlán** (50 kilometers/31 miles), the "Mezcal Capital of the World," will attract others.

After Mitla and Matatlán, Hwy. 190 continues to the Isthmus of Tehuantepec; from Teotitlán, a very good dirt road (rather than taking paved Hwy. 175 from San Andrés Huayapan) leads into the Sierra Juárez Hwy., arriving in Benito Juárez, the gateway to the Pueblos Mancomunados.

OCOTLÁN ROUTE

Hwy. 175 south of Oaxaca City traverses a fertile valley passing through three unmissable artisanal towns: **San Bartolo Coyotepec** (15 kilometers/9 miles), famed for its luminous black pottery and excellent state museum; **San Martín Tilcajete** (20 kilometers/12 miles), known for its *alebrijes*, and **Santo Tomás Jalieza** (29 kilometers/18 miles), where you can watch women weave their famous cotton fabrics with waist looms in the market. The final destination, **Ocotlán de Morelos** (35 kilometers/21 miles), is a bustling agribusiness powerhouse with the excellent Rodolfo Morales Museum and exquisite cathedral. Tours run from Oaxaca City on Friday, to take advantage of the Jalieza and Ocotlán markets.

This is also the most direct route to the popular beach town of Puerto Escondido. Almost halfway between them, about 2 hours south of Ocotlán, is the high-altitude town of **San José del Pacifico** (132 kilometers/82 miles), famous for great trips.

GETTING AROUND

The Central Valleys is the most developed region in the state, with excellent public transportation and, for the most part, very good paved roads. Regardless, the region is usually seen on guided tours arranged in Oaxaca City.

Buses and Colectivos

Public buses, as well as *colectivo* taxis and shuttle vans, serve almost all major towns and destinations in the Central Valley. Most public transport from Oaxaca City leaves from the Abastos Centro second-class bus station, covered in the Transportation chapter.

For buses and shuttles back to Oaxaca (or headed elsewhere in the Central Valley), ask anyone *"¿Donde esta el autobus para [Oaxaca]?"* They may point you to a *colectivo,* or collective taxi. These leave for specific destinations once they have four passengers; if they are headed back to Oaxaca City, they usually drop you near Abastos.

Some towns and attractions are located a kilometer or two from the main highway. Thus, if your bus doesn't go to the *mero centro* (actual center) of the town, you'll need to walk from the highway bus stop. It's worth asking if you're headed to Mitla, Jalieza, or Tilcajete. Most archaeological sites are also a hike from the bus stop; most tourists will find it worthwhile to rent a car or private taxi.

Private Taxis

Taxis are a convenient way to see the Central Valleys, and can be arranged directly with the driver if you speak a bit of Spanish; expect to spend about US$20 per hour, US$100 per day, for up to four people.

Your hotel or any tour outfit can also arrange private taxis and English-speaking guides. Larger vans are available for groups of three or more people.

The efflorescence of frescos at San Jerónimo Tlacochahuaya, painted with natural dyes, needs a little TLC every century or so.

Rental Car

It's easy to drive in the Central Valleys, with one major exception: Oaxaca City, with its clogged 16th-century streets and chaotic urban sprawl. Most visitors find it easier to take taxis or buses to attractions within the greater metropolitan area, including Monte Albán, Santa María Atzompa, and San Antonio Arrazola.

Once you're out of town, however, it's quite easy to navigate the paved, well-signed roads, and parking is usually a breeze. The road from Mitla to Hierve el Agua is unpaved.

Even secondary roads tend to be well signed in Oaxaca.

Guided Tours into the Oaxaca Valley

So, you've only got a few days and a lot to see. Why not book a guided day trip from Oaxaca City? These are the most commonly offered tours, which usually leave at 10 AM:

Mitla Route: After a quick stop at the Tule Tree, it's on to Teotitlán del Valle, the *tapete*-weaving town where you'll probably enjoy an hour-long dyeing and weaving demonstration, and the fantastic ruins of Mitla. After a pricey lunch, full-day tours continue to Hierve el Agua, returning via the mezcal distilleries, complete with free shots. Offered daily, but go on Sunday, market day in Tule, Mitla, and the less-visited town of Tlacolula.

Monte Albán and Zaachila: You can easily visit Monte Albán by shuttle bus, or book a Thursday tour that includes the Zaachila Market, Cuilapan's amazing church, and the *alebrije*-carving town of Arrazola.

Ocotlán Route: Visit San Bartolo Coyotepec's black ceramics workshops and museum; stop for lunch in the *alebrije*-production town of San Martín Tilcajete, then move to the picturesque market in the weaving center of Santo Tomás Jalieza, and finally Ocotlán's famous cathedral and excellent museum. Tours run daily in high season, and always on Fridays, to take advantage of Jalieza's and Ocotlán's festive market days.

Etla Valley: Wednesday tours visit the excellent market, Dominican church, paper factory, and the ruins of San Jose El Mogote. Operators also arrange custom tours, which are a bit more expensive but not a bad deal if you've got a group. Popular options include archaeology tours to less-visited ruins, or shopping tours to the surrounding artisanal towns. Check the Shopping chapter for more information on those.

During the Day of the Dead, the most authentic and interesting celebrations take place in *panteones* (cemeteries) in the Central Valley. The easiest way to attend these festivities is on a guided tour, offered almost everywhere.

Continental-Istmo Tours (951-516-9625; www.continentalistmotours.com; Alcalá 201, Centro) The company offers all the usual tours, plus trips to Cuajimoloyas in the Sierra Juárez, with waterfalls, hiking, and traditional medicine demonstrations; stay overnight and enjoy a *temazcal*.

Dominicos Tour (951-132-9006; Calz Porfiro Díaz 102, Hotel Misión de Las Angeles) All the standard tours plus the Dominican Route, visiting several truly astounding 16th-century churches, covered in the Northern Oaxaca chapter.

✪**Lescas Tours** (951-515-5400; lescastour@yahoo.com) Eduardo and Omar Lescas are both knowledgeable, professional guides often hired by the big companies, but they also offer quality custom tours at great prices.

✪**La Mano Mágica** (951-516-4275; www.lamanomagica.com; Alcala 203, Centro) This exceptional crafts store also runs Casa Sagrada B&B, in Teotitlán, from which it organizes *temazcals*, horseback riding tours, guided hikes, market tours, cooking classes, and other activities.

Monte Albán Tours (951-520-0444; www.montealbantours.com; Alcala 206F, Centro) The reliable, convenient, large-scale operator on Alcalá offers good-quality generic tours.

✪**Sierra Norte** (951-514-8271; www.sierranorte.org.mx; Bravo 210-1) Organizes overnight ecotourism trips to the high-altitude Pueblos Mancomunados, covered in the Northern Oaxaca chapter.

Turísticos Marfils (951-516-8138; turisticosmarfil@hotmail.com; Acalá 407; V, MC) Inexpensive, at least hourly shuttle service to Monte Albán, the company offers all the tours plus easy transfers to Puerto Escondido and Huatulco.

Viajes Xochitlán (951-514-3620; www.oaxaca-travel.com; M Bravo 210-A, Centro) Viajes has all the regular tours, plus daily Etla trips, and visits to ecotourism sites in the surrounding mountains, including the Sierra Norte.

Villa de Etla's wonderful Wednesday market is a feast of energy and color.

LODGING

Almost all of the destinations in this chapter are within an hour's drive of Oaxaca City, where most visitors make their base. There are alternatives, however, for those who seek quieter solace in the starry heart of the Zapotec kingdom. Most Valley hotels are geared toward budget and local travelers, comfortable but unremarkable. They offer clean, fan-cooled rooms, cable TV, and private hot water baths; the good ones are listed under "Other Hotels," at the end of the section.

Less adventurous travelers may be more comfortable in the mid-range hotels in Mitla and Ocotlán, or the sprinkling of B&Bs in the rolling hills, most catering to handicrafts shoppers.

Lodging Price Code

Cost of lodging is based on an average per-room, double-occupancy during peak season (July; November through mid-January), not including the mandatory 18 percent tax, which may be waived for cash payment. Rates are often reduced during low season (June and August through September), and can double during the Christmas–New Year's holidays, Día de los Muertos, and Semana Santa, when the best hotels are booked weeks and months out. Costs are calculated at 10 pesos to the US dollar.

Inexpensive	Up to US$50
Moderate	US$50 to US$100
Expensive	US$100 to US$150
Very Expensive	More than US$150

Hotels

Hotel Don Cenobio
Manager: Marina
951-568-0330
www.hoteldoncenobio.com
informes@hoteldoncenobio.com
Mitla, Avenida Juárez 3, Centro
Price: Moderate
Credit Cards: Yes
Handicapped Access: Challenging

The town of Mitla is certainly an atmospheric spot to spend the night, thanks to the wonderful ruins scattered scenically around town. In addition to several budget hotels, an excellent family run four-star hotel is just a few blocks from the city center. Modern, inviting rooms, all equipped with hot water baths, cable TV, hair dryers, WiFi, and all the amenities, have cheerful jungle-themed furnishings, and colorful hand-woven bedspreads. Suites have full kitchens. Kids will love it, along with the sprawling, grassy central courtyard where a fairly fabulous buffet *comida* is served to day-trippers. For budget options in town, see "Other Hotels," below.

Hotel Rey David
951-571-1248
Ocotlán, 16 Septiembre 248, south end of town
Price: Inexpensive
Credit Cards: Cash only
Handicapped Access: None

Much nicer than you'd imagine from the outside, this historic adobe on the busy main drag has a wonderful artistic touch. Cool, cavernous rooms (some with very small windows) have hand-painted murals and detailing, combined with strategically revealed adobe brick. Furnishings are made locally, with lots of hand-carved wood and colorful woven bedspreads and curtains. Private hot bath, cable TV, air conditioning, heat, and free parking are all part of the package, just a 10-minute stroll from the city center.

Bed & Breakfasts

Casa Linda
Owner: Linda Hanna
951-540-8020
www.folkartfantasy.com
linda@folkartfantasy.com
Huayapan, 6 kilometers (3 miles) from Oaxaca Centro
Price: Moderate
Handicapped Access: None
Special features: Folk-art immersion: tours, books, and remarkable examples.

Tranquil three-room B&B in the hills east of Oaxaca City has everything you'd expect in a quiet mountain retreat: lovely gardens, a full breakfast, drinking water, and pleasant rooms with TV, CD/DVD player, WiFi, private bath, and truly exquisite décor.

If you want to learn more about Oaxacan handicrafts, take advantage of the library and guided tours, or ask the owner to arrange lunch with artists, or schedule any class or demonstration you wish. These can be arranged separately, by non-guests, or as part of a package. Dinners can also be arranged. Hanna also rents a nice little guesthouse in town.

Casa Sagrada
Owners: Arnulfo and Mary Jane Mendoza
951-516-4275, 310-455-6085 in the United States and Canada
www.casasagrada.com
info@casasagrada.com
Teotitlán del Valle; offices at La Mano Mágica, Alcala 203, Oaxaca City, Centro
Price: Moderate to Expensive

Credit Cards: Yes
Handicapped Access: None

The owners of the fascinating La Mano Mágica handicrafts store in downtown Oaxaca operate this B&B, decorated with exquisite *artesanías.* Intricate embroidery and elegant weavings are displayed in every room, and French doors open onto the patio. Outside, enjoy the shaded porch, with bougainvillea-framed views over the valley.

La Casa Sagrada offers tours and activities, open to non-guests who book them as day-trips from Oaxaca: guided hikes, horseback rides, birding tours, cooking classes, and even a *temazcal.* Or relax in a hammock, enjoy a yoga class, get a massage, or stroll down into Teotitlán to admire the rugs. Rates include a full breakfast and dinner, and there's a two-night minimum.

Casa Raab
Owners: Tony and Rebecca Raab
951-520-4022
www.casaraab.com
casaraab@gmail.com
San Pablo Etla
Price: Moderate to Expensive
Credit Cards: Cash only
Handicapped Access: None
Special Features: You can rent the entire ranch.

The Central Valleys' poshest accommodation is just outside the ancient village of San Pablo Etla (as distinct from Villa de Etla or San Agustín). A classic hacienda-style ranch house, with a ceramic *tejas*-tiled roof, has all the modern comforts, including a great pool. Rent the entire casa, or just one room in the Casa Grande, which has four huge, airy bedrooms impeccably decorated with ceramics, *tapetes,* fresh flowers and wood furnishings that elegantly set off the ceramic floors and cane ceilings. The smaller Casita has two rooms sleeping a total of five, and an outstanding porch,

Weaver Edgar Mendoza shows off some of Teotitlán del Valle's famous tapetes, or wool weavings.

perfect for families. Both houses have full kitchens.

Though the setup is exquisite, this isn't a full-service luxury hotel. A full breakfast is provided and dinner can be arranged; talk to the cook, and she might even offer a tour of the market while you shop together. Staff is off, however, from Saturday afternoon until Monday morning, so you'll be on your own.

Las Granadas Bed & Breakfast
Manager: Roberta Christie
951-524-4232
www.lasgranadasoaxaca.com
lasgranadasoaxaca@gmail.com
Teotitlán del Valle, 2 de Abril 9
Price: Inexpensive

Credit Cards: Cash only
Handicapped Access: None

This two-story guesthouse is in tiny Teotitlán, which is famed for its family owned *tapete* workshops, weaving natural-dyed wool rugs, and wall hangings. Local weavings are also on display, decorated with fresh, bright colors and handy wooden and wicker furnishings.

Adorable first-floor rooms have shared showers, and a pleasant patio with wonderful valley views. The second-floor "deluxe" room has a private hot-water bathroom and balcony. A full, cooked breakfast is included. The B&B is just a few blocks from town, and the staff can arrange guided workshop tours, birding walks, and Spanish classes.

Nature Lodges

There are *very* basic accommodations at Hierve el Agua and Gruta San Sebastian, covered in Parks and Protected Areas, below.

Cabinas Guacamaya

951-510-9482
15 kilometers (9 miles) from Villa de Etla, well signed from Hwy. 131
Price: Inexpensive
Credit Cards: Cash only
Handicapped Access: None

This relatively new ecotourism project sits atop a mountain covered in cool pine forests, with outstanding views of the valley and Villa de Etla. Cozy adobe cabins have fireplaces, and there's a small lake with playground equipment for kids. There's an onsite restaurant, but be sure to bring your own snacks. Make and confirm reservations, as there's no one permanently on site.

El Rincón de San Agustín Etla

951-521-2526, 951-510-3902
cury9ja@yahoo.com, amaliacruz@hot mail.com
San Agustín Etla
Price: Inexpensive
Credit Cards: Cash only
Handicapped Access: None
Special features: Great camping.

Occupying an old farmhouse in the relaxed village of San Agustín Etla, this pastoral paradise occupies a grassy riverbank surrounded by pristine forest and acres of farmland. Cabanas are cozy and adorable, with full kitchen, fireplace, and private bath. There's also a nice campsite. Staff can arrange guided hikes, birding tours, visits to the paper factory, and dance classes. The outdoor restaurant offers breakfast and *comida*.

San Miguel El Valle y El Carriza

951-520-9058
200-123-7372 (Palacio Municipal)
San Miguel El Valle, Mitla Route
Price: Inexpensive
Credit Cards: Cash only
Handicapped Access: None

Adventurous types might want to try the tiny, ancient town of San Miguel El Valle, just south of Santa Ana del Valle. The brand-new ecotourism project offers one cabin and one dorm, all with hot-water baths, and a good restaurant. Activities include trout fishing and visiting the *tapete* workshops, the ornate 18th-century church, and Cueva Iglesia, an underground grotto.

Tourist Yu'u Santa Ana del Valle

951-562-0419
Santa Ana del Valle
Price: Inexpensive
Credit Cards: Cash only
Handicapped Access: None

This tourist *yu'u*, or community center, offers clean, basic lodging in simple rooms and dorms for people who would rather spend money on rugs than lodging. Close to the market and museum, it's clean, well-kept, and well-attended, with nice gardens for relaxing.

Other Hotels

ETLA VALLEY

Villa de Etla (951-521-5148; Morelos 40, Villa de Etla; cash only; $) Three blocks from the market, the villa has 12 refurbished, modern rooms with gleaming tile floors, homey furnishings, local television, private bath with 24-hour hot water, WiFi, and a great porch. The front rooms, with big windows and archways, are the best.

MITLA

In addition to the excellent Don Cenobio, reviewed above, there are a handful of budget hotels by the ruins, including:

Hotel and Restaurant Mitla (951-568-0112; Juárez 6; cash only; $) Family run with a wonderful garden and very basic rooms; the ones upstairs are better.

Zapotec Hotel and Restaurant (951-540-0020; 5 de Febrero 12; $; cash only) Spacious, basic rooms with private baths and a great onsite restaurant.

SAN BARTOLO COYOTEPEC
Hotel El Angel (no phone, San Bartolo Coyotepec; cash only; $) This very basic hotel and restaurant right on the main plaza, across from the Museo Estatal, offers clean, fan-cooled rooms with hard beds, mismatched furniture, and tiny (the shower is right over the toilet) bathrooms with hot water in the morning.

SAN JOSÉ DEL PACIFICO
About two hours south of Ocotlán, on the way to Puerto Ángel, is the mountain town famous for its traditional indigenous medicine. It's also a great place to spend a night between Oaxaca City and the beaches.

Cabañas Puesto del Sol (951-100-8678; www.sanjosedelpacifico.com; sanjosedelpacifico@yahoo.com; Hwy. 131, just north of town; cash only; $$) This posh spot between Oaxaca and Puerto Ángel has a collection of whitewashed duplex cabinas, with colorful gardens and semi-private porches overlooking the awesome mountain scenery. Each has cable TV, mellow furnishings, and a private hot bath; for US$10 extra, you get a fireplace. The onsite **restaurant** (B, L, C, D; $–$$) has huge windows over all that scenery as well.

Restaurant y Hotel El Pacifico (951-505-4353; www.cabanaspacifico.com.mx; reservaciones@cabanaspacifico.com.mx; Hwy. 131, kilometer 135; cash only; $) A variety of rooms are homey with outstanding views. The simplest, built of polished wood with big windows, have shared hot-water bathrooms and cozy comforters. The bigger, second-floor rooms have private hot-water showers and a terrace; one has a fireplace. All come with WiFi, and the owners can arrange any tour or *temazcal*.

SANTA MARÍA EL TULE
Posada El Niño (951-518-0936; Calle 2 Abril; cash only; $) Right on the central plaza, with views of the city's famed Tule Tree, this basic family run posada has fan-cooled rooms with soft beds, cable TV, and private hot-water bath; request one with a balcony.

TEOTITLÁN DEL VALLE
In addition to the B&Bs, there's a tradition of housing visitors at artist cooperatives or in private homes, usually in conjunction with workshops or private weaving classes. Ask at any workshop, or try **Cooperativa de Artesanos** (951-524-4092, 951-124-1947; viridiana_loom56@hotmail.com, gaspar_chavez@hotmail.com; Juárez, kilometer 2.5).

TLACOLULA
La Calenda (951-562-0660; Avenida Juárez 40; credit cards accepted; $) The best hotel in town offers 45 freshly-painted, smallish rooms on three floors, surrounding a pleasant courtyard. All have new mattresses, cable TV, WiFi, and fan, but no seats on the toilets. The onsite **restaurant** (B, L, C, D; $) specializes in barbecue.

Hotel Restaurant Guish Bac (951-562-0080; Zaragoza 3; cash only; $) Good vibes warm the basic rooms in a family run, three-story building. The restaurant serves regional cuisine all day long in the informal atrium.

Hotel Restaurant Regis (951-562-0332; Juárez 33; cash only; $) Also perfectly acceptable, it's on the main drag and has a parking lot and, for US$4 extra, cable TV. Four rooms have small balconies.

RESTAURANTS AND FOOD PURVEYORS

Though the Central Valleys and their cultural bounty almost certainly inspired many of Oaxaca's renowned recipes, it simply isn't a foodie paradise. In general, restaurants fall into two classes: small *comedors,* or vendors, with inexpensive regional dishes found in and around the town market; and large restaurants (often buffet-style) geared to large groups and families.

Restaurants and Food Purveyors Price Code

The following prices are based on the cost of a dinner entrée with a non-alcoholic beverage, not including the usually voluntary (but check your receipt) 10–15 percent gratuity. The coding "B, L, C, D" refers to U.S.-style meals (breakfast, lunch, dinner), as well as the typical Mexican *comida,* traditionally the biggest meal of the day, served in lieu of lunch from about 2 PM to 6 PM. Prices are calculated at 10 pesos to the dollar.

Inexpensive:	Up to US$5
Moderate:	US$5 to US$10
Expensive:	US$10 to US$20
Very Expensive:	US$20 or more

Restaurants

MONTE ALBÁN—ZAACHILA ROUTE
The ruins at Monte Albán have a nice **restaurant** (B, L; $$) serving solid Oaxacan cuisine for predictably inflated prices. There's a full bar and a great view.

✪ **La Capilla de Zaachila**
951-528-6011
zaachila_lacapilla@msn.com
Carretera Oaxaca-Zaachila, kilometer 145, across from Pemex
Price: Moderate to Expensive
Credit Cards: Yes
Cuisine: Oaxacan
Serving: B, L, C, D
Reservations: For groups, on market day

Since 1972, La Capilla has served wonderful Oaxacan cuisine, traditionally cooked in its shady gardens. Today, it can serve some 3,000 people at its long wooden tables, something for which you'll be grateful if you do the Zaachila market tour in high season. Grab an oversized menu and consider some of the truly authentic offerings, such as *vino*

de nogal, a non-alcoholic red tea made from a local bark. There are platters for every budget and appetite, including *platones,* "big plates," for four to seven people, featuring most of the foods you've planned to try, including *tasajo,* moles, chile rellenos, *memelitas,* and of course *chapulines,* for starters.

Restaurant Familiar Los Alebrijes
951-152-5066
Road to Atzompa, 1.5 kilometers (1 mile) south of town.
Price: Inexpensive
Credit Cards: Cash only
Serving: C, D
Handicapped Access: None
Reservations: No

A short walk or drive toward Oaxaca City from Arrazola (right on the bus line), you can find this cute bamboo restaurant with plastic chairs and a big dance floor, locally known for its barbecue and rabbit dishes. You can also get burgers, *tortas, tlayudas,* and other Oaxacan fast food. It becomes a bar and disco after dark.

MITLA ROUTE

Caldo de Piedra

951-550-8486
www.youtube.com/watch?v=1usn_Eu015E
Hwy. 190, kilometer 9
San Felipe Usila, 1 kilometer (.6 miles)
west of the Tule Tree
Price: Inexpensive to Moderate
Credit Cards: Cash only
Serving: C, D
Reservations: No

Planeta.com considers this modest eatery
"The Best Food Experience in Mexico," and
it's certainly one of the most unique. The
specialty is a classic Chinanteco dish from
the Papaloapan region: *caldo de piedra,*
stone soup. After preparing the ingredients—shrimp, vegetables, herbs, broth—in
a simple ceramic bowl a red-hot river rock
is dropped into the mix, cooking the soup
from the inside out.

✪ El Patio

951-562-2947
patios@prodigy.net.mx
Hwy. 190, kilometer 28; Macuilxochilt,
Tlacolula
Price: Moderate to Expensive
Credit Cards: Cash only
Cuisine: Oaxacan
Serving: L, C, D
Reservations: For groups

This classic roadside rest stop offers breezy
patio seating overlooking lovely gardens
and incredible views that bring tourists
and locals alike. You can't miss it: It's a
pink-and-white wedding cake of a Colonial
hacienda, complete with its own adobe
chapel for a reproduction Virgen of Juquila.
Try great Oaxacan cuisine, including the
recommended mole *almendra* and chiles
rellenos, and starters such as *tlayudas* or
a quesadilla hot off the wood-fired *comal.*
Make reservations for Sunday at 2 PM, when
the Badu Huinni Cusia (Angel Dancers)
youth troupe performs the Guelaguetza.

La Perla

951-449-5117
San Andrés Huayapan, overlooking the dam
and reservoir
Price: Moderate to Expensive
Credit Cards: Cash only
Cuisine: Oaxacan, Seafood
Serving: C, D
Reservations: No

Just 4 kilometers (2.5 miles) from Oaxaca
City, the tiny town of San Andrés Huayapan
is technically within Benito Juárez National
Park, protecting the artificial lake at the
entrance to town. Right above the water is
Restaurant La Perla, with huge windows to
enjoy the view, great seafood dishes from
the coast, and trout from the neighboring
mountains. There's a large children's playground out front.

Restaurant El Descanso

951-524-4125
Teotitlán, Avenida Juárez, Centro
Price: Moderate
Credit Cards: Yes
Cuisine: Oaxacan
Serving: B, L, C
Reservations: For groups

Rejuvenate while perusing Teotitlán's famous
tapete shops, right in the center of the lovely
little town. The shady Colonial surrounds a
lovely interior courtyard, and the whole place
is hung with wonderful rugs, which you can
admire over lunch (and, of course, purchase
along with your meal). Moles and other
Mexican food are the highlights, but there are
a few international options as well.

Restaurant Tlamanalli

951-524-4006
Teotitlán, Juarez 39
Price: Moderate to Expensive
Credit Cards: Cash only
Cuisine: Oaxacan
Serving: C, D
Reservations: For large groups

This well-loved restaurant in scenic environs is all about the experience: The Mendoza sisters greet you in full indigenous outfits, backed by what may be one of the most marvelous ceramic-tiled kitchens in the state. Start off with one of their many mezcals, then try the *comida,* which changes daily and usually has four or five options. The Mendozas' black mole is regionally revered. It's a bit overpriced, but best quality.

ETLA VALLEY
The Etla Market, at its busiest on Wednesday, is well known for its *quesillo,* a skimmed cheese usually served melted, *pan amarillo,* rich "yellow bread," and *tasajo,* thinly sliced beef.

Hacienda San Agustín
951-517-6477
Kilometer 2 a Carretera a San Agustin Yantareni
Price: Moderate to Expensive
Credit Cards: Yes
Cuisine: Oaxacan, buffet
Serving: C
Reservations: No

It claims to be the biggest, best buffet in Oaxaca. In addition to award-winning moles, accompanied by well over 100 sides, there's grilled steak and other meats at **La Caballeriza,** the grill restaurant next to the buffet. The restaurant is also well known for its homemade tortillas (worth taking home), and caters to families with kids' prices and a big playground.

Hacienda Santa Martha de Barcéna
951-521-2835
www.restaurantelaescondida.com.mx
Hwy. 131, San Sebastián de las Flores
Price: Moderate to Expensive
Credit Cards: Yes
Cuisine: Oaxaca, buffet
Serving: C
Reservations: For groups

Convenient to San José El Mogote, the spectacular buffet has hundreds of choices: dozens of mains, moles, soups, salads, as well as a *comal* and grill making more food to order, and far too many desserts. Grab an outdoor table in the expansive, wedding-ready grounds, which come complete with a small church, a children's playground, and even a real plane you can board for fun. Service starts at 1:30 PM daily.

OCOTLÁN ROUTE
Azucena Zapoteca
951-510-7844
www.tilcajete.org
San Martín Tilcajete, kilometer 23.5, Hwy. 175
Price: Inexpensive to Moderate
Credit Cards: Yes
Cuisine: Oaxacan
Serving: B, L, C
Reservations: For groups

Right on the highway, at the turnoff to the famous *alebrije*-carving town of San Martín Tilcajete, this colorful restaurant makes a very pleasant stop. Try the *tasajo* stuffed with cheese and vegetables in a rich bean sauce, the pork enchilada in a light green salsa, or the stuffed pumpkin flowers.
The restaurant, bar, and gift shop are run by renowned woodcarvers Jacobo and María Angeles, whose naturally dyed *alebrijes* are displayed in the Smithsonian.

✪ La Taberna de los Duendes
951-585-4353
Hwy. 131, San José del Pacifico
Price: Inexpensive to Moderate
Credit Cards: No
Cuisine: International
Serving: B, L, D
Reservations: No

"The Tavern of the *Duendes,*" loosely translated as "mischievous elves," is almost halfway between Oaxaca City and the Pacific, about two hours south of Ocotlán.

The cave-like space, hung with moss and polished-wood art, has plenty of room for live bands, fire dancers, and other entertainers. The food has Italian flair and uses local and organic ingredients, as well as imported European cheeses, meats, and liquors. Locally caught trout is a favorite, and on chilly nights, try a *vin brulé,* a spiced red wine. For romantic views, reserve the single upstairs table, surrounded with windows.

The owners sell an excellent assortment of local wool handicrafts, and can arrange guided hikes and horseback riding trips. There are also several more traditional, locally operated restaurants serving simple fare for cash only within walking distance, including pretty **Restaurant Rayita del Sol** (951-547-4225; Hwy. 131; B, L, C, D; $), with a sunny back patio overlooking a steep canyon; and **Restaurant La Montaña**, just a few steps farther up the hill, with free WiFi.

Food Purveyors

Most villages in the Central Valleys are centered on a market, where you can find inexpensive eateries, fresh-baked goods, tamales, and other great food at local prices.

Cafés

Café Express (no phone; San José del Pacifico, Hwy. 131; B, L, D; $) This café sells coffee, snacks, sweaters with mushroom patterns, crocheted mushrooms, carved wooden mushrooms, and other mushroom-related paraphernalia.

Sacred Bean Café (Teotitlán, Juárez 49, Centro; L, C; $) Refuel after a hard morning of *tapete* shopping with an espresso, pastry, or hot chocolate. The café also sells *tapetes.*

El Valle Café (Tlacolula, North Colas Bravo, Edificio Eden; L, D; $) This brand-new coffee shop on the second floor of the tallest building in town does espresso beverages, pastries, and light meals.

Specialty Foods and Grocers

The small towns of the Central Valleys rarely have full-service supermarkets, though there are always grocers selling the basics.

Guish Bac Chocolate (951-526-1321; Tlacolula, Avenida Juárez 36) Tlacolula's *molina,* or community grinder, offers custom mixed and ground chocolate, mole, and other spices without the fuss you'll find at Oaxaca City's markets.

Inalim (951-515-9507; www.inalim.com .mx; Calle Libertad, Santa María Coyotepec) Inalim produces unique Oaxacan condiments, including *sal de chapulin* (grasshopper salt), *sal de guisano* (worm salt) made with real worms and grasshoppers, and many other insectalicious items, the perfect gift. There's another branch in Oaxaca City (951-515-9507; Quinceo 103, Colonia Volcanes), but look for their products at any grocer.

CULTURE

This is the cradle of Oaxacan culture, embracing almost every possible expression of spirit in the Valleys' long history. Important pre-Columbian cities and Spanish Colonial churches are complemented by heartfelt community museums. Markets dating back to Monte Albán's reign still serve ancient dishes alongside recipes improved with each generation.

This is a region rich with wonderful handicrafts, where you can spend hours exploring workshops where woven wool *tapetes,* colorful hand-carved *alebrijes,* delicate filigree jewelry, and all sorts of iconic ceramic and textiles are made. Each town has its own specialty, and families devote their days to the perfection of their craft. Tours, workshops, and classes can be arranged. For more information, see the Shopping chapter.

The carmine color of cochineal, a natural dye made with a tiny insect that inhabits the prickly pear cactus, can be manipulated with the addition of lime or calcium, or simply by using different colored wool.

Architecture

This rich and relatively well-watered agricultural region has been a population center for perhaps 3000 years, with thousands of architecturally significant indigenous ruins. There are also scores of magnificent churches.

Churches

Baroque lovers and history buffs can explore an incredible assortment of churches in the Central Valleys, some part of the Dominican Route, covered in the Northern Oaxaca chapter. In addition to the big churches, consider visiting Zaachila's **Nuestra Señora de la Natividad**; Teotitlán's 1751 **Preciosa Sangre de Cristo**, a classic of Colonial architecture with a feast day celebrated with the *Danza de la Pluma;* **Iglesia de la Asunción Tlacolula**, with loads of silver and famous examples of "folk baroque" murals and sculpture; and **San Pablo Mitla**, usually overshadowed by the ruins, though its monumental neoclassical bulk protects several graceful *retablos* inside.

Iglesia Villa de Etla The fertile valley of Etla, and former estate of conquistador Hernán Cortés, supports dozens of small pueblos, many of them with the name Etla. The most important is Villa de Etla, its Dominican church rising above the city's famed Wednesday market and broad plaza. The original church, built in the 1550s, has been destroyed and remodeled several times; the current incarnation dates to 1636, after the nearby aqueduct was completed.

Though called "The Dancers," the people who posed for these ancient Olmec-style portraits actually may have been under medical observation.

There are dozens of other churches in the Etla Valley, including the 1726 church of **San Andrés Zautla**, with what's recognized as Oaxaca's most beautiful organ, a gilded four-pedal masterpiece covered with angels and restored in the 1990s.

San Andrés Huayapan (4 kilometers/2 miles) Though the rich ochres and ambers of the exterior are impressive enough, you're here to see the "gilded lace" *retablo,* considered Oaxaca's finest, created in the late 1700s by artist Andrés de Zarate. Other artifacts include a silver tabernacle and several expressive sculptures that are also probably Zarate's work.

San Jerónimo Tlacochahuaya (Hwy. 190, 23 kilometers/14 miles east of Oaxaca) Once a remote and austere monastery, this 1558 Dominican church has since developed into a folk-baroque showpiece. Wonderful frescos, emblazoned with brilliant flowers, were originally painted with natural dyes. Several ornate altars and *retablos* within the sanctuary seem to correspond with older divinities. The church has been rebuilt numerous times and was last completed in the 1730s, when the recently restored pipe organ was constructed. You can hear its pure tones all over the cute cobblestoned town, especially during the fun, five-day Feast of San Jerónimo.

To see another important example of folk-baroque painting, take the paved road 10 kilometers (6 miles) south to **San Juan Teitipac**, where the 16th-century church, built atop an old Zapotec pyramid, has some of the region's most mysterious murals, perhaps depicting the Inquisition here in Oaxaca.

✪ **Santiago Apostal Cuilapan de Guerrero** (12 kilometers/7.5 miles) This unfinished masterpiece, begun by the Dominicans in 1550 at the "River of Palms," was ambitious: Its iconic, arcaded basilica still graces many brochures. Though it is unfinished (construction

Mezcal, Buzz of the Gods

"Para todo mal, mezcal; para todo bien, también."

"For everything bad, mezcal; for everything good, as well."

In the beginning, the maguey "blue" agave, a dangerous-looking bouquet of thick-spined leaves sprouting dramatic and bush-sized across the high desert, was considered a vital food (as well as a conveniently ready-made needle and thread, but that is another tale), like corn and beans. Sacred to the Mixtec goddess Mayahuel, it held much of Oaxaca's sweetness, and was made into candy called mexcalli.

The Spanish, however, experts in the sugary chemistry of alcohol, saw more potential in this humble crop. They introduced a type of Moorish distillery, made of copper and ceramic, to the region, and began perfecting that beverage considered the most Oaxacan of them all.

They called it mezcal, from mexcalli, and like Champagne declared that it could be brewed only here. For seven to 10 years the maguey grows, its floral stem cut to concentrate the scenery's sweetness in its heart. When the time comes, the center is cut away from the rest and called a piña, literally "pineapple." It is aged, then traditionally wood-fired for 72 hours with mesquite or oak, in clay or loam, depending on the flavor desired.

Other flavorings are added as the charred piña ferments: fruit, nuts, flowers, chocolate, even chicken breast (considered a delicacy by connoisseurs). The type of container—tree trunks, stone, steel, clay, leather—also affects the taste.

Most famously, however, mezcal's bite is made smoother, more suave, by the addition of a worm. This is actually a caterpillar, picudo del agave, Scyphophorus acupunctatus, which infests the agave and can destroy an entire crop if left to itself. But it is (evidently) quite tasty when toasted, used as a spice, or consumed whole. Oaxaqueños have always incorporated troublesome insects, deliciously prepared, of course, into their diet. And the maguey worm was no exception.

No one knows when the first worm was dropped into a bottle of mezcal. Its presence certainly serves several purposes beyond its primary job of mellowing the liquor. Once upon a time, it proved that the brew was strong enough to preserve the little worm. Today it serves as an advertisement, a gimmick, proclaiming the vintage authentically Oaxaqueño. And, of course, according to legend, eating the protein-rich tidbit will cause the drunkard to hallucinate. Promises, promises.

Mezcal comes in dozens of different flavors, and hundreds of different decorative bottles, making it the perfect gift for almost anyone.

But, finally, mezcal's promise as an art form and export is being fulfilled. Mezcal is now available around the world, thanks to the efforts of some 25,000 families and 700 factories (perhaps two-thirds of them registered) scattered across the countryside. Only half, it's estimated, have access to electricity and running water, but with each handcrafted bottle of Oaxaqueño mezcal consumed, their world becomes a little bit easier. And that is something to drink to.

was halted in the 1580s), it was designed as an outdoor church, so Mixtecs would feel more comfortable attending the weddings and baptisms of their converted neighbors.

This wasn't just any church, either. It was Cortés's summer home; what may be the regally carved archways of his old residence are still standing, closer to town. July 25, the feast day of Santiago Cuilapan, is celebrated with the *Danza de la Pluma,* commemorating Cortés's defeat of the Aztecs.

✪ **Santo Domingo Ocotlán** (Ocotlán Centro) An elaborate baroque showpiece at the heart of Ocotlán, this 17th-century beauty rises in rich blues and delicate detail above one of the loveliest central parks in the state. Begun in the 1500s but not finished until Oaxaca's more romantic and extravagant style—flutes, flowers, curlicues, pilasters, and more—had reached its pinnacle, it shouldn't be missed. The impeccable restoration was completed by world-famous artist and Ocotlán favorite son Rodolfo Morales, whose Morales Foundation also operates his eponymous museum in the convent.

Though never included on standard tours, it's worth visiting the other churches Morales helped restore, such as colorful **Santa Ana Zagache**, about 10 kilometers (6 miles) northwest of Ocotlán, another 17th-century folk-baroque masterpiece transformed by the artist's vibrant paint schemes.

Other Morales Foundation churches are on the Mezcal Route, a good paved secondary road that connects Ocotlán with Santiago Matatlán, "Mezcal Capital of the World." These include (from Ocotlán to Matatlán): 18th-century **Santa Catarina Minas**, home of the Black Christ; the enormous 16th-century Dominican **San Baltazar Chichicapan**, with an elaborate well system (Chichicapan means "Bitter Water"); **San Pablo Guila**, with Mitla-style décor, a site of pilgrimage since the Zapotec Empire; and **San Dionisio Ocotepec**, with another outrageously painted church protecting huge Churrigueresque *retablos.*

Museums

One of the best museums in the state is at Monte Albán, the region's most important archaeology site. Note that community museums may have irregular hours; if you show up and it's closed, ask at the Municipal Palace or any shop about finding someone with a key.

✪ Museo Comunitario Baala Xtee Guech Gulala

951-524-4463
Teotitlán del Valle
Open: 10 AM—6 PM
Admission: US$1

Teotitlán del Valle's excellent community museum has extensive signage in English, detailing the town's foundation as the Zapotec city of Xugui, "Below the Hill." This was a bustling city of 8,000 people during its heyday, around 200BC—450 A.D. The museum displays period artifacts from all over the region, including the pre-Columbian villages of Macuitlxochitl, Teitipan, and Yagül.

The highlight is the history of weaving in Teotitlán, with dioramas, exquisite examples, and centuries-old looms. As a weaving center under Aztec rule, tributes were paid with cotton blankets woven on backstrap looms. Floor looms and wool came with the Spanish, courtesy of Bishop Lopez de Zarate. My favorite exhibit shows how the distinctly Zapotec fashion of serapes spread from Teotitlán to the rest of the world, following the hippie movement of the 1960s.

Museo Comunitario Cerro de la Campaña Santiago Suchilquitongo and Ruinas Huijazoo
951-528-4616
mx.geocities.com/binnigulazaa/principal
Hwy. 131/190, Santiago Suchilquitongo, Municipal Building
Open: 10 AM–2 PM and 4 PM–8 PM Tues.–Sun.
Closed: Mon.
Admission: US$1 donation

Suchilquitongo, about 35 kilometers (21 miles) from Oaxaca City, is a very worthwhile stop on your way to Apoala Valley and the Mixteca. From the museum doorway, you can see the *cantera* mines. Just above, the partially excavated pyramids of Ruinas Huijazoo are visible. The museum is constructed with a cool, "you're in the tomb" theme, displaying impressive artifacts from Tomb Five, including an effigy of the Zapotec rain goddess, an inlaid skull incense holder, and lots of jade and obsidian, most dated between 300 and 800 A.D. There are also photos of the largest mural in Oaxaca, a 40-meter (120-foot) fresco of Zapotec ball players, locked within that hill, but you'll have to make special arrangements to see it.

Visit the exterior of the ancient ruins on your own, or the museum may be able to arrange guides. Any Mixteca-bound bus can drop you on the highway, where you can catch a three-wheeled mototaxi for the 2-kilometer (1-mile) trip to the museum, or get a **Suburban Blancos** (US$1.20; every 10 minutes) from Centro de Abastos in Oaxaca City. Huge civic fiestas go off around July 24th.

The Spanish deemed the well-fortified city of Yagul too strong to leave inhabited, thus the entire population was marched to Talcolula.

Museo Comunitario San José el Mogote ex-Hacienda El Cacique
Hwy. 190, kilometer 12 to Etla
Open: 10 AM—2 PM and 4 PM—6 PM, or ask for Señor Agustín Mendez in the store across the street
Admission: US$1

The ruins of Oaxaca's first major city, San José el Mogote, are interspersed with the Spanish Colonial buildings of this "modern" version of the village, including the elegant sprawl of the former Hacienda El Cacique. The old adobe now houses some of Oaxaca's finest archaeological pieces, most dating to 1150–500 B.C.

Exquisite figurative ceramics, expertly worked iron mirrors, bone-and-shell jewelry, stone tools, and much more are displayed in modest cases. The most remarkable pieces are huge jade statues, including the famed *El Diablo Enchilado*, a large red-jade effigy depicting a rather unhappy-looking gentleman. The ruins are about two blocks away, though you'll find remnants of ancient walls and buildings all over town.

The ruins are 12 kilometers (7 miles) northwest of Oaxaca City, about half an hour on Hwy. 190; make a left at Nazareno. The ruins are visible from the road, and the museum is clearly marked, about two blocks from the heart of the old ceremonial complex.

Museo Comunitario San Pablo Huitzo
951-528-4209
Hwy. 170, Ex-Convento de San Pablo Huitzo, Plaza Cívica

Temporarily closed when I visited, this community museum inhabits the former convent of one of the Etla Valley's most important Dominican churches, San Pablo Huitzo. The church, presiding over an agricultural town well known for its impressive aqueduct, has stylized stone carvings of fish and water, as well as a few preserved Zapotec glyphs on the cloister fountain.

Museum Comunitario San Pablo Huixtepec
951-571-5505
Hwy. 175, 31 kilometers (19 miles) from Oaxaca City
Open: 3 PM—8 PM
Admission: US$1

This small community museum includes a large Colonial section with oil paintings and other art, as well as artifacts and dioramas. Several photos from the early 20th century offer insight into local life, and there is a section on community fiestas. Halcones (Bustamante 606-B, Centro) runs regular buses from Oaxaca City.

Museo Comunitario Shan-Dany
951-562-1705
Santa Ana, Centro
Open: 10 AM—2 PM
Admission: US$1 donation

This small museum right next to the market has a selection of archaeological treasures, and interesting photos of the excavation that uncovered the tools, jewelry, ceramics, and stone carvings. Other exhibits include cool dioramas of the Mexican Revolution, lots of old guns, iconic headdresses from the local *Danza del las Plumas,* and a large section on weaving, natural dyes, and old looms. There's also a small **religious museum** in the atrium of the church.

✪ Museo Estatal de Arte Popular Oaxaca
State Museum of Oaxacan Folk Art
951-551-0036
www.oaxaca.gob.mx/cultura/meapo
San Bartolo Coyotepec, Calle Independencia
Open: 10 AM–6 PM Tues.–Sun.
Closed: Mon.
Admission: US$2 adults, US$1.20 children

This outstanding museum features the region's handicrafts, focusing on the gleaming black ceramics for which the town is famed; the huge Day of the Dead altar by artist Carlo Magno may be my single favorite piece of art in all Oaxaca. Other ceramics, in particular the richly detailed and figurative painted red forms distinctive of Octolán de Morelos, are also on awe-inspiring display.

Beautiful jewelry, *alebrijes,* and delicate hammered tin pieces are exhibited in their finest incarnations. The museum also hosts gallery-style openings, competitions, and other events for upcoming artists, as well as workshops and markets for collectors. The gift shop is top-notch.

Rodolfo Morales Foundation Museum and Home
951-571-0198
Morelos 105
Open: 10 AM–2 PM and 4 PM–8 PM
Admission: US$3

Revered Mexican artist Rudolfo Morales's renovation of the beautiful ex-convent at the heart of Ocotlán also includes this collection of Spanish Colonial paintings and sculptures. The displays give deference to artistry over historic importance. Not that these centuries-old oils are without symbolic grace; the painting of St. Francis and St. Dominic embracing confirms the partnership of their respective orders here in Oaxaca. Pre-Columbian pottery, Spanish Colonial artifacts, and Morales's own work complement exhibits such as a scale model of a Oaxacan Pueblo.

Morales's house and studio is open to visitors, with personal items, private collections, and the artist's archives. The Morales Foundation offices are also here, offering services such as a computer lab to the community.

RECREATION

Parks and Gardens

Hierve el Agua

Mitla Route, 2 hours from Mitla
Admission: US$2

Pouring from a terraced cliff face into the eastern chasm of the Tlacolula Valley, this glistening white flow of frozen calcium carbonate is one of Oaxaca's iconic sites. Short hiking trails, unequalled photo ops, and the single best swim in the Central Valleys can be found at the beautiful spot, whose the name translates as "Boiling Water." These aren't hot springs, however. The way the mineral-laden water bubbles up from the calcium-encrusted rock below gives the waters their name. Sulfur gives the water a distinctive smell and certain healing properties, and you just can't beat that view. There are ramshackle restaurants serving basic grub close to the parking area, and one simple cement room with bare light bulbs and dorm beds for seven, with a shared, warmish shower, operated by the **Presidencia de San Ysidro Roguia** (951-105-2722; cash only; $).

Gruta San Sebastián

San Sebastián, 84 kilometers (53 miles) south of Oaxaca, off Hwy. 131
Admission: US$1.50, guided tour US$6

Only a fraction of this enormous cave system is open to visitors, its chambers up to 400 meters (1,300 feet) long and 70 meters (230 feet) high, with interesting formations and small pools. There's a shady rest area with grills, *palapas,* and simple cabins for rent ($) on the San Sebastian river. To get here, take Hwy. 131 84 kilometers (52 miles) south of Oaxaca, and make a right at the signed town of El Vado. It's a bumpy, unpaved 12 kilometers (7.5 miles) to town; the cave is about five minutes up the road. Guides are available through the Palacio Municipal.

Orquidario La Encantada

951-119-4214
Mitla Route, San Andrés de Huayapan
Open: By reservation
Admission: US$5

There are almost 700 orchid species in Oaxaca, about half of Mexico's total. Octavio Gabriel Suárez shows off about 900 species native to Mexico, including many from Chiapas, on the paths around his home. Visitors can arrange tours for groups or individuals in advance.

Salina Blanca

951-501-2282
armandoeric@hotmail.com
Hwy. 190, San José de Gracia
Offices in Oaxaca City: Cinco de Mayo 204, Centro

About an hour and a half from Oaxaca City, on the way to Tehuantepec, this ecotourism project offers adventures on 15 hectares (37 acres) of dry tropical wilderness, centered on several calcium-deposit structures. Guided hikes, caving (lamps can be rented), white-water rafting, and swimming are available, and there are several restaurants onsite.

The cool, mineral-rich waters of Hierve el Agua flow into the Tlacolula Valley, leaving behind these sacred sculptures.

Tule Tree
Mitla Route
Santa María El Tule, 9 kilometers (5 miles) east of Oaxaca on Hwy. 101
Open: 9 AM–6 PM
Admission: US 30¢

Top tourist attraction is an enormous Montezuma cypress *(Taxodium mucronatum)* towering over the pretty, but seemingly minuscule, church of Santa María, built atop the foundation of an old pyramid. According to legend, a local priest planted the tree 1,400 years ago (a claim supported, incidentally, by tree rings); it now measures 58 meters (190 feet) at the widest point of the endlessly chasmed and buttressed trunk. Once a wetland, the town of Tule has become quite dry in recent decades, and in the 1950s an extended drought endangered the tree. So the town built an irrigation system that provides some 5,000 liters (1,300 gallons) per day.

Archaeological Sites
This is one of the most archaeologically rich regions in the world, and one of the finest sites is the monumental Zapotec capital, Monte Albán. Other spectacular sites are relatively easy to visit, on guided tours or by public transportation, including Mitla, a must-see with its unusual geometric frescos; Zaachila, in the center of the famed market town; and San José El Mogote, the first true city in Oaxaca State.

Dainzú
Mitla Route, Hwy. 190, 20 kilometers (12 miles) east of Oaxaca City
Open: 8 AM–5:45 PM
Admission: US$2.90

Though the Valleys seem almost a desert at times, in the highlands rainforest species like these beautiful bromeliads thrive.

It is hard for mere humans to really comprehend the Tule Tree's true girth—until we try to fit the entire tree into a single photographic frame, anyway.

This fascinating and photogenic archaeological site is best described by its Zapotec name, "Hill of the Organ Cactus." Set into the mountain itself, the main pyramid and plaza face the golden sunset and sparkling Río Salado, a small river attended by several other unexcavated cities along its meandering shores. This lovely, possibly ceremonial center was founded around 600 B.C., just before Monte Albán, and includes wealthy tombs, one guarded by carved jaguars. Jaguars (perhaps the home team's mascot?) also guard a ball court with great views from the stands; several large slab stone carvings, probably portraits of players, come complete with helmets and pads. This site is rarely visited on standard Mitla day-trips, but easily can be worked into custom tours. Buses drop you off about 1 kilometer (.5 mile) from the ruins on Hwy. 190, a shadeless walk. A taxi from Oaxaca City runs about US$20 round-trip, including a couple of hours at the site.

Lambityeco
Mitla Route, Hwy. 190, 27 kilometers (17 miles) east of Oaxaca
Open: 8 AM–6 PM
Admission: US$2.40

Once a major salt producing town (Labityeco may translate as "Mounds of Salt"), the region's saline water was boiled in special ceramic vessels, the residue traded throughout the valley. It was a good living, and supported the city from 600 B.C. to 800 A.D., but collapsed when Monte Albán was abandoned. Though there are evidently murals inside the closed buildings, the most important and impressive artifacts are the stucco carvings of what was apparently a royal couple, and two detailed stone carvings of Cosijo, Lord of Rain.

Mitla

951-568-0316
San Pablo Mitla, 45 kilometers (28 miles) north of Oaxaca; ruins are a 15-minute walk
from the bus stop.
Open: 9 AM–5 PM Tues.–Sun.
Closed: Mon.
Admission: US$3.50

Extravagantly frescoed in geometric, almost hallucinogenic patterns, the ancient city of
Mitla was once painted entirely red with cinnabar. The site is enormous, and only partially
enclosed by the area of the archaeological park that requires a few; ruins rise in many
places through the bustling agribusiness town of San Pablo Mitla.

This is one of the oldest inhabited sites in Oaxaca, close to an important chert mine
with stone suitable for tools. Evidence of permanent settlement dates to around 900 B.C.,
but the city began to thrive at the same time as its important trading partner, Monte Albán,
between 200 A.D. and 800 A.D. It became the Central Valleys' most important city after the
collapse of Monte Albán, and maintained its autonomy under Aztec rule as well. Unlike
other Tlacolula Valley cities, Mitla was not abandoned, and many buildings were used well
into the Spanish occupation.

Five major complexes within the fee area, including the Column and Church groups,
comprise several palaces, tombs, and temples in a stone labyrinth. Archaeologists have
refurbished some of the tombs and rooms with cane roofs, to give a sense of place. Just
outside the entrance, surrounded by a permanent *artesanías* market, the Spartan church
of San Pablo Mitla rises above far more ancient buildings, betraying its own mestizo birth
with glyph-engraved stones above the doors of the interior patio.

There are three other major groups of buildings in town. The Arroyo Group, well signed
from the road and close to the river; the Adobe Group, just west of the ruins; and the oldest buildings, Grupo del Sur, located three blocks south of the ruins. Sadly, the respected
Museo Frissel has shut down. It apparently has been robbed of many artifacts, and will
remain closed for the foreseeable future.

Monte Albán

951-516-1215
Oaxaca State, off Mex 190, 8 kilometers (5 miles) west of Oaxaca City
Open: 8 AM–6 PM
Admission: US$4.80

Rising 400 meters (1,300 feet) above Oaxaca, the ruins of Monte Albán are what remain of
what was once Oaxaca's most important city, a Zapotec capital of more than 30,000 spread
across six hilltop hectares. Perhaps 5 percent of the ancient city has been excavated, as the
complex actually spreads unseen as far as Atzompa, Paragüito, and the El Gallo hills.

The site was chosen for its strategically important views and its natural resources,
including clay for ceramics, spring water, and forests. When the first settlers, probably
political exiles from San Jose El Mogote, arrived in 500 B.C., they had a plan.

These ancient engineers actually flattened the entire mountain and shaped it into the
enormous plaza you see today. Everything is designed to withstand earthquakes, with
sturdy stone foundations conveniently riddled with subterranean drainage systems, cis-
terns, and secret passageways.

Construction of the stone city was carefully planned, from the Gran Plaza, with incredible views, bounded by pyramids and palaces aligned to the cardinal directions. The South Platform displays more than 300 carefully carved stone slabs that appear to be detailed portraits of real people, displaying birth defects, serious wounds, ejaculation, and birth. Theories suggest that they may be medical documents, records of captured enemies, or some sort of early writing, but no one knows. Similar stone slabs that show healthy people and families are commonly found (often displayed in private residences) throughout the Central Valley.

In 800 A.D., Monte Albán was mysteriously abandoned, perhaps because of overpopulation or political collapse. The Mixtecas continued using the city, which they called Sahandevul, "At the Foot of the Sky," as a burial place for important figures; some 170 Mixtec tombs have been discovered.

The onsite museum is one of the best in the state, with detailed signage in English. Guides can be hired at the entrance of the ruins; they offer tours in English and other common languages for US$15-20 per group. There's an onsite **cafeteria** (credit cards accepted; $$–$$$) with great views, a full bar, and a good gift shop. The ruins are fully wheelchair accessible.

It's about US$4, round-trip, from Oaxaca City on **Autobuses Turísticos** (951-516-5327; Mina 509, Centro; across from Hotel Riviera del Ángel), with shuttle buses running hourly to the ruins, half-hourly in high season. Most tour operators offer guided trips as well.

San José el Mogote
Hwy. 190, Kilometer 12 toward Etla; exit at Nazareno.
Open: 8 AM–6 PM
Admission: US$2.90

The Central Valleys' first major urban center was San José El Mogote, occupied for thousands of years at the entrance of the fertile Etla Valley, about 10 kilometers (6 miles) north of Oaxaca City. Evidence of permanent settlement dates to around 2000 B.C., and by 1500 B.C. it was a powerful city with ties to the Central Mexican Basin's far-ranging trade routes. The city foundry produced polished metal mirrors and exquisite gray and white pottery prized as far away as Veracruz and Tenochtitlán, traded for obsidian tools and other goods.

By 1150 B.C., El Mogote was a major city of more than 1,000 inhabitants, aligned with the powerful Olmec Empire, and exercising political control over dozens of neighboring towns. This was the region's first chiefdom, site of Mexico's oldest known 260-day calendar—and Oaxaca's oldest examples of irrigation, agricultural terracing, and defensive architecture. There are several pyramids and monuments to see, as well as incredible carved stone slabs. The community museum, nearby, displays many artifacts discovered here.

Xaaga
Mitla Route, Hwy. 190, 3 kilometers (2 miles) south of Mitla
Admission: Free; local guide, US$6

Apparently the center of Oaxaca's art scene between 10,000 and 3,000 years ago, the tiny town of Xaaga, south of Mitla, displays some of the oldest relics of human habitation in the Central Valleys, dozens of petroglyphs and tools. Nearby, on a private ranch, a tomb and several other buildings contemporary to Mitla, still vividly painted, have also been discovered.

Yagül

Mitla Route, Hwy. 190, kilometer 42
Open: 8 AM–5 PM Tues.–Sun.
Admission: US$3.50

As you make the well-signed turnoff to these little-visited ruins, look east toward the great stone cliffs. A massive petroglyph, depicting a pattern from Mitla and a stick figure of a man, is visible for kilometers. Welcome to Yagül, "Ancient Tree."

The city rose to prominence almost concurrently with Monte Albán, between 750 B.C. and 950 A.D. Its massive ball court is Mexico's second largest (after Chitchen Itza's). Also striking are the formidable defenses and watchtower overlooks utilizing the area's massive cliffs. After the Zapotec Empire collapsed, Yagül continued to thrive under Mitla rule, and was never abandoned.

The Spanish, however, were not keen to leave the Zapotecs in their fortified village, and in the early 1500s they moved the townspeople to what's now Tlacolula. The ruins are in excellent shape, with awesome views and a couple of tombs you can enter partway. Note that most buses drop you at the turnoff from the highway, more than 3.2 kilometers (1.9 miles) from the ruins. Consider taking a bus to Tlacolula, and catching a cab from there.

✪ Zaachila

Zaachila, 16 kilometers (10 miles) south of Oaxaca City, 30 meters (100 feet) behind the church
Open: 8 AM–6 PM
Admission: US$2.90

It's easy to spot the turnoff to Yagül; it's been well signed for centuries.

Right above the central plaza (look for the mural, pointing the way) are the ancient, partially excavated pyramids of the last capital of the Mixtec Empire. Zaachila was occupied when the Spanish arrived, and had been a thriving city since at least 1200 A.D. The Dominicans clearly used a much older foundation for the pretty, if unremarkable San Sebastian Church, visible from the vistas atop the temples.

The treasures discovered in the Tomb of Lord Nine Flower have been shipped to Mexico City, but park rangers have a stack of laminated 8-by-10 photos of the finds, such as a gold-and-precious stone calendar, a jade death mask, and much more. They display the photos outside their tiny booth when groups are there, or by request.

You can go into two of the elaborately carved and painted tombs, usually forbidden at more popular archaeological sites. Anthropomorphized owls and swimming turtle-men, with a bit of the original paint still intact in those damp depths, make one wonder what else lies beneath the grass.

Tours and Workshops

Most tours are organized through companies based in Oaxaca City; see the sidebar at the beginning of this chapter. The Shopping and Cuisine chapters have information about handicraft workshops, cooking classes, and more.

Casa Sagrada Guided Horseback Adventure (951-516-4275; www.casasagrada.com; Teotitlán) The neat B&B also organizes horseback riding tours; from Oaxaca City, you can make reservations through Mano Mágica (same phone, Alcalá 203, Centro), right downtown. They also offer full- and half-day guided hiking treks in and around Teotitlán, including lunch and round-trip transportation from Oaxaca City.

Centro de las Artes San Agustín (951-521-3042;Calle Independencia, Barrio Vista Hermosa San Agustín Etla) The outfit offers workshops, classes, events, art exhibits, and free movies on Sundays at 4 PM and 6 PM. It's a beautiful building in wonderful rural setting.

Etla Market Tour (951-518-8432; US$10 per person) Yolanda Girón Morales gives enthralling three-hour English-language tours of Etla and other markets, explaining the history, use, and flavor of each ingredient you buy.

Taller de Arte Papel Oaxaca (951-516-6980; San Agustín Etla, Vista Hermosa; open 9 AM–3 PM; free) Innovative paper factory in an adorable town offers tours explaining the all-natural papermaking process, which use bark, berries, or shimmering mica to add texture. Excellent gift shop.

Turismo de Aventura Teotitlán (951-524-4371; Avenida Juárez 59,Teotitlán del Valle) Three-hour horseback rides to the ruins originate in Teotitlán, then continue to the Dainzu archeological site. Reserve a day in advance.

Vida Nueva Women's Weaving Cooperative (951-524-4250; www.zapotec.com; estrella delvalle@hotmail.com; Centenario del Valle 1, Familia Gutierez, Teotitlán del Valle) A women's collective with a wonderful workshop and showroom offering weaving and dying demonstrations and several other services, including a *temazcal,* massages, basic accommodations (US$15), meals, and various walking tours of the town and surrounding wilderness.

Wildlife Displays

Divertigranja Selva Magica Zoo

951-522-9512
www.divertigranja.org
Santiagüito Etla; 1 kilometer (.6 miles) after the Municipio from Hwy. 131
Open: 10 AM–4 PM Sat. and Sun., by reservation only during the week
Admission: By donation

Kids will enjoy this petting zoo, geared toward local children with disabilities. There are
more than a dozen types of animals, including goats, deer, cows, hamsters, foxes, monkeys, dogs, and the original manx cat, all patient and professional. The "Five Exercise
Challenge" teaches healthy children what it's like to live with disabilities. Weekdays are
generally reserved for school groups, but anyone can visit on weekends.

Parque Zoológico Yaguar

951-502-0132
Tanivet, Hwy. 190
Open: 10 AM–2 PM Tues.–Fri., 10 AM–5 PM Sat.–Sun.
Admission: US$6.50 adults, US$5 children on foot; US$9 adults, US$7.50 children in air-
conditioned van; some activities US$2 extra

This smallish safari park displays an assortment of endangered species that once roamed
Oaxaca. An entire section is home to some of the hemisphere's flashier species, including
spider monkeys, Mexican cats, llamas, buffalo, raccoons, saraguato monkeys, black
jaguars, turtles, and others; there's a petting zoo here as well.

The Oaxacan wilderness is home to a few things that get your attention the hard way.

The park also offers a small camping area and food service, as well as rock climbing and other kid-friendly activities, and there's a small waterslide park nearby. The turnoff is well signed from Hwy. 190; it's about 2 kilometers (1.2 miles) past the women's prison.

Spas

Though there are other *temazcals* in the Central Valleys, the beautiful mountain **San José del Pacifico** offers something a bit different. The scenic town is famed for its traditional medicines, specifically the *teonancatl*, or hallucinogenic mushroom, which is illegal under Mexican law. Several local shamans offer guided trips, often including *temazcals* and other activities.

Maliollin Medicina Tradicional Indigena (951-515-8612; www.oaxaca-mio.com/ maliollin.htm; maliollin@hotmail.com) Healers Manuel García Ramírez and Irma Guadalupe Martínez Blás have more than 30 years of experience offering *temazcals*, massages, healing rituals, and workshops in both Spanish and English.

Luis García Blanco, of the ceramics stronghold of Santa María Atzompa, displays one of her highly polished, hand-built pots.

Ritual del Temazcal (irma_guadelipe_martinez@yahoo.com.mx, iguadelupe@latinmail .com.mx) Not your average sauna, this offers a celebrated psilocybin mushroom sauna, as a stand-alone or part of a three-day ritual involving meals, rituals, and working with ceramics.

SHOPPING

The Central Valleys' handicraft tradition makes this one of the most unusual and rewarding shopping experiences ever. Sure, you can pick up all your gifts at one of Oaxaca City's massive handicrafts malls, but why not take a local bus into the countryside, to one of the tiny, scenic towns specializing in each different art form? Workshops are open to the public, and you can meet the artist, and watch him or her work.

The Valleys' handicrafts and artisan towns are thoroughly covered in the Shopping chapter, with hints and tips for finding that perfect rug or *alebrije*.

Malls and Markets

Each town in the Valleys has its own market day, when people come from all over the region to sell their wares and produce. It's worth the effort to experience a small-town market, whether on a guided tour (Oaxaca City operators offer different market trips throughout the week), or on your own.

Monday: Miahuatlán, Ixtlán de Juárez

Tuesday: Atzompa, Ayoquezco, Santa María de Etla, Soledad Etla

Wednesday: Villa de Etla, Zimatlán

Thursday: Zaachila, Ejutla de Crespo

Friday: Ocotlán, San Bartolo Coyotepec, Santo Tomás Jalieza, San Antonio Castillo Velasco

Saturday: Oaxaca City, Mercado de Abastos, Tlaxiaco

Sunday: Tlacolula (the Valleys' largest market, after Abastos), Ayutla Mixe

EVENTS

January
San Pablo Apostol (San Pablo Huitzo) Pilgrimages to a small shrine in town are met with fireworks, traditional dances, and other festivities.

February
La Candelaria (February 2; Santa María El Tule) *Calendas* (processions), a guelaguetza, and *mayordomía* celebrate the Blessing of the Infant Jesus.

March
Señor de las Peñas (Two weeks before Good Friday, Villa de Etla) Celebrations, fireworks, and dances.

Good Friday (Friday before Easter; Zaachila) There's a passion play.

May
El Señor de la Sacristia (May 18, Ocotlán) The Ocotlán Valley's biggest fiesta, with religious processions, a huge market, traditional dances, cockfights, and fireworks the third weekend in May.

July
Lani Xte Llub (mid-July; Teotitlán) This "Celebration of Corn" brings out the Pluma dancers, partiers, and local cooks, who serve every possible corn-based dish at stands set up all over town.

Guelaguetza (last two Mondays in July; Zaachila) The last Zapotec capital has its own smaller and less commercial Guelaguetza celebration.

Feast Day of Santiago Apóstal (July 24–25; Cuilapám) Celebrated with special outdoor Masses and a performance of *Danza de la Pluma*, this festival commemorates Cortés's victory over the Aztec Empire.

August
Festival of San Bartolo (San Bartolo Coyotepec) A carnival, processions, and traditional feather and gardener dances go on in the third week in August.

September
Virgin of the Nativity (Ejutla de Crespo) This village famous for its 17th-century church and handmade knives celebrates the entire week around September 8 with processions, fireworks, rodeos, and mock battles.

October
Day of the Dead is celebrated throughout the Valleys from October 31 to November 2, with several Oaxaca City operators offering night tours to rural *panteones* (cemeteries), usually in Xoxocotlán and Villa de Etla.

Battle of Walnut Hill (Miahuatlan de Porfiro Díaz, Hwy. 175, 105 kilometers/65 miles south of Oaxaca) Battle reenactments are accompanied by horse parades, goat barbecue, traditional dance, and beauty queens.

Fiesta del Alebrije Shin Naa Lasn Arte del Pueblo (951-524-9228; www.feriadelalebrije .org.mx; San Martín Tilcajete; October 31-November 8) *Alebrije*-producing towns hold a huge handcrafts market the first week in November, with more than 300 artists as well as food, music, and other festivities.

Friends of Oaxacan Folk Art (www.fofa.us/eventsinoaxaca.html) This well-received jur-ied exhibition of up-and-coming folk artists at the Museo Estatal de Arte Popular Oaxaca in San Bartolo Coyotepec will hopefully be repeated every October–November.

Santa María El Tule Civic Fiestas (Second Monday in October; El Tule) It's an unofficial day of pilgrimage, when people from all over the Valleys come to see the Tule Tree deco-rated (respectfully) by the locals, and enjoy something to eat at the fiesta.

December
Santo Tomás Jalieza Civic Fiestas (December 21) The famed weaving town holds tradi-tional fiestas and a huge market, conveniently right before Christmas.

5

Pacific Coast

Beaches, Bays, and Cultural Waves

Beautiful beaches and a blissful climate make Oaxaca's 600 kilometers (375 miles) of Pacific Coast one of Mexico's most relaxing destinations. Long separated from the heavily populated Central Valleys by the mountains of the Sierra Madre del Sur, Oaxaca's beaches are among the least touristed of the Mexican Pacific. By road, it is at least six hours of steep but scenic hairpin turns to the sea, though beginning in 2011, a new toll road will cut the trip in half. In addition, the two major regional airports, in Huatulco and Puerto Escondido, have expanded and improved with added national and international flights.

The majority of tourists visiting the "Oaxacan Riviera" will spend most of their vacation in either Bahías de Huatulco, a planned resort community with family friendly beaches, or festive Puerto Escondido, a chaotic, sprawling beach town with wonderful surfing and rollicking nightlife.

Perhaps confusingly, the coast doesn't run north-south as in much of Mexico; Hwy. 200 follows Mexico's plump little mezcal belly from east to west, from the Isthmus of Tehuantepec along the resort-lined Oaxacan Riviera to the Mixtec Coast. Few beaches face the setting sun straight on, and instead look southward over the sea.

This chapter begins with the sunrise, on the fascinating **Isthmus of Tehuantepec**, famed for its indigenous culture and exquisite fabrics, with untouristed beaches to spare. Next, it's on to **Huatulco** (wa-TUL-co), the newest, and greenest, of Mexico's five integrated resort communities.

The beautiful, bohemian beaches of **Puerto Ángel** offer the best bargains on the coast, not to mention nesting sea turtles from May through December. Or continue west to Oaxaca's original resort town, **Puerto Escondido**, on the Emerald Coast. Tourists thin as you continue west on the Pacific Coast Hwy. 200, to the heart of the Mixtec Coast: **Santiago Pinotepa Nacional**, renowned for its African Oaxacan communities, wonderful handicrafts, and undiscovered beaches.

TOURIST INFORMATION

Most major towns have tour offices stocked with pamphlets and local information; Huatulco and Puerto Escondido also have numerous private tour operators offering guides and advice.

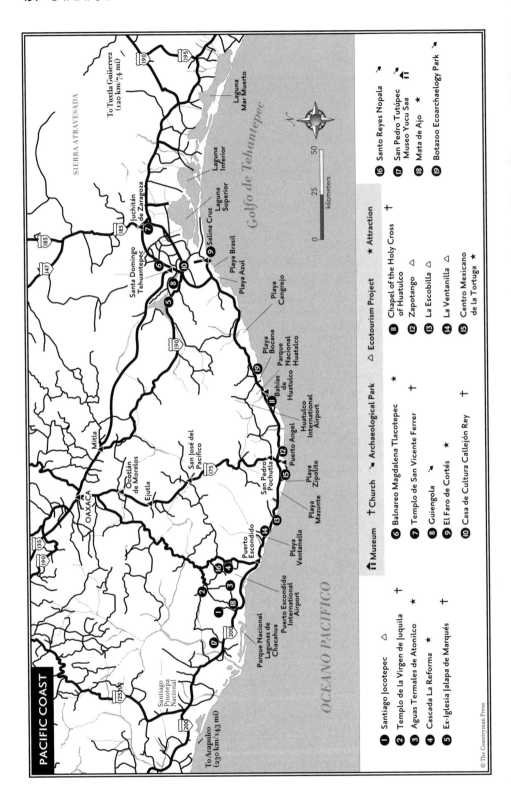

PACIFIC COAST

To Tuxtla Gutierrez
(120 km/74 mi)

SIERRA ATRAVESADA

Laguna
Mar Muerto

Laguna
Inferior

Golfo de Tehantepec

Laguna
Superior

Juchitán
de Zaragoza

Santa Domingo
Tehuantepec

Salina Cruz

Playa Brasil

Playa Azul

Playa
Cangrejo

Playa
Bocana

Parque
Nacional
Huatulco

Bahías
de Huatulco

Huatulco
International
Airport

Puerto Angel

Playa
Zipolite

San José del
Pacífico

San Pedro
Pochutla

Playa
Mazunte

Guiengola

Mitla

Ocotlán
de Morelos

Ejutla

OAXACA

Playa
Ventanilla

Puerto
Escondido

Puerto Escondido
International
Airport

Parque Nacional
Lagunas de
Chacahua

Santiago
Pinotepa
Nacional

To Acapulco
(230 km/143 mi)

OCEANO PACIFICO

N

0   25   50
kilometers

🛈 Museum   † Church   ↗ Archaeological Park   △ Ecotourism Project   ★ Attraction

① Santiago Jocotepec △
② Templo de la Virgen de Juquila †
③ Aguas Termales de Atonilco ★
④ Cascada La Reforma ★
⑤ Ex-Iglesia Jalapa de Marqués †

⑥ Balneario Magdalena Tlacotepec ★
⑦ Templo de San Vicente Ferrer †
⑧ Guiengola ↗
⑨ El Faro de Cortés ★
⑩ Casa de Cultura Callejón Rey †

⑪ Chapel of the Holy Cross
of Huatulco †
⑫ Zapotango △
⑬ La Escobilla △
⑭ La Ventanilla △
⑮ Centro Mexicano
de la Tortuga ★

⑯ Santo Reyes Nopala ↗
⑰ San Pedro Tutúpec
Museo Yucu Saa 🛈
⑱ Mata de Ajo ★
⑲ Botazoo Ecoarchaelogy Park ↗

© The Countryman Press

BAHÍAS DE HUATULCO

To Tehuantepec (149km/147 mi)
Oaxaca (237 km/147 mi)

To airport
(17km/10 mi)
Pochutla
(52 km/32 mi)
Puerto Escondido
(124 km/77 mi)

LA CRUCECITA

Parque Ecológico
Rufino Tamayo

Boulevard Benito Juarez

TANGOLUNDA

Bahía de Chahue

Bahía
Santa
Cruz

Playa La Entrega

OCEANO PACIFICO

Parque
Nacional
Huatulco

Crucecita

*OCEANO
PACIFICO*

① Church of Santa Cruz
   (Parroquia Señora de Guadalupe)

② Tourist Information Kiosk

③ Tourist Information Kiosk

④ Tetro del Mar

⑤ Chapel of the Holy Cross of Huatulco

⑥ Huatulco Delegación de Turismo

⑦ Huatulco Hotel & Motel Association

⑧ Second-Class Bus Station

⑨ First-Class Bus Station

⑩ Museo de Artesanias Oaxaqueñas

© The Countryman Press

Delegación de Turismo en Huatulco (958-581-0176, 958-581-0177; delhuatulco@prodigy.net.mx; Boulevard Benito Juárez, Bahía Tangolunda) The most professional tourism office in the state has a very helpful staff and all sorts of information.

Puerto Ángel Information Cabaña (no phone; Puerto Ángel, main road; open 9 AM–5 PM Mon.–Fri., 9 AM–2 PM Sat.) Not the most professional outfit in Oaxaca (blaring music, eye-rolling teenagers), but it has a nice collection of flyers. And the teenagers did make good recommendations.

Puerto Escondido Tourist Information Module (954-582-0175; delpuerto@aoaxaca.com; Boulevard Benito Juárez) Like the town itself, this is an informal affair, but exceptionally helpful, with multilingual staff and tons of information.

Tehuantepec Modulo de Información Turistica (Tourist Information Module; no phone; delistmo@prodigy.net.mx, delistmo@aoaxaca.com; kilometer 283 Hwy. 185; open 8 AM–

8 PM Mon.–Fri., 9 AM–8 PM Sat., 9 AM–noon Sun.) Friendly tourist center offers information about the city and isthmus.

WEATHER

Temperatures along the Pacific Coast average 30 degrees Celsius (85 degrees Fahrenheit), but can rise well into the 40s (100s) on dry-season afternoons, or drop to the teens (60s) in the evenings.

The rainy season usually runs from mid-June through October (with September and October the rainiest months), characterized by sunny mornings and afternoon showers, though it can certainly rain for days on end. Foliage is greener and destinations cheaper, but bring your umbrella.

SAFETY

Though the beach communities have statistically lower crime rates than Oaxaca City, party towns, such as Playas Zipolite and Zicatela, report late-night muggings on darkened beaches. Never leave valuables unwatched on the beach. Though you may be offered drugs, or see locals smoking marijuana openly, remember that police, as well as criminals looking for an inebriated victim, are keeping an eye on you.

The main dangers are the strong currents that plague all beaches, in particular Zipolite and those surrounding it. These may become worse a few days after a full or new moon. Though many beaches have caution flags, ask the locals about current conditions before going in past your knees.

GETTING AROUND

Oaxaca City is connected to the coast by four major roads, all of them narrow, winding, and paved. By car it takes five to seven hours, depending on the route; a bus trip adds four hours. Bring Dramamine if you're prone to motion sickness. A new toll road, cutting the time to three hours, is scheduled to open in 2011.

Bus service is excellent between major destinations, but smaller beach and mountain towns may require a taxi from larger cities or the Pacific Coast Hwy. 200. Boat taxis also ply the coast, and are a scenic way to get around.

Air

The vast majority of tourists will use the **Huatulco International Airport** (HUX; 958-581-9000; Carretera Pinotepa Cruz kilometer 237) or **Puerto Escondido International Airport** (PXM; 954-582-2023, 954-582-2024; Playa Bacocho, 5 kilometers (3 miles) east of Puerto Escondido on Hwy. 200).

Both have daily service with various airlines to Oaxaca City (30 minutes) and Mexico City (45 minutes), but only Huatulco had direct international flights (from the United States and Canada) at press time. International charters often serve Huatulco in high

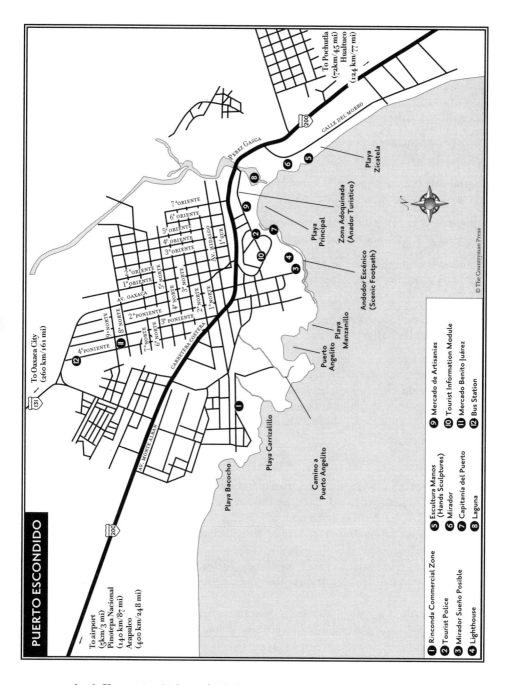

PUERTO ESCONDIDO

To airport
(5km/3 mi)
Pinotepa Nacional
(140 km/87 mi)
Acapulco
(400 km/248 mi)

To Oaxaca City
(260 km/161 mi)

To Pochutla
(72km/45 mi)
Hualtuco
(124 km/77 mi)

CALLE DEL MORRO
PEREZ GASGA

7ª ORIENTE
6ª ORIENTE
5ª ORIENTE
4ª ORIENTE
3ª ORIENTE
2ª ORIENTE
1ª ORIENTE
AV. OAXACA
2ª PONIENTE
3ª PONIENTE
4ª PONIENTE

9ª NORTE
8ª NORTE
7ª NORTE
6ª NORTE
5ª NORTE
4ª NORTE
3ª NORTE
2ª NORTE
1ª NORTE

AV. HIDALGO
1ª SUR
CARRETERA COSTERA
AV. MONTE ALBÁN

Playa Zicatela
Zona Adoquinada
(Andador Turístico)
Playa Principal
Andador Escénico
(Scenic Footpath)
Playa Manzanillo
Puerto Angelito
Playa Carrizalillo
Camino a Puerto Angelito
Playa Bacocho

© The Countryman Press

1 Rinconda Commercial Zone
2 Tourist Police
3 Mirador Sueño Posible
4 Lighthouse
5 Escultura Manos (Hands Sculptures)
6 Mirador
7 Capitanía del Puerto
8 Laguna
9 Mercado de Artisanias
10 Tourist Information Module
11 Mercado Benito Juárez
12 Bus Station

season; check **Skyservice Airlines** (416-679-1273 Canada, 1-800-701-9448 U.S. and Canada; www.skyserviceairlines.com) in Canada, or **USA 3000** (877-872-3000; www. usa3000.com) in the United States.

Aerotucán (951-502-0840; 1-800-640-4148; www.aerotucan.com.mx; Macedonio Alcala 201, Huatulco) The tiny airline flies its zippy Cessna Caravan 208Bs between Oaxaca City and both Huatulco and Puerto Escondido twice daily.

Aerovega (951-516-4982 Oaxaca City, 954-582-0151 Puerto Escondido; aerovegaoax@ hotmail.com; Puerto Escondido, corner of Avenida Pérez Gazga and Marina Nacional) Another small airline, Aerovega has direct flights from Oaxaca City to Puerto Escondido.

American Airlines (1 800-904-6000 Mexico; 1-800-433-7300 U.S. and Canada; www .aa.com) American has one flight daily between Huatulco and Mexico City.

Continental (1-800-523-3273 U.S. and Mexico; www.continental.com) Continental flies once a day between Houston and Huatulco.

Interjet (1-800-011-2345 Mexico; 1-866-285-9525 U.S. and Canada; www.interjet.com .mx) Interjet has five weekly flights between Huatulco and Toluca (Mexico City).

Mexicana (1-800-531-7921 U.S. and Canada, 1-800-502-2000 Mexico; www.mexicana .com) Five direct flights weekly between Huatulco and Oaxaca City, three weekly to Mexico City.

Mexicana Click (1-800-531-7921 U.S. and Canada, 1-800-502-2000 Mexico; www .clickmx.com) Daily flights between Puerto Escondido and Mexico City.

Note that airport taxis serving HUX are expensive; if you're planning to go much farther than the resorts, take one to La Crucecita and get a regular taxi there. **Servicios Turísticos del Sur** (958-581-0512; www.huatulcodmc.com; stshuatulcosdmc@prodigy.net.mx) arranges cheaper airport shuttles from Huatulco. In Puerto Escondido, **Aerotransportes Terrestrials** (954-582-0734; Avenida Pérez Gags) offers hotel pickup in collective vans headed to the airport.

Driving

Hwy. 200, running east to west, is attached to Oaxaca City by four major roads: Hwy. 190 via Mitla, convenient to Tehuantepec, Huatulco, and Chiapas; Hwy. 175 via Ocotlán, through San José del Pacifico to Puerto Ángel; Hwy. 131 via San Bartolo Coyotepec, straight to Puerto Escondido; and Hwy. 125, running from Tlaxiaco to Pinotepa Nacional, convenient to Acapulco.

Allow between six and nine hours for any of these routes. A new toll road between Oaxaca and Puerto Escondido, which will shave travel time to three hours, is due to be completed in 2011.

In general, these main highways are narrow and twisting, but paved and in good shape, if a bit potholed. Most destinations are well signed, though smaller mountain and beach towns may not be. Some secondary roads are unpaved, and may be four-wheel drive only in rainy season.

Rental Cars

Unless you're planning to do some serious off-road exploring, a normal two-wheel drive car should be sufficient.

Online Resources

All these sites are in English unless otherwise noted.

Bahías de Huatulco (www.baysofhuatulco.com.mx) Spanish-language site has information and links (some outdated) for Huatulco.

Costa Chica (www.costachica.net) Listings and information about the Puerto Ángel Beaches.

✪Huatulco Adventure (www.huatulcoadventure.com) This excellent site offers photos and insight into Huatulco's natural attractions and more adventurous undertakings, and includes links to top outfitters.

Huatulco Magazzine (www.huatulco.magazzine.net) The tourist 'zine available all over town offers excellent online information and links to hotels and tour operators.

Intro Magazine (www.revistaintro.com) A great bilingual lifestyle magazine covering Puerto Escondido.

Jalapa de Marqués.com (www.jalapadelmarques.com) The site features photos, videos, and Spanish-language information about this Tehuantepec town and Reservoir Benito Juárez.

✪Pacific Coast of Mexico (www.tomzap.com) Tom Penick's excellent online guide to Oaxaca, Colima, and Jalisco beaches offers hundreds of regularly updated, info-packed pages covering the Oaxacan Riviera, and lots of inland destinations as well.

✪Puerto Ángel (www.puertoangel.net) An excellent site with comprehensive coverage of the Puerto Ángel beaches, it includes maps, photos, hotel and restaurant listings, links, and more.

Puerto Escondido (www.puertoescondidovisitalo.com) Information in Spanish.

Salina Cruz En Linea (www.salinacruzenlinea.com.mx) A Spanish-language guide geared to residents, it has a solid map collection.

Salina Cruz Municipal Site (www.salinacruz.gob.mx) Spanish-language information about the city and municipality.

El Sol de la Costa (www.elsoldelacosta.com) This bilingual magazine covers Puerto Escondido happenings.

Todo Huatulco (www.todohuatulco.com) Huge, hip, Spanish-language guide has excellent online maps plus the local lowdown on bars, discos, restaurants and more.

Viva Mazunte! (www.vivamazunte.com) Small site has basic information about Mazunte.

Zicatela.net (www.zicatela.net) This small site with several links to Mexico's best surfing beach promises to grow.

HUATULCO

Advantage and Dollar (958-587-1381; www.advantage.com, www.dollar.com; Boulevard Chahué Lot 22, Manzana 1, Sector R) The companies share the same office.

Auto-Car Rental Oaxaca (800-714-4600, 958-581-0293; www.oaxacacarrental.com.mx; Tangolunda, Centro Comercial las Conchas L-5) Independent agency promises "flexible rates."

Europecar (958-581-9094; www.europcar.com; Boulevard Chahué Lot 164, Plaza Camelinas) Gets complaints.

Funny Cars for Rent (958-581-0516; Tangolunda, Plaza Las Conchas) Rents motorcycles, dirt bikes, *cuads,* and even cute three-wheeled mototaxis.

Hertz (958-581-0588; www.hertz.com; Hotel Crown Pacific) Hertz also has a module at the ADO station.

Kawasaki (951-583-4104) Rents motorcycles.

PUERTO ESCONDIDO
Bacocho Rent-A-Car (954-582-0312; budget@grupobacococho.com.mx; Bacocho, Boulevard Benito Juárez) This independent dealer near Playa Carrazillo works with Budget.

Dimar (954-582-0737; www.viajesdimar.com; viajesdimar@hotmail.com) The full-service travel agency rents cars from Playa Zicatela (954-582-2305; Calle del Morro) and Playa Principal (954-582-0734; Avenida Pérez Gasga 905).**Económica Rent-A-Car** (954-582-2579; www.economica.com.mx; Playa Zicatela, Bajada Las Brisas 7) Económica rents scooters, motorcycles, and cars, including some sweet custom-painted VW Beetle ragtops.

Rent-A-Car (954-582-0179; www.hotelsantafe.com.mx, Hotel Santa Fe) Another option.

Taxis
Taxis are widely available and almost always unmetered; ask at your hotel about appropriate fares, and settle with the driver before getting in. In addition to quick city and regional rides, many people use taxis for long-distance runs between different beach towns. Once again, find out appropriate fares from a third party, and negotiate with the driver before the trip.

Huatulco is too spread out to stroll, so you'll either need to rent a car or rely on collective taxis, which can take you most places for between US$2 and US$3. Boat taxis are another great option, but are considerably more expensive.

Experienced travelers who think they've seen everything should head straight to Tehuantepec, where they can catch a ride on the city's signature ✪ *motocarros,* tiny, three-wheeled flatbed trucks with motorcycle engines. Ride standing up, and watch locals for hints on a graceful dismount.

Buses
Buses run along the Pacific Coastal Hwy. 200, as well as between coastal towns and Oaxaca City and Mexico City. For more contact information about bus lines, including offices on the coast and routes to and from Oaxaca City, check the Transportation chapter.

Turistar (800-000-3355; www.turistar.com.mx) runs luxury buses on Hwy. 200, with stops in Huatulco, Pochutla (Puerto Ángel beaches), Puerto Escondido, and Pinotepa Nacional.

TEHUANTEPEC
Tehuantepec City is a convenient transport hub for the rest of the isthmus, with a main bus terminal (971-715-0108; Hwy. 185, 1.5 kilometers (1 mile) north of town) served by

Tehuantepec's cool motocarros *make getting around town an adventure.*

first- and second-class buses. Istmeños buses to Juchitán leave from across the street every half hour or so, while Transportes Tehuantepec leaves hourly for Oaxaca City, Salina Cruz, and other destinations from the Tourism Module parking lot, where *colectivo* taxis also congregate.

Salina Cruz has a first-class station (971-714-0703; corner of Calle Laborista and Avenida Ferrocarril) on the outskirts of town, served by Autobuses del Oriente (ADO), Ómnibus Crístobal Colón (OCC), and Estrella Blanca. City buses run between the first-class station and the city center on Avenida Ferrocarril. The second-class bus station (Avenida Heroes, between Calles Acapulco and Coatzacoalcos), right off the plaza, serves most of the same destinations.

PUERTO ÁNGEL BEACHES

Pochutla, about 12 kilometers (7.5 miles) north of Puerto Ángel, is the transportation hub, with three bus terminals close to the corner of Avenida Lazarus and Calle Las Palmas. These are served by Estrella del Valle, with service to Oaxaca City (nine times daily), Mexico City, and Puebla; OCC, with service to Chiapas and Guatemala; Estrella Blanca, running buses to Acapulco and Mexico City; and Sur, serving Huatulco and Puerto Escondido.

From Pochutla, you'll need to grab either a *colectivo* taxi (US$2-4) or *camioneta* (pickup truck; US 50¢-$1) to the beach of your choice. You can also hire taxis from the Huatulco (45 minutes) or Puerto Escondido (1 hour) airports.

PUERTO ESCONDIDO

Bus lines serving Puerto Escondido include Estrella Blanca (954-582-0086), Estrella del Valle (954-582-0050), Estrella Roja (954-582-0875), and OCC (954-582-1073).

LODGING

Most of the beachfront hotels are concentrated in Oaxaca's two resort towns, Huatulco and Puerto Escondido, with several more in Puerto Ángel. The inland communities of the Isthmus of Tehuantepec, Pochutla, and Pinotepa Nacional offer basic lodging, geared more to Mexican travelers than international tourists. Cabanas geared to surfers and ecotourists can be found in quieter communities, both on the beach and in the mountains, but don't expect much in the way of service or amenities.

Lodging Price Code

Cost of lodging is based on an average per-room, double-occupancy during peak season (July; November through mid-January), not including the mandatory 18 percent tax, which may be waived for cash payment. Rates are often reduced during low season (June and August through September), and can double during the Christmas–New Year's holidays, Día de los Muertos, and Semana Santa, when the best hotels are booked weeks and months out. Costs are calculated at 10 pesos to the U.S. dollar.

Inexpensive	Up to US$50
Moderate	US$50 to US$100
Expensive	US$100 to US$150
Very Expensive	More than US$150

Hotels

TEHUANTEPEC AND THE ISTHMUS
There aren't many standout hotels in this region, which includes the relatively untouristed towns of Tehuantepec, Juchitán, and Salina Cruz; most are basic budget rooms, and listed under "Other Hotels" later in this section.

Hotel Oasis
Owner: Julia Isabel Contreras Cabrera
971-715-0008
h.oasis@hotmail.com
Melchor Ocampo 8
Price: Inexpensive to moderate
Credit Cards: Yes
Handicapped Access: Yes

"*Bueno, bonito, barrato,*" an enthusiastic guest explained to me in halting Spanish: "Good, pretty, cheap." Rising above Tehuantepec to four simple stories (and some nice views from the upper floors, with big windows and wide-open terraces), this solid hotel offers clean, basic rooms with good beds and hot water in the morning. Choose whether you want a basic, fan-cooled room (US$20), with cable TV (US$35), or with air conditioning and TV (US$40). There's WiFi in the excellent **Restaurant Almendres** (B, L, C, D; $) on the first floor, serving Oaxacan and Tehuana classics in an appealing dining room.

HUATULCO

There are scores of hotels, some 2,300 rooms, in Huatulco, and it would be impossible to list them all here. Surprisingly, there's no comprehensive list available online, either, though the **Huatulco Hotel Association** (www.hotelshuatulco.com .mx) lists many of the top-end offerings, while **Huatulco Magazzine** (www.huatul co.magazzine.net), **3w.Huatulco** (www .huatulco.com.mx), and Pacific Coast Mexico (www.tomzap.com/huatulcohotels .html) list dozens of other options.

Most of the luxury resorts cluster around Bahías Tangolunda and Chahué, though there are fine properties scattered throughout the community. Budget travelers will find solid options in the US$25–35 range in La Crucecita, a 15-minute walk from the beach, but home to Huatulco's best restaurants and nightlife.

Camino Real Zaashila
Director General: Yvonne Kraak
958-583-0300; 1-800-901-2300
www.camino-zaashila.com
zaares@prodigy.net.mx
Playa Tangolunda
Price: Very Expensive
Credit Cars: Yes
Handicapped Access: None

This gracefully aging Mexican-Mediterranean masterpiece remains one of Oaxaca's nicest properties. The whitewashed architecture fronts one of the prettiest beaches in Tangolunda, perfect for swimming. All 148 rooms and suites offer views to the sea, lined with thatched umbrellas and beach chairs, and a small outdoor massage table offers the ultimate in relaxation.

The beach club serves cold drinks and light meals. For dinner, however, you'll want reservations at elegant, open-air ✪ **Azul Profundo** (D; $$$$), a romantic restaurant with a few tables right on the water, worth visiting even if you aren't a guest. It and **Chez Binni** (D; $$$$), another gourmet restaurant beneath an epic vaulted ceiling, offer excellent service and gourmet takes on Oaxacan and international cuisine. A third restaurant offers buffet breakfasts, as well as dinner buffets in high season. Then relax at one of the two free-form pools, one of them Huatulco's largest, or work out at the tiny gym or two tennis courts. Staff can arrange any sort of tour.

✪ Hotel Mision de los Arcos
General Manager: Magdalena Rodriguez
958-587-0165
www.misiondelosarcos.com
La Crucecita, Gardenia 902
Price: Moderate
Credit Cards: Yes
Handicapped Access: None

Relaxed and wonderful, this beautiful hotel may be the best deal on the Oaxaca Coast. Elegant and understated rooms are spotless and freshly painted, with elegant handwoven bedspreads and curtains adding natural textures to the ambience. Standard rooms are cozy, but the clever layout, built-in furnishings, and mounted lighting put the available space to excellent use. All the rooms include air-conditioning, cable TV and WiFi; request one with a tiny private balcony, perfect for enjoying those refreshing Huatulco evenings.

The two suites are much larger: The Garden Suite has its own private garden and a handmade bathtub, while the Junior Suite has two double beds and two balconies overlooking the town square. Room service is provided by the very pretty onsite **Terra Cotta Restaurant and Café** (B, L, C, D; $$), serving excellent coffee, salads, and Oaxacan classics. The French toast is truly outstanding.

Hotel Posada Eden Costa

958-587-2480
www.edencosta.com
info@edencosta.com
Calle Zapoteco s/n, Chahué
Price: Expensive
Credit Cards: Yes
Handicapped Access: Yes

This lovely little guesthouse, conveniently located between La Crucecita and Chahué Beach, offers spacious rooms with tiny private balconies overlooking the pool. Each room has ceramic tiles and colorful décor, including hand-woven bedspreads and painted details, air conditioning, fan, Sky TV, and WiFi. Three larger suites on the ground floor have small stoves and refrigerators, always convenient for longer stays.

But the best amenity of all—and do consider dropping by even if not as a guest—is the excellent restaurant, ✪ L'Echalote (L, C, D; $$$). Earning accolades from critics and locals alike, this exquisite spot is renowned for its international cuisine, prepared with Oaxacan flair, thanks to local ingredients and techniques. Dishes hail from African, Belgian, French, and Indian traditions—both the curries of the subcontinent and local pre-Columbian specialties, such as a soup made with *nopales* (prickly pear pads) and dried shrimp. Make reservations during high season.

Hotel Villas Coral

Manager: Luisa Hori
958-581-0500
www.hotelvillascoral.com
hotelvillascoral@gmail.com
Playa Arrocito, 2 Paseo El Arrocito
Price: Expensive
Credit Cards: Yes
Handicapped Access: None

This quiet cove beach, one of Huatulco's most beautiful, is primarily the province of pricey vacation rentals and luxury condominiums. However, this gracefully aging four-star hotel, a confection of whitewashed balconies and terraces connecting just 26 rooms, offers quiet contemplation of "Little Rice Beach," just a five-minute stroll away.

Rooms are large and comfortable, if not extravagant, with wonderful views, simple furnishings, and hand-woven bedspreads. Suites are much nicer, with built-in furnishings and private porches, as well as coffee makers, microwaves, and refrigerators. Villas sleeping six, with full kitchens, are in the oldest part of the hotel, and are a great deal for families. There's an onsite restaurant, a nice pool, and a wonderful staff.

Ocean Park Condominium Hotel

Manager: Rebeca Anaya Cardenas
958-587-0440
www.huatulcorealestate.com
rentalsoceanpark@yahoo.com
Santa Cruz, Calle Mitla 402
Price: Expensive
Credit Cards: Cash only
Handicapped Access: Yes

Right in the heart of Huatulco, overlooking the original fishing village and its collection of shops, restaurants, bars, and boats, Ocean Park offers some of the loveliest family friendly accommodations on the coast. There are 18 privately owned condominiums, all independently, and tastefully, decorated. Even the smallest options are fairly spacious, with full kitchens, satellite television, pool access, maid service, and small terraces. The larger suites have separate rooms, and better views over the central plaza and sea.

Quinta Real

Manager: Dieter Holfort
958-581-0428, 1-800-500-4000
www.quintareal.com
reser-hux@quinta-real.com
Tangolunda, Juárez Lote 2
Price: Very Expensive

Credit Cards: Yes
Handicapped Access: None

This small, 28-room boutique hotel sits on a gorgeous wooded property, inset with stunning views, tennis courts, and numerous sparkling pools. Master suites lack the awesome 180-degree vista some of the pricier suites enjoy, while nine offer tiny plunge pools angled for privacy. All are romantic and spacious, with river-pebble inlaid floors and magnificent beds attended by columns, arches, and wrought-iron lamps offering flattering light.

Jacuzzi tubs and fireplaces in each suite lend an aura of romance, but separate living spaces, babysitting services, large-screen televisions, a lovely children's pool, and other kid-friendly amenities make this a great spot for families. Lovers and parents alike will appreciate the enormous porches, hung with handmade fiber hammocks and furnished with table and chairs.

Las Cúpulas (B, D; $$$–$$$$), the hotel's beautifully decorated fine dining restaurant, has an outstanding view, hand-carved furnishings, and a breezy outdoor patio. In addition to perfectly prepared international and Oaxacan cuisine, traditional dishes from throughout Mexico are offered. Beneath the restaurant's twin dome is **Las Cúpulas Bar**, offering the same stunning vistas in a more casual ambience. And for those who prefer that nothing come between them and the stars, the outdoor ✪ **Sky Lounge** offers cocktails overlooking the moon-streaked bay.

The views over Bahía Tangolunda are the only thing better than Las Cupulas restaurant's classic Mexican cuisine.

Villa Escondida

Manager: Elsa María García
958-587-9293
www.villaescondida.com.mx
g2elsa@hotmail.com
Playa Bocalito, on the beach
Price: Very Expensive
Credit Cards: Yes
Handicapped Access: None

This brand-new boutique hotel built in classic Spanish style offers four stunning suites right on the almost undeveloped Playa Bocalito, at Huatulco's eastern edge. The long, pearl-gray stretch of sand, with surfing and a small indigenous village nearby, has a handful of restaurants selling seafood and renting surfboards, and little else. It is the anti-Tangolunda.

The hotel, filled with hand-carved, dark wood furnishings, and elegantly appointed with fine bedding, tropical plants and fresh flowers, walk-in closets, private terraces, a rooftop Jacuzzi, and richly decorated lounging areas, offers Colonial ambience with every modern amenity, and personalized attention that may inspire you to spend a week right here. Packages include everything from surfing lessons to beach bonfires, and staff can arrange spa services and fine dining right here.

PUERTO ÁNGEL BEACHES

The blue-collar port town of Puerto Ángel offers a range of accommodations. Budget backpackers can head straight for Playa Zipolote, where they can get their own ramshackle room right on the beach for US$10 double, though there are a few much nicer spots. Several beautiful B&B-style spots overlook Playas Agustinillo and Mazunte, while Playa Ventanilla has just one excellent beachfront ecolodge.

Luxury lovers should note that one of Oaxaca City's best hotels, Los Laureles, will open a five-star beachfront property close to Puerto Ángel, **Boutique Hotel Bichu** (www.hotelhaciendaloslaureles.com/ english/casa_bichu.php) before this book goes to print. It looks divine.

✪ El Alquimista

General Manager: Marcelo Barbas
958-587-8961
www.el-alquimista.com
el-alquimista@zipolite.com
Playa Zipolite, west end
Price: Moderate
Credit Cards: Yes
Handicapped Access: None

Easily the most comfortable lodging on Playa Zipolite, The Alchemist offers 14 gorgeous rooms right on the (clothing-optional) east end of Playa Zipolite. Each is unique, ranging from older, rather basic stone cabanas, spacious and airy with high ceilings, handmade wooden furnishings, private hot-water baths, and appealing décor, to open-air, *palapa*-topped beach-front cottages, overlooking the shore from your big double bed. The deluxe rooms and suites offer some of the nicest lodging on the beach, with polished wooden floors and sliding Japanese-style doors, swinging beds, bamboo furnishings, even smooth rock arches above the air-conditioned space. Private porches, hung with good hammocks, make this absolute perfection.

The excellent **restaurant-bar** (B, L, C, D; $$) is a popular spot for pizzas, seafood, salads, and more, with live music some evenings, when the mood strikes. An outstanding spot, perfect for the softer adventurer.

✪ Cabañas Punta Placer

Manager: Claire Dailly
No phone
www.puntaplacer.com
info@puntaplacer.com
San Agustinillo
Price: Moderate to Expensive
Credit Cards: Cash only
Handicapped Access: None

On a Budget in Huatulco

Huatulco may be Oaxaca's most exclusive resort community, but there are dozens of excellent lodging options for travelers on a budget. On weekdays and during low season, your best bet is to just roll into La Crucecita, where less expensive hotels and guesthouses congregate, and have a look around. During Christmas, Semana Santa, and on weekends, consider making reservations in advance. Here are a few solid options.

Hotel Flamboyant (958-587-0113, 1-800-670-6996; www.hotelesfarrera.com/flamboyant; credit cards accepts; $$–$$$) Next to the Templo of Guadalupe, right on the main plaza, this perfectly acceptable choice has dozens of clean, pleasant rooms, cheerfully painted with images of local churches , and newer family sized suites with full kitchens overlooking the pool.

Hotel María Mixteca (958-587-2336; andreal00@prodigy.net.mx; Guamuchil 204; credit cards accepted; $$) The small, 14-room hotel surrounding a courtyard and overlooking attached (and excellent) restaurant Sabor de Oaxaca is outfitted in cheerful yellows and soft browns and creams, with built-in furniture, great bathrooms, air-conditioning, TV, and WiFi.

Hotel Montserrat (958-587-0724; posadamonserrat@hotmail.com; Macuith 209; cash only; $) This impeccable, family run guesthouse offers excellent deals on pretty (in pink!) rooms with air-conditioning and cable TV, and some with tiny balconies. The family owns another similar hotel nearby.

Hotel Plaza Conejo (958-587-0054; Guachumil 208; MC, V; $$) Don't let the strip-mall ambience fool you, the 10 pretty rooms are great deals, with air-conditioning, cable TV, WiFi, and lots of attention to detail. Beds are firm but a bit low, perhaps not for folks with back problems.

✪**Huatulco Trailer Park** (no phone; http://www.tomzap.com/HUATULCOtrailerpark. html; Huatulco, Playa Tangolunda; $) Famously posh Playa Tangolunda is home to glamorous five-star hotels, rolling golf greens, and . . . this scruffy vacant lot with a few bathrooms in the weeds. The owner refused to sell his premium slice of beachfront property when the resort crowd came to town, and now offers free access to their gorgeous golden sands, along a swampy, barely maintained trail involving old pallets and logs. Camp, park your RV (US$5 per person), or just drop by for the lulz; somewhere, they're most appreciated.

This hotel is the labor of love, from an adventurous French and American trio who show impressive attention to detail in the beautiful gardens and every corner of these eight absolutely flawless rooms.

Though, to be precise, there aren't any corners in these gracefully rounded bungalows, with smoothly built-in furnishings, shelves, and pedestal beds topped with premium mattresses and bedding, including mosquito netting. The effect is rather regal, particularly in the upstairs units, where conical *palapa* ceilings and fine beachfront views from your private porch and hammock seem fit for royalty. Each comes with a pretty, hand-tiled hot-water bath and fans (but not air conditioning). There's also a good **restaurant** (B, C, L, D; $$) offering Mexican, American, and French-accented favorites.

Also check out **Mexico Lindo y Que Rico** (no phone; www.mexicolindoyquerico.com; cash only; $), just west of Punta Placer, geared to surfers but with surprisingly good rooms.

Made in the shade at Playa Agustinillo.

Hotel La Cabaña
958-584-3105
hotellacabanaapto.angel@gmail.com
Puerto Ángel, Playa del Panteón
Price: Inexpensive
Credit Cards: Cash only
Handicapped Access: None

A step above (literally; it's a steep walk to the beach) Puerto Ángel's plethora of solid budget lodging, this comfortable, *tejas*-topped lodge amid well-maintained gardens offers great views over the bay. Rooms are basic but appealingly decorated, with fresh paint and colorful *telas* atop beds with new mattresses. All the rooms have private hot-water bath and cable television; some also have air conditioning. Or just lounge on the shady terrace, and enjoy the view.

Hotel Puesta del Sol
Owners: Maria and Harold Ferber
958-584-3315
www.puertoangel.net/puesta_del_sol.html
puestasol@puertoangel.net
Puerto Ángel, Barrio del Sol
Price: Inexpensive to Moderate
Credit Cards: Cash only
Handicapped Access: None

This homey spot, overlooking Puerto Ángel with wonderful sunset views, has a variety of fan-cooled, tiled rooms, all with rather frilly, floral décor inside a modern Mission-style building surrounded by gardens. Budget travelers can save on rooms with immaculate shared bath, while folks willing to splash out can enjoy spacious doubles and triples with hot-water baths and some with private terraces. All guests have access to the rooftop terrace, hung with hammocks, and a television lounge with a multi-lingual library. The friendly owners are a wealth of knowledge, and really make the place.

Shambhala
Owner: Gloria Johnson
958-584-3151
shambhalavision.tripod.com
shambhala_vision@excite.com
Playa Zipolite, west end
Price: Inexpensive to Moderate
Credit Cards: Cash only
Handicapped Access: None

Climb from the white-sand nudist beach up wooden stairs to Shambhala. Mandalas and murals, relaxing open spaces and polished natural wood details, enhance the eco-zen vibe and one of the most beautiful views in Oaxaca State.

The hotel itself, "Where the '60s never end," seems a work in progress, with several rustic but comfortable private rooms (most with shared bathrooms), good beds and good vibes. The dorms are wonderful, boasting the best views on the property. There's plenty of space for a group retreat, or just a gathering in the beautifully simple **vegetarian restaurant** (B, L, D;

On a Budget in Puerto Escondido

Barlovento Hotel (919-582-0220; www.rincondelpacifico.com.mx; Camino Al Faro 6a. Sur 3; credit cards accepted; $–$$) Three blocks north of the lighthouse, this comfortable option has magnificent views from the pool and the big windows of the pretty, air-conditioned rooms, equipped with cable TV, minifridges, and phones.

Hostal Frida (954-582-3064; Centro; Avenida Oaxaca 110; credit cards accepted; $–$$) This standout among budget hotels surrounding the old Centro plaza (three blocks north of Hwy. 200) does it right, with a marble entryway, fine original artwork, new furnishings, big windows, and nice bathrooms—all for about US$15 more per night than the competition, which includes the clean, basic **Hotel Fatima** (954-582-2448; 3n Norte 103; $), with 24-hour hot-water bath and parking lot.

✪**Hotel Ines** (954-582-0416; www.hotelines.com; Playa Zicatela, Calle del Morro; Playa Zicatela, Calle del Morro; $–$$) Peter and Inez Voss's immaculately clean, freshly painted, beautifully maintained rooms and bungalows have great built-in furnishings, thoughtful décor, and your choice of fan or air conditioning; rooms with kitchens are available for weekly or monthly rates. The lovely property has terraces and a wonderful pool; the owners are a terrific source of information. A great value. Make reservations.

Hotel Tucán (954-104-2588; Centro, Calle Puerto Angelito corner of 3a; MC, V; $) This family run hotel high atop central Puerto Escondido has clean, nicely decorated rooms, a few balconies, and great staff. An excellent value, but quite a workout walking back from the beach.

✪**Villa Mozart y Macondo (**954-104-2295; www.villamozart.de; villamozart@gmx.de; Playa Carrizalillo, cash or PayPal only; $) This tranquil spot near Playa Carrazilillo is an excellent deal on clean, basic villas with built-in furniture, great bathrooms, artsy towels and telas, high ceilings, refrigerators, and a few full kitchens—but no air-conditioning or televisions. All surround tidy tropical gardens (which, along with some of the rooms, have WiFi), maintained by Manfred Rehse, the conscientious owner.

$-$$), with free movies Sunday through Thursday. Or retreat on your own on one of the hiking trails into the hills. Note that reservations are not accepted; if you're meant to be here, the perfect spot is sure to be open.

PUERTO ESCONDIDO

As with Huatulco, there are far too many options to list here, and as yet, no comprehensive online directory. The **Puerto Escondido Hotel Association** (954-582-3740; www.amhmpe.com) lists a solid selection of two- and three-star properties; click *Afiliados*.

Hotel Santa Fe

General Manager: Roberto Lepe Cameros
1-800-712-7057, 954-582-0170
www.hotelsantafe.com.mx
info@hotelsantafe.com.mx
Playa Zicatela, Avenida del Morro (north end)
Price: Expensive to Very Expensive
Credit Cards: Yes
Handicapped Access: Yes

A local landmark and certainly the best hotel on Playas Zicatela or Principal, the Santa Fe lounges in the shadow of the rocky point dividing the region's most popular beaches. Several types of rooms sprawl across the plazas and porticos punctuating the palm-shaded gardens and pools. The standard rooms really are quite standard, albeit tastefully arrayed in terra cotta tile and varnished wood details and furnishings. All the amenities you'd expect—air conditioning, cable television, etc.—are furnished and well-maintained.

The several classes of suites, however, are exceptional, and the two Bungalows Santa Cruz atop the rise behind the hotel property are perhaps the best rooms in Puerto Escondido. The comfortably elegant **Santa Fe Restaurant** (B, L, C, D; $$-$$$) keeps the focus on excellent, traditionally prepared vegetarian cuisine, although there

are plenty of meat and seafood dishes to keep everyone satisfied.

✪ Villas Carrizalillo

Owners: Amy Hardy and Edward Mitchel
954-582-1735
www.villascarrizalillo.com
info@villascarrizalillo.com
Playa Carrizalillo, Avenida Carrizalillo 125
Price: Expensive to Very Expensive
Credit Cards: Yes
Handicapped Access: None

In a privileged spot, atop a forested cliff over blue-green Playa Carrizalillo, this plush boutique property perfectly fulfills the promise of its unparalleled location. Follow cobbled paths past the flowers to your spacious room, remodeled to a sort of modern Spanish Colonial elegance. Villas have one, two, or three bedrooms, usually with wood or ceramic-tile floors, huge windows overlooking the dramatic bay, wonderful woodwork, and elegant, often artsy furnishings. Some have full kitchens, private terraces or balconies, and bathtubs; all the outstanding bathrooms include wonderful Mazunte personal products.

The grounds come complete with a pretty pool, surrounded by comfortable covered lounge areas fit for royalty. But you'll want to descend to the beach below, lined with *palapa*-style restaurants (only one has electricity) with umbrellas, lounge chairs, seafood, and cold drinks all right on the sand; surf lessons are also available.

But do indulge yourself with dinner at the excellent onsite (though separately owned) restaurant, consistently ranked the best in Puerto Escondido. ✪ **Las Tugas Cozhína** (954-582-0995; lostugas@gmail.com; B, D; closed Wed.; credit cards accepted; $$$-$$$$), with that same unbelievable view over the picture-perfect cove, is run by a cheerful Portuguese-Mozambiquian couple who offer an outstanding international menu.

The view over Puerto Escondido from the Hotel Santa Fe's breezy Presidential Suite is one of the best in town.

Portuguese-style fish, cooked with wine, onion, and bell pepper, or the *caldierada,* an Iberian fish stew, are favorites. Or go for the Mozambiquian-style shrimp, cooked in white wine, cream, and potatoes, and a variety of curries, including lamb.

Bed & Breakfasts

Huatulco

Agua Azul la Villa
Owners: Brooke and Richard Gazer
958-581-0265
www.bbaguaazul.com
gaurei@hotmail.com
Huatulco, Playa Tejoncito
Price: Moderate
Credit Cards: Yes
Handicapped Access: None

Within walking distance of secluded white-sand Playa Tejoncito, the six lovely rooms of this B&B, paved in ceramic tiles and furnished with handmade tables, chairs, lamps, and décor, come complete with stunning views from the hammock-hung private terraces to the sea. Sweet-smelling gardens surround a small and very pretty pool, its ambience enhanced by the breezy tropical architecture, all whitewashed walls and palm-thatched roof. Service is personalized, and both owners get raves from former guests for their local knowledge and helpful demeanor—not to mention the excellent breakfasts, with homemade breads and cookies, yogurt, fresh fruit, and more.

This is a traditional B&B, with a three-day minimum stay and no children younger than 18 permitted. Thus it is the perfect spot for a romantic getaway, perhaps a honeymoon, beneath the Huatulco sky.

Villa Sol y Mar

Owners: Wayne and Marcy Overby
763-300- 5815 Mexico, 763- 300- 5815 U.S.
www.villasolymar.com
villasolymar@yahoo.com
Huatulco, Playa Conejos
Price: Moderate
Credit Cards: Yes
Handicapped Access: None

This lovely B&B is situated in a quiet residential neighborhood, with views across Bahía Tangolunda from the large infinity pool. And you're just steps from lovely Playa Conejo, a sweet crescent of sand protected by a small coral reef (snorkel equipment is available).

There are only five spacious suites, with built-in furniture, colorful accents, wonderful double showers, and private porches to settle in and enjoy the sea. A hot breakfast is included, and the kitchen is open to guests for the rest of the day (you can arrange other meals as well). In high season, rooms are usually rented individually, and children younger than 17 are not permitted. In low season, however, you can rent the entire villa, in which case all ages are welcome.

PUERTO ÁNGEL BEACHES
(ZIPOLITE, AGUSTINILLO, MAZUNTE)

✪ Casa Pan de Miel

Owner: Anne Gillet
958-100-4719
casapandemiel@yahoo.com.mx
Between San Agustinillo and Playa Mazunte
Price: Expensive
Credit Cards: Cash only
Handicapped Access: None

Perched atop the rocky headland that separates San Agustinillo from Playa Mazunte, with views of the shoreline from the Jacuzzi and infinity pool, is this perfectly executed B&B. Four standard rooms and one expansive suite are tastefully decorated, with beautiful furnishings, air conditioning, WiFi, Sky TV, and private terraces where you can relax in your hammock and enjoy the view.

Guests enjoy a full breakfast each morning, and kitchen access throughout the day, as well as use of the expansive outdoor lounge, with library, and other amenities. Facilities are adults-only, and while the B&B is walking distance from either beach, it's a steep hike and not for the mobility impaired.

Ecotourism Projects

It's always best to make advance reservations for these community-run ecolodges.

✪ **La Escobilla** (958-589-9745, 958-587-9882 cell; santurioescobilla@yahoo.com.mx; Hwy. 200, kilometer 181 from Puerto Escondido to Pochutla; $) Cute, clean, cement cabins with private cold-water baths and a seafood restaurant overlook Mexico's most important turtle nesting beach. Turtle nesting season runs from May to February, peaking during the rainy season in September and October. *Arribazones,* or mass arrivals, can cover the beach with turtles, day and night, for a week; these may be more likely four days after a full moon. La Escobilla also rents kayaks.

Lachiguiri (971-717-5564, 971-717-5723; Istmo; $) When you really want to escape from it all, head 45 kilometers (28 miles) north of Jalapa de Marqués (follow the signs to Llano de la Cumbre), a coffee-growing area and rainforest with dramatic limestone cliffs and caves. Guided hikes, mountain biking, and environmental-education workshops are offered, and you'll stay in a thatch-roofed dorm.

Santa Ana (954-541-0273; www.ocho venado.wikispaces.com/inglessantaana; ecosta@laneta.apc.org; Santa Ana, 17 kilometers (11 miles) north of Hwy. 200 on the

While Playa Zipolite is most famous for its dangerous surf, always ask about conditions before swimming on the Oaxacan Pacific.

road to Tuxtepec; $; cash only) Rustic cabins and home-cooked meals in this small, coffee-growing village offer "active adventurers" a great base for hiking, horseback rides, and swimming in waterfalls.

Santiago Jocotepec (954-506-4131 after 6 PM, 954-543-8284; www.ochovenado .wikispaces.com/inglesjocotepec; Jocotepec; $; cash only) Make advance reservations for quaint *cabinas* in this high-altitude coffee town offer. Santiago Jocotepec features horseback rides, camping, archaeological sites, stunning views to the sea, and a deer and *jabali* (wild boar) breeding area. A map on the Web site offers driving directions (it's about an hour from Puerto Escondido). The staff also makes those awesome gum-wrapper purses.

✪ **La Ventanilla** (958-589-9277; Playa Ventanilla) The westernmost coast of the Puerto Ángel beaches remains almost wild, an endless white-sand beach of rough, rather unwelcoming water and absolute beauty. The well-managed ecotourism project offers horseback riding tours and guided hikes through the mangrove-fringed lagoon, as well as basic cement cabins with private cold baths. There are a couple of restaurants, a competing ecotourism project offering slightly different tours, and the "little window," a rock formation defining the beach. La Ventanilla also rents boats, horses, and tents, and has a camping area.

Beaches Less Traveled
Several beaches between Salina Cruz and Puerto Escondido offer very basic lodging, often geared to ecotourists, surfers, or locals. These are listed from east to west.

Cabañas Playa Cangrejo (971-728-9604; 33 kilometers (20 miles) west of Salina Cruz; $) Look for the poorly signed exit at kilometer 27 west of Salina Cruz on Hwy. 200, from which a good dirt road leads 5 kilometers (3 miles) to Playa Cangrejo, a picturesque fishing village offering great swimming, thatched-roof seafood restaurants, and these very basic, fan-cooled cabins in paradise.

✪ **Bahía de la Luna** (958-589–5020; www.bahiadelaluna.com; Playa la Boquilla; cash only; $$) A step above the usual beach cabanas, this sublime spot offers pretty cement cabins with thatched roofs, private cold-water showers, a basic restaurant (there's nothing else around), and access to isolated Playa la Boquilla, a gorgeous little inlet that's truly away from it all. Access is via pricey boat taxi from Puerto Ángel (there's also terrible road access; not recommended), and it's a bit overpriced, but undeniably beautiful.

Other Hotels

SANTO DOMINGO DE TEHUANTEPEC

Guiexhoba Hotel Tehuantepec (971-715-0416; kilometer 250.5 Hwy. 200; credit cards accepted; $$–$$$) Just outside town on the coastal highway, Guiexhoba (named for a local flower) offers spacious, modern rooms with locally woven bedspreads, pretty wooden furniture, and amenities including air conditioning, minibar, telephone, WiFi, and room service. There's also a sparkling indoor pool, an excellent restaurant, and a private tour operator who may be able to arrange guides to local sites if the Tourism Module cannot.

Hotel Donaji (971-715-0064; Juárez 10, near Iglesia Laborio; credit cards accepted; $$) This solid mid-range choice centers on a relaxed interior courtyard, flowing into a coffee shop and out onto the small plaza of pretty Laborio Church. Rooms are shabby

but clean, most with two double beds, cable TV, soothing Spanish tiles, and your choice of air conditioning or fan. There's hot water in the mornings. Bathrooms are sort of open, which might make some guests uncomfortable.

JUCHITÁN DE ZARAGOZA

Hotel Lopez Lena Palace (971-711-1388; Belisario Dominguez 59; cash only; $-$$) Against the dramatic Moorish architecture and excellent, almost upscale **Restaurant La Califa** ($–$$$), the clean, spacious rooms with air conditioning, cable TV, and 24-hour hot water seem a bit basic by comparison.

SALINA CRUZ

Hotel Altagracia (971-726-6225; Avenida Cinco de Mayo 520; cash only; $–$$) Clean, modern rooms with TV, air-conditioning, WiFi, and other amenities arc a good deal; the penthouse suites, overlooking the city, are designed for families, sleeping five comfortably, with a full kitchen.

Hotel Lena Real (971-714-2657; hotellenareal@hotmail.com; Avenida Avila Camacho 514; credit cards accepted; $$) The most comfortable lodging in town is at this four-ish star sprawler with 70 clean, modern rooms, all the amenities, and not much else. A small gym, pool, WiFi, guarded parking, and good restaurant, all just outside of the bustling center, make this a convenient place to overnight.

✪ **Hotel Vinisa** (971-720-2451; hotel.vinisa@hotmail.com; Avenida Manuel A. Camacho 405; cash only; $–$$) This beautifully detailed, family run hotel has small, lovely rooms with original art, big windows, handmade bedspreads, air conditioning, cable TV, WiFi, and pretty terraces. Cute.

PINOTEPA NACIONAL

The heart of the Mixtec Coast isn't really geared to international tourists, though it makes a comfortable base for exploring the fascinating surrounding towns, or a convenient overnight on your way to Acapulco.

Hotel Carmona (954-954-3222; Avenida Díaz 127; credit cards accepted; $) The nicest hotel in town has large rooms, some with air conditioning and cable TV, surrounding a small pool and good restaurant.

Hotel Las Gaviotas (954-954-3262; Calle 3 Poniente; cash only; $) Close to the shady central plaza and adorable church, this good hotel in town offers basic rooms, some with air conditioning and television.

Vacation Rentals

HUATULCO

Huatulco Reality (958-587-0218, 1-800-561-6331 Mexico; www.huatulco-realty .com; La Crucecita, Bugambilia 303, Plaza Continental) The company rents posh villas and condominiums throughout Huatulco.

Ideal Real Estate (958-587-0440; www .huatulcorealestate.com) Full-service villas and condos are listed here.

Resort Real Estate Services (958-585-5950, 818-424-9997 U.S.; www.rrestate services.com; Bahía Chahué) This outfit handles Huatulco's most luxurious rental properties.

PUERTO ESCONDIDO

Blue Horizons (954-102-8003; www.blue horizon.com.mx; Rinconada, Boulevard Benito Juárez, at Restaurant El Nene) Blue Horizons has a great variety of listings, from full luxury mansions (butler, maid, cook, and driver included) to fine family oriented and more rustic options.

Puerto Real Estate (954-582-3130; www .puertorealestate.com) Luxury rentals in and around Puerto Escondido.

RESTAURANTS AND FOOD PURVEYORS

While the resort towns offer a range of international cuisine, be sure to try some of the Oaxacan Riviera's signature seafood dishes, served at the *palapa*-topped restaurants that line almost every populated beach on the coast.

Restaurants and Food Purveyors Price Code

The following prices are based on the cost of a dinner entrée with a non-alcoholic beverage, not including the usually voluntary (but check your receipt) 10–15 percent gratuity that should probably be added. The coding "B, L, C, D" refers to U.S.-style meals (breakfast, lunch, dinner), as well as the typical Mexican *comida,* traditionally the biggest meal of the day, served in lieu of lunch from about 2 PM to 6 PM. Prices are calculated at 10 pesos to the dollar.

Inexpensive:	Up to US$5
Moderate:	US$5 to US$10
Expensive:	US$10 to US$20
Very Expensive:	US$20 or more

Restaurants

TEHUANTEC AND THE ISTHMUS

Perhaps the region of Coastal Oaxaca with the most distinctive cuisine. The Isthmus has been a melting pot where European, American, Chinese, Spanish, and indigenous cooks have swapped recipes for generations. Inspired gourmands can peruse the markets for exotic meats, including armadillo, iguana (which is illegal), and pigeon, or perhaps enjoy them in tacos, *guisados, relleno de papas* (seasoned mashed potatoes baked in banana leaves, like tamales), and the signature Tehuana dish, *garnachas,* stuffed corn tortillas topped with pickled veggies.

Restaurant Casa Grande

971-711-3460
Juchitán; Juárez 12
Price: Moderate to Expensive
Credit Cards: Yes
Cuisine: Tehuana, Oaxacan
Serving: B, L, C, D
Handicapped Access: Challenging
Reservations: Weekend dinners

Juchitán's finest dining is here, in what may be the city's oldest building, a beautiful Spanish Colonial overlooking the plaza. The menu is upscale Tehuana; the ambience is elegant, attracting business people for *comida,* going a bit more romantic at dinner.

Though many of Oaxaca's beaches aren't outfitted for tourism per se, there's almost always someone who'll fix you a wood-fired fish dinner.

The menu features the best of the state and isthmus, with upscale *tlayudas* at lunch and a delicious red mole anytime. But the real draw is the seafood, shrimp and fish from the neighboring lagoons, served *al ajillo* (in garlic sauce), fried, or in delicious soups and preparations.

Restaurant Scarú

971-715-0646
mx.geocities.com/sscaru/index.html
Tehuantepec; Callejon Leona Vicario 4
Price: Moderate to Expensive
Credit Cards: Cash only
Cuisine: Tehuana-style seafood
Serving: B, L, C, D
Reservations: Yes, especially for groups

Tehuantepec's most elegant evening out is inside a beautifully maintained 18th-century adobe mansion with wonderful murals, just up the twisting old road from the Iglesia Laborio. Though Scarú clearly caters to international tourists more than anywhere else in town, it's popular for weddings, baptisms, and other important events which call for a spectacular selection of fresh seafood, Oaxacan classics, and arguably the best sangria on the coast. Specialties include *filete relleno de mariscos* (US$14), fish filet stuffed with shrimp, tomato sauce, and the local yellow cheese; and *camarones aselga* (US$13), shrimp sautéed with a local vegetable. Big breakfasts, burgers, and international options are also on the menu. Finish off with the flan.

Restaurant Viña del Mar

971-714-2657
Salina Cruz, Camacho 110, corner of Guaymas
Price: Moderate to Expensive
Credit Cards: Cash only
Cuisine: Seafood
Serving: B, L, C, D
Reservations: No

Salina Cruz may not be a top tourist destination, but if you find yourself in this busy port town, be sure to stop by its favorite restaurant. The specialty, of course, is seafood, and depending on what the city's serious fishing fleet caught that day, you'll find shrimp, lobster, and a variety of *pescado* cooked to perfection.

But the restaurant is also well known for offering the best breakfasts in town, as well as a variety of Oaxacan classics, from chicken in mole to *tlayudas* and more.

HUATULCO

✪ La Bohéme

958-587-2250
www.laboheme.com.mx
Paseo Chahué Lote 5, Manzana 3, Sector M
Closed: Tues.
Price: Expensive to Very Expensive
Credit Cards: Yes
Cuisine: French
Serving: C, D
Reservations: Yes

Often described as the best restaurant on the Oaxacan Coast, this beautiful spot offers a few fusion dishes, but it's the classic French recipes that make this restaurant a very special place. Begin with the foie gras, in raspberry chutney with onion, or perhaps escargots de Bourgogne. Though there are several tempting salads, pastas, and meat dishes (aged beef, of course, with several prime cuts available, or as *estofada a la provençal*), traditional *coq au vin* and *moule a la mariniere* are the chef's recommendations. Pair your meal with one of more than 40 wines, many of them French but with reds and whites from Italy, Spain, Chile, and elsewhere. Then settle in for something from the scrumptious selection of desserts.

Reservations are recommended in the evening, but drop by earlier for the more affordable executive menu, served starting at 2 PM. The restaurant can also arrange to send a chef to your hotel or yacht, and prepare whatever your heart desires.

Il Giardino de Papa

958-587-1763
La Crucecita, Flamboyant 204
Price: Expensive to Very Expensive
Credit Cards: Yes
Cuisine: Italian
Serving C, D
Reservations: Yes

Casual elegance and excellent Italian cuisine earn this Crucecita eatery raves. Aged steaks, tender veal dishes, homemade pastas, and plenty of vegetarian options are all excellent choices, but fresh seafood is the standout on the menu. Start with a Caesar salad or a bowl of perfectly seasoned minestrone soup, then try the spaghetti frutti di mar, pasta with the fresh catch, or perhaps the garlic shrimp.

Pair with one of several fine wines, all served with panache by the attentive staff. There are several desserts on offer, but the tiramisu is, of course, the favorite.

El Grillo Marinero Restaurant-Bar

958-587-0783
www.grillomarinero.huatulco.tv
La Crucecita, Carrizal 908
Price: Moderate to Expensive
Credit Cards: Cash only
Cuisine: Seafood
Serving: L, C, D
Reservations: No

Palapa-topped restaurant on a quiet Crucecita side street is a local favorite for its friendly staff, casual ambience, and excellent, good-value seafood. Try the octopus cocktail, *caracol* steaks, or shrimp served any number of ways. The most popular dish is the lobster, perhaps best when grilled with cheese and flavorings. Owner Doña Pola is a sweetheart who can recommend the freshest item on the menu, then cook it however you choose. Wash it all down with a cold beer, and be glad that you're alive.

Restaurant Bar Doña Celia Lobster House

958-587-0128
Bahía Santa Cruz, on the beach
Price: Moderate to Expensive
Credit Cards: Yes
Cuisine: Seafood
Serving: B, L, C, D
Reservations: Yes

There are dozens of thatched-roofed restaurants lining the various beaches and bays of Huatulco, all offering ice-cold beer and coconut milk alongside the catch of the day, plus a shady, comfortable spot to enjoy the sand and sea. But the accepted best of the bunch is Doña Celia, serving dishes that are now considered classic Huatulqueño cuisine.

The star of the show, in season, is lobster, cooked eight different ways. But many folks come just for the *piña rellena,* a pineapple stuffed with seafood, avocado, mayonnaise, and other deliciousness. Or stick with the excellent ceviche. The popular eatery (a favorite with tour buses, among others) also offers big breakfasts, grilled meats, and a good-value *comida* every afternoon, probably featuring the catch of the day.

Restaurant Onix

958-587-0520
La Crucecita, Bugambilias 603, Plaza Principal
Price: Moderate to Romantic
Price: Expensive to Very Expensive
Credit Cards: Yes
Cuisine: Gourmet international
Serving: C, D
Handicapped Access: None
Reservations: Yes

This sleek, polished spot, all gleaming hardwoods and frosted lights, seems more suited to Southern California than little old Huatulco. Climb the stairs to this second-story bistro, where the professional staff will guide you to your table overlooking La Crucecita's Zócalo. The *mejillones medeterráneos,* mussels baked with ham and cheese, are outstanding, though the vegetarian ceviche and *sopa Donaji* (with cactus, garbanzos, and dried shrimp) also get accolades. Then move on to the mains, perhaps the exquisite *fusilli onix,* with pine nuts and calamari served in its own ink, or one of the many delicious steak, poultry, and seafood entries. It all comes beautifully presented, sauces and garnishes artistically arranged, and service is impeccable. Call for reservations.

Rollo Chino
958-587-2900
Santa Cruz, Calles Monte Alban and Mitla, second floor
Closed: Mon.
Price: Inexpensive to Moderate
Credit Cards: Cash only
Cuisine: Chinese
Serving: L, C
Handicapped Access: None
Reservations: No

Serving some of the best Chinese food on the Oaxacan Coast, this unassuming restaurant offers a few tables overlooking Santa Cruz's pretty downtown plaza. The charming Russian-Chinese owners (who speak fluent English and Spanish) offer a short menu of well-done dishes, including fried rice, chop suey, chow mein, and different soups, plus more expensive (but still very reasonable) shrimp dishes. "Lunch boxes," or combo deals, are basically the Chinese answer to *comida,* which makes sense as Rollo Chino is only open from 1 PM to 6 PM, perhaps a bit later in high season.

El Sabor de Oaxaca
958-587-0060
La Crucecita, Avenida Guamuchil 206
Price: Expensive
Credit Cards: Yes
Cuisine: Oaxacan
Serving: B, L, C, D
Reservations: Yes

For a taste of Oaxaca's own renowned cuisine, come here. The ambience is elegant, a high-ceilinged yellow dining room with hand-carved wooden furnishings and original art, accented by locally woven fabrics. Prices may seem a bit steep, compared to similar offerings elsewhere, but there simply aren't better traditional treats, such as *tasajo* (thin slices of grilled, spiced beef), tamales, *tlayudas,* chiles rellenos, and more. Breakfasts are outstanding.

PUERTO ÁNGEL BEACHES
This less-touristed collection of beaches may not offer the same variety of international and upscale cuisine as the resort communities of Huatulco and Puerto Escondido, but there are still a few gems worth visiting; don't miss the restaurant at Hotel El Alquimista in Playa Zipolite. In Puerto Ángel proper, which supplies seafood to the entire state, several *palapa*-style restaurants serve the best seafood you've ever had.

La Calenda
958-107-6547
www.hostallacalenda.blogspot.com
Playa Zipolite, mid-beach
Price: Moderate
Credit Cards: Cash only
Cuisine: French and Mexican
Serving: B, L, D
Reservations: No

Though there are more than a dozen perfectly acceptable seaside restaurants lining Playa Zipolite, all serving solid seafood and Mexican cuisine, La Calenda offers a little more elegance atop the sand.

Follow the smoky sounds of Edith Piaf to this spot, marked with a red sign, plastic tables, and a smattering of hammocks. The restaurant is well regarded for its excellent breakfasts: Oaxacan classics, Western favorites, and outstanding sweet or savory French crepes, and that's just the beginning of your day. The French owner also uses techniques and recipes from his native Bretagne to create tasty seafood dishes, vegetarians items, and an affordable menu of the day. There's live music every night at 10, and La Calenda also rents some of the sturdier-looking budget rooms on the beach, with mosquito nets and fans.

La Dolce Vita

958-584-3464
Playa Mazunte, Calle Paseo de Mazunte
Price: Moderate to Expensive
Credit Cards: Cash only
Cuisine: Italian
Serving: D
Reservations: Yes

For more than a decade, this breezy, open-air Italian restaurant has earned raves for its outstanding and authentic Italian cuisine. Delicious thin-crust pizzas are topped with the familiar and the exotic, while handmade pastas are perhaps best with the freshest seafood possible. Choose a delicious salad or antipasto to accompany your meal, as well as a bottle from a selection of at least 10 Italian wines. Finish off with an espresso, expertly prepared, and perhaps something off their dessert menu.

If there's a dish you desire but don't see on the menu, feel free to request it several hours in advance. La Dolce Vita also shows movies in high season, and welcome input on that selection as well. The owners also rent three delightfully simple rooms ($) with wonderful décor, private baths, and fans.

PUERTO ESCONDIDO

The beaches are lined with *palapa*-topped restaurants at which the specialty is seafood, served with an ice-cold beer. Budget travelers can head inland, across Hwy. 200, where the old city center has a range of inexpensive *comedors,* the cheapest inside the market. If you're looking to splash out on excellent international cuisine, your options are almost endless. Be sure to check under lodging, as several of the region's best restaurants are inside hotels.

La Galera (Hotel Arco Iris)

954-582-1494
www.hotel-arcoiris.com.mx
Playa Zicatela, Calle del Morro
Price: Moderate
Credit Cards: Yes
Cuisine: International
Serving: B, L, C, D

Fantastic views and stunning sunset happy hours (5 PM to 7 PM) are already big draws to this third-story restaurant overlooking Playa Zicatela. Add a big menu of well-prepared seafood and solid international cuisine, and you've got a winner. Many ingredients are grown right here on the grounds (the staff will show you around the eco-friendly gardens), and cooked atop a traditional *comal.* They roast their own coffee, as well, perfect with a big breakfast. There are several vegetarian dishes, and all sorts of Oaxacan options, from full lobster dinners to crispy *tlayudas.* And everyone raves about their burgers.

The hotel ($$) is a great Playa Zicatela option, too, though the clean, colorful rooms, surrounding a huge pool, are somewhat dated. Try to get one with a balcony boasting those same great views; some have kitchenettes as well.

Guadua

954-107-9524
www.guadua.com.mx
Playa Zicatela at Tamaulipas
Closed: Mon.
Price: Expensive
Credit Cards: Yes
Cuisine: Gourmet Oaxacan, international
Serving: C, D
Reservations: Yes

Your best beachfront choice for an elegant evening is this exquisite open-air restaurant, where chef Ricardo Morales takes Oaxaca's best culinary traditions and freshest ingredients, and interweaves them with the best international cuisine. Presentation is at a premium; your perfectly rice-paper wrapped spring rolls aren't just served, they are displayed. Slow-simmered sauces swirl across subtly seasoned fish dishes, while tender couscous is tossed with ripe vegetables and fruits. The wine list is good; the dessert list is better. There's live music on weekends

Las Margaritas

954-582-0212
8a Norte, next to Mercado Benito Juárez
Closed: Tues.
Price: Inexpensive to Moderate
Credit Cards: Cash only
Cuisine: Oaxacan
Serving: B, L, C
Reservations: No

What's arguably the best restaurant in town is also one of the most reasonably priced: relaxed Las Margaritas. Grab a seat on the pleasant patio and watch as tortillas are made by hand, creating the perfect accompaniment to well prepared Oaxacan classics, including a variety of moles and wonderful soups. Budget travelers come for one of the best *comidas* in town, while others try the excellent seafood. Service is good, the ambience is casual, and the location—right next to Mercado Benito Juárez—is convenient for souvenir and grocery shoppers.

✪ Sabor a Mar

954-102-7090
Playa Principal, east end
Price: Moderate to Very Expensive
Credit Cards: Yes
Cuisine: Seafood
Serving: B, L, C, D
Reservations: Yes

For more than 40 years, this breezy point between Playas Principal and Zicatela has been home to the best seafood restaurant in town. You can tell right away this is no ordinary *palapa;* professional, uniformed waiters usher guests into the open-air restaurant, tablecloths fluttering in the breeze, with a certain formality belying a commitment to offering a great experience. The menu is huge, with dozens of delectable seafood dishes; ask what's fresh, then choose your preparation. The surf-and-turf kebobs get high marks, as do the shrimp quesadillas. Sabor has earned raves from all the food critics for the best seafood in town, but budget travelers have a soft spot for its perfect fries. A huge roster of wines, tequilas, and mezcals lubricates the stunning sunsets, and adds a little romance to each starry night.

La Torre

954-582-1119
Juárez 427, Rinconada
Closed: Mon. and Tues.
Price: Moderate to Expensive
Credit Cards: Yes
Cuisine: Steakhouse
Serving: D
Reservations: Yes

This longtime favorite is known for its cozy atmosphere and excellent steak, your choice of rib eye, New York, and real filet mignon, cooked with a Northern Mexican flair. The chef also serves up great chicken and seafood dishes, as well as a popular Thursday Chinese special. Rib lovers, however, should be sure to show up on Friday, when slow-cooked barbecued pork ribs are on the menu. The specials are always excellent, and a good wine list provides fine compliment to the flavors.

MIXTEC COAST

Though there are few notable restaurants (for international visitors, at least) in this little-touristed region, the Mixtec is well known for its distinctive cuisine, available at tiny *comedors* and colorful festivals throughout the area. Juquila is considered the culinary capital of the region, known for delicacies such as deer tamales, pickled pigs' feet, cornbread *memelas,* and *nanacates* (corn fungus) made into a delicious yellow mole. Chocolate beverages and *bocadillos de coco,* made of *piloncillo* and shredded coconut, are widely consumed during the Festival of the Virgen of Juquila. Also try the excellent regional breads, baked in the beehive-shaped ovens you see outside local homes: *tarazones, betunes, pan con azúcar y betún,* and others.

Food Purveyors

Cafés

TEHUANTEPEC AND THE ISTHMUS

Italian Coffee Company (Cinco de Mayo, on the plaza; B, L, C, D; $) Salina Cruz loves its lattes done right.

Terra Nova Restaurant (971-715-0794; Juan C Romero 70, Barrio Laborio; B, L, C, D, closes at 5 PM Sun.; $) Family run spot in central Tehuantepec offers outdoor seating with street scene views, and great local dishes.

Yizu Coffee Place (971-715-1199; Tehuantepec City, Juárez 10, off Plaza Laborio; open 8 AM–11 PM daily; $) Espresso beverages plus traditional *bocas* (snacks); *chavindecas,* a Michoacan-style fried quesadilla with meat; and mains such as chicken stuffed with ham and two kinds of local cheeses. It's part of the Donaji Hotel.

HUATULCO

Café Gourmet (958-587-1881; La Crucecita, 601 Bugambilia; B, L, C, D; $$) Enjoy organic Pluma coffee beneath a spreading mango tree at this nice café overlooking the plaza.

✪ **Café Huatulco** (958-587-1228; www.cafehuatulco.com.mx; Santa Cruz, on the plaza; $) This cool outdoor café in the center of the original Huatulco community, Santa Cruz, offers bistro seating on the plaza where you can enjoy espresso made with locally grown Café Pluma, light meals, and live music on weekends.

Ice Caffe Venezia (958-109-7313; La Crucecita, Macuhitle 312; closed Mon.; $) Friendly, Italian-owned spot with sidewalk seating specializes in espresso beverages, gelato, and light meals—try the crepes (sweet or savory) or vegetarian lasagna, perhaps paired with one of several Italian wines.

PUERTO ÁNGEL BEACHES

El Bohemio Café (958-584-3151; Playa Zipolite, west end; $) Organic coffee and light vegetarian meals right on the beach.

Café Sol (no phone; Puerto Ángel, main road; $) Cozy spot for espresso beverages, ice cream, and great meals—steak, burgers, *chilaquiles,* and more—offers an alternative to the *palapa* restaurants lining the shore.

Dolce Passione Gelato Italiano (Playa Zipolite, town center; $) Gelato, espresso beverages, and light meals; try the pizza or salads.

PUERTO ESCONDIDO

✪ **El Cafecito** (954-582-0516; Calle del Morro; B, L, D; $–$$) Excellent breakfasts, homemade breads, fresh-squeezed juices, and kick-ass coffee, right on the beach. There's another location on the Rinconada (Juárez 10), close to Playa Carrazillo, but without the view.

The Italian Coffee Co. (Avenida Peréz-Gazga) Hey, you couldn't call it the Mexican Starbuck's if there *wasn't* one on every corner, could you?

✪ **Vivaldi Baguetteria** (954-582-0800; Avenida Peréz-Gazga, Playa Principal; open 7 AM–2 PM; credit cards accepted; $$) Excellent espresso beverages (illy, not Pluma), 17 smoothies, sushi, sandwiches, and crepes keep this place packed with locals and tourists, everyone's favorite spot to hang out.

Pizza

✪ **Cafeteria Jardín** (954-110-0412; Puerto Escondido, Playa Zicatela; Calle del Morro; $$) Popular, open-air eatery offers tasty, creative wood-fired pizzas and salads, plus one of the best vegetarian selections on the beach. Homemade breads and pastas, great ice cream, and real Italian iced coffee make this a fine place to enjoy the sea breeze.

La Crema Bar (958-587-0702; Huatulco, La Crucecita; Gardenia 311; $$) Right in the heart of La Crucecita, this festive bar also makes excellent thin-crust pizza.

✪ **Empenada** (958-587-9175; Puerto Ángel Beaches; Playa Mazunte, Bugambilia; D; $) On the west end of tiny Playa Mazunte, Empenada serves spectacular pizza, sushi, seafood, and Mexican classics beneath a basic *palapa,* for dinner only.

Mixtú Guiishi (971-711-3945; Juchitán, Colón 7; D; $) This popular spot for pizza and beer shows free movies after sunset. If you'd rather talk, try **La Vianda**, off the Zocaló, in an atmospheric 19th-century mansion.

Vittorios Pizza (971-714-4349; Salina Cruz, Cinco de Mayo 404) Popular spot in downtown Salina Cruz serves pizza and more.

Grocery Stores

Plaza La Sevilla (Salina Cruz, Hwy. 190) The largest grocery store on the Isthmus of Tehuantepec is conveniently located (for drivers) just outside Salina Cruz, right before you hit Pacific Coast Hwy. 200. There's an HSBC ATM, too.

Super Che (Huatulco, Boulevard Chahué) This huge grocer offers acres of foods, from local produce and baked goods to foreign cheeses and brand names from home.

Super Mini Mart Rockaway (Playa Zicatela) The only 24-hour grocer in Puerto Escondido also has the best selection of liquor and snacks.

CULTURE

Though the Oaxacan Riviera is better known for its beach scene, pre-Columbian ruins, Spanish Colonial churches, fabulous fiestas, tasty cuisine, and colorful handicrafts can be found all along the stunning Pacific coast.

The **Isthmus of Tehuantepec**, first settled some 4,000 years ago, was ruled by the Huaves people until the mid-1300s, when it became part of the Zaachila kingdom of the Zapotec Empire. From the city of **Santo Domingo Tehuantepec**, still presided over by ruins of mighty Guiengola Fortress, King Cocijoeza successfully fended off attacking Aztecs in 1486, six years after founding what's still Tehuantepec's cultural capital, the **Heroic City of Juchitán de Zaragoza**. (Originally called Ixtaxochitlán, or "Place of the White Flowers," the "Heroic" title was bestowed by the Mexican government after Jachuteco battalions beat back French invaders.) Cocijoeza's son, Cosijopíi, would later join with the Spaniards to overthrow the Aztec Empire.

Though Cosijopíi and the Zapotecs converted to Catholicism shortly after the defeat of the Aztecs, the local population actively resisted much further Spanish meddling. The March 22, 1660, Rebellion of Tehuantepec, while unsuccessful, convinced the Spanish to allow more autonomy here than elsewhere in New Spain. Thus, Istmeños have retained much of the indigenous American heritage snuffed out elsewhere in the name of Catholicism, including relative social equality between men and women, and tolerance for gay men, or "muxes."

When the Tehuantepec National Railway began construction in the late 1800s, European and Chinese immigrant railroad workers enriched this vibrant community. The resulting cultural mix is most beautifully expressed in the traditional women's *traje,* a velvet or satin *huipil* blouse and full skirt, richly embroidered with flowers, and accented with lace petticoats, and perhaps the lace headdress that has become the regional symbol.

HUATULCO

The freshly scrubbed resort community of Bahías de Huatulco, built by Fondo Nacional de Fomento al Turismo (FONATUR) (www.fonatur.gob.mx), the national tourism ministry created in 1983, may not appeal to those in search of the "real Mexico." It seems too clean, too new, with the best infrastructure in Oaxaca; you can even drink the tap water.

Huatulco is, however, arguably more authentically Mexican than any of the other resort communities along this coast. The Mexican government worked overtime making this an ecologically sound development, and won the prestigious Green Globe 21 award for its efforts. The family friendly resort, with calm, protected swimming beaches and plenty of activities for kids, is more popular with wealthy Mexican vacationers than the international jet-set crowd, which has yet to discover (or learn to pronounce) this newest resort community.

PUERTO ESCONDIDO

Originally christened Punta Escondida (Hidden Point), Oaxaca's original beach resort town was, since around 2300 B.C., a quiet fishing village and part of the Chatino Empire, the capital of which, now called Santo Reyes Nopala, is in the hills above town. Coffee growers developed the town into a major shipping port beginning in the late 1800s, and by the 1930s it was the most important port in Oaxaca, shipping coffee, tropical hardwoods, and other products to the rest of the world.

But it was the completion of the Pacific Coast Highway 200 from Acapulco in the 1960s that brought in tourists eager to escape the overdeveloped beaches to the north. Tourism has grown steadily since, and today this is Oaxaca's most popular beach town.

MIXTEC COAST

The bustling urban center of the Mixtec Coast is the decidedly untouristy town of Santiago Pinotepa Nacional, an ancient city whose name means "Palace of *Pinol,*" a sweetened corn drink. Indigenous culture remains strong in the region, well known for its exquisite handicrafts, particularly the textiles, ceramics, and carvings. The *Costa Chica,* however, is a place of stunning human diversity, famed for its fascinating African Oaxacan community.

Though the origins of this distinctive culture are shrouded in history, tales of wrecked slave ships and abandoned plantations may explain the unusual mix. No matter what the truth may be, the African immigrants intermarried with the local Mixtecas, settling comfortably in communities near the Lagunas de Chacahua, San Pedro Tututepec, Santa María

Boat taxis and tours are the most scenic way to visit Huatulco's bays and beaches, even those, such as Playa El Arrocito, that you can reach by car.

Huazolotitlán, Pinotepa Nacional, Santo Domingo Armenta, Santiago Tapextla, and Santa María Cortijos. A wonderful place to learn more about this unique culture's traditions, dances, and cuisine is at the Collantes Civic Fiestas, held every September.

Archaeological Sites

El Faro de Cortés (Playa Ventosa) On a picturesque point just east of Salina Cruz, this surprisingly well-maintained lighthouse allegedly dates to 1526. Part of the region's first European-style shipyard, it was commissioned by conquistador Hernán Cortés.

✪ **Guiengola** (no phone; delistmo@prodigy.net.mx, delistmo@aoaxaca.com; 14 kilometers/9 miles west of Tehuantepec; open 8 AM–6 PM daily) Just west of Guiga Roo Guisii, or the City of Tehuantepec, is the almost unexcavated Zapotec fortress of Guiengola, or "Big Rock." Once strategically important, the remarkably well-preserved fortress is still protected by a 3-meter (10-feet) high, 2-meter (6-feet) wide stone wall that once encircled the entire mountain. A dirt road goes partway up the mountain, but you'll eventually need to park and walk another hour to what was probably a summer home for Zapotecs who lived in Tehuantepec.

Built in the 1300s by Zapotec leaders getting increasingly jittery about aggressive Aztecs, fortifications include two terraced plazas and two pyramids marking east and west. Several other buildings and tombs are open to adventurous visitors, those atop a 400-meter (1,300-foot) hill offering incredible views over the Guiengola River. The ruins were abandoned shortly after the Spanish conquest, and have remained unoccupied since.

Arrange a guide through the **Tehuantepec Tourism Module** (no phone; delistmo@

prodigy.net.mx) or speak directly to guide **Victor Velasquez** (971-714-4660, 971-122-3966), in Spanish. Guides run about US$30 per group. If you have a four-wheel drive car or are springing for a taxi, it's a 3-kilometer (1.8-mile) hike from the parking area; buses drop you off about 6 kilometers (3.5 miles) from the ruins.

The Tourism Module also arranges guides for the 90-minute tours to the hidden ruins atop **Cerro del Tigre**, Jaguar Hill, or *tecuani-tepec,* rising from the center of Tehuantepec City; and **Piedra San Vicente**, in the nearby village of San José el Progreso, covered with ancient paintings, most dating from the Postclassic Period (900–1521AD). For tours, contact guides **Francisca Bustamante** (954-541-9029) or **Eusebio Sabas** (954-541-9238).

Santo Reyes Nopala (San Gabriel Mixtepec, 32 kilometers (20 miles) north of Puerto Escondido) The quaint coffee town's name means "Valley of the Prickly Pears" in Nahuatl, and it has been inhabited since 800 B.C. The ruined city peaked between 500 A.D. and 700 A.D., part of the Mixtec Empire ruled by Chief Ocho Venado Garra de Tigre, portrayed in full regalia

San Pedro Tututepec (from Hwy. 200, 81 kilometers/49 miles west of Puerto Escondido, north 9 kilometers/6 miles from Santa Rosa de Lima) This quiet, traditional town has been occupied for millennia, but was officially incorporated on April 3, 357 A.D., by Prince Matatzín of Tilantongo. Matatzín had been ordered by his father, the king of the Upper Mixtec Empire, to settle thousands of families along the resource-rich coast.

Throughout the Postclassic period (900 A.D.–1521 A.D.), Matatzín's descendents would begin ambitious expansion. King Eight Deer Tiger Claw led his people into Guerrero and Eastern Oaxaca. This was at first successful, but led to wars with the Aztecs, then the Zapotecs, and finally with the latter's powerful new allies, the Spanish. They killed the final Coastal Mixtec king and settled the valley themselves. The town was christened San Pedro Tututepec in 1623.

In addition to the excellent Yucu Saá Museum, displaying pieces from the Mixtec and Spanish eras, you can also see ancient Colonial era bells near the gracefully arched 18th-century adobe church.

Architecture

The Spanish never settled the Pacific coastline with the same enthusiasm that developers show today, thus the region's colonial architecture is modest, and usually found well inland from the resort towns. There are a few gems, however.

ISTHMUS OF TEHUANTEPEC

This region, with its population centers well inland, offers the most impressive colonial architecture.

Casa de la Cultura Callejón Rey Cosijopíi (971-715-0114; Tehuantepec, corner of Guerrero and Dr. Liceaga; www.itistmo.edu.mx/) The former Convent of Santo Domingo was probably constructed during the 16th century, as part of the **Cathedral**. Both buildings have been well maintained, with faded original frescos adorning each soaring archway. Today the graceful stone edifice holds a community cultural center, with a library and displays of old Spanish and Mixtec artifacts, and runs various workshops and classes. The cathedral is also lovely, most notable for its impressive altar, commissioned by Zapotec King Cosijopíi.

Visitors are welcome to both buildings, where they can search for secret entrances to a system of tunnels that allegedly runs under the entire town, perhaps connecting the Cathedral well to **La Gruta** (The Cave), visible above town and across the river, and several other historic buildings. These include **Iglesia Dolores**, with its panoramic view over Tehuantepec; charming **Templo de la Natividad Excelsa**, fronting pretty Laborio Plaza; and lovely blue-and-white **Templo de la Virgen de la Asunción**. Other points of interest include the 1793 **Escuela Benito Juárez**; and the **Chalet de Juana Cata**, where prominent businesswoman Juana Catalina Romero received her close friend President Porfiro Diáz via the railroad he built right to her door.

Old Church of Jalapa de Marqués (Reservoir Benito Juárez, Jalapa de Marqués) About 45 minutes from Tehuantepec, the town of Jalapa de Marqués was completely rebuilt when the Benito Juárez Dam flooded its original site. The lake, lined with simple restaurants serving *mojarra,* or rainbow bass, is an attraction in itself, but history buffs can rent boats to see the partially submerged old church, rising in domes and arches above the blue water. There are also a few more ancient indigenous ruins nearby, as well as a popular public hot spring (clothing mandatory) just outside town. A small museum, **Casa del Gobierno**, will re-open while this book is on the shelves.

Templo de San Vicente Ferrer and Casa de la Cultura Juchitán (971-711-1351; Juchitán, corner of Belisario Domínguez and Colón) A classic 17th century church, with adobe arches, a gently curved façade, an ornate, gold-gilt altar, and the figure of San Vicente Ferrer. Saint Vincent was a Dominican monk born on January 23, 1350, in Valencia, Spain, who is best remembered for his good looks and ability to convert Muslims peacefully. His escapades in Juchitán, however, are quite a different story.

According to local legend, God gave Saint Vincent a bag full of *muxes* (see sidebar), or gay men, and instructed him to leave a few in every village in Mexico. When he got to Juchitán, however, the bag broke and all the muxes escaped, and are still a prominent part of Juchitán's cultural scene. There's no telling how these legends became intertwined, but the priests of Templo San Vicente happily accept gays and lesbians in the church community, and support several *velas,* or festivals, where they are top performers.

Next door is the interesting **Casa de la Cultura**, founded in 2000 by famed local poet Macario Matus. Shows and *velas* are held here, and the central library boasts a collection of indigenous and colonial-era artifacts. If you want to learn more about the socialist worker-peasant-student coalition of Tehuantepec (COCEI), democratically elected in 1981 and violently ousted by the federal government in 1983, this is a great place to start.

HUATULCO

Huatulco features whitewashed, resort-style architecture, combining the Mexican, Moorish, and Mediterranean attributes seen from Cancún to Cabo, but with a three-story limit. Though the resort was developed in 1984, there are a few architectural gems. The 1870 **Church of Santa Cruz** (958-587-0944; La Crucecita; Avenida Gardenia), at the heart of "downtown" Huatulco, La Crucecita, is more often called the Parroquia de Nuestra Señora de Guadalupe. The Mission-style edifice is famed for what may be Mexico's largest painting of the Virgin of Guadalupe, a contemporary take on the country's patron saint, measuring 87 square meters (935 square feet).

The **Chapel of the Holy Cross of Huatulco**, in the original fishing village of Santa Cruz, is supposedly set upon the very spot where some 2,000 years ago, the god Quetzalcoatl brought the first cross to Huatulco, a name meaning "where the wood is venerated."

Though this was long before the Spanish officially arrived, the "Christian" cross remained here well into the conquest. In 1587, pirate Thomas Cavendish attacked and looted the village. He attempted to steal, then cut with axes and saws, and finally burn the sacred cross, but could not. The Catholic Church was more successful. In 1612 Bishop Juan de Cervantes of Oaxaca took the cross to the Vatican, though fragments are preserved at cathedrals across Mexico. Today, a beautiful and breezy open-air church has been erected upon the place where this mysterious cross once stood, and is the focus of Holy Cross festivals held in February.

Mixtec Coast

Templo de la Virgen de Juquila Oaxaca's most famous pilgrimage site is this 18th century sanctuary, with slim Doric columns, elegant red-and-white façade, and beautiful gold *retablo* framing the revered image of the Virgin of Juquila. Much older than this church, she arrived here from the tiny town of Amialtepec after surviving a fire that destroyed her first church in the 1600s. Though her feast day is December 8, when the town comes alive with entertainment, food stands, and pilgrims enjoying the excitement, visitors arrive year-round to pray for a miracle. Even if you don't believe, she will grant petitioners one wish. La Solteca and Estrella Roja del Sureste run between Juquilla and Oaxaca City, or take the, unpaved road (usually passable to normal cars) 20 kilometers (12 miles) from kilometer 78 on Hwy. 131 north of Puerto Escondido.

Museums

Museo Yucu Saa

No phone
San Pedro Tututepec, central plaza
Hours: 10 AM–5 PM Tues.–Sat., 10 AM–2 PM Sun.
Admission: US$1 donation

The indigenous town of Tututepec (90 kilometers/56 miles west of Puerto Escondido) was founded on April 3, 357 A.D. by Prince Matatzín of Tilantongo of the inland Mixtec Empire. He was enchanted by "The Hill of Birds," with its view to the sea, and so chose it as the capital of the Coastal Mixtec people. It rose to prominence during the Postclassic Period (900 A.D.–1521 A.D.), but eventually fell to the Spanish.

Today, Tututepec is home to this fascinating museum. The first floor exhibits the pre-Columbian treasures, with lots of ceramics, a few pieces of jewelry, and a couple of outstanding stone *stellae* dating to this rural backwater's reign as an imperial capital. The upstairs exhibits artifacts of the early Spanish Colonial period, and photos of nearby archaeological sites. Museum staff should be able to arrange guides to see those sites, or go through the municipality, right on the plaza.

Music and Nightlife

Huatulco

Though Huatulco can't compare with some of Mexico's other resort towns, there are plenty of places to let your hair down.

Café Dublin (La Crucecita; Carrizal between Flamboyan and Chacah) This cozy bar serves a wide variety of beers and liquors, plus a short list of great bar food, including what's lauded as the best burger in Huatulco. Closed Monday.

Camelot (958-585-8148; www.bar-camelot.com; Vialidad 14, Boulevard Juárez; open 8 PM) The Medieval castle has German beer and food, as well as wenches in period clothing, but no jousts. There is live rock music some nights.

Noches Oaxacaqueñas: Guelaguetza en Huatulco (958-581-0001; www.donwilo.com; Bahía Tangolunda; Boulevard Juárez; 8:30 PM nightly; US$12.50 cover) Enjoy traditional dances from Oaxaca's seven provinces by the beach; order dinner from the attached **Don Porfiro Restaurant** ($$$$), with top-notch seafood and steak, cooked on the outdoor grill. Reservations recommended.

La Papaya (958-587-2589; Chahué Bay, Boulevard Juárez; open 9 PM Thu.–Sat.; $10 cover) Popular disco has two stories of go-go dancers, bars, flashing lights, and loud music. Other discos worth checking out include **La Mina** (958-587-2731; Bahía Chahué, Mixie 770 at Hotel Real Aligheri; opens 10 PM; $10 cover), with a more international crowd, and **Baby Kiss** (Boulevard Chahué, Lote 30, Manzana 3, Sector R; open Thu.–Sat.; $10 cover), with Latin rock and sometimes live music.

✪ **Tipsy Blowfish** (958-587-2844; La Crucecita, Calle Flamboyant 30; open 10 AM-2 AM daily) This family friendly bar and grill is everyone's favorite place to hang out. It's owned and operated by helpful English-speaking travelers who rock out to a great, mellow soundtrack, offer board games and kids' meals, and have live music most evenings.

PUERTO ÁNGEL BEACHES
The beaches of Puerto Ángel, Playa Panteón, and especially Playa Zipolite are lined with watering holes, many with live music.

Disco-Bar La Puesta (Playa Zipolite; open Thu.–Sat. 10 PM) This is the best place to dance on the beach.

Livelula Bar (Playa Zipolite, east end; open Wed.–Sat. 8 PM; credit cards accepted) This popular open-air bar has pool and ping-pong tables, plenty of hammocks, snacks, and sometimes live music.

PUERTO ESCONDIDO
There are plenty of bar-restaurants where you can enjoy a drink, and perhaps a shrimp cocktail, on the sands of playas Principal and Zicatela.

Bar Fly (www.barfly.com.mx; Playa Zicatela) Dancing, DJs, performances, and fun until the wee hours.

Casa Babylon (no phone; Playa Zicatela, Calle del Morro) A mellow bar known for its mojitos and board games, it gets going after 10 PM with DJs or live music.

✪ **Cinemar Zicatela and PJ's Book Bodega** (954-102-2007; Playa Zicatela, Calle del Morro) This small bookstore selling new and used, mostly English-language titles also rents surfboards and has a 15-person, air-conditioned cinema. Movies, ranging from Hollywood blockbusters to foreign art flicks show nightly at 7 and 9 for US$3, and beer and snacks are available.

Danny's Terrace and Bar (954-582-0056; Playa Principal; B, L, C, D; closed Wed. in low season; $$) A full bar, a full menu, and candlelit tables right on the sand make this a fine (and rather romantic) place for an early drink or late meal.

Split Coconut (954-582-0736; Guelatao and Tlacochahuaya, Bacocho) Awesome burgers and barbecue, NFL, pool tables, and sometimes live music.

Surface (954-109-1405; www.surface.com.mx; Playa Zicatela, Hwy. 200 and Bajada de las Brisas) Relaxed surfer lounge has hammocks, cold drinks, snacks, and movies on Thursday, Saturday, and Sunday at 8 PM.

Wipeout (954-582-2302; Avenida Peréz-Gazga) This longtime favorite disco keeps the music pumping all night; ladies' night is Saturday.

Spanish Classes
All are in Puerto Escondido.

Instituto de Lenguajes Puerto Escondido (954-582-2055; www.puertoschool.com; Puerto Escondido, Hwy. 200 above Playa Zicatela, across from Cemento Cruz Azul) Private or group lessons, homestays, and activities.

MARESS Spanish School in Puerto Escondido (954-582-4159;Centro, corner of 2da Norte and 1a Oriente) Several types of classes and activities, organizes homestays.

Oasis Language School (954-582-7827; www.oasislanguageschool.com; Juárez 2, Rinconada) Puerto Escondido's top surfing school also offers Spanish classes.

RECREATION

Oaxaca's endlessly varied coastline, developed resort communities, and stunning mountains offer almost unlimited recreational opportunities. Here's a taste of what's available.

Beaches
While the vast majority of visitors to the Oaxacan Riviera stick to the stunning beaches of Huatulco and Puerto Escondido, scores of less-touristed shores await more adventurous souls. Note that many beaches, most notably Playa Zipolite, can be unsafe for swimming, particularly just after a full moon or new moon. If the sea seems rough, or you don't see other swimmers, ask about current conditions before going in.

ISTHMUS OF TEHUANTEPEC
Though less known for its beaches than its cultural riches, the Isthmus offers several untamed stretches of sand.

Juchitán boasts several beaches, all on protected Laguna Superior, about 4 kilometers (2 miles) from the city center on good dirt roads: Playa Santa María del Mar, Santa Cruz Primero de Mayo and, most accessible, Playa Vicente. From here, you can arrange boats to smaller Laguna Inferior and Laguna Oriental, or any of several islands within these calm waters, or to the rough wild Pacific beaches on the barrier. From **Tehuantepec**, grab a cab (45 minutes; US$1 *colectivo*) to Moro Mazatan, Santa Gertrudis Miramar, and **De Pacolín**, the last of which has restaurants, boat trips, and horse rentals geared to locals.

Though right on the sea, the shores of **Salina Cruz** are dominated by an artificial port, oil refineries, and shrimp farms. Head north, however, to swimmable Las Salinas del Marques, Las Escolleras, and ✪ **Bahías La Ventosa**, with basic lodging and restaurant options. **El Faro de Cortés** and **Santa María del Mar** also offer fishing trips and basic

The entire Oaxacan coastline is a fishing paradise, and boats can be arranged at any glittering resort town or tiny village on the shore.

restaurants, all just southeast of town. **Punta Conejo** has great surfing. Heading west on Pacific Coast Hwy. 200, you'll pass **Playa Azul**, best known for its popular baby sea turtle release. Or try **Playa Cangrejo**, with very basic cabinas ($) and good swimming, or **Bahía Chipehua**, a long, white beach good for swimming, dune walking, fishing, and several *palapa*-topped restaurants with beach chairs.

HUATULCO

Chosen for its spectacularly scalloped shoreline, most of Huatulco's nine bays and 36 beaches remain undeveloped and accessible only by boat, with many, almost pristine, set aside as part of Huatulco National Park.

At the eastern edge of the resort community, delineated by the Río Copalito, is **Playa Bocana**, with surfing, a few restaurants, some indigenous mud baths, and the five-star Villa Escondida all alone on the endless, white-sand shore.

Bahía Conejos is the farthest bay east in Huatulco proper, with diving, swimming, and sportfishing. Five beaches stretch along the water in one long, almost contiguous stretch of sand: **Playa Conejos**, with vendors on weekends and holidays; **Magueyito**, with interesting tide pools; **Punta Arena**, a broad kilometer of rough white sand and rocky outcroppings; **Playa Arena**, just beyond; and tiny **Tejoncito**, a small, intimate cove.

The next bay westward is posh **Bahía Tangolunda**, with five beautiful beaches lined with Huatulco's very best hotels, a rolling golf course, and one scruffy trailer park operated by the last original resident. **Playa Tangolunda**, a long, broad beach of coarse golden sand is the bay's beautiful centerpiece; walk east to the finer sands and stronger surf of **Playa Rincón Sabroso**. Rent a boat to visit the clear emerald waters of **Playa Ventura**, perfect for diving and snorkeling; **Isla La Montosa**, close to tiny **Playa Mixteca**; and swimmable **Playas Manzanillo** and **Tornillo**.

Just west is **Playa Arrocita**, soon to be developed, and **Playa Consuelo**, both occupying a resort-studded headland. The polished **Bahía Chahué**, with a 180-slip marina, a strollable breezy jetty, and picturesque **Playa Chahué**, 600 meters (1,800 feet) of white sand rapidly developing into a resort community, is also the closest beach to La Crucecita, a 10-minute walk from town. **Playa Esperanza**, about 1.5 kilometers (1 mile) south of Chahué, offers excellent swimming, while tiny **Playa Tejón** offers access to a 10-meter (30-foot) deep bay of calm, turquoise water.

Bahía Santa Cruz was the original heart of the ancient, indigenous settlement, and Playa Santa Cruz now boasts a beautiful little marina and village, with shops and restaurants surrounding a picturesque square. Take a boat to tiny **Playa Yerbabuena** or more developed **Playa La Entrega**, also accessible by road, with family friendly surf, great snorkeling, and several restaurants.

Just east are the twin bays of **Maguey**, lined with restaurants renting snorkel gear for visiting the wonderful reefs, and virgin **Organo**. Both fine white-sand beaches are usually visited by boat, though some mountain bike tours also end up here.

The next three bays, well within Huatulco National Park, are usually visited by boat: mangrove-lined **Cacaluta Bay**, surrounding a small island with good snorkeling, is most popular with sportfishers, but the area also boasts broad, 1-kilometer (.62 miles) long **Playa Cacaluta**, with strong waves, and **Playa Arroyo**, a tiny, swimmable white-sand cove. **Bahías Chachacual** and **Riscalillo** are almost virgin, protecting **Playa Chachacual**, stretching more than a kilometer along the pounding surf; secluded and swimmable **Playa La India**, has deep, clear water for snorkeling among the rock formations, while **Playa Jicaral** sports exceptional reefs.

The final, westernmost bay, **San Agustín**, is also most easily reached by boat, but a rough, well-signed dirt road runs 18 kilometers (11 miles) from Hwy. 200 at Santa María Huatulco. Endless white-sand **Playa San Agustín** offers excellent snorkeling, several restaurants, and very basic lodging; **Cacalutilla**, just north, is a smaller and calmer spot with good snorkeling.

PUERTO ÁNGEL (ZIPOLITE, MAZUNTE, VENTANILLA)
Modernized in the late 1800s by local coffee barons, at the southern terminus of Hwy. 175 from Oaxaca City, **Puerto Ángel** remains more a blue-collar fishing village than a glittering resort town, centered on a colorful marina lined with simple seafood restaurants. There is a good swimming beach, **Playa Principal**, where you can arrange boats for fishing, diving, or exploring. Nearby, **Playa Ixtacahuite** has good fishing and diving in the impressive coral reef, while **Playa La Boquilla** is shallow enough for snorkeling. **Playa Panteón** is the city's best swimming beach, with restaurants renting snorkel gear for appreciating the undersea scenery.

Most international tourists continue west along the potholed coastal road, running parallel to Hwy. 200. First up is broad **Playa Zipolite**, a budget backpacker haven lined with inexpensive lodging, restaurants, and bars. The name supposedly means "Beach of Death" in Nahuatl, and true or not, dangerous currents mean that swimming (or going in past your knees) is not recommended. You can, however, sunbathe *au naturel* in several spots, most famously the cove at the western end of Zipolite, **Playa del Amor**; locals seem accustomed to the show.

Or continue west to more elegant, and (usually) swimmable, **San Agustinillo**, stretching almost a beautiful mile, with great lodging options and good restaurants. On the other side of a steep and scenic headland is **Playa Mazunte**, also swimmable and one of the primary sea turtle nesting beaches in Mexico, and home to the Mexican Sea Turtle Center. Just west is the southernmost point in Oaxaca, **Punta Cometa**, popular for watching sunsets. Just beyond, **Playa Mermejita** is another popular nesting beach for leatherback and other sea turtles.

La Ventanilla, the westernmost of Puerto Ángel's beaches, is almost wild, with a small, mostly indigenous pueblo of some 25 families, beautiful Laguna de Tonameca, mangrove forests, and a baby crocodile farm.

PUERTO ESCONDIDO

Perhaps the more authentic of the Oaxacan Rivera's two resort towns, this festive spot has accommodation for every budget, cuisine from all over the globe, and beaches offering everything from world-class surfing to calm, clear coves. At the center of it all is **Playa Principal**, 700 meters (2,100 feet) of soft gray sand lined with tourist claptrap, all overlooking a supremely swimmable (but boat-filled) bay.

Just east is a world-famous surf destination, **Playa Zicatela**, stretching 4 kilometers (2.5 miles) past one of the world's best beach breaks, and scores of restaurants, hotels, and arguably the best bars on the coast.

West of Playa Principal, ✪ **Andador Escénico** has a stone walkway that hugs the wave-crashed cliffs beneath the lighthouse and Mirador Sueño Posible ("Possible Dream Overlook"), all the way to tiny **Playa Manzanillo**, with warm, transparent water and fine

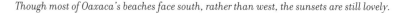

Though most of Oaxaca's beaches face south, rather than west, the sunsets are still lovely.

white sand. *Palapa*-topped restaurants sell seafood and rent snorkels. Continue west to **Puerto Angelito**, another clean, white crescent beach overlooking calm, shallow water perfect for a swim or snorkel; it has a convenient parking lot and family friendly restaurants.

Though the footpath ends here, you can continue west on regular roads to **Playa Carrizalillo**, a tiny, tranquil, white-sand beach bookended by steep, rocky formations. There are a handful of restaurants and a mellow point break perfect for beginning surfers; lessons can be arranged right here.

On the western edge of developed Puerto Escondido is long, wild **Playa Bacacho**, perfect for a walk, but not good for swimming; two beach clubs offer pools and food service.

Costa Mixteca

Some 36 kilometers (22 miles) west of Puerto Escondido, **Roca Blanca** is a long, broad beach stretching some 15 kilometers (9 miles) along the rough open sea, facing a small island also called "White Rock." Several *palapa*-style restaurants rent hammocks and cater to surfers, including ✪**Restaurante Roca Blanca**, where Señor José Galán can offer advice about diving and snorkeling, and point you toward basic cabañas for rent.

The road then turns inland, though there are still wonderful beaches accessible through the no-nonsense town of Pinotepa Nacional. On the *bocabarra*, or barrier sandbar, sepa-

Descending the stone staircase to Playa Carrizalillo, perhaps the most perfect beach of them all.

rating the Laguna de Corralero from the Pacific, **Playa Corralero** has restaurants, basic lodging, and a long beach facing the open Pacific on one side, and on the other the calm protected waters of the lagoon, with flocks of migratory birds October through January. Basic cabins are available and collective taxis make the hour-long 27-kilometer (17-mile) trip from Pinotepa Nacional.

Parks and Preserves

El Botazoo Ecoarchaeological Park

555-449-7006
www.conanp.gob.mx
Huatulco, east of Playa Bocalito
Hours: Sunrise to sunset

This 20,000-hectare (50,000-acre) park, close to the Playa Bocalito, is still being developed for tourism, and is most easily visited on a guided tour from Huatulco. FONATUR began developing the park in the late 1990s, but when it came across the 2,500-year-old Zapotec ruins of Punta Celeste, had to pause while archaeologists studied the area. Today, the smallish ruins can be visited, though they aren't really ready for tourists.

Most people visit the park, which stretches across several lagoons, on guided birding hikes (more than 200 species have been recorded), or as part of rappelling and rock-combing trips which take on the 50-meter (150-foot) rock walls with views to the sea.

Escobilla Natural Reserve

Playa Escobilla, 34 kilometers (21 miles) southwest of Pochutla
555-449-7006
www.conanp.gob.mx
Hours: Turtle tours usually run 9 PM to midnight
Admission: US$10

This white-sand beach facing the open sea is the sight of one of nature's most impressive pilgrimages, played out by some graceful olive ridley turtles at only a handful of beaches in the world. Called *arribadas, arribazones,* or arrivals, mother turtles arrive by the tens of thousands, piling themselves on the beaches day and night for almost a week. It only happens four or five times between June and September, according to lore, just after the full moon. **Escobilla Turtle Camp** works with several ecotourism agencies, offering one-night visits and voluntourism that lets you patrol the beaches at night, to protect eggs and turtles from poachers.

Huatulco National Park

555-449-7006
www.conanp.gob.mx
Huatulco, west of Bahía Santa Cruz
Hours: Sunrise to sunset
Admission: US$1 land; US$2 sea

Officially protected in 1988, this 11,885-hectare (29,368-acre) park stretches across the bays west of Huatulco. The water portion of the park, which extends about 3.5 kilometers

(2 miles) from shore, begins just west of Santa Cruz; the larger landed expanse, at Bahías Chachacual and Riscalillo, stretches north and east into the surrounding hills.

Most of the broad beaches, mangrove forests, and picturesque coves are accessible by boat only. San Agustín, at the western edge of the park, can be reached by car or taxi, a 45-minute trip (longer if the 18-kilometer/11-mile dirt road from Hwy. 200 is washed out) from Santa Cruz. Bahía Cacaluta can be reached by a rough dirt trail through the park, usually on guided mountain bike or *cuad* tours, though it could be hiked independently.

The park preserves the largest coastal area in Mexico, as well as the nation's most important reef systems. Sunscreen (which causes coral bleaching and death) is absolutely forbidden. The reefs, mangroves, and dry tropical forests protect a number of species, including 430 plants, 15 amphibians, 282 birds, 130 mammals, 73 reptiles, 121 fish, 12 types of coral, and 96 marine invertebrates; 130 species are protected by law.

There's no official entrance or office for the park; in general, pay your fees to the boat captain or tour operator guiding you into the park.

Laguna de Manialtepec
18 kilometers (11 miles) east of Puerto Escondido, well signed from Hwy. 200

The "Place of the Alligators" is easy to visit on a day trip. Any hotel will organize transport, or catch a bus to ✪**Isla del Gallo Restaurante** (954-107-5718; Laguna de Manialtepec, off Hwy. 200, kilometer 124.5; B, L, C, D; $$), right on the water, with good seafood, lots of hammocks, and boat tours for birders (tours leave Puerto Escondido at 6 AM), or to see the luminescent algae that glows when swept by the tides (tours leave at 8 PM). You can also rent kayaks, skis, and motorboats for waterskiing or wakeboarding. You could even stay overnight at the brand-new **Best Western Hotel La Laguna** (954-588-7280, 1-800-713-0204; www.bestwestern.com; Hwy. 200, kilometer 124; credit cards accepted; $$–$$$), large, clean, and modern with all the amenities you'd expect, including Sky TV, WiFi, a great pool, and nice restaurant, as well as authentic extras including pretty tile work and tours to local villages.

Laguna de Zapotengo
958-109-7827
www.zapotengo.net
Exit at kilometer 217 Hwy. 200, 3.5 kilometers (2 miles) to the beach

Just 40 minutes from Huatulco, and usually arranged as a day trip from either there or the Puerto Ángel beaches, this family-run ecotourism operation offers boat tours of this pristine lagoon, as well as a good restaurant and basic campsite. There's also a turtle incubation center, where you might get to see newborn babies waiting to head out to sea, and a small zoo with birds, crocodiles, *jaguarundis,* deer, and other local animals.

Lagunas de Chacahua National Park
555-449-7006
www.conanp.gob.mx (official); www.lagunasdechacahua.com (private)
Laguna de Chacahua, 50 kilometers (30 miles) west of Puerto Escondido

This stunning series of mangrove-lined lagoons was declared a national park in 1937, protecting 14,187 hectares (55 square miles) of wetlands, at least a dozen endemic species, and the nesting grounds of both olive ridley and leatherback turtles. There are also several beaches, perfect for swimming or surfing, with places to eat and stay at Cerro Hermoso and Chacahua.

Birding tours from Puerto Escondido arrive early in the morning, in search of roseate spoonbills, perhaps the most sought-after species, though several types of storks, herons, pelicans, and other waterfowl are plentiful.

It's easy for independent travelers to drive (or hire a private taxi) to either well-signed park entrance off Coastal Hwy. 200. It's more challenging by public transportation: From central Puerto Escondido, take a Transportes Unidos de Río Grande truck to the community of Río Grand, then get a taxi to Zapotalito, at the eastern edge of the park. From there, you can rent boats or take advantage of the several small communities which offer boat tours, inexpensive seafood with a view, and basic lodging.

Very basic accommodations include **Hotel-Restaurant Kassandra** (954-544-7198; $), offering three cement, fan-cooled rooms with mosquito-net covered windows and shared bath, and even simpler **Chacagua Cabanas** (no phone; $), which offers bamboo shacks built on top of the roof. Take a boat to **Cabañas Don Carlos** (954-540-6903; $) on the open sea. **Hotel y Restaurant Jenni** (954-559-3826; Playa Cerro Hermoso; $) has eight freshly painted rooms with cool tile floors, decent beds, big windows and fans, and private cold-water bathrooms. The restaurant downstairs has great, inexpensive food and hammocks.

Boats can be hired at El Zapotalito through **Paraíso Escondido Zapotalito Sociedad Cooperativo Tourist Services** (954-588-6721, 954-544-9326), with a stand on the beach, offers set rates for several tours.

Manglar Birdwatching (954-559-2431; www.manglarbirdwatch.blogspot.com; manglarbirdwatch@hotmail.com; Las Negras; Hwy. 200, kilometer 123) At the Flor del Pacifico Restaurant ($$–$$$), several tours, that include hotel pickup in Puerto Escondido, are offered, including sunrise and sunset birding tours (US$35, 7 AM and 4 PM respectively) and nighttime phosphorescence tours (8 PM, $25). **Lalo Ecotours** (954-588-9164; www.lalo-ecotours.com; Las Negras, Centro Turistico) offers the same tours for the same prices.

ATV Tours

Jungle Tour (958-0587-1381; jungletour1@hotmail.com; Huatulco; Boulevard Chahué L22 M1 Sector R, across from FONATUR) Organizes ATV jungle tours, and also rents a yacht equipped for sport fishing.

Tres Reyes ATV Tours and Rent-A-Car (954-114-0157; a_payan@live.com.mx; Puerto Escondido, Playa Zicatela; east end) At the end of the road, you'll find this spot renting ATVs, organizing beach tours, and renting a few cars, too.

Bicycling

✪**Rutas de Aventura** (954-582-0170; www.rutasdeaventura.com; Puerto Escondido, Playa Zicatela) This excellent adventure outfitter offers unique tours to area coffee fincas, archaeological sites, and small Colonial towns, as well as hiking, biking, kayaking, canoeing, and other activities.

Boat Tours

You can arrange boat tours on any beach in Oaxaca, just ask around.

HUATULCO

Boat tours visit the many bays and beaches of Huatulco, most of which are inaccessible by car. From small boats to catamarans and yachts, every type of water travel can be arranged here.

Atlantis Adventure (958-581-0012; www.atlantis-adventure.com; Plaza Chahué 15, Boulevard Benito Juárez) Groups of up to 12 can rent this fabulously outfitted yacht, *Presidente Juárez,* comfortably equipped with leather seats, satellite TV, a full bar, and everything you need for snorkeling and fishing. Several trips are offered, including sunset cruises, whale watching tours, and more.

Fortuna Huatulco (958-581-0491; fortunahuatulco@msn.com) Deep-sea fishing is the specialty aboard this pretty yacht.

Paseo a las Bahías (958-587-2080; boulevards Chahué and Juárez, near Hotel El Castillo) Tour the bays in 120- to 300-person catamarans, leaving at 10 AM daily with a stop for lunch and snorkeling in Bahía San Agustín.

Tequila Catamaran (958-587-2303; marinautica@hotmail.com) See the bays, perhaps in double, from this party cat with open bar.

Velero Luna Azul (958-587-2276; www.lunaazul.netfirms.com) Enjoy the bays, or just a sunset cruise, on this beautiful sailboat.

PUERTO ÁNGEL BEACHES

Any hotel or independent captain can arrange boat tours to swim with turtles and dolphins, or try **Coco Loco Surf Club** (see below) in San Agustinillo.

Puerto Escondido's Anandor Escénico, a scenic footpath following the sea, braves the mist and crashing waves beneath the old lighthouse.

✪**Montate a la Aventura Tours** (958-584-0549; www.laventanillamx.org; laventanilla mx@yahoo.com.mx; Playa Ventanilla) This indigenous, grass roots tour operator offers several tours around Playa Ventanilla, including boat trips through the lagoons and mangrove forests, visits to a crocodile farm, birding walks, night tours, and even turtle conservation tours where you can help collect eggs to protect them from (usually human) predators. They also rent very basic cabinas ($) right on the beach.

Nativo Tours (958-107-0389; Puerto Ángel, main road across from Villa Florencia) This outfit arranges fishing, snorkeling, and sightseeing tours.

PUERTO ESCONDIDO

The **Prestadores de Servicios Turisticos** (954-582-1426, 954-114-3528; Playa Principal) has a big booth right on the main dock, and representatives fanned out across the beach. They offer set prices on popular tours for boats of up to seven people: beach tours (US$30), turtle tours (US$50), and fishing tours (US$40).

Puerto Escondido is considered the best sport fishing spot on the Mexican Pacific, with boats heading out in search of sailfish, marlin, dorado (all shallow-water fish), *pez gallo, pesca de mero, barrilete sierra,* and in the cold deep water, yellowfin tuna. But you can also arrange sightseeing tours to beautiful beaches, snorkeling reefs, and areas where you can swim with sea turtles or dolphins.

Cooperativa Local de Pesca Deportiva (Local Sportfishing Cooperative; 954-821-1678; Avenida Marina Nacional) The best place to rent four-person *lanchas* with all fishing equipment.

Omar Sportfishing (954-559-4406; omarsportfishing-1@hotmail.com) An English-speaking guide offers sportfishing and dolphin tours.

Robert's Sportfishing (954-108-3547; fishingbobmarlin@hotmail.com) Private fishing and sightseeing trips.

Rodolfo's Sport-Fishing (954-111-2781; Playa Zicatela, Avenida del Morro) Fishing, snorkeling, and sight-seeing trips.

Coffee Tours

In the mid- to late-1800s, German families arrived in the high, forested mountains of the Sierra Madre del Sur and planted coffee. Several coffee fincas offer day trips, arranged in any beach town or directly with the finca. Tours take in the fields, in full flower through March and April, as well as the processing facilities, which differ from farm to farm. The most interesting time to visit the farms is in November or December, during harvest.

Several also offer lodging and hiking trails through the hills, a great escape from the steaming beaches any time of year.

Finca Cafetalera El Refugio (958-583-5021; hotelrefugio.xauki.com/English.html; robert @hotelrefugio.xauki.com; $) Close to Huatulco (the Web site has directions), this well-organized option offers an excellent deal on basic, modern rooms with private hot baths, right in the middle of the tropical forest. Amenities include a small pool and a big outdoor playground; guides offer coffee tours and longer hikes into the wilderness.

Roasting local organic coffee over a traditional wood-fired stove.

Finca La Gloria (958-587-0697; lagloria@hispavista.com; Santa María Petatengo) Often visited as part of a day trip to the waterfalls from Huatulco, this breezy finca offers tours, frequently led by owners Maria Isabela and Don Gustavo Scherremberg, who explain the coffee production process. Onsite waterfalls offer a refreshing finish.

Finca Las Nieves (954-582-0170; www.fincalasnieves.com.mx) This beautiful finca close to Puerto Escondido is one of the region's best developed, offering organic coffee tours, birding, and three-day, two-night stays (US$150) in its simple, beautifully appointed adobe cabins, including two meals daily. Everything, including transportation, can be arranged through Hotel Santa Fe in Puerto Escondido.

Finca Monte Carlo (951-514-7038; www.fincamontecarlo.com; ricaemax@hotmail.com; Santa María Xadani) Two hours from Huatulco, at more than 1,000 meters (3,000 feet), the plantation offers tours and hiking trails through the forest above it, as well as over-nights in the romantic, century-old mansion, which has a pool and room for up to 15 people. Make reservations two weeks in advance; meals and tours are included, transportation from Huatulco can be arranged.

Finca El Pacifico (958-584-6094; pacifico34@hotmail.com; kilometer 204 on Hwy. 175 Oaxaca-Puerto Ángel) One of the region's oldest organic coffee farms, making the transition in 1988 and becoming officially certified in 1997. Tours of the finca are arranged in Puerto Escondido, or personal tours can be scheduled in advance. In addition to fields and processing, tours of banana, *guanabana,* and *cacao* (chocolate) plantations are also offered. With advance arrangement, you can stay overnight in one of their guest rooms ($).

Rancho El Sagrado (951-169-6343; www.ranchoelsagrado.com; $) Signed from Hwy. 131, kilometer 195, about an hour north of Puerto Escondido, the ranch offers coffee tours, trout fishing (the restaurant will cook your catch for you), and basic cabañas. Geared to Mexican tourists from the big city who want to teach their kids about country living.

Diving and Snorkeling

The use of sunscreen is prohibited by law, as it is toxic to coral reefs. Your operator probably won't enforce the restriction, but please comply.

HUATULCO

Huatulco's 13 dive sites are the largest, most diverse, and most important reefs on Mexico's Pacific coast, and local operators finally have a decompression chamber at the local naval hospital. Most excursions visit Bahías Santa Cruz, with the Cave of the Vampire, La Entrega, and San Agustín, with a sunken boat some 30 meters (98 feet) deep, but ask about less-visited sites.

Centro de Buceo Sotavento (scubasota@hotmail.com) The trusted operator offering tours and lessons has three convenient locations: Crucecita (958-587-2166; Plaza Oaxaca, across from Zócalo), Bahía de Chahué (958-587-1389; Sector M, Manzana 7), and Tangolunda (958-581-0051; Edificio Las Conchas 12).

✪ **Hurricane Divers** (958-587-1107; www.hurricanedivers.com) This excellent dive shop has two offices, in Santa Cruz and Tangolunda. A variety of tours include boat, beach, and kayak trips, and several courses are offered. The Web site offers a wealth of knowledge about the region's underwater attractions.

PUERTO ÁNGEL

There are several good snorkel spots in and around Puerto Ángel, including Playa Panteón, close to the town center and accessible by boat, Playa Estacahuitea, and Playa La Boquilla. All have places to rent snorkel equipment.

Azul Profundo (958-584-3109; azul_profundomx@hotmail.com; Puerto Ángel, Playa del Panteón) Azul Profundo offers a variety of snorkel and dive tours, and can arrange diving lessons with advance notice. Ask around for "Chepe."

PUERTO ESCONDIDO

Aventura Submarina (954-582-2353, 954-544-4862; asubmarina@hotmail.com) The long-standing diving operation knows the best sites.

Deep Blue Diving School (954-582-0416; www.hotelines.com; Playa Zicatela) Hotel Ines arranges diving lessons and trips.

✪ **Puerto Dive Center** (954-102-7767; www.scuba-diving-mexico.com; Peréz Gazga, near Mayflower Hotel) This professional operation offers tours and classes; the Web site has great photos of the area's undersea wildlife.

Golf

Campo de Golf Tangolunda (958-587-0350, 877-847-8183 U.S. and Canada; Tangolunda; US$52 for nine holes, US$65 for 18 holes) The Oaxacan Riviera's only golf course is this challenging 18-hole green with shade trees, tennis courts (US$11), **Restaurant Hoyo 19**

(B, L; $$–$$$), and ocean views from the 13th hole. The staff can arrange lessons and equipment rentals.

Horseback Riding

Rancho Caballos del Mar (958-587-0366; Huatulco, Playa Bocalito) Several Huatulco operators offer horseback tours, most through Caballos del Mar, with routes for every age and riding level, along the beach or on more challenging mountain trails.

Sociedad Cooperativa Produccion y Servicios Lagarto Real (954-588-9161; Puerto Ángel; Playa Ventanilla) This new tour operator, which competes with more established Montate a la Aventura Tours (see Boat Tours) across the street, offers horseback rides into the surrounding mangrove forests and lagoons, as well as boat tours and guided hikes.

Other Tours

HUATULCO

Aqua y Terra (958-581-0012; aqua_terra@terra.com; Plaza Las Conchas L-6, Tangolunda) Organizes all sorts of tours—rafting, horseback rides, day trips—and rents cars.

Aventuras Huatulco (958-587-1695; www.avesdemexico.com; erastorojas@hotmail.com; Boulevard Guelaguetza lote D) Adventuras offers tours of the national parks, waterfalls, and Moro Rock, and can arrange biking, kayaking, and other activities.

Bird Watching Tour (958-589-1211; birdguidecornelio@yahoo.com.mx) Cornelio Ramos Gabriel offers birding hikes in and around Huatulco National Park.

Malibu Disco Bus (958-587-1429; johny_malibu@hotmail.com) Day trips take in the mezcal factories, bays, mud baths, and other intoxicating sites, then end up in the party zone of downtown La Crucecita. Very popular with young Mexican tourists.

✪ **MPG Wheelchair Tours** (958-100-4517; info@mpgtours.com; Andador Cacaluta 93 Fracc, Residencial San Agustín) Mario Pedroarena Guzmán offers tours for serious wheel-chair adventurers, including whitewater rafting, sea kayaking, snorkeling, fishing, even zip-line canopy tours. Tours are primarily in Spanish, but you're not going to let that stop you, right?

Plaza de Mezcal (958-581-0001; www.donwilo.com/mezcal; Bahía Chahué) Not the most authentic demonstration of mezcal production in all Oaxaca, but you do get a traditional buffet lunch and free shots of their different mezcals.

PUERTO ESCONDIDO

✪ **Agencia de Viajes Dimar** (www.viajesdimar.com; viajesdimar@hotmail.com) Established, full-service travel agency organizes everything from local tours to inter-national travel, car rentals to bus tickets. There are two locations, on Playa Principal (954-582-0734; Avenida Pérez-Gasga 905-B, next to Hotel Casa Blanca) and Playa Zicatela (954-582-2305; Calle de Morro, next to Bungalows Puerta del Sol).

Gina Machorro Espinosa (954-582-0276; ginainpuerto@yahoo.com) Tomzap.com calls her "The Information Goddess," and her multilingual guided tours of the city and surrounding sites get raves. Look for her at the Tourist Information Module by Playa Principal.

Skydive Cuautla (555-517-8529 Mexico DF, 555-103-3862 cell; www.skycuautla.com) The Acapulco-based skydiving operation now offers trips from Puerto Escondido with advance notice.

Waterfall Tours

The mountains inland from the popular beach communities offer a refreshing escape from the steamy coastal climate. While it's possible to visit these waterfalls on your own, the rural dirt access roads are poorly signed, by design. Tours are arranged by any hotel or tour operator.

Cascada La Reforma (Puerto Escondido, 15 kilometers (9 miles) north on Hwy. 131 to Oaxaca) A short drive north of Puerto Escondido, close to the village of San Pedro Mixtepec, flows the Río Chiquito. From the town, it's a 7-kilometer (4-mile) hike to the impressive 60-meter (180-foot)-tall cascades from a wall of rock, emptying into several swimming pools. Ask around town for recommended guide Albino Lara Gijón.

Llano Grande Cascadas (958-587-9629; Puerto Ángel Beaches) Your hotel or tour operator can arrange a trip to these scenic waterfalls, which come complete with a *mariposario* (butterfly garden), herb and medicinal plant gardens, and crafts.

✪ **Magic Waterfalls of Copalitilla** (958-587-2954, 958-587-1470; Huatulco, La Crucecita, Colorin 404, corner of Avenida Gardenia; daily trips 10 AM–6:30 PM) The company's popular day-trip, arranged all over Huatulco, takes you to the site of more than 30 waterfalls, the highest 20 meters (66 feet), as well as caves, tunnels and swimming holes. You'll also visit **Piedra de Moros**, a smooth and sacred 20-meter (66-foot)-tall rock dome (some tour outfits arrange rappelling and climbing here, as well), medicinal gardens, artist workshops, and coffee farms as part of the tour.

Surfing

The world-famous waves at Playa Zicatela are just the beginning; there are scores of breaks along the Oaxaca coastline. Most of them are "secret," at least no one's going to tell the guidebook writer, so befriend a local or hook up with a surf school offering tours. Huatulco's bays are primarily for swimming, though Playa Bocalito and El Mojon have okay breaks.

ISTHMUS OF TEHUANTEPEC

Salina Cruz Surf Tours (905-228-0507; www.wavehunters.com/salina/salina.asp; surfing mexico@yahoo.com; Salina Cruz) This untouristed port town is better known for its oil rigs than beach breaks, but bilingual local brothers César and David Ramirez organize surf tours, lessons, and fishing trips from **Hacienda Pescador** ($), their cute guesthouse 15 minutes from the waves. The Web site has descriptions of area breaks.

Barra de la Cruz (between Salina Cruz and Huatulco) A tiny sign from Hwy. 200, about 20 kilometers (13 miles) east Huatulco, points to this world-class beach break that used to be secret, but is becoming overcrowded thanks to guidebooks like this one. Basic cabinas are available right on the beach.

PUERTO ÁNGEL BEACHES

✪ **Coco Loco Surf Club** (www.cocolocosurfclub.com; balamjuguc@hotmail.com; Hotel Mexico Lindo y Que Rico, San Agustinillo) Offers surf lessons, tours, and trips, as well as surf and boogie board rentals, massages, tours to area coffee fincas, and other services.

PUERTO ESCONDIDO

Bazar Puerto Escondido (954-582-7065; jaramirez773@hotmail.com; Playa Zicatela) Private surf instruction.

Oasis Surf Factory and Language School (954-104-2330; www.rpmsurfer.com; Boulevard Juárez 2, Puerto Escondido) Surfing and Spanish classes, plus tours and multi-day surf trips around Puerto Escondido.

Ody Boards (954-540-1980; www.odyboards.com) Ody custom builds surfboards and will have them waiting for you when you arrive.

Pablo Surf Lessons (954-100-2338; pablopte@hotmail.com; Playa Carrizalillo) Look for the "surf lessons" sign on this tiny, beautiful beach, where more manageable waves than, say, the Mexican Pipeline, make this a much better spot for beginners.

Wakeboarding in Paradise (954-582-1703; www.wakeboardparadise.com; Laguna de Manialtepec) Learn to wakeboard in a pristine, protected lagoon 18 kilometers (11 miles) west of Puerto Escondido.

The "Mexican Pipeline" at Playa Zicatela always gets a thumb's up.

Wildlife Displays and Rescue Centers

✪ **Centro Mexicano de la Tortuga (Mexican Turtle Center)**

958-584-3376
www.centromexicanodelatortuga.org
Playa Mazunte
Hours: 10 AM–4:30 PM Wed.–Sat., 10 AM–2:30 PM Sun.
Admission: US$2

For centuries, locals have harvested sea turtles and their eggs from these important nesting grounds. In the 1980s, however, overhunting threatened to drive the turtles to extinction. In an effort to save them, the federal government banned the harvest entirely, destroying the regional economy. Founded in 1991, the center educates and employs the locals, advancing turtle research and tourism in the region. Here, sea, freshwater, and land turtles frolic in outdoor tanks, hatcheries, and a large aquarium. Tours are offered in English and Spanish, explaining the center's work and its prized inhabitants. Staff can also arrange night tours to visit nesting beaches between May and December: **Playa Escobilla**, where thousands of olive ridley turtles arrive several times annually, and **Playa Mermejita**, where you may see the very endangered leatherback turtle, a world-roving species and the world's largest reptile.

Whitewater Rafting

Río Copalito, close to Huatulco, offers Class II-V whitewater rafting and kayaking. Children as young as three are generally accepted on the Class II rides, with age minimums increasing with difficulty. You need at least four people to fill a raft (solo travelers can ask different operators about space), with costs running about US$30–70 per person, depending on difficulty, including transportation and lunch. Most companies offer the option of going in kayaks.

✪ **Aventura Mundo** (958-581-0371; Tangolunda, Juárez 23) This professional outfit with English-, French-, and Spanish-speaking guides offers rafting and kayaking trips.

Eco Tours (958-105-1331; Plaza Las Conchas, Tangolunda) Rafting and kayak tours are available here.

Explora México (958-587-2058; exploramex@prodigy.net.mx) Several rafting and hiking trips are on offer, as well as custom multi-day adventure tours.

Rancho Tangolunda (958-587-2126; www.ranchotangolunda.com; Tangolunda, Boulevard Juárez 5; Huatulco) The company offers rafting and kayaking trips, as well as hiking, rappelling, and *tirolesa* (zip-line canopy) tours.

PUERTO ÁNGEL BEACHES
Rafa Kayak (958-587-9175; rafakayak@hotmail.com; Playa Mazunte, Bugambilia) The owner of Empenada Restaurant (open 4 PM daily) also organizes kayak and rafting trips on area rivers.

Spas and Gyms

HUATULCO
Clínica de Masaje (958-583-4257; La Crucecita, Colorín 303) Therapeutic massage, acupuncture, and traditional herbal medicine.

Eco Spa (958-581-0025; www.ecoyspa.com; Tangolunda, commercial center) Tiny spa offers wraps, massages, and more.

Huatulco Fitness (958-587-2633; Chahué, Plaza Camelinas, Boulevard Chahué 164) This huge, modern gym caters to travelers with day and week memberships.

Temazcal de Santa Cruz (958-587-2179; Plaza Las Conchas, Tangolunda) The package includes transport from your hotel, massage, and traditional *temazcal* sauna, all for US$30 per person.

Women of La Bocana Cooperative Zapotec Mud Bath (Huatulco, near mouth of Copalita River; US$5) Local Zapotec women offer access to healing mud springs.

Xquenda (958-583-4448; www.huatulcospa.com; Chahué) This beautiful spa with exquisitely muralled *temazcal* also offers massages, facials, and other services.

PUERTO ÁNGEL BEACHES

Centro Nijo (958-585-7263; www.centronijo.com; near Playa Ventanillas) Beautiful holistic healing center offers classes and treatments using traditional and Chinese medicine; basic accommodation is also available.

PUERTO ESCONDIDO

Healing Hands Massage (954-107-1056; Playa Zicatela, Bajada las Brisas) A spa hidden inside a hippy haven hostel ($).

Lotus Spa (954-582-1691; lotus-spa@hotmail.com; Bacocho) Make an appointment for facials, massages, permanent makeup, and Pilates.

Spa Prehispánico (954-582-0508; www.aldeadelbazar.com.mx; Playa Bacocho, Juárez 7) This lovely spa, with a *temazcal,* massages, facials, and other treatments is within the somewhat surreal Moorish wonderland that is **Hotel Aldea del Bazar** (credit cards accepted; $$), offering large, unremarkable rooms with all the amenities. The extravagant pool area and Mandil Restaurant will have you humming the soundtrack from Disney's *Aladdin.* Seriously.

Temazcalli Puerto Escondido (954-582-1023; www.temazcalli.com; Avenida Infraganti y Calle Temazcalli, Lázaro Cárdenas) Take a Zapotec-style steam bath, perhaps in combination with one of several massages.

Yoga

La Loma Linda (no phone; www.lalomalinda.com; info@lalomalinda.com; Playa Zipolite; $$) This gorgeous retreat offers six spacious bungalows, some large enough for families and with full kitchen access, all overlooking the beach. Offers group and individual classes specializing in the Feldenkrais method, for both guests and visitors, as well as retreats.

Poorna Rishi Yoga (954-103-2622; e.libelula33@gmail.com; Puerto Ángel, Casa Penelope) Group and individual classes.

Solstice Yoga and Vacations (no phone; www.solstice-mexico.com; Playa Zipolite; $–$$) The neat spot in Zipolite centro has cute but basic stone bungalows and dorms, and offers several classes and workshops.

Yoga Huatulco (958-100-7339; Huatulco, La Crucecita, Palo Verde 406) Group classes (US$10 a day, $48 a month), private lessons, plus workshops and retreats.

SHOPPING

Though street dealers often offer wonderful goods at fabulous prices, please refrain from buying jewelry made with coral or tortoise shell, which are illegal.

ISTHMUS OF TEHUANTEPEC

Though most people come to the Isthmus in search of the famously floral embroidered women's costumes, the satin and velvet *trajes* and *huipiles* that can be had for a fraction of what's charged in Oaxaca City, there are other handicrafts worth seeking out: excellent leather goods, in particular *huaraches* (sandals), belts, purses, and other items, with distinctive stamps and decorations; pottery, both plain and utilitarian or colorful and figurative; *cestería,* or basketry; colorful hammocks, and *orfebrería;* or the delicate gold filigree jewelry prized all over the country.

Tehuantepec Market (22 de Marzo and Plaza Central) sprawls from the official edifice across the plaza and railroad tracks, with a wide selection of medicinal plants, cheap eats, and other typical fare. Serious shoppers, however, head to **Juchitán Market** (16 de Septiembre and Jardín Central), the cultural capital of the Tehuantepec Isthmus, when Sunday brings in vendors from all over the state. Hidden amid the usual *comedors* and food stalls, you may find turtle and iguana, both meat and eggs, all of which are illegal.

HUATULCO

Huatulco offers excellent shopping, though prices may be higher for handicrafts. Dozens of shops, selling everything from ticky-tacky souvenirs to fine art, are concentrated in La Crucecita, though several upscale stores can be found in Santa Cruz. **Plaza El Madero** (La Crucecita, Guamuchil, entrance), a smallish mall, has a few clothing stores and surf shops, an Internet café, fast food, and a four-screen cinema.

El Buen Mezcal (958-587-1249; La Crucecita, Bugambilia 102) Taste-test several mezcals, then try chocolates, moles, and other Oaxacan specialties.

La Casa de Tobaco (Plaza Las Conchas, Bahía Tangolunda) A shop to meet most of your smoking needs, catering to deprived U.S. citizens with a wide variety of Cuban cigars.

Coconuts (958-587-0279; Huatulco, corner of Gardenia and Flamboyan) In the center of La Crucecita, downtown Huatulco, this small shop sells scores of magazine titles, many in English and other languages.

Foto Conejo (958-587-0054; Avenida Guamuchil 208-A) The store sells film and all sorts of cameras, and also burns CDs.

María Bonita Fine Jewelry (958-587-1400; www.mariabonitajewelry.com.mx; Santa Cruz, 3 Darsena) This fine designer jewelry shop offers free transport from your hotel.

Manteleria Escobar (958-587-0532; La Crucecita, Cocotillo 217) Watch as high-quality hammocks, bedspreads, and curtains are loom-woven, and perhaps take home a souvenir.

La Probadita (958-587-1641; www.laprobadita.com.mx; La Crucecita, Bugambilia 501, corner of Chacah) If this is just a beach vacation, and you won't make it to Oaxaca City (or don't want to waste time shopping while there) stop in for a taste *(probadita)* of the state's fine moles, chocolates, mezcals, and even *chapulines* (grasshoppers).

Santa Cruz Jewelry (958-587-1273; Santa Cruz, Lote 8 and 9) More fine jewelry.

Puerto Ángel Beaches

Though you can find basic necessities at small stores on any of the Puerto Ángel Beaches, note that **San Pedro Pochutla,** with grocery stores, ATMs, and a huge Monday market, is the place to stock up.

Mazunte Natural Cosmetics (958-587-4860; Mazunte) Body Shop founder Anita Roddick, hoping to create new business opportunities for former turtle harvesters, asked her chemist to concoct beauty products using only local and mostly organic ingredients. Since 1993, this co-op has appealingly packaged products that are quite nice, but the factory, usually visited by tour groups, seemed abandoned when I dropped by; I got my products at the Hotel Santa Fe gift shop in Puerto Escondido.

Rancho de las Hamacas (No phone; kilometer 7.4 Carretera Puerto Ángel, between Zipolite and San Agustinillo) Oaxaca's most relaxing shopping experience offers some of the state's most beautiful hammocks, for sale or just to try out overlooking their private, clothing-optional beach. Enjoy a drink, meal, or even an overnight at one of their very basic cabinas ($).

Puerto Escondido

Scores of stores selling just about everything imaginable can be found along Avenida Pérez Gazga, on Playa Principal in the pedestrian-only **Zona Adoquinada**, often packed with street dealers selling wonderful art, clothes, handicrafts, and knick-knacks. More stores line Calle del Morro, running parallel to Playa Zicatela. **Mercado Municipal Benito Juárez** (corner of 3a Poniente and 9a Norte) has the best deals on almost everything.

Amazonia do Brasil (954-582-2023; Playa Zicatela; Calle del Morro) Brazilian bikinis and fashions.

Arte Textil (954-109-3738; Avenida Pérez Gazga 205) Watch as artisans weave fine textiles, then buy some of the region's best right here.

Casa de Bambole (954-582-1331; Pérez Gazga 707) This neat store has colorful fabrics and handicrafts, most from the indigenous areas of neighboring Chiapas State.

Plateria Ixtlán (954-582-1672; Playa Zicatela, Pacific Surf Building) The best selection of silver jewelry, from workshops all over the country.

Mixtec Coast

Mixtec artisans are best known for outstanding, naturally dyed fabrics. In Pinotepa Nacional, stop by the **Women's Collective** (corner of Calle 17 Sur and Venustiano Carranza), where you can watch the women weave, then purchase their work.

Santiago Pinotepa Nacional's enormous market is busiest on Wednesday and Sunday, when you can find colorful cedar masks from **Huazolotitlán** (16 kilometers/10 miles east of Pinotepa), worn during local fiestas, as well as fine leatherwork. Also look for beaded *chiquira* blouses from **Santiago Yaitepec**; distinctively beribboned *huipiles* from **San Andres Huaxpaltepec**; and the white-on-white embroidered *huipiles* and wrap skirts from **Santiago Jamiltepec,** among many other regional crafts. Or, better yet, use Pinotepa as a base to visit area handicraft villages.

EVENTS

January

Festival of San Sebastian (Pinotepa Don Luis, 28 kilometers (17 miles) north of Pinotepa Nacional) Traditional Mixtec celebration for the town's patron saint occurs on January 20; other big bashes are held during Carnaval and Semana Santa.

February

Celebrate democracy and the Anniversary of the Constitution (Pochutla) February 5 with flag waving, soccer competitions, rodeos and more.

La Candelaria (San Pedro Tututepec) The huge festival for the Virgin of the Candlemas, housed in a beautiful 18th-century church, features live music, sporting events, parades and more.

Carnaval (Puerto Escondido) Festivities begin with the "Burning of Negative Thoughts" and selection of the King and Queen, then devolve into parties, parades, night-time boat parades, eating, drinking and other merrymaking.

March

Guendalizaa (Tehuantepec) On March 22, this indigenous festival celebrates the 1660 Rebellion of Tehuantepec with different indigenous dances.

Festival of Jesus the Nazarene (San Andres Huaxpaltepec) This tiny Mixtec pueblo goes all-out with a massive three-day party and market, beginning four weeks before Good Friday.

Semana Santa (Everywhere) The week before Easter, "Holy Week" brings most of Mexico to the beaches; make reservations well in advance, and expect to pay high-season prices. To see more traditional celebrations, check out Pinotepa Nacional, with a public Passion Play, cock fights, folkloric dance, and other festivities.

May

Día de la Cruz (Santa Cruz) May 3 is celebrated across Latin America, usually with processions to hilltop crosses presiding over most towns. In Santa Cruz, it's an especially big party.

Vela Istmeña (Tehuantepec) The second week in May brings people from all over the Isthmus for 10 days of dancing, parties, food, parades, and Masses.

Vela Guiexoba (Tehuantepec) This popular fiesta with food, folkloric dance, parades, floats, and fireworks takes place the last two weeks in May, culminating with the **Vela Sanduga** (last Saturday in May), a huge ball.

Fiesta San Vicente Ferrer (Juchitán) Huge traditional festival.

Salina Cruz Fishing Tournament (Salina Cruz; 971-720-2062) Annual fishing tournament each May.

June

Cacahuatepec Civic Fiestas (www.cacahuatepec.gob.mx; Cacahuatepec, Hwy. 125 north of Pinotepa Nacional) The small indigenous town, centered on a Spanish Colonial church and ancient stone ruins, honors Saint John the Baptist with a week of traditional food and dancing, soccer tournaments, fireworks and more, culminating on June 24. Fiestas are also held here during Semana Santa and the Day of the Dead.

August

Santa María Huazolotitlán Civic Fiestas (East of Pinotepa Nacional) The picturesque farming town and seat of Mixtec culture offers outstanding traditional fiestas in mid-August, when you can see the region's colorful dances, including "The Tiger," "The Turtle" and "Dance of the Chareos" (the last more Catholic than indigenous).

September

Collantes Civic Fiestas (Collantes, 25 kilometers/16 miles southeast of Pinotepa) African Oaxacan and Mixtec cultures mix at these colorful civic fiestas traditionally held on September 27. The "Dance of the Diablo" is Collantes's signature folkloric dance, but troupes come from all over the Mixtec Coast to perform their own masked numbers.

Day of the Angel (Puerto Ángel) From September 30 to October 2, the church's angel statue is paraded around the town and bay, accompanied by live music, dances, street food, Masses, and parties.

October

Day of the Dead (Everywhere) All the beach communities and *panteones* (cemeteries) have their own Day of the Dead traditions and events. Juchitán puts an indigenous spin on Xhandú (as the Zapotecs call it) with amazing altars and parades.

Huatulco Film and Food Festival (Huatulco; 958-981-0176; www.filmfoodfestival.com) Concurrent with Day of the Dead, cinema, cuisine, and fun.

Octoberfest (Huatulco; www.oktoberfesthuatulco.com) Beer and German culture. Really.

San Pedro Amusgos Civic Fiestas (San Pedro Amusgos) This indigenous town celebrates the Virgen de la Rosario with a famous market, traditional dances, sporting events, and more the first Sunday in October.

November

PMX International Surf Tournament (Playa Zicatela) A totally tubular way to spend the second week in November.

Festival Costeño de la Danza (Puerto Escondido) Festival of dance, with the Mixteca well represented.

Fiestas de Noviembre (Puerto Escondido) Puerto Escondido's biggest party is the last week of November, with folkloric dancing exhibitions, surfing, the International Sailfishing Tournament (www.pescandopuertoescondido.com), live music, donkey polo, street food, rides, parades, art exhibits, and more.

Mazunte Jazz Festival (Playa Mazunte) Musicians from all over Mexico and the world perform.

Vela Muxe (Juchitán) This traditional Zapotec drag festival is more properly known as *La Vela de las Auténticas Intrépidas Buscadoras de Peligro* (the Festival of the Authentic, Intrepid Danger Seekers), when Muxes, Tehuana gays and transvestites, break out the ball gowns and peacock feathers for some fierce and fabulous fun. Curious? Download *The Muxes of Juchitán*, part of filmmaker Yorgos Avgeropoulos's Exandas Documentary Series.

December

Fiesta de la Virgen de Juquila (Juquila) December 8 marks one of Oaxaca's biggest religious festivals. Pilgrims pay their respects to the miraculous, 30-centimeter (12-inch)-tall statue of Santa Catarina, brought here in 1633 after surviving a fire in nearby Amialtepec. Fiestas are fun, with plenty of Masses and mezcal. Some of the faithful prefer to avoid the whole circus and make their requests on less crowded occasions.

Oaxaca Fiesta del Mar (Salina Cruz) Spend the week between Christmas and New Year's enjoying live music, boat parades, and other activities in this blue-collar seaside town.

6

Northern Oaxaca

*Deserts, Cloud Forests, and
Lush Tropical River Valleys*

The big skies, undeveloped vistas, and vast cultural and ecological wealth of the great
Oaxacan North offer endless opportunities for ecotourism, adventure, and exploration. It
is most famously home to Oaxaca's finest collection of massive Dominican churches, but
there are so many other reason to make this journey.

Dozens of quaint Colonial towns, with their own less-famed 16th century churches,
are often quite close to partially excavated Mixtec ruins; some, like Cerro de las Minas in
Huajuapan, are an easy stroll from downtown. Wonderful community museums offer cultural excuse to explore this scenic region well away from the beaten path. Colorful *tanguis*,
traditional markets, are full of crafts that, yes, you could probably find in Oaxaca City, but
here you're buying direct from the source.

And best of all, nature lovers, this region boasts ecological riches unparalleled in the
nation. Within a few hours' drive (or convenient bus ride) you can go from cactus-studded
deserts rent asunder with sandstone canyons, to misty cloud forests marbled with cool
waterfalls; chilly pine-covered mountains with granite-strewn peaks, to lush tropical lowlands where lake islands arise. And all these exquisite regions are relatively easy to access,
thanks to an innovative system of grass roots ecotourism projects, cabins and activities
operated by indigenous pueblos scattered through paradise.

I've divided this enormous region into three major areas, all of which can be explored
in a rental car, or with time and persistence, public transport.

Mixteca

This is the land of the Mixtec, a high-altitude escape into an ancient indigenous stronghold. Most famously, it is home to the Dominican Route, boasting some of the hemisphere's finest 16th-century stone churches. But if you do the entire Mixtec loop, you'll
see so much more.

Hwy. 190 heads north into the Mixteca Alta (High Mixteca, referring to the altitude)
where towns such as Noxchitlán, Tlaxiaco, and several smaller villages offer access to
partially excavated Mixtec ruins and several fascinating community museums. Do the
route counterclockwise, and you'll pass through the Dominican heartland, including
Tamazulapam, before arriving at the region's most important city, bustling Huajuapan.

On a mountaintop just above Huahuapan de León, the original city's pyramids and plazas remains partially unexcavated.

Head south for lakeside lodging, or the incredible Canyon of Tonalá, then continue through the highlands where Triqui Indians, in their signature red wool *huipiles,* make their way through the lush high-altitude forest.

Wend back around, past Juxtlahuaca's enchantments and several other tiny towns whose community museums beckon you well off the paved road, to Tlaxiaco, famed for its market and fine church. Make your last stop Valle de Apoala, "Cradle of the Mixtec," one of the most beautiful places this writer has ever seen.

La Cañada and the Papaloapan

It's a fierce, dry drive through the desert's burned hues, past the no-nonsense agribusiness center of San Juan Bautista Juicatlán, framed in dramatic red cliffs, to the turnoff to La Cañada. Make a right at Teotitlán del Camino (if you get to Puebla State, you've gone too far) and then head up into the misty, bromeliad-strewn wilderness of La Cañada's cloud forest. Remarkably, this rare and magical region is little developed for tourism; save for pilgrims in search of María Sabina's spirit and a single ecotourism project, this is unexplored wilderness in the mysterious Mazatec heartland.

You can continue east through Huautla, when the road begins to drop into the Papaloapan River Valley. A handful of ecotourism cabins offer access to this humid rainforest wonderland centered on quaint Jalapa de Díaz, framed with huge tsunami-shaped mountains foaming green at the crest. The region is anchored by a huge reservoir, above which rise the churches of Ixcatlán and Isla Soyaltepec, both with wonderful lodging options awaiting your arrival; and the Río Papaloapan, the River of Butterflies, upon whose banks Tuxtepec thrives.

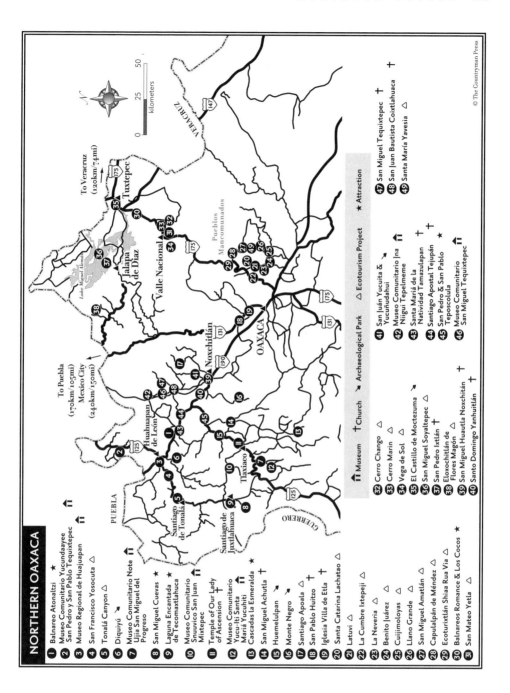

© The Countryman Press

NORTHERN OAXACA

1 Balnareo Atonaltzi ★
2 Museo Comunitario Yucundaayee San Pedro y San Pablo Tequixtepec
3 Museo Regional de Huajuapan
4 San Francisco Yosocuta △
5 Tonalá Canyon △
6 Diquiyú 🏹
7 Museo Comunitario Note 🏛 Ujia San Miguel del Progreso
8 San Miguel Cuevas ★
9 Laguna Encantada de Tecomaxtlahuca
10 Museo Comunitario Snuuvico San Juan Mixtepec
11 Temple of Our Lady of Ascension †
12 Museo Comunitario Yucu-Iti Santa Mariá Yucuhiti 🏛
13 Cascadas La Esmeralda ★
14 San Miguel Achutla †
15 Huemelulpan 🏹
16 Monte Negro 🏹
17 Santiago Apoala △
18 San Pablo Huitzo †
19 Iglesia Villa de Etla
20 Santa Catarina Lachatao △
21 Latuvi △
22 La Cumbre Ixtepeji △
23 La Neveria △
24 Benito Juárez △
25 Cuijimoloyas △
26 Llano Grande △
27 San Miguel Amatlán △
28 Capulalpán de Méndez △
29 Ecoturistán Shiaa Via Via △
30 Balnareos Romance & Los Cocos ★
31 San Mateo Yetla △

🏛 Museum † Church △ Archaeological Park 🏹 Archaeological Park ★ Attraction

32 Cerro Chango △
33 Cerro Marin △
34 Vega de Sol △
35 El Castillo de Moctezuma 🏹
36 San Miguel Soyaltepec †
37 San Pedro Ixtlán △
38 Eloxochitlán de Flores Magón †
39 San Miguel Huautla Noxchitán †
40 Santo Domingo Yanhuitlán †

41 San Juán Yucuita & Yucuñudahui 🏹
42 Museo Comunitario Ĵna Niigui Tepelmeme 🏛
43 Santa Mariá de la Natividad Tamazulapan †
44 Santiago Apostal Tejupán †
45 San Pedro & San Pablo Teposcolula ★
46 Museo Comunitario San Miguel Tequixtepec 🏛

47 San Miguel Tequixtepec †
48 San Juan Bautista Coixtlahuaca △
49 Santa María Yavesia △

This fascinating city, at the heart of the lush and fertile region, makes a very comfortable base for further exploration. Or head south on Hwy. 175, past Valle Nacional and another collection of ecotourism projects (these surrounding brilliant blue *Balnearios,* or artesian swimming holes) and back into the mountains.

SIERRA JUÁREZ

Only an hour or two from Oaxaca City, depending on where you're headed, these pine- and oak-carpeted dry mountains are the easiest to access, thanks to the Pueblos Mancomunados (see sidebar, later) inviting even the most timid ecotourist to partake of Oaxaca's natural wonders. But there are other options for enjoying this refreshing world, where Benito Juárez once tended sheep for the weavers of Teotitlán del Valle, far below.

SAFETY

While this region is very safe for travelers (but, as always, stay alert and don't take chances), be prepared for extreme variations in temperature and altitude. Bring warm clothes to the mountains, and allow yourself to acclimate for a few days in Oaxaca City if you're coming from sea level, particularly if you plan to do any strenuous hiking in the Pueblos Mancomunados.

Online Resources

Most of Northern Oaxaca's Web sites are in Spanish only; others also use various indigenous languages.

Huajuapan Portal (www.portalhuajuapan.com) The Mixteca's biggest town has a sprawling Web site for locals, as well as videos, photos, and famous Mixtec myths and legends.

Juxtlahuca.net (www.juxtlahuaca.net) Currently almost a placeholder; hopefully more information about this little-visited town will be posted soon.

Portal Tlaxiaco (www.tlaxiacoenlinea.com.mx) Information about Tlaxiaco and the surrounding area.

San Andrés Chicahuaxtla Official Page (www.san-andres-chicahuaxtla.8m.com) The de facto Triqui capital in the very High Mixteca doesn't have much on its Web site, yet.

Tamazulapam del Progreso (www.tamazulapan.org) Spanish-language site about this little-visited Mixtec town describes eco-adventures and has a news feed.

Tlaxiaco en Linea (www.tlaxiaco.com) Articles, forum, links, and lots of photos.

Triquis en Linea (www.triquis.org) This most reclusive of indigenous groups, speaking their own separate branch of Mixtec and best known for the ladies' beautiful, warm, floor-length red *huipil*, has this sort of messy but fun Web site.

Tuxtepec en Linea (www.tuxtepecenlinea.com) Community resource with some information for tourists.

Getting Around

There are no major airports in Northern Oaxaca.

Buses

Major cities are served by **ADO** (Autobuses del Oriente; 1-800-702-8000 Mexico, 1-800-950-0287 United States; 951-515-1248 Oaxaca City; www.ado.com.mx); **OCC** (Ómnibus Crístobal Colón; 951-515-1214; www.occbus.com.mx); **Sur**; and other first-class buses; check **Ticket Bus** (1-800-702-8000; www.ticketbus.com.mx) to see what schedules work for you. **AU**(Autobuses Unidos; superbussesmex.galeon.com/amigos1389306.html) runs between Oaxaca City and Tuxtepec.

Many smaller bus companies run from Oaxaca City directly to different destinations throughout Northern Oaxaca; check the Transportation chapter for details. Here are other options. This is *not* a comprehensive list; ask at your hotel about what else is available if these don't work for you.

Apoala Valley

A private shuttle runs from Apoala to Noxchitlán on Wednesday, Saturday, and Sunday at 8 AM, returning from the Noxchitlán market at 5 PM.

Huajuapan

Most second-class buses and van lines leave from Calle Nuyoo, across the highway from the first-class ADO station. *Colectivo* taxis leave from around the central plaza.

Costa de Oro (953-503-4309; Nuyoo 35) The nationwide bus line runs to Mexico City, Tijuana, Tapachula (the Guatemalan border), and other destinations, as well as Oaxaca destinations including Juxtlahuaca, Pinotepa Nacional, Puerto Escondido, and Huatulco.

Tequixtepec Colectivos (Mercado Zaragoza) Take a collective taxi to visit Tequixtepec's excellent community museum.

Tonalá Colectivos (5 de Febrero, in front of Aurora Bodega supermarket) Throughout the day, shuttles run from Huajuapan to Tonalá Centro (US$2.50); from there you can get cabs to the canyon entrance.

Transportadora Turista de Oaxaca (953-533-0023; Nuyoo 40) The company runs vans at least hourly to Oaxaca City (US$7).

Turisticos Huajuapan (953-532-0534; Calle Trujano) Vans run hourly to Oaxaca City (US$7) and shuttles head for Juxtlahuaca every 40 minutes (US$3), and can drop you off in Noxchitlán or Coixtlahuaca.

Yosocuta Colectivos (Calle Allende corner of Guerrero) It's only US$1 to go to the lake!

Tlaxiaco and Teposcolula

CUMSA Camionetas de Lujo (J.P. García 209, Centro Oaxaca) Runs several times daily to the Mixteca town of Teposcolula (20 de Noviembre 15).

Autotransportes Tlaxiaco (Trujano 505, Oaxaca Centro) Runs buses between Oaxaca City and Tlaxiaco (Independencia 19).

Transportadora Mixteca Baja (Hidalgo 208, Oaxaca Centro) Runs buses from Oaxaca City to Tlaxiaco (corner of Independencia and Hidalgo).

TUXTEPEC

Al Istmo (951-516-1674) Runs between Tuxtepec and Oaxaca City daily.

Transportes Tuxtepec runs minivans between Tuxtepec and Valle Nacional every 10 minutes. Covered trucks run from Valle Nacional to Yetla every few minutes.

Sociedad Cooperativa Benito Juárez (951-516-5768) Runs between Oaxaca City and Tuxtepec seven times daily, stopping in Guelatao, Ixtlán, and Valle Nacional.

Rental Car

Northern Oaxaca is an excellent region to explore in a rental car, and even unpaved roads are well maintained for regular two-wheel-drive cars. Be aware that distances, particularly on secondary roads (even paved) are misleading. Because of rough roads, speed bumps, and communities where you are required to slow to a crawl when passing through, it can easily take an hour to go 40 kilometers (25 miles). While seasoned budget travelers will almost always be able to find acceptable lodging, hotels with hot water and cable television are fewer and farther between. If you have your heart set on a certain type of accommodation, leave a little earlier than you think is necessary.

Boat

Boat trips can be arranged on the Temazcal Reservoir (sometimes called Miguel Alemán, after the dam) from almost anywhere along its banks, most conveniently in San Pedro

Friendly guides at Isla Soyaltepec meet your boat, and will even carry your luggage up to the Mazatec town's new ecotourism cabins. That reservoir view is well worth the climb.

Ixcatlán. There, try **Manuel Segura** (287-871-3108; blue house near Hotel Villa del Agua). Motorboats (*tzutzus* in Mazatec) seating eight or so generally cost US$10–20 per hour, depending on the length of the trip, about $35 to take you to Isla Soyaltepec and pick you up another day.

Lodging

Though Northern Oaxaca has much to offer, few international tourists, save the more independent and adventurous backpacker types, have struck out on a quest to discover its riches. Thus, lodging options are rather limited. The major cities—Huajuapan, Tlaxiaco, and Tuxtepec—all offer a small selection of excellent hotels, with comforts that should satisfy all but the most delicate luxury lovers.

Elsewhere, however, rooms are for the most part basic. Almost every town of any size offers two- and three-star lodging, clean, comfortable, with cable television, fine views, and hot private showers. They will be perfectly acceptable to most seasoned travelers, but don't expect turndown service. That's probably not why you've chosen to travel north, however; you're here to experience a world few people even realize exists.

Which brings us to Northern Oaxaca's most exquisite offerings, rather unpoetically called "ecotourism projects" and scattered through the chill mountains and lush river valleys. Created with a community effort by isolated indigenous pueblos eager to share the fantastic beauty they've inherited, these usually offer quite similar amenities. Fairly basic cabañas that sleep up to five people run about US$30, even if it's just you. Some offer dorm beds that are a better deal for solo folks, US$10–15 for the night. There's usually hot water, but no air conditioning or television.

They do include, however, amenities such as the world's deepest cave, ravishingly blue artesian springs, achingly beautiful limestone canyons, crystalline waterfalls pouring through refreshing pine forests, and the usual assortment of guided hikes, horseback rides, and mountainbike tours. As with all indigenous ecotourism projects, it's best to make reservations or show up early in the day, to give everyone time to prepare your room.

Lodging Price Code

Cost of lodging is based on an average per-room, double-occupancy during peak season (November through mid-January), not including the mandatory 18 percent tax, which may be waived for cash payment. Rates are often reduced during low season (June and August through September), and can double during the Christmas–New Year's holidays, Guelaguetza (all of July), Día de los Muertos (October 31–November 2), and Semana Santa (the week before Easter), when the best hotels are booked weeks and months out. Costs are calculated at 10 pesos to the U.S. dollar.

Inexpensive	Up to US$50
Moderate	US$50 to US$100
Expensive	US$100 to US$150
Very Expensive	More than US$150

Hotels

Most are listed under "Other Hotels," later in this section.

MIXTECA

✪ Hotel García Peral

Owner: Carlota Manzanarez
953-532-0777
www.hotelgarciaperal.com
hotel_garciaperal@hotmail.com
Huajuapan de León, H Colegio Militar 1, Centro
Price: Moderate
Credit Cards: Yes
Handicapped Access: None

Perhaps the nicest hotel in the Mixteca, the García Peral is a classy spot right on the shady Zócalo of Huajuapan de León. With elegant Spanish Colonial style, rooms rise to three stories above a vine-covered central courtyard paved with two sparkling blue pools.

Rooms aren't extravagant, but are lovely, showcasing the intricate inlaid wood furnishings typical of the region. Original art, chosen to match the freshly painted, colorful rooms, also adds character. Suites, which only cost about US$10 more, include an entirely separate bedroom, refrigerator, and a terrace overlooking the street scene and cathedral. All the rooms include cable TV, modern hot-water bathrooms, security boxes, and other amenities. Some have air conditioning.

The excellent ✪ **restaurant** (953-532-1532; B, C, L, D; credit cards accepted; $$–$$$), right on the plaza, is a local favorite and roundly respected for its outstanding Mixtec-style moles (served in ceramic tripod bowls, like those uncovered around here by archaeologists), and serves what are considered the best steaks in town.

Hotel del Portal

Owner: María Magdalena Justina Hernandez Martínez
953-552-0154

www.hotelestlaxiaco.com
Tlaxiaco, Constitución 2, Centro
Price: Moderate
Credit Cards: Yes
Handicapped Access: None

This unique hotel is Tlaxiaco's best, surrounding an outstanding Spanish Colonial courtyard of colorful columns, trickling fountains, and graceful archways, where the onsite restaurant, El Patio (B, L, C, D; $$) serves a great *menú* and a well-regarded Sunday buffet.

Rooms are just lovely, with lots of hand-carved headboards and antique furnishings collected over the years. Skylights, archways, brick floors, big windows, beautiful rugs, lovely bathrooms, cable TV, WiFi in some rooms; this is a class act. There's also an onsite events salon.

Hotel Los Mangos

953-531-0023
Santo Domingo Tonalá, Lazaro Cardenas 27, Centro
Price: Inexpensive
Credit Cards: Cash only
Handicapped Access: None

The pretty town of Tonalá's premier hotel and restaurant (okay, only hotel and restaurant) is Los Mangos. The basic, family-run spot is also the nerve center of Ecomixtonalli, the new ecotourism project offering guided hikes of the nearby canyon and transportation to the cabins there. It offers three brightly painted cement rooms with big windows onto the slightly overgrown gardens. Each fan-cooled room has a private hot-water bath, desk, television, and homey touches such as lace doilies on the mismatched end tables. One room, the double, is much bigger.

The onsite **Restaurant Los Mangos** (B, L, C, D; $–$$) serves good Oaxacan grub every day except Sunday, Tonalá's market day, when dozens of different stands set up next to the church.

PAPALOAPAN

With the widest range of services in the Papaloapan, Tuxtepec is an excellent base for further exploration. But there are many other options listed in Ecotourism Projects and Other Hotels.

✪ Hotel Villa de Agua

Owner: Patricia Sarmiento Castillo
287-871-3090
San Pedro Ixcatlán Centro
Price: Inexpensive
Credit Cards: Cash only
Handicapped Access: None

This charming hotel in this beautiful backwater town, overlooking Lake Miguel Alemán, is an unexpected island of comfort and detail-oriented care. In a white, Victorian mansion close to Iglesia San Pedro, this sweet spot offers seven immaculate, muted white rooms with lots of light and graceful white wood and wicker furnishings, some with king-sized beds (and new, firm mattresses), cable television, air conditioning, and modern, tiled, hot-water bathrooms (though you'll need to request hot water about 20 minutes in advance). Oddly, considering how nice everything else is, the toilets don't have seats.

There's an onsite restaurant with wonderful views, overlooking a superb little pool. Perfection. The staff can help arrange boats to Isla Soyaltepec, with one of the best ecotourism projects in Oaxaca.

✪ Mesón de Rivera Bed & Breakfast

Manager: Edgardo Asamar Peña
287-877-9427, 287-875-4738
www.mesondelarivera.com
Muro Boulevard Francisco Fernández Arteaga 2931
mesondelariverahotel@prodigy.net.mx
Price: Moderate to Expensive
Credit Cards: Yes
Handicapped Access: Yes

This beautiful, brand-new boutique hotel offers almost world-class amenities. It's well away from town (which may count as a positive, if you have a car; it's about US$2 for a taxi into the center of things), but close to the river and several family parks and soccer fields, tranquil.

The professional staff welcomes you to the modern, California stucco-style main entrance, before guiding you back to the elegant rooms surrounding the sparkling pool. Each is spacious and elegantly outfitted with dark wood furniture, lighter polished wood floors, beautiful modern bathrooms with personal products, and all sorts of amenities including WiFi, coffee maker, ironing board, and cable TV. Suites and king-sized rooms are larger and nicer; some have balconies. There's even a tiny business center, with computers and fax, and a small gym.

They're still working on room service, but currently you can order out from the steakhouse next door, **El Asadero** (287-875-8695). A full, hot complimentary breakfast is served buffet-style.

Villa Blanca Suites

Manager: Antonio Sacre
287-871-6250
villablancasuites.blogspot.com
villa_blanca@prodigy.net.mx
Tuxtepec, Avenida Mexico s/n, Frac La Esperanza
Price: Moderate
Credit Cards: Yes
Handicapped Access: Yes

This new, upscale hotel brings another level of luxury to Tuxtepec. On the other side of the river from the downtown Tuxtepec (a short walk from the US$1 ferry to downtown, or US$2.50 by taxi), next to Club Palapas, it's a family oriented recreational area with pools and restaurants.

Villas and suites surround a lovely pool with a shaded restaurant and lounge area nearby. They aren't extravagant by Oaxaca

City standards, but the brand-new, modern rooms, with lovely ceramic tiles, locally made bedspreads, flattering lighting, and big bathrooms are definitely comfortable. Some also come with air conditioning, minifridge, cable TV and microwave. There's a good restaurant onsite, in a modest adobe overlooking the quiet side of the river, **Restaurant El Faro** (287-875-0465; B, L, C, D; $$), specializing in steak and seafood, with cheaper *comidas* and big breakfasts.

Ecotourism Projects

Nature lovers, rejoice. Northern Oaxaca offers one of Latin America's most impressive collections of easy-access ecotourism opportunities, allowing you to stay on cloud-forested peaks, rainforest-shrouded river valleys within awe-inspiring canyons, or even on an island in the middle of Lake Temazcal.

The easiest to visit are the Pueblos Mancomunados, just an hour or two from Oaxaca City, through English-speaking representatives downtown. But if you're willing to carry a Spanish phrasebook and either use local transportation or rent a car, there are even more magnificent options for eco-escape.

Be aware that at some of these projects, management can be . . . flaky. Many people working on these projects are fulfilling their monthly community service (local indigenous governments require communal work), rather than full-time hoteliers. While most ecotourism projects that I visited had someone right there with the key, others took more than an hour, and a bit of asking around, to locate the guy. Your best bet is to either make reservations, or show up by early afternoon, to give everyone time to get your room ready. All ecotourism projects accept cash only.

MIXTECA

✪ **Comité de Turismo de Santiago Apoala** (555-151-9154; Santiago Apoala; $) They

Escape crowded downtown Tuxtepec by ferry across the Río Papaloapam.

say this is the cradle of the Mixtec People, who emerged from the deep caverns which riddle the stunning white limestone cliffs, hung with bromeliads, that rise shear and magnificent 100 meters (300 feet) above this perfect valley. It's only 30 kilometers (19 miles) from Noxchitlán on a good dirt road through the *milpas* (corn patches), *maguey*, and tiny log and adobe cabins to this idyllic spot, where one of Oaxaca's best-managed and most beautiful ecotourism sites is nestled.

The Tourism Committee offers two types of lodging: simple rooms with private baths in the communal lodge, where you take your meals, or larger and more comfortable cabins, with fireplaces, a short walk away. The committee offers one day-long tour, inspiring (if not requiring) you to spend two nights. It takes in two small archaeological sites with ancient paintings, underground rivers, huge caves, 30-meter (90-foot) waterfalls, and a hike along the Río Que Arranca, which must have carved those stone cliffs reaching straight up into sky.

The easiest way here is with a rental car; the dirt road is excellent. You can get a taxi here from Noxchitlán for about US$20 each way, while one bus (US$4) leaves Noxchitlán at 11 AM daily, and returns at 8 PM.

San Francisco Yosocuta (953-534-8082, 953-532-2842; Hwy. 125, 12 kilometers (7 miles) south of Huajuapan; $) Just 10 minutes south of Huajuapan's hastily constructed outskirts, Yosocuta Lake, artificially created in 1969, offers sport-fishing, boat tours to a little island, and several breezy restaurants serving cold beer, fresh fish, and wonderful views, just a US$1 cab ride from town. The "ecotourism project" isn't particularly rural (it's right by the always busy parking lot, just off the main road), but offers six slightly musty cabins with shared bath, plastic table and chairs, and two soft double beds. It's not the Ritz, but you're right on the water. Rent *lanchas* for about US$25 per hour, for up to eight people. Fishers can supply rods, or **Richard's Tackle Shop** (953-532-347; Río Tlapaneco 16, Colonia La Merced) in Huajuapan can hook you up. The **Mixtec Fishing Club Tournament** (www.clubpesca mixteca.com) goes off in early November.

Santiago Tilantongo (951-510-4970; 30 kilometers (19 miles) south of Noxchitlán; cash only; $) Fascinating high-desert town has a 16th-century Dominican church and access to the impressive Mixtec ruins of Monte Negro. Guided hikes can take in both, or head further out into Ñuu Tnou countryside. The ecotourism project offers four private cabins and a dorm, as well as bicycle rental and camping.

Tonalá Canyon (953-531-0010; www .ecomixtonalli.com; Santo Domingo Tonalá, Parque la Sabinera, Interior; $) Carved over the millennia by the seemingly innocent Río Salto into a smooth and stunning sandstone canyon, this is El Boqueron, "The Big Mouth," and it is impressive. A walkway—itself something of an architectural marvel—clings to the cliffside above the water complete with railings that are fine for small children. It's a leisurely half-hour stroll to the end of the paved walkway, to a small 1968 dam, swimming area, and shady spot with grills and picnic tables. Trails continue another 5 kilometers (3 miles) further upstream. The ecotourism project operator, based at Los Mangos Hotel (see earlier), Ecomixtonalli, offers cabins close to the canyon (US$15 per person), tent rental (US$10), bicycle rental (US$10 per day), and several different guided hikes and bike rides, including overnights, ranging from US$17–60.

LA CAÑADA AND PAPALOAPAN

Arroyo Zapotillo (287-877-2071; 1.5 kilometers (1 mile) west of Jalapa de Díaz; $) If you're hoping to climb the massive limestone tsunami of rainforest-carpeted, cavern-riddled beauty that is Cerro Rabón, this is the best place to arrange a guide. In addition to this epic hike, with views over Lake Temazcal, the project offers fine swimming holes in the river, camping, a picnic area, and lodging for 12 people.

Eloxchitlán de Flores Magón (555-151-1165; Carretera Huautla–Tuxtepec, signed turnoff west of Huautla; $) Your best option for exploring Oaxaca's small swath of misty cloud forest is here at Eloxchitlán, with dorm-style lodging and a group kitchen. Your fee includes a complimentary tour of San Antonio Papua church, built atop a Mazatec temple. Guided hikes take you to several waterfalls and caves.

Oaxaca, including the cloud forests of Huautla, has become increasingly eco-conscious in recent years, so please, "No Littering."

✪ **San Miguel Soyaltepec** (287-745-9636, 287-871-3090; ecoturismo@bioplaneta .com; Soyaltepec Island, 30 minutes by boat from San Pedro Ixtlán; $) This incredible spot, the "Hill of Palm Trees," was once merely a mountain overlooking the fertile Mazatec homeland. In 1954, however, Miguel Alemán Dam was completed, and the population evacuated—save for here, on the hill, and in nearby San Pedro Ixcatlán. Today, it is an island of impressive beauty, to which Hotel Villa de Agua (see earlier) in Ixcatlán can help arrange boats. There you'll be met by young guides who'll escort you up the slippery and steep 20-minute climb to the rocky headlands and 18th-century stone church. Several circular, thatch-roofed cabanas with shared cold bath and no showers sleep up to five. Meals (US$4–5) are served in the adjacent restaurant. Tours take you to see cave paintings and ancient carvings, bat caves and waterfalls. But somehow, those views are almost enough in themselves.

SIERRA JUÁREZ
In addition to the Pueblos Mancomunados, there are several other ecotourism options in the Sierra Juárez.

Capulálpam de Méndez (951-539-2168; www.capulalpam.com; beenegaguieco turismo@yahoo.com) Just beyond Ixtlán, this "Magic Village" (a nationwide tourism designation recognizing a commitment to tradition) is known for its 1731 church with a stunning interior of ornate gold-leafed *retablos,* and a history of medicinal healing. Arrange a visit to the Centro de Medicina Tradicional, with professional herbalists and a *temazcal,* or a guided tour to see the unusual formations of massive, limestone Cueva del Arroyo ("Cave of the Creek"). You can arrange lodging, horseback rides, trout fishing and other activities through the contact information above. Flecha del Zempoaltépetl buses leave Oaxaca's second-class bus station daily for Villa Alta at 8:45 AM and 5:45 PM and Zoogocho at 7 AM and 2 PM. You can catch a cab from Ixtlán.

La Cumbre Ixtepeji (200-125-7099, 200-125-7100; www.lacumbreixtepeji.com; Hwy. 175, kilometer 24 from Oaxaca City; $) Within Benito Juárez National Park, this 900-hectare (2,223-acre) semi-private, well-run preserve offers day-use visits, cabins, camping (tents can be rented), and dorm-style accommodations for up to 32

Magic María and the Holy Children
By Beth Penland

Before New Age healers and naturopaths, there were shamans or *curandera,* a village elder and go-to person for healing salves, herbal remedies, and spiritual guidance. María Sabina is one of Mexico's most famous shamans, credited with introducing the "magic mushroom" to the Western world.

Born in 1888 in the mountain town of Huautla de Jiménez, where she lived until her death in 1985, Sabina used various species of psychoactive mushrooms, or "holy children," for a ceremony called *velada,* to open the mind and guide her practice.

The *velada* was one of Mexico's best-kept secrets until 1955, when Sabina allowed U.S. banker and fungus fan R. Gordon Wasson to experience the vigil with her. In 1957, Wasson wrote about his trip in the *Life* magazine article "Seeking the Magic Mushroom," alerting a developing American counterculture to new and exciting ways to get a buzz. Sabina initially welcomed and befriended the visitors, but grew bitter as many sought fun and frolic rather than a true spiritual and religious experience.

Today the Mexican counterculture still holds her up as a hero, and her image adorns everything from T-shirts to tote bags in local markets.

Ecotourism Papaloapan

"The River of Butterflies," Río Papaloapan, flows through a fantastic tropical region of lush, humid, rainforest-cloaked mountains, endless acres of coconut palm and papaya, vibrant blue artesian springs . . . all just four hours from Oaxaca City. Four Chinanteca Indian pueblos, all close to the friendly service town of Valle Nacional, have constructed four marvelous ecotourism projects, called **Ecopapaloapan**, modeled on the Pueblos Mancomunados.

Prices are the same across the board: Cabins sleeping one to four people run US$35. Meals cost US$4–8 (try the river shrimp, a local specialty). All are cash only, and the closest ATM is in Tuxtepec. Camping costs US$1 per person, but bring your own tent. There are four affiliated ecotourism projects:

Cerro Chango (287-406-9906; San José Río Manzo [Manso]) The most remote of the projects is atop a jungled mountain known and named for its spider monkeys. The site has three lovely wooden cabins with tiny private porches, and a larger dorm, guided hikes, an observation tower, boat trips, and several incredible caves (guides can explain which animals each formation resembles), one of which has been transformed into a small Catholic church, Iglesia de Nuevo San José Río Manzo.

Cerro Marín (200-123-0589, 200-123-0590; Hwy. 175, 40 kilometers south of Tuxtepec) Idyllic and Eden-like, this professional, well-managed spot is right off the highway, overlooking Balneario Monteflor's naturally vibrant blue waters, surrounded by lushly landscaped tropical flora. Sturdy wooden cabins with *palapa* roofs and elaborate hand-carved doorways have two floors connected by a ladder, with a double bed below and twins above; there's a hammock for a fifth person. Guided hikes

Cabins are simple and services basic, but indigenous Oaxaca's "ecotourism projects" boast some of Mexico's most brilliant settings, such as San Miguel Amatlán's hilltop retreat among the Pueblos Mancomunados.

Brilliant blue Balnareo Zuzul, hidden in the lush rainforested hills of the Papaloapan, is a great place to bathe or stay overnight at Vega del Sol's ecotourism project.

can take you to the deepest cave in the world, San Agustín; archaeological sites; coffee farms; and the fascinating community museum.

San Mateo Yetla (200-125-1360; 200-125-1379, 200-125-1380; Hwy. 175, 50 kilometers (31 miles) south of Tuxtepec) Perhaps the best developed and most popular of the projects are these *palapa*-topped adobe cabins with ceramic floors, 24-hour hot water, fans, a bit of mold, and cute porches overlooking the river. A huge cement swimming pool filled with natural artesian spring water lazes right by the rushing river, and there's a good restaurant (B, L, C, D; $–$$) next door specializing in tamales, trout, and river shrimp (and just eating here earns you admission to the pool). It's 2 kilometers (1 mile) from Valle Nacional, with cabs.

Vega del Sol (283-101-7247, 283-101-7169; Santa María Jacatepec, 47 kilometers (29 miles) south of Tuxtepec) About 10 kilometers (6 miles) from Valle Nacional, 3 kilometers (2 miles) off Hwy. 175 on a well-signed dirt road (covered *camionetas* meet the buses), Balneario Zuzul is a gem, a partially developed artesian spring flowing into the clear Río Valle Grande. Overlooking the serene scene of women washing and kids diving off the platform are two polished cedar caverns on stilts. Beautiful. Except no one could find the key to let me in. Theoretically, the site offers guided hikes, horseback rides, and the whole bit, but the operators may still be working out some kinks.

people, in pine-forested paradise. Food is served when there's a group of more than 10 people, but otherwise bring your own (a kitchen is available). Guided tours—biking, hiking, waterfalls, a mushroom farm, trout fishing, 3,185-meter (10,500-foot) Mirador Pelado Chiquito—run US$10 per group, rooms US$15 per person, dorms US$13. Make reservations at least two weeks in advance, if possible. The staff can arrange transport, but suggest renting your own car.

Ecoturixtlán Shiaa Rua Via (951-553-6075; Ixtlán 16 Septiembre, corner of Revolución, Ixtlán Centro) An excellent alternative to the Pueblos Mancomunados is this well-run ecotourism project in the cute, Colonial town of Ixtlán de Juárez, 60 kilometers (37 miles) (a little more than an hour) from town by convenient direct buses. The very professionally managed spot offers cabins in the pine-filled mountains and hiking, biking, and canopy tour. The company has offices in Oaxaca City (951-514-1104; Calle Rayón 608, Centro), where you can reserve

Los Pueblos Mancomunados

The easiest way into the pine-carpeted mountains that make up most of Oaxaca State is a visit to the well-organized Mancomunados Villages, which have pooled the natural resources of their 290-square-kilometer (112-square-mile) territory into endless ecotourism opportunities. Just 60 kilometers (37 miles) from Oaxaca City, via either Hwy. 175 or on a dirt road heading north from Teotitlán del Valle, are eight cool mountain towns offering comfortable cabins, dorm beds, and campsites in paradise.

The Zapotec-speaking "People of the Clouds," founded the region's first ecotourism projects, an innovative program that combines great lodging with guided hikes, mountainbike rides, and horseback tours, on dirt roads and well-worn paths connecting the villages. Guides help you explore.

All the villages manage their projects separately, but work through a central office in Oaxaca City, ✪**Sierra Norte** (951-514-8271; www.sierranorte.org.mx; sierranorte@oaxaca.com; Bravo 210-1). Based on your personal needs (how many days you have, your fitness level, what you want to see) this group arranges treks to and between the villages. They have photos of what each community has to offer, can explain the options in English, and will recommend public and private transport options once you've purchased the tour.

You're more than welcome to work with the projects directly, but either make reservations, or show up early to give folks time to prepare your room. Prices are consistent, US$15 per person for private lodging, US$13 for a dorm bed, and US$4 per person camping; most pueblos rent tents. Guided hikes usually run US$12–20 per day. Cabins are not heated, but have fireplaces. Simple food is either provided by your hosts, or at one of a very few *comedors* in town. Kitchens are usually available. It's worth bringing your own food from town.

Elevation ranges from well over 3,000 meters (10,000 feet) in Cuajimoloyas and Llano Grande, to a more temperate 2,400 meters (7,900 feet) in Latuvi. Consider acclimating in Oaxaca City for a couple of days before taking on a serious trek. Note that it's much cooler in the mountains, and can drop almost to freezing at night, so dress accordingly. Use a hat and sunscreen.

Benito Juárez (951-545-9994, 951-172-1581; 54 kilometers (33 miles) from Oaxaca City via Teotitlán) The gateway to the Pueblos, this well-managed flagship operation is one of the best and most convenient. Spectacular views, a glass-topped dorm that lets you sleep beneath the stars, trout fishing, and a 340-meter (1,115-foot) *tirolesa* (canopy tour) also set this spot apart. There are hiking, biking, and horseback trails, including the popular trek to Pico de Orizaba, a 3,100-meter (10,170-foot) slice of granite from which you can see Oaxaca City and the Central Valleys. Collective taxis run here from Teotitlán on Tuesday, Friday, and Saturday afternoons, or just get your own cab (US$15).

Llano Grande (via Sierra Norte only) Almost at the altitude of a cloud forest, Llano Grande offers trails through the cool, misty pre-montane forests, on bikes. Adobe cabins have fireplaces and hot water, and you can also rent tents. Flecha del Zempoaltepetl runs buses from the second-class bus station in Oaxaca City daily; go to Villa Alta, and catch a cab.

La Nevería (951-516-6837, 951-514-2999; ecoturismo_neveria@yahoo.com.mx, omstour@prodigy. net.mx) Right next door to Benito Juárez (7 kilometers/4 miles), this adorable Colonial town offers cute cabins and comfortable homestays, camping, horses, waterfalls, a reforestation project, and the *pozo de hielo*, or cave of ice, where ice has been produced for centuries. Learn Zapotec language and recipes from village elders. You can also see military trenches from the Mexican Revolution.

San Antonio Cuajimoloyas (via Sierra Norte only) At 3,000 meters (10,000 feet) above sea level, this neat spot offers access to the canyonlands with rappelling, biking, and trails. Locals also practice weaving and can offer demonstrations and workshops in the fiber arts, or in astronomy, traditional medicine, or cooking. They also have a village *temazcal*.

San Miguel Amatlán (200-125-7300 Efrén Yescas, 200-125-7302 town phone; 200-125-7304 municipal offices, 951-210-0544 cell; yexe_28@hotmail.com) Atop a steep and rocky hill overlooking the agricultural valley, this spot offers world-class views. Birding, biking, hiking, a 1910 church, waterfalls, mushroom farms, and a deer nursery run by the local women's collective make this a full package. You can walk 1 kilometer (.62 miles) up the hill to the neighboring town of Santa Catarina, with its own ecotourism projects. To get here, get a *colectivo camioneta* from Ixtlán (US$2), or the 5:30 AM bus from Abastos Centro.

San Pedro Nexicho (555-151-9135) At a rather lower elevation, these lusher pine-oak forests were preferred by the ancient Zapotecs, who left behind carvings, ceramics, and tools now displayed at a tiny community museum. There's also a 16th-century church, guided hikes and horseback rides, and a pretty adobe cabins in the woods.

Santa Catarina Lachatao (951-193-3565; Roberto Hernández Cruz; www.lachataoexpediciones. com; ecoturlachatao@hotmail.com) Right above San Miguel Amatlán, this stunning hilltop town is crowned by a 16th-century stone church, Iglesia Santa Catarina. There are two lodging options, dorm-style in what appears to be an old monastery, or larger, more comfortable cabins a 10-minute walk from town. There are two restaurants, including **Los Pinos**, which specializes in organic and vegetarian cuisine. There's a market Friday and Saturday, and plans are afoot to build a community museum. One Benito Juárez bus leaves Abastos in Oaxaca City at 5 AM daily, returning at 4 PM.

Santa Marta Latuvi (200-125-7108 town phone, 200-125-7111 municipal phone; 13 kilometers (8 miles) from kilometer 176, 53 kilometers (33 miles) from Oaxaca City) Latuvi, or "rolled leaf," is named for a landmark tree that once guided Zapotec refugees escaping from the Spaniard-infested lowlands to this safer altitude. The region is well known for its apples, pears, *chilacayotas*, and preserves, as well as its signature crusty bread, which you can learn to bake in a traditional adobe oven. Guided hikes, trout fishing, and pretty cabins with ceramic floors and fireplaces are all on offer. Buses run Tuesday and Friday from the Abastos Centro.

lodging and tours, and arrange transportation. To get here, take Flecha del Zempoaltépl buses to Villa Alta, or Benito Juárez buses to Zoogocho, leaving from Abastos Centro.

San Pablo Guelatao (951-553-6028) The name means "Small Lagoon," a pleasant place where you can still walk around the water where beloved native son Benito Juárez used to herd his sheep. There are no hotels, but private homes set up for visitors; call the number above or arrange lodging though the Municipal Palace (or just ask around).

San Pablo Mancuiltanguis (951-524-0030; Hwy. 175, halfway between Ixtlán de Juárez and Valle Nacional; $) This peaceful mountain town at an altitude of 2,200 meters (7,200 feet) must have bustled at one point; the name means "Place of Five Markets." Today it is a quiet rural village, with eight family oriented cabins surrounding a swimming pool and playground. Guided hikes take you to rivers, mountaintops, and the Spanish cave, where you can see petroglyphs.

Other Hotels

The smallest pueblos often have private homes (*casas particulares*) that will rent rooms and provide meals for a small fee. Ask about these at the municipal palace, usually located on the town plaza, close to the church.

THE MIXTECA

HUAJUAPAN DE LEÓN

The nicest spot is the Perla, reviewed above, but also consider these good choices.

Hotel Casa Blanca (953-532-9363; Amatista 1 Santa Teresa; credit cards accepted; $) Industrial-sized three-star hotel has 73 rooms, a pool, WiFi, bar, air-conditioning, room service, cable TV, and gift shop selling tobacco products and local *artesanías*.

Hotel Laredo (951-532-0402; Antonio de León 13; $) Good choice for budget travelers with rental cars. Clean, basic, cement rooms with TVs, nice furniture, fans, and hot water until midnight surround a tightly packed parking lot.

Hotel María Luisa (953-532-5801; hotel ml@hotmail.com; Huajuapan, Colegio Militar 5; credit cards accepted; $) Right on the Zócalo, this adorable option offers 18 homey, comfortable rooms with mismatched furnishings, private hot-water baths, cable television, air conditioning, and other comforts. The tiny courtyard houses a few squawking parrots, while the onsite restaurant offers room service.

NOXCHITLÁN

Pickings are slim in the windswept, high-desert town of Noxchitlán, a pretty place with a beautiful blue-and-white Colonial church and lovely central park, not to mention a festive market with fresh-squeezed juices and everything else you'll ever need.

Hotel Independencia (951-522-0463; Indepencia 6, Noxchitlán, behind the Municipal Palace; cash only: $) A great choice, with several classes of rooms; the cheapies are small and dark but the nicest rooms, on the third floor, are spacious and well decorated with tiny private balconies overlooking the church. All have WiFi, cable TV, telephones, and private hot bath.

Hotel and Restaurant Juquila (951-522-0581; Hwy. 135 on the south entrance to town; $) Spotless tiled rooms with windows facing an interior courtyard are large, plain, and whitewashed, with good beds, cable television, small desks, and hot water in the morning and evening. An upstairs *terraza* with desert views, onsite parking, and a downstairs restaurant, Yamuchilan Anapola (open 9 AM–8 PM daily; $) with inexpensive Mexican food make this a decent option.

Hotel Roma (951-522-0219; Morelos 34, Barrio Chocano; credit cards accepted; $$) Noxchitlán's finest hotel, with four stars and 10 rooms, has WiFi, a parking lot, and cable TV. It also boasts the best restaurant in town.

SANTIAGO JUXTLAHUACA
Sunday is market day, when the very inexpensive hotels fill up.

Hotel Eden (953-554-0706; Calle México 309; credit cards accepted; $) Juxtlahuaca's finest lodging is also its tallest building, six stories of surprisingly comfortable, modern rooms with Sky TV, great beds with new mattresses, telephones, WiFi, air-conditioning, a parking lot, new bathrooms, and great views. Standard rooms are cramped; spend US$5 more for a slightly larger deluxe. Bonus: You're right across the street from the laundry.

Hotel San Miguel (Melchor Ocampo 203, Centro; $) On the main road heading into town, it has clean basic rooms with private hot-water bath, cable TV, firm beds, and a good restaurant onsite.

TLAXIACO
This pretty Colonial city, centered on a monumental Dominican church, has hotel listings, photos, events information, and more at **Hoteles Tlaxiacao** (www.hoteles tlaxiaco.com).

Hotel Misión Tlaxiaco (953-552-1156; Carretera a Yucuda kilometer 55, Barrio San Diego; $$) Clean, modern rooms, including a few spacious suites with sofas and sitting areas, are attractively outfitted with nice furnishings, cable TV, and other amenities, surrounding a parking lot.

Hotel San Mishell (953-552-0064; Independencia 11, Centro; cash only; $) This fabulous Colonial mansion has been faithfully maintained with wonderful courtyard gardens and even a small chapel. Rooms in the "old section" are larger and

more atmospheric, with mismatched furniture and cable TV; the "new section" is more modern, but a bit sterile. Parking is free, and there's an onsite restaurant.

VILLA DE TAMAZULAPAM DEL PROGRESO
Casa Perla Mixteca (953-533-0280; 2 de Abril 3, Centro; $) This hotel, well signed from Hwy. 190, offers three-star comforts in a pretty, new, Colonial-style building. Bright colors, evocative archways, and gleaming hardwood floors, plus modern amenities such as cable TV and WiFi, make this a welcoming spot in the rural Mixtec. There's a kids' playground outside.

Hotel Puerto Mexico (953-533-0044; Colón 12, San Cipriano) Probably your second-best bet, this hotel offers clean, basic rooms with private hot showers, plenty of light, cable TV, and a good onsite restaurant/bar for a bit less.

LA CAÑADA AND PAPALOAPAN
HUAUTLA DE JIMÉNEZ
This city's unbelievable cloud forest location provides awesome opportunities for ecotourism, but the hotel situation is a bit grim. The ecotourism project may be a better bet.

Hotel Julia (236-378-0586; Hwy. 182; cash only; $) Huautla's best hotel, which isn't saying much, is right on the freeway, with clean, tiled rooms (some with balconies overlooking the road rather than the rainforest), decent beds and televisions, as well as a great seafood restaurant downstairs. The rooftop terrace is nice.

JALAPA DE DÍAZ
Casa de Huespedes Lili (128-877-7209; Jalapa Centro, across from a two-story yellow building; cash only; $) Jalapa's most comfortable lodging is basic: 10 spotlessly clean, windowless (some ventilation is provided by open cement bricks at the top) cement rooms, some with a private cold-water bath. Ask anyone in town for the

"hotel" and they'll point the way. There's another, even more basic spot, **Hospedaje Gallegos** ($) about two blocks away, with tiny rooms and a shared bath, that might do in a pinch.

SAN JUAN BAUTISTA CUICATLÁN

No Cuicatlán hotels accept credit cards or have email addresses.

Casa Riviera Hotel (236-374-0257; Cinco de Mayo Centro; $) Since 1947, this very basic, truly Colonial option next to the plaza has offered five large, clean adobe rooms around a quiet patio, now furnished with private cold-water bathrooms (no toilet seats), decent beds, and regular television, for the lowest price in town.

✪ **Hotel Real Sochiapan** (236-374-0001; one block east of the bus station; $–$$) Cuicatlán's best hotel, close to the highway and bus station, offers 32 spacious, modern rooms with handsome wood furnishings, excellent beds, big hot-water bathrooms, and access to the Vueltas River, where guests can swim. There's a parking lot and pleasant restaurant (open 7 AM–9 PM; $–$$) onsite.

Hotel Tijuana (236-374-0116; Juárez 9 Centro; $) This site offers 13 cool, tiled, modern rooms, with hot water, air conditioning, and access to a great third-floor *terraza* with city views. Note that it's also home to a popular bar/billiards room that shuts down at 1 AM.

TUXTEPEC

In addition to the better hotels given full coverage above, try one of these less expensive, but still comfortable, options.

Hotel Mirador (287-875-0500; Independencia 985; cash only; $) A perfectly acceptable budget hotel with fairly large rooms and the option of air-conditioning and cable TV, this has the best view of town, over the river, right where the ferry crosses the soothing Río Papaloapan. There's onsite parking.

Hotel Tuxtepec (287-875-0934; Matamoros 2, corner of Independencia; credit cards accepted; $) The best (and most expensive, by a few dollars) of downtown's plethora of good cheapies, this three-story has been wonderfully well maintained. Rooms are large, freshly painted in quiet pastels, with good mattresses and better-than-average bedding, extra-fluffy towels, and huge windows with lots of light. Each is also outfitted with modern hot-water bath, cable TV, WiFi, phone, and air conditioning, as well as ceiling fans. Rooms are still simple, and the hallways less well maintained than the rooms, but if you get a room with a balcony, they're among the best in town.

VALLE GRANDE

If, for some reason, you don't want to stay in the area's lovely ecotourism projects, there are a couple of options in town.

Hotel del Valle (283-877-4218; one block off Hwy. 175; $) This hotel has 16 eclectically furnished cement rooms with private cold-water showers and broadcast television. The owners are sweethearts.

Valle Real Hotel (283-877-4405; Hwy. 175, town center; $) It's the nicest hotel in town, apparently, but it was closed when I was there.

SIERRA JUÁREZ

In addition to the excellent area ecotourism projects, there are a few privately owned hotels.

La Sierra El Punto Ixtepeji (951-560-3002; Hwy. 175 ; cash only; $) Cute, high-altitude cabins are professionally managed and right on the highway. The cozy restaurant serving savory stews and big breakfasts right off Hwy. 175 has two spacious, basic brick cabins with fireplaces, private hot-water showers, reed mats, and two big beds. Next door, **Cabaña Cucurri** (951-560-3021) offers similar accommodation.

La Soledad Hotel and Video Club
(951-553-6171; e_jimenez_r@hotmail.com; Ixtlán, Francisco Javier Mina 4, Barrio Soledad; cash only; $) Picturesque, cobblestoned, and ancient Ixtlán de Juárez, the gateway to the Sierra Juárez, has a few basic hotels, the best of which is this simple spot, close to Soledad Church. Simple, cement rooms, most with a private bath, surround a parking lot. Bathrooms are tiny but freshly painted; rooms have lots of light, good beds and pretty bedspreads, cable TV, and WiFi. The staff can cook meals and arrange tours.

RESTAURANTS AND FOOD PURVEYORS

This rather rural region isn't exactly a gastronomical wonderland; basic bakeries and no-frills *comedors,* serving big breakfasts and scrumptious set *comidas,* fill you up during the day, while greasy taquerias serving tacos, and ubiquitous stands with *elotes* dish up dinner. Consider self-catering at area grocery stores.

On the upside, however, mountain streams and lakes yield freshwater delicacies, including trout, river shrimp, and *mojarra,* served baked, fried, in soups, as ceviche, in garlic sauce, layered with herbs and broiled, and so on. Since these are indigenous areas, many familiar recipes are made with slightly different flavors, thanks to unusual herbs and spices. The tamales are bigger and better up north as well.

Note that the stretch between Tuxtepec and Oaxaca can be considered the state's fruit basket: The fertile Papaloapan river basin is carpeted with orange, mandarin, papaya, banana, grapefruit, and coconut trees, while the Sierra Juárez grows apples, pears, and all manner of vegetables. Tiny roadside stands sell all these very fresh fruits for pesos on the dollar compared to what you'd pay in Oaxaca.

Restaurants and Food Purveyors Price Code

The following prices are based on the cost of a dinner entrée with a non-alcoholic beverage, not including the usually voluntary (but check your receipt) 10–15 percent gratuity that should probably be added. The coding "B, L, C, D" refers to U.S.-style meals (breakfast, lunch, dinner), as well as the typical Mexican *comida,* traditionally the biggest meal of the day, served in lieu of lunch from about 2 PM to 6 PM. Prices are calculated at 10 pesos to the dollar.

Inexpensive:	Up to US$5
Moderate:	US$5 to US$10
Expensive:	US$10 to US$20
Very Expensive:	US$20 or more

Restaurants

Ajos y Cebollas

953-532-0795
Huajuapan, Madero 1, Zócalo (second floor)
Price: Inexpensive to Expensive
Credit Cards: Cash only
Cuisine: Oaxacan, seafood
Serving: B, L, C, D
Reservations: Weekend evenings

On a second-story balcony overlooking
the busy Huajuapan Zócalo may sit the best
tables in town. This beautiful restaurant,
decked out in ancient archways and bright
gem tones, brings in the ladies who brunch
by late morning for espresso beverages,
fruit salads, and an array of pastries and
desserts. Businesspeople pack the place
for *comida,* as well as the locally revered
tlayudas and enchiladas verdes. Light
lunches such as crepes, sandwiches, and
seafood spaghetti are also on the menu, as
is a very full bar. It's a very romantic place
for dinner.

Espadas Casa Blanca

287-875-6520
espadascasablanca@hotmail.com
Cinco de Mayo 438, corner of Hidalgo
Price: Moderate
Credit Cards: Yes
Cuisine: Mexican
Serving: B, C, D
Reservations: Yes

This top-notch buffet restaurant offers
dozens of items, including grilled meats,
within rather formal and air-conditioned
environs. The setting, a pretty old Colonial,
is whitewashed and rather elegant; uniformed waitstaff attend to your almost
every need.

Of course, choosing which salads, soups,
moles, and other main plates, not to mention desserts, is up to you. Just don't skip
the big pot of hot chocolate simmering in a
ceramic urn off to one side.

Restaurant-Bar Malagon

287-875-4445
Tuxtepec, Cinco de Mayo 425, corner of
Hidalgo
Price: Inexpensive to Moderate
Credit Cards: Yes
Cuisine: Oaxacan
Serving: C, D
Reservations: Yes

In the city center (though not out over the
water), this spot has a great US$3.50 *comida*
starting at 2 PM, as well as a huge Sunday
buffet, and excellent seafood and northern Oaxacan items such as empanadas and
arracheras. But the real reason to come is
the live mariachi music most evenings, as
well as tango on the dance floor.

Restaurante Rana Feliz

953-556-8876
Tlaxiaco, José Domingo Vazquez 5, between
Hidalgo and Independencia
Price: Inexpensive to Moderate
Credit Cards: Cash only
Cuisine: Oaxacan
Serving B, L, C, D
Reservations: No

This above-average budget restaurant
sticks with a theme, the "Happy Frog," with
several ceramic frogs decorating the cute
two-story interior. It's easy being green
here, with specialties such as *filete a la
rana,* a fish filet in parsley sauce with rice;
or enchiladas *a la rana,* made with chicken
in a salsa verde. The service is good, the
location is convenient (just a block from
the plaza), and the food is great.

✪ El Rincón de Gon

953-552-0608
cussilvia2_66@yahoo.com.mx
Tlaxiaco, Aldama 1, Heroica Ciudad
Price: Moderate to Expensive
Credit Cards: Yes
Cuisine: Tlaxiacan

Serving: B, L, C, D
Reservations: Yes

Don't miss this classic Mixtec fine-dining experience, in an atmospheric old Colonial that surrounds a fabulous courtyard often decorated for the region's many wonderful festivals and seasonal events. Original art, candles, photos of old Tlaxiaco, and staff in traditional outfits complete the pretty picture.

Reserve some courtyard seating, and consider some of the more authentic Mixtec items on the menu, such as the *tutuñis,* balls of corn tortilla mix fried with dried chiles and herbs, then served with eggs or *tasajo;* or perhaps a sandwich, hamburger, or seafood soup. The signature dish, for US$10 per person, is the *Tlaxiaqueña.* A small ceramic charcoal grill is brought to your table, where you cook your own meat, *nopales,* onions, and other goodies to taste. There's live music Wednesday through Friday, and a very full bar (including more than a dozen homemade flavored mezcals) to keep things fun. A memorable evening out.

✪ Sal y Pimienta

287-875-8293
Libertad 1115, between Matamoros and Ocampo
Price: Inexpensive
Credit Cards: Cash only
Cuisine: Vegetarian, Oaxacan
Serving: B, L, C
Reservations: No

Vegetarians who need a break from rice and beans should find this tiny diner not far from the first-class bus station. The emphasis is on traditional Mexican cuisine made with vegetarian "meats," including *al pastor* tacos, enchiladas, *syncronizadas, chilaquiles* with chorizo sausage, and other tasty snacks. Soups, salads, and vegetable dishes are available for folks who'd rather not bother with fake meats, however. The

comida is a great deal, just US$4 for four courses and the day's fruit juice, though you may want to splurge on something more exotic, such as the seaweed-pineapple beverage. Great service, nice people, good karma. Enjoy.

LA CAÑADA AND PAPALOAPAN

Como Yo No Hay Dos

287-871-1304
Entry road, San Pedro de Ixcatlán
Price: $30–80
Credit Cards: Cash only
Cuisine: Seafood, Oaxacan
Serving: B, L, C, D
Reservations: No

There are dozens of *palapa*-topped restaurants lining the shores of the Temazcal Reservoir, but though there may be others, this restaurant's name proclaims, "Like Me There Are Not Two." The breezy, thatched-roof restaurant with outstanding lake views is Ixcatlán's best, where couples celebrate their anniversaries over fried *mojarra* and ceviche (the house specialties), or *mojarra* served half a dozen other ways; try it in garlic sauce. River shrimp are also available in season. You could stop in for a beer, but you must have snacks as well.

Palapas Mingo

287-874-7070
Hwy. 175, Chiltepec
Price: Moderate
Credit Cards: Cash only
Serving: C, D
Reservations: No

But if you want to dine right on the water, Palapas Mingo is more than just another ramshackle restaurant serving the freshest fish imaginable, however. It's a destination.

In addition to the restaurant, you can rent your own private *palapa,* basically a shaded table and chairs strung with hammocks, to enjoy the breeze off the river.

There are also swimming pools and a large playground for kids, as well as a relatively full bar for parents. The food is authentic, cooked over wood-fired grills and served with the region's wonderful fresh salsas. Awesome.

SIERRA JUÁREZ

Parador and Campamento del Monte
951-560-3052, 951-172-7277
delmontemx@hotmail.com
Hwy. 175, kilometer 27 from Oaxaca City
Price: Moderate
Credit Cards: Cash only
Serving: B, L, C
Reservations: No

As the steep rise out of the hot, arid Oaxaca Valley begins to mellow, wending through the rustling pine forests, you'll come to this wonderfully rustic roadside restaurant with huge picture windows overlooking the forested mountains. It's a favorite for folks from the Valleys escaping the heat below,

and the weekend braised-rabbit special packs the house. The restaurant also rents several **large cabins** (US$50), comfortably sleeping six in mostly dorm-style beds, with fireplaces, refrigerator, stove, but no cookware or dishes. It's a great deal for DIY travelers who don't need a lot of supervision.

Food Purveyors
Bakeries
Centro Ovolactovegetariano (Tuxtepec, 20 de Noviembre 913; closed Sun.) This organic grocery and health-food store also has an excellent bakery, with heavy wholegrain breads to compete with the dozens of regular bakeries nearby.

Espiga de Oro (953-532-3432; Huajuapan, Nuyoo 9, Centro) This excellent and inexpensive bakery sits just off the main plaza.

Pastelería D'Claus (Noxchitlán, Calle Independencia) Specializing in pastries and cakes, D'Claus also serves ice cream.

Though the Spanish introduced wheat only five centuries ago, there are already scores . . . hundreds . . . maybe thousands of distinct regional breads and pastries.

Pastelería Gloria's (953-532-2923; Huajuapan, Allende 10, Centro) Specializes in sweets.

Cafés

El Faisan (Ixtlán, Central Plaza) Juices and snacks, as well as good, hot coffee (if not espresso).

The Italian Coffee Company (951-530-5842; Huajuapan, Trujano 1) Your new guilty pleasure has invaded Huajuapan.

Café Pagticel (951-532-0018; Huajuapan, Antonio de León 2; B, L, C, D; $) Escape that chain feeling at this local café, in an old adobe Colonial wrapped around a tiny green courtyard and fountain. The tables have cheerful red-and-white tablecloths, the coffee menu includes frappes and other espresso beverages, and there are fruit salads and pastries.

Grocery Stores

Gran Bodega (20 Noviembre, right off Hwy. 175) A huge grocery store, the largest in the Tuxtepec area.

Super del Centro Rosy (Tuxtepec, 20 de Noviembre) A good grocer in Tuxtepec; San Gabriel Verderas y Frutas sells fresh produce right next door.

Supermarket El Molino (Cuicatlán) The biggest selection for 50 kilometers (31 miles) around is right off the plaza.

Tienda Comunitaria Dicona (Ixtlán de Juárez, Venustiano, two blocks uphill from the plaza) This basic grocery is this small community's biggest.

CULTURE

This region's cultural wealth has never been developed for tourism, as the Central Valleys' has. Many of the indigenous populations, in particular the Triquis and Mazatecs, seem to have little interest in entertaining tour groups; that's why they go to Oaxaca City.

That said, if you're willing to visit the museums, explore the small towns, and learn from observation rather than demonstrations, this may well be the richest region, culturally, in Oaxaca.

Archaeological Sites

Though this region is replete with archaeological riches, most are undeveloped for tourism, though area community museums and municipal palaces can usually find Spanish-speaking guides to take you there. You'll need to provide your own four-wheel-drive transportation, and/or do some hiking. Less adventurous travelers, however, can easily visit Cerro las Minas, below.

Two of the earliest known caches of pre-Columbian artifacts discovered in Oaxaca were found in two caves, located in the cloud-forested Mazateca, near present-day Huautla. **Blade Cave**, which may have been a workshop or ritual site, was filled with hundreds of chipped obsidian and chert tools, while **San José Tenango** contained incredible ceramics, jewelry made of gold, silver, and precious stones, obsidian tools, and many other artifacts.

✪ Cerro de las Minas Huajuapan

Huajuapan, 2 kilometers (1 mile) from central plaza; parking lot on Heladio Ramirez Lupez
Open: 8 AM–6 PM
Admission: Free

Misty and mysterious Valle de Apoala calls itself the "Cradle of the Mixtecs," a claim corroborated with archaeological evidence.

The best-explored and most-accessible archaeological site in the Mixteca is in a city park in walking distance from central Huajuapan. The permanent stone structures were begun around 400 B.C., with a major expansion during Monte Albán's lucrative heyday of 300–800 A.D., when the massive ball stadium was added. Today, it's a pleasant place for a picnic on the pyramids.

There's no signage, so stop first at the Museo Regional museum downtown, where you can find maps, artifacts, and information about the site. For guided, Spanish-language tours of the ruins, contact the **Palacio Municipio** (953-533-0017; Plaza de la Constitución) at least five days in advance, though they may be able to arrange guides on shorter notice. The museum may also be able to find a guide.

Diquiyú
One hour from Huajuapan

A good dirt road leads from Huajuapan to the partially excavated ruins of "On Top of Stones," built into a cliff. There are buildings, slab stone carvings, but no infrastructure for visitors. The museum or municipal palace in Huajuapan should be able to find you a Spanish-speaking guide for about US$25, but you'll need to supply transportation, either a rental car or taxi.

Huamelelulpan
Hwy. 125, 20 kilometers (12 miles) north of Tlaxiaco, toward Teposcolula

This small town was once a regional trade center, and the remains of the old city are still preserved amid the Spanish Colonial buildings. The church incorporates stones carved in an earlier era. Several pyramids, buildings, and walls are extant, as are the ball court and auditorium. There's a small community museum displaying the relics uncovered during the incomplete excavations.

These ruins, while undeveloped for tourism, are quite easy to visit, and any bus can drop you at the entrance to town.

Monte Negro (Tilantongo)
Southwest of Noxchitlán

Serious explorers willing to make a two-hour, mostly uphill hike from the tiny town of Tilantongo (where you'll need to ask around for guides and permission; begin at the Palacio Municipal) can visit this isolated site of vast mountaintop plazas and precisely oriented temples. The site probably predates Monte Albán, and features similar city planning. Pottery, architecture and other cultural quirks seem quite similar to those of its contemporary, Yucuita, which is visible from Monte Negro.

San Juan Yucuita and Yucuñudahui
North of Noxchitlán, 86 kilometers (53 miles) from Oaxaca City

The "Hill of Flowers," atop a strikingly conical hill visible for kilometers around, was one of the first and most important settlements in the Noxchitlán Valley. Occupied as a permanent settlement since 1400 B.C., the sprawling community, still marked by high stone walls broken by narrow doorways, probably peaked at 3,000 inhabitants by 200 B.C. Though it was never abandoned completely, the region's political center shifted 4 kilometers

The Dominican Route

Oaxaca's Dominican Route actually begins at Santo Domingo in Oaxaca City, then follows the friars into the Central Valleys, whose monumental churches include San Jerónimo de Tlacochahuaya, and Cuilapan de Guerrero, San Pablo Huitzo, and Villa de Etla.

But here in Mixteca, where the busy Dominicans built scores of area churches, the three most impressive and important examples are the "Splendid Trinity" of Yuhuitlán, Coixtlahuaca, and Teposcolula, just north of Noxchitlán. Keep an eye open for Dominican symbols such as the eight-sided cross, fleur de lis, and the "Dominican dog" with a torch in its mouth illuminating the world with the word of God (yes, it's a pun). For more information, check out *Exploring Colonial Oaxaca* author Richard D. Perry's Web site, **Colonial Mexico** (www.colonial-mexico.com).

San Juan Bautista Coixtlahuaca
113 kilometers (70 miles) north of Oaxaca City (1.5 hours)
This was once the regional capital, its wealth woven from palm thatch in the cool caverns still hidden beneath modest homes scattered through the hills. It was also the site of the main Mixtec temple to Quetzalcóatl, the Plumed Serpent.

It was with the stones of this older edifice that the Dominicans began construction of Oaxaca's purest example of Renaissance architecture. The open chapel allowed un-baptized Indians to watch their friends accept the sacraments, while the distinctive *tequitqui* carvings in the interior used Mixtec styles and symbols—including some that look suspiciously like plumed serpents—to portray traditional Christian themes. The wonderful altarpiece, dating to the 1600s, was painted by Andrés de la Concha.

San Pedro and San Pablo Teposcolula
Hwy. 125, 149 kilometers (92 miles) northwest of Oaxaca (2 hours)
The graceful open chapel, an arcade of enormous *cantera* arches, is considered the finest in Mexico.

The churches of the Dominican Route, such as Santo Domingo Yanhuitlán, are monumental echoes of their surroundings.

Construction began in 1538, and included the open "Chapel of the Indios" that let locals appreciate the Gothic marvel, an enormous central nave supported by five splendid arches.

Several original treasures remain, not least the very syncretized *tequitqui* carvings and murals that seem to portray angels as deities from the Mixtec codices; the floral motif was apparently more sacred to the locals than Europeans. The remarkable interior paintings probably launched the careers of *retablo* specialist Andrés de la Concha and Flemish painter Simón Pareyns, who likely collaborated on the five spectacular Churrigueresque naves. An 18th-century bellows organ has recently been restored inside.

Santo Domingo Yanhuitlán
Hwy. 190, kilometer 119, 93 kilometers (58 miles) from Oaxaca City (1.5 hours)

Yanhuitlán, once a powerful city, had been utterly crushed just prior to the Spanish Conquest for refusing to pay taxes to the Aztec Empire; soldiers rounded up a thousand survivors and marched them to Mexico City to be publicly sacrificed. When the Spanish arrived, Yanhuitlán rolled out a warm welcome to the Dominicans.

A small adobe chapel was dedicated in 1529, and construction on the stone temple began in 1541 atop the foundation of an ancient pyramid. Perhaps 500 people worked onsite for more than 20 years, completing the temple just as smallpox began to sweep the countryside. The huge Renaissance–baroque structure would remain well used and loved, as its ornate altars and vestibules, stunning ribbed arcades, and enormous nave were used as a school where Spanish and Mixtec, woodworking and stone carving were taught to students who included de la Concha. The church is also home to a restored 17th-century organ.

The interior, said to be second only to Santo Domingo de Oaxaca, was to be renovated at press time, as were the outer buttresses damaged by earthquakes in the 1990s. When the church reopens, there will also be a small religious museum onsite.

Other Important Dominican Route Churches
Nuestra Señora de la Asunción Tlaxiaco (Hwy. 125, 175 kilometers/109 miles, 2.5 hours northwest of Oaxaca) This towering church, with an immense façade, was built in the 1550s and modeled after the Dominican church in Plascencia, Spain. The nave features neoclassic altarpieces, gold *retablos*, a huge Spanish organ dating to 1794, and other treasures. The adjacent convent was dedicated in 1607.

Santa María de la Natividad Tamazulapam (141 kilometers/87 miles north of Oaxaca City) The façade of this church, first constructed in 1542 and most recently rebuilt after an 1814 earthquake, is awe-inspiring, as are the grounds. But the real reason you're here is for the amazing *retablo*, de la Concha's masterpiece.

Santa María Tiltepec (10 kilometers/6 miles west of Hwy. 190, near Yanhuitlán) This classic 1575 church displays Spanish royal insignia and a Mixtec "House of the Chief" design, suggesting the presence of Mixtec Royalty, on one of the doors. The baroque church, with its broad columned façade and thick stone interior arches, has several ornate *retablos* as well as an unrestored 18th-century organ.

Santiago Apostolo Tejupán (Hwy. 190, 119 kilometers/74 miles north of Oaxaca City; open 10 AM-6 PM Mon.-Fri., until 1 PM Sat.) Well worth a stop just to wander this once-prominent Mixtec town, this pretty painted church recently restored its 17th-century organ and three fantastic Churrigueresque *retablos*, which they discovered had once boasted an entirely different paint scheme. Entry is free, but you must get permission from the Palacio, also on the plaza. On Sunday, the church is open for noon Mass.

(2 miles) away, to Yucuñudahui, with a ball court and pyramids, today accessible only on foot. It's also possible to visit these sites from the towns of Yucuita or Santa María Chachoapan, where you may be able to find guides (highly recommended), and you should definitely get permission to visit. The Community Museum may also be able to find guides.

Museums

The Mixtec is home to many "community museums," basically repositories of impressive archaeological finds (uncovered, perhaps, by the plow), old photos, and other historic mementos donated by area elders and generally housed in a historic building close to the plaza. Some are incredible; the treasures protected within Huajuapan are worth the trip just to see. Others are smaller and less impressive . . . in a way. But even these provide a great excuse to escape into the wild Mixtec, and see a world well off the beaten path.

Museo Comunitario Ihitalulu

951-510-4949
San Martín Huamelulpan, Hwy. 125
Open 10 AM–5 PM Tues.–Sun.
Closed: Mon.
Admission: US$1

Of the many community museums on this route, "Beautiful Flower" is one of the best and most easily accessible. The archaeological salon, with pieces from the nearby ruins, is the standout, with skeletons, ceramics, and stone tools on display. A scale model of the archaeological dig puts it all in perspective. Other exhibits include reproductions of the Mixtec codices and a discussion of medicinal plants.

Museo Comunitario Monte Flor

200-123-0589, 200-123-0590
Next to Balneario Monteflor
Open: 7 AM–7 PM daily
Admission US$1 adult, 50¢ child

This small community museum has several exhibits, the most striking a model of pre-Columbian Chinanteca tombs discovered nearby. Scores of artifacts from the tombs and elsewhere in the area, mostly ceramics, are also on display. The Spanish-language signage has fascinating and detailed information about the Chinanteca Indians. The museum staff, or folks manning the local *balneario* and ecotourism cabins, can arrange guided hikes to nearby caves, including one that may be the deepest in the world.

Museo Comunitario Note Ujia San Miguel del Progreso

San Miguel del Progreso, right off kilometer 125, 207 kilometers (128 miles) from Oaxaca
Open: 10 PM–2 PM Wed.–Sun.
Closed: Mon.–Tues.
Admission: US$1

The Museum of the Seven Rivers is in a privileged location, a high-altitude (2,780 meters/9,121 feet), Mixtec-speaking village in the chill high in the mountains. The museum is divided into three sections: dioramas and displays about belt-weaving; com-

munity history; and archaeological treasures. This is also a center for the study of traditional Mixtec culture and language, with displays about that as well.

Museo Comunitario Snuuvico San Juan Mixtepec
San Juan Mixtepec, between Tlaxiaco and Juxtlahuaca
Hours: Vary
Admission: US$1

Way off the beaten trail, the museum "Between the Clouds" preserves the cultural heritage of this small community straddling the High and Low Mixtec. Accessible via good dirt
roads from Tlaxiaco and Juxtlahuaca (it's slow going, so don't consider this a shortcut),
this is a visit you make mostly to enjoy the steep and cactus-studded scenery. Exhibits
cover the tradition of the *mayordomo,* or competitive gift-giving parties; the Mexican
Revolution of 1910–1920; community legends; and an impressive archaeological salon,
comprising only donated pieces.

Museo Comunitario Yucu-Iti Santa María Yucuhiti
954-553-4140 (community telephone)
presidencia-yucuhiti@hotmail.com; yeni-eu@hotmail.com
About 30 kilometers/18.6 miles (1.5 hours) south of Hwy. 125 at San Miguel Progresso
Open 10 AM–2 PM Tues.–Sun.
Admission: US$1 donation.

The real reason to make the trek to this isolated community museum is to visit the tidy
town itself, fronted by the pretty adobe church of Santa María. The community museum,
one of the region's first, is in the small blue building next door. It's a small one, with photos and artifacts illustrating community history, local weaving techniques, and the foundation and growth of the pueblo, using the words of local elders (in Spanish and Mixtec).

Museo Comunitario Yucundaayee San Pedro y San Pablo Tequixtepec
Tequixtepec Centro, 38 kilometers (24 miles) north of Huajuapan on Hwy. 25; 4 kilome-
ters (2.5 miles) from the signed turnoff
Open: 10 AM–2 PM and 4 PM–8 PM Mon.–Sat., noon–3 PM Sun.
Admission: US$1

This small, sparkling clean little pueblo was once an important city and ceremonial center,
the remains of which still lie, unexcavated and little visited, somewhere near town; you
may be able to find a guide. The museum is excellent, with scores of artifacts uncovered
in the 1960s by archaeologist John Paddock, and of course uncovered by farmers plowing
their fields around town. The murals are especially intriguing, depicting a terrible fire,
the revolution, and a horrible cholera epidemic, as well as the car that the doctor finally
arrived in, the first the villagers had ever seen. To get here, take a collective taxi from the
corner of Nuyoo and Hwy. 125, across from the ADO station in Huajuapan.

Museo Ñuu Kuiñi (Pueblo del Tigre)
museo_cuquila@yahoo.com
Santa Maria Cuquila, Hwy. 125
Open: 10am–2pm Wed. and Sun.
Admission: US$1

This "Heroic Town" has a small community museum with a great exhibit on waist-loom weaving, lots of artifacts, mostly ceramics and tools, from the nearby archaeological site. The museum can also arrange tours of the site, which is mostly unexcavated. There are also several *artesanías* workshops in town, mostly working in ceramics and embroidered cloth.

✪ Museo Regional de Huajuapan

www.mureh.org.mx
Nuyoo 15, Centro
Open: 10 AM–2 PM and 4 PM–8 PM Tues.–Sun.
Closed: Mon.
Admission: US 50¢ adult, US$1 family, free Sun.

This fascinating museum focuses on the impressive assortment of artifacts uncovered at nearby Cerro de las Minas, including carved stellae, ceramics, and many other items. But there are also several excellent murals, and exhibits from both the Colonial era (including some 1590 maps) and the Mexican Revolution, during which Huajuapan became a "Heroic City" for resisting a 112-day siege by better-armed Spanish forces. Look for the 1921 photo of the city; it was taken at the Calavario Church, above town.

My, how things have changed.

Tepelmeme Museo Comunitario Jna Niigüi

130 kilometers (80 miles) northeast of Oaxaca, 13 kilometers (8 miles) from Coixtlahuaca
Open: 9 AM–3 PM Thurs.–Tues.
Closed: Mon.
Admission: US$1

The region around Coixtlahuaca, famed for its fabulous Dominican church, was once entirely supported by the expert weaving of *palma,* or palm fronds, into sombreros, baskets, and other items. Many of the tiny homes you see in the dry, sunny hills around you are actually much larger than they appear, with large natural caves underneath providing the cool damp climate such artistry requires.

This small museum, founded in 1996, has photos, dioramas, and examples (some on sale, very inexpensively) of the *palma*-weaving art, as well as ceramics and stone carvings from the area's more ancient inhabitants. There's also a display on traditional medicine.

RECREATION

There aren't many organized tour operators based in the Northern Zone. Your best bet is to work with an ecotourism outfit based in Oaxaca City and arrange specialized tours with English-speaking guides, or ask at any Municipal Palace to find guides, most of whom will only speak Spanish, to the attractions that interest you.

Parks and Preserves

The best outdoor experiences in the region—Apoala Valley, Tonalá Canyon, and the Papaloapan region around Valle Nacional—are all home to wonderful ecotourism projects, discussed earlier.

Steep-walled Tonalá Canyon is threaded by a hiking path suspended above the river, following the trail of an old aqueduct bored through the rock itself.

Centro Educativo Ambiental Las Huertas
(953-522-6020; cealashuertas@hotmail
.com; Carretera Huajuapan-Juxtlahuaca
kilometer 26) Just 6 kilometers (3.5 miles)
south of the San Marcos Arteaga (look for
the waterslide and church), this agricultural
education center offers tours of the gardens
and guided hikes.

Cueva San Miguel (25 kilometers/16 miles,
1.5 hours south of Juxtlahuaca) A wonderful boondoggle just for the scenery, which
takes you from the hot Mixtec Baja into the
crisp mountain air. And at the top of the
climb? Pretty Cueva San Miguel (also the
name of the town), with a hilltop Palacio
Municipal decorated with circus animals,
and a precious blue-and-white adobe
church. But you're really here for the *cueva*,
or cave. Technically, you must hire an official guide from the Palacio (953-112-6956;
7 AM–9 PM daily), for US$6. But if no one is
around at the Palacio, pretty much anyone
can take you down to the enormous limestone cave just outside town. The remnants
of an old church, long ago flooded away, are
here.

*Oaxaca's mountains are riddled with underground
rivers and immense caverns, including scenic San
Miguel Cuevas, where the remains of a Colonial-era
church are slowly calcifying into the cave.*

**Reserva de la Biosfera Tehuacán-
Cuicatlán** (Oaxaca: 236-374-0115; San
Juan Bautista Cuicatlán, ex-estacion del
ferrocarril; Puebla: 238-372-0470; Reforma Norte 1209 Interior 7, Colonia Buenos Aires,
Tehuacán; www.conanp.gob.mx/anp/tehuacan-cuicatlan) Stretching from the state of
Puebla through the northern Mixteca, this enormous and poorly developed park attempts
to protect some 490,817 hectares (1,895 square miles) of vast and arid big-sky country,
little visited by even the most intrepid tourists. Most people enter the park and arrange
guides through the Puebla office, in the large metropolitan city of Tehuacán (www.puebla
-tehuacan.wexico.com).

Tuxtepec River Walk

The western side of the river offers the opportunity to stroll for kilometers along the
waterfront, punctuated by parks and playgrounds that take full advantage of the views and
breeze. It's beautiful, but as you leave the city center, it gets very poor; this may not be the
place for an evening stroll alone.

Balnearios (Swimming Holes)

Don't miss Balnearios Monteflor and Zuzul, part of the Ecopapaloapan ecotourism project,
covered earlier.

Arroyo de Banco (6 kilometers/4 miles from Valle Nacional) This tiny community has an absolutely lovely *balneario* complete with a small waterfall. The road from the regional hospital leads here, or just take a taxi.

Balneario Atonaltzi (Tamazulapam; open 9 AM–3 PM; admission US$1) The slightly warm sulfur springs just outside Tamazulapam del Progreso were once the province of Coixtlahuaca royalty, who considered the waters curative. Several pools, including one 4 meters (12 feet) deep, today are open to everyone.

Balneario Río Uluapan (10 kilometers/6 miles from Jalapa de Díaz) A walled-off swimming hole on the crystal-clear Uluapan River is just a 45-minute hike from a waterfall. Ask at your hotel or the Municipal Palace about finding a guide; any taxi driver can take you to the springs.

Chiltepec (15 minutes from Tuxtepec) Chiltepec offers two *Balnearios*, El Romance and Los Cocos. El Romance is the prettier of the two, with that stunning blue water and palm-jungle shore, while Los Cocos is larger, with a better beach. Urvans (with continuing service to Valle Nacional) runs *camionetas* from Tuxtepec to the springs.

Laguna Encantada de Tecomaxtlahuca (Hwy. 125, just north of Juxtlahuaca) The brilliant blue "Enchanted Lagoon" is popular with families and teens on weekends, when its shady parking area becomes a virtual campground and community barbecue. Weekdays are a more sedate time to visit this magical place, which has healing springs whose remarkable color is caused by a sulfurous hot spring mixing with regular groundwater. There's a small restaurant and snack bar onsite; campers can use the bathroom facilities.

SHOPPING

Both Tuxtepec in the Papaloapan and Huajuapan in the Mixteca have a wide variety of goods and services difficult to find elsewhere in these more rural regions.

Of course, all the towns and pueblos have market days, but the most famous of these is the enormous Saturday *tanguis* in Tlaxiaco, considered the best and most authentic market in the Mixteca. It's the best place to find the warm woolen *huipiles* and other wonderful woven goods from the Mixteca Alta, as well as everything else you could imagine. Other days, sellers cluster on the main plaza, near Hotel Portal, and you can find items much less expensively than you would in Oaxaca City.

Casa de la Cultura Huajuapan (953-532-0540; Huajuapan Zócalo) Right on the Huajuapan plaza, the shop sells dozens of small-print-run books about Mixtec history, legends, and culture.

EVENTS

March
Feria de la Mojarra (Third week in March; Isla Soyaltepec) Local residents put Laguna Temazcal to work with this celebration of fishing. It includes sporting events, parades, and the election of a beauty queen.

May

Expo Fair Tuxtepec (Second week in May; Tuxtepec) Tuxtepec's biggest party brings in folks from all over the Papaloapan for live entertainment, a huge fair and art show, and more.

June

Feast Day of Saint John the Baptist (June 24; Tuxtepec and Huajuapan) Tuxtepec celebrates with boat races, live music and traditional dance, carnival rides, and more. Huajuapan has a lower-key party.

July

Fiesta of the Señor de los Corazones (July 15–23; Huajuapan) The Mixteca Baja's biggest party goes on all month, with big-name musicians, a huge market, and lots of food. The party culminates on July 23, when the streets are decorated with murals of colored sawdust, across which the image of Jesus is paraded. Another big fiesta, for Santiago Apostal (St. James), takes place July 25.

August

Fería de los Hongos (Late August; San Antonio Cuajimoloyas;) The Festival of Mushrooms is celebrated in the Sierra Norte, where July showers mean August mushrooms, harvested and prepared by experts.

Fiesta of the Virgen de la Asunción (August 15; Noxchitlán) Noxchitlán's big civic fiestas, with traditional dances, live music, sporting events, fireworks, parades, and more, go all month long. It's a great place to see *La Mascarita,* the region's traditional dance.

October

Festival of the Mole de Calderas (Third weekend in October; Huajuapan) Goats, introduced in the 1500s, were an economic boon to Huajuapan. The locals sold goat meat and hides throughout the Spanish Empire; today, they market throughout the world. But it's all preceded by *La Matanza,* "The Slaughter," when thousands of goats are killed over three weeks. The Mixtecs quite rightly added ceremony to the bloody proceedings, adorning the first sacrificial goat with flowers and carrying her to her fate in solemn procession. The Matanza is followed by this festival, when "thigh mole," made with goat hindquarters and flavored with avocado leaves, *costeño* chiles, and *guajes,* is made in vast quantities and served all over town.

November

Day of the Dead (Oct. 31–Nov. 2) *Día de los Muertos* is considered an authentically Mixtec tradition, and it's less diluted with Halloween and tourism here than the Central Valley.

7

Cuisine

Rich, Spicy, and Full of Love

Oaxaca's vast and varied geography, offering any number of fertile microclimates within a day's walk of the market, and its history, thousands of years nurturing cultural diversity and expression, have conspired to make *la comida Oaxaqueña* one of the finest cuisines in all the world.

The basis of the Oaxacan diet, as throughout Mesoamerica, was once the pre-Columbian triad of maize (corn), beans, and squash. These fundamentals were joined, over the centuries, by other crops first domesticated elsewhere in the Americas and introduced by early visitors: tomatoes, onions, garlic, tomatillos, *nopales* (prickly pear cactus), *maguey*, chiles, cacao (chocolate), pineapple, and various herbs, such as *herba santa*.

To this, the Spanish added ingredients from all over their world, including wheat, the European staple; tamarind, from North Africa; goats and sheep, from the Middle East; and sugarcane, from Southeast Asia. One wonders what the first cook to combine that sweet addition and the native cacao must have thought.

Oaxaca's cosmopolitan appeal has mixed into this rich stew any number of other cultures, as visitors from all over the world, many specifically intrigued by the region's culinary wealth, have come to add their own unique flavor. The result? You'll have to taste for yourself.

Mole colorado *only has 15 or so ingredients;* mole negro *can have twice that.*

On the Menu

Abarrotes: Neighborhood grocery, selling the basics, often in single-use sizes.

Aguacate: Avocado.

Aguardiente: Potent, inexpensive sugar-cane liquor.

Aguas Frescas: A sweet drink made with blended water, sugar, and fruit.

Antojitos: Snacks, usually finger foods such as tacos and *empanadas* (*botanas* are more like bar food).

Asiento: Liquid pork fat, usually drizzled over a crispy tortilla and served with fresh cheese, thinly sliced onions, and chile.

Atole: A thin cornmeal gruel (or thick drink) served piping hot, perhaps with a tamale or pastry, from tiny stands that set up at 6 AM all over town. Comes sweet, *de panela,* or, even better, *con chocolate.*

Bolillos: White rolls, like softer French bread, available cheaply at any normal Mexican bakery (look for a huge bin, in the back) and perfect for sandwiches.

Botanas: Snacks, usually bar food such as peanuts and plantains.

Buñuelo: Fried bread with cinnamon and sugar.

Calabazas: Squash and pumpkins.

Calabazas en dulce: Candied squash, often sold at street stands.

Carnitas: Michoacan-style pork barbecue.

Cazuela: Large pot.

Chayote: A pear-shaped squash often served boiled on the side of the road. The large inner seed is edible (and quite delicious); the tough skin, not so much.

Cecina: Thinly sliced pork.

A piping hot cup of corn atole, perhaps flavored with spiced chocolate, is just the thing to get you going on a chilly Oaxaca morning.

Chapulines: Grasshoppers. The insects are collected in the field, stored for 24 hours (to work out the waste) then simmered with lemon juice and chile.

Chia: A nutritious seed made into aguas frescas—and, yes, Chia Pets.

Chicharones: Pork rinds.

Chichilo (mole stew): One of the rarer moles, made with toasted seeds from several chiles, oregano, and avocado leaves, it's usually served over heavy pork and beef dishes, often with slices of lime.

Chilacayota: Fruit often made into aguas frescas.

Chilaquiles: Hearty breakfast dish made with strips of leftover corn tortillas, cooked with sauce, served with cheese, chicken, onions, etc.

Chiles rellenos: Chiles stuffed with meat, seafood, cheese, beans and/or vegetables, then lightly breaded and deep fried.

Choyones: Corn dumplings.

Churro: Long, fried, cream-filled donut.

Cochinita pibil: Like pulled pork, cooked with *anchiote*, peppers, and onions, traditionally served in banana leaves.

Comal: The clay griddle above an outdoor fire at the heart of any traditional Oaxacan meal, used since the heyday of Monte Albán for making corn tortillas, roasting chiles, and preparing all sorts of other delectables.

Elotes: Corn on the cob is a popular street food, served either boiled or roasted. Choose your ear and order it *con todo* (with everything: lime juice, mayonnaise, cheese and chili powder) or customize to your own tastes.

Enmoladas: Tasty, economical dish of tortillas in mole negro.

Epizote: Herb used as a seasoning, as well as an anti-parasitic. Some folks recommend taking this tea in addition to antibiotics or other modern medical treatments.

Esquitas: Often served at the same stands as *elotes,* this is a Styrofoam cup of stewed corn, with your choice of the same toppings.

Garnachas: Small corn tortillas topped with meat, pickled cabbage, carrot, onion, and tomatoes, sauce and cheese, native to the Isthmus.

Guajolote: Turkey, or *pavo.*

Guia: Edible squash vines, cooked and served like green vegetables.

Gusano: Worm, powdered mixed with salt and chile to make *sal de gusano,* or "worm salt." Served with lime and mezcal.

Hierba sagrada: Sarsaparilla, a broad-leafed herb with a slight anise flavor, is often steamed with other foods, particularly fish.

Horchata: Sweet, rich rice drink often flavored with chocolate, almonds, or fruits.

Huachinango: Red snapper.

Manchamanteles (table-cloth stainer mole): This rich, thin mole often served in a soup bowl involves several chiles, fruits, sweet herbs, and sesame seeds.

Masa: Pre-made corn flour dough, often available from specialty stores that also sell fresh, inexpensive tortillas.

Metate: The traditional, rough stone corn grinder, used since the Olmec era, but today largely replaced by the community *molina.*

Molcajete: Stone mortar-and-pestle-style grinder, sometimes designed to resemble pigs.

Mole amarillo (yellow mole): This light mole can be prepared in an afternoon using fresh herbs, squash, wild mushrooms, and several types of chiles. It's often served over wild game.

Mole colorado (red mole): Perhaps the oldest of the moles, this fiery dish is served with the most traditional meals, such as tamales and enchiladas.

Mole coloradito (little red mole): This fresh-tasting mole has a roasted tomato base, with raisins, plantains, chocolate, allspice, and cinnamon to give it a sweet taste.

Make Mine a Mole
By Beth Penland

They say that those who come to Oaxaca and don't enjoy a rich mole were never really here. The traditional sauce is the centerpiece of holidays and family celebrations, with unique recipes handed down through the generations.

While there is no definitive mole, there are seven basic recipes with up to 30 ingredients that create a rich companion for everything from roast turkey to enchiladas. Mole negro is the most famous and most complex of the sauces to prepare. Ingredients include six types of chiles, plantains, ginger, tomatillos, cloves, squash seeds, almonds, sesame, peanuts, avocado leaves, cinnamon and chocolate.

Creating the sauce from scratch is a painstaking task. Chiles are roasted, seeds and nuts toasted, then carefully blended into a creamy sauce with other ingredients. An all-day simmer results in the kind of mouthwatering, flashback-inducing meal that will haunt you for years after your travels are complete.

While there's no substitute for the real thing, concentrated mole paste produces an amazing result with little effort, and can be found in most grocery stores and online. Diced tomatoes and chicken broth bring the sauce to life and like most things, the longer it simmers the better it gets. For proof, soak cooked, shredded chicken in the sauce and serve with tortillas for a simple but delicious taste of Oaxaqueño cuisine.

If you don't have time to prepare all the 30-plus ingredients for your mole negro tonight, buy paste by the kilo and mix it up at home.

Mole negro (black mole): The "King of the Moles" is also the most complex, a symphony of some 30 ingredients smoothly prepared with precision and dedication, often over the course of days by multiple chefs.

Mole verde (green mole): Light mole is one of the simplest to cook, without the days of preparation required by the more complex negros and colorados. Made with fresh herbs, tomatillos, and stock, it's served over light dishes such as fish or vegetables.

Molina: The community grinder, where people take the ingredients for tortillas, mole, chocolate, and other important foods to be ground to their specifications. You can see them in action on the road next to Mercado 20 de Noviembre.

Nieves: Oaxacan ice cream, usually closer to a sherbet.

Nopal: Prickly pear cactus. After removing the spines, the paddles are sliced, roasted, and used as a green vegetable, while the fruit, or *tuna,* is served as juice or nieves.

Pan de muertos: Egg-yolk bread especially baked with tiny faces for use during Day of the Dead.

Pan de yema: Rolls of dry, tasty egg-yolk bread are perfect alongside a cup of rich, spicy hot chocolate.

Picante: Spicy hot (as distinct from temperature hot, which is *caliente*). Often waiters will ask you *"Picante?"* to determine the level of spice you can manage. A simple *si* or *no,* with an appropriate level of enthusiasm, allows them to season your dish.

Pilloncillo: The thick cones of distinctively flavored brown sugar sold throughout Mexico.

Pan de yema, *best enjoyed with a cup of hot chocolate at Mercado 20 de Noviembre, is called* pan de muerto *when it's decorated with faces for the Day of the Dead.*

Holy Mole! Learn to Cook Oaxacan-style

Can't get enough of that incredible Oaxacan cuisine? Try a cooking class. Most are taught in English, last around four hours, and may include a market tour (highly recommended), during which you'll learn more about Oaxaca's incredible variety of ingredients.

Casa Crespo Cooking Classes (951-514-1102; www.casacrespo.com; Crespo 415, between Allende and Bravo; $60 per person) The professional, four-hour classes are designed for people who already love to cook but want to learn more about Oaxacan ingredients and methods. Classes start at 10 AM and 2 PM and include coffee, pastries, beer, and mezcal.

Non-chefs can enjoy the process at **El Teatro Culinario** (951-514-1102; elteatroculinario@go-oaxaca.com; MC, V; US$65 per person), which offers an eight-course tasting menu of experimental Oaxacan cuisine, by reservation only.

Casa del Tio Güero (951-516-9584; daphneugalde@hotmail.com; García Vigil 715; $40 per person, including lunch) With a less formal approach (and lower prices), chef Alfredo Ugalde offers Latin fusion and vegetarian versions of moles, chiles rellenos, and more in the spare upstairs kitchen.

Cocina de Nora (951-515-5645; 877-234-4706 United States and Canada; www.almademitierra.net; Aldama 205) Run by the wife of Casa de mis Recuerdos, this outfit offers classes in English or in Spanish for groups of up to 10 people. Classes include a market tour and meal, prepared in a fully-equipped kitchen. Vegetarian classes are also available, and Nora can arrange multi-day package deals and tours.

Hacienda Los Laureles (951-501-5300; www.hotelhaciendaloslaureles.com) The renowned gourmet Oaxacan restaurant also offers cooking classes.

Even in the afterlife, this obviously beloved soul is still preparing the perfect mole.

Mano Mágica (951-516-4275; www.casasagrada.com; Alcalá 203) This fabulous handicraft store offers cooking classes at their Teotitlán B&B.

Mexican Cooking with Pilar (951-516-5704; 201-255-6104 from the U.S.; www.laolla.com.mx) Pilar Cabrera of the celebrated La Olla restaurant and Casa de los Sabores B&B offers four-hour classes for every skill level.

Seasons of My Heart (951-504-8100; www.seasonsofmyheart.com) Cookbook author and respected chef Susan Trilling offers a day-long trip into the Etla Valley, where you'll tour the Wednesday market before heading to her impossibly scenic cooking school.

Toni's Tours (951-517-5947; toni_sobel@hotmail.com) A thirty-year resident of Oaxaca with a fan club that includes Rick Bayless, Toni Sobel offers cooking classes and a variety of fully customizable tours that cover the region's handicrafts, history, and of course, cuisine.

Pipián: Rich pumpkin-seed sauce.

Pulque: Cheap, local liquor made from agave and often sold out of large, plastic containers.

Raspado: Snow cone made with freshly shaved ice and your choice of mostly fruity toppings.

Semilla: Seeds, usually served toasted with spices. Semilla chilacayota are the black-and-white calabaza seeds.

Sopa: Soup, but in Oaxaca, *sopa de arroz* and *sopa de pasta* basically means rice pilaf or a light pasta dish.

Tacos Arabes (Arab tacos): A variation on *tacos al pastor,* rotisserie-grilled pork with different (though not particularly Middle Eastern) spices.

Tamales: A satisfying cornmeal dumpling, stuffed with every type of savory filling (meat, mole, vegetables), wrapped in corn husks or banana leaves, boiled, and served steaming hot.

Tasajo: Thinly, delicately sliced beef.

Téjate: You'll see big bowls of this chocolate-colored sweet drink, topped with foamy-looking residue, on sale at markets and plazas all over the state. It is made with corn cooked with senisa, *flor de Rosita*, and *mamuey,* which makes the amazing foam.

Tomatillos: Green berry very similar in taste and appearance to tomatoes, usually used in salsas.

Tortillas: Flatbread cooked on a *comal,* available absolutely everywhere. In Oaxaca, the vast majority of tortillas are corn, but you may be asked if you prefer wheat tortillas

Tutelas: Triangle-shaped tortillas with beans from Tlaxiaco.

8

Shopping

You could spend an entire month in Oaxaca just shopping—for that one perfect *tapete* (wool rug), *huipil* (cotton blouse), or *alebrije* (carved wooden figure)—and some people do. If you're just looking for a beautiful *recuerdo* (memento), your options are endless and relaxed: stroll Oaxaca City's markets and boutiques, or wander the artisanal towns of Central Valleys.

The best strategy for finding the perfect *artesanía* is to find one that you believe is beautiful, no matter who carved, painted, or wove it. Buy it when you see it, as it may not be there tomorrow. And bargain gently; most vendors will quote a price like M$110, to give you the thrill of knocking off the extra 10 pesos. Too shy? Just stand there, examining the piece, and the salesperson will probably offer you a lower price. Over-bargaining, however, is a bit of a social faux pas.

If you are a serious shopper, here to invest in collectors' pieces, or perhaps help finance your trip by bringing home handicrafts, you'll benefit by planning ahead. Invest in a photo guide to Oaxacan handicrafts, such as the indispensable *Mexican Folk Art* by Arden Aibel Rothstein and Anya Leah Rothstein, detailing the Central Valleys' major craft towns and families, with maps of the most important small artisan villages and their workshops. Other worthwhile books are listed in the Recommended Reading chapter.

Consider packing a suitcase within a suitcase, to fill with new treasures for the ride home. Also check out the museums exhibiting your favorite crafts, such as the *tapetes* displayed in Santa Ana and Teotitlán's community museums. High-end craft stores, such as ✪ Mano Magíca in Oaxaca City, are also great places to educate yourself about quality.

Most tour companies include one or more of the artisan towns on their Central Valleys day trips. You'll probably be taken to a single workshop, where you'll spend perhaps an hour watching a demonstration before hitting the road. That's enough for some people, but shopaholics would do better to hire a specialty guide (listed below), or visit the towns on their own. Bus service throughout the Central Valleys is inexpensive and excellent, and taxis are fairly cheap as well. Artists are more than happy to welcome you to their homes, and can usually offer an impromptu demonstration, since they're usually working anyway.

I've listed a few of each town's top artists, but both **Oaxacaoaxaca.com** (www.oaxaca oaxaca.com/artisans.htm) and **Oaxaca Wiki** (oaxaca.wikispaces.com/artesanos) have compiled more comprehensive lists of local artisans. **PROFECO** (951-513-4555; www.profeco .gob.mx; Colegio Militar 1109, Reforma), the Mexican Consumer Protection Agency, accepts Spanish-language complaints about shady businesses.

Handicraft Tours
Several outfits offer tours that introduce you to the artisans.

Casa Linda (951-540-8020, www.folkartfantasy.com, San Andrés Huayapam) Linda Hanna offers custom tours all over the Central Valleys, and runs a cute B&B just outside Oaxaca City with DVDs, books, and other information about Oaxacan *artesanías*.

Manos de Oaxaca (www.manos-de-oaxaca.com) This outfit specializes in tours, workshops, and custom trips for ceramics enthusiasts.

Oaxaca Culture, Art, Tradition (www.oaxacaculture.com) Teotitlán resident and "cultural naviga-tor" Norma Hawthorne offers weaving, dyeing, and other workshops. Her Web site has great photos and information.

Traditions Mexico Hands-On Tours (951-571-3695; www.traditionsmexico.com; Camino a Guadalupe, Etla s/n, Colonia Rabiz) These unique, all-inclusive tours can incorporate classes and workshops.

ALEBRIJES

Oaxaca's most photogenic *artesanías* are the *alebrijes,* colorfully painted wood carvings that depict animals and more fantastic creatures carved from the soft, light wood of the copal tree.

Though the art is sometimes traced back to much older traditions of carving fanciful wooden masks or children's toys, *alebrijes* have existed in their current form only since the 1980s. In recent years, they have transcended simple craftsmanship and entered the realm of fine art, with masterpieces fetching thousands of dollars. But you can still find simpler critters cheap.

When choosing an *alebrije,* the most important quality is that it appeals to you. Objectively, however, the "best" *alebrijes* are larger, smoothly finished, and without removable pieces (though I actually quite like those). Paint is also important, with softer natural dyes more highly prized than vibrant artificial colors.

Men generally do the initial carving and sanding. Many say they "recognize" the figure within the wood, then use simple tools such as machetes, carving knives, and chisels to bring out the shape. The piece is then sanded to a smooth finish and dried for months.

Next, the painters, usually women, begin adding the intricate colors and designs, often inspired by Zapotec and Mixtec motifs. Though the art form may be relatively new, carvers have conscientiously researched and resurrected many of the old images, deities, and pat-terns used by their forebears, such as rabbits, jaguars, owls, and Olmec dragons.

The most famous *alebrije* towns are San Antonio Arrazola and San Martín Tilcajete, while La Unión Tejalapan is becoming famed for its more primitive figures. Less well-known carving towns include neighboring San Pedro Ixtlahuaca, which also produces masks; San Pedro Cajonos, between Ocotlán and San José del Pacífico, where the Blas family paints *alebrijes* with hallucinogenic detail; San Agustín de las Juntas (4 kilo-meters/2 miles south of Oaxaca), known for its skeleton dioramas and nativity scenes; and San Pedro Taviche (2 kilometers/1 mile south of Ocotlán), which produces handsome unpainted wooden figures.

Each brightly painted, hand-carved alebrijes *seems to have its own distinct personality.*

In addition to the resources noted earlier, serious shoppers can look for two guides available at either Amate Books in Oaxaca City, or through the author, Christopher Stowens (cstowens@gmail.com): *The Carvers of La Union Tejalapam* (2008; US$9), with Abigail Andrea Meja; and *The Carvers of San Martín Tilcajete* (2008; US$9), with Rogelio Sosa Ortega.

Oaxaca City
You can find *alebrijes* in almost any shop or market, but some of the finest can be found at **ARIPO** (951-514-0861; García Vigil 809), an artists' cooperative with a wide selection of crafts; **Artesanía Teresita** (Murgia 100-B, just north of the Zócalo), with new *alebrijes* from top-tier carvers arriving almost daily; and the **Mercado de Artesanías** (Matamoros and García Vigil), with more inexpensive items.

San Antonio Arrazola
9 kilometers (6 miles) northwest of Oaxaca
In the shadow of Monte Albán is one of Oaxaca's best-known carving towns. For centuries, it specialized in masks, until innovator **Manuel Jiménez** (951-510-4036; Tabasco 1) began making wooden *nahuals*, or animal guides, painted with bright colors and patterns. Today, his family (who live nearby) is one of the most respected carving families in Oaxaca.

When you arrive in Arrazola, with neither a hotel nor formal restaurant—it does have an ice cream parlor and a couple of *comedors*—you'll see the **Casa de Artesanías** (10 AM–7 PM daily), where several families ply their wares and demonstrate painting and carving. About a block away is another large workshop, **Sergio Santiago** (951-124-2062; sergiosantiago@ yahoo.com; Zapata N 2-B), with a huge selection of high-quality *alebrijes*. But there are scores of workshops worth perusing around town, the most famous belonging to the Ramirez, Castellanos, and Morales families.

Urbanos buses leave Abastos Centro for the Arrazola Casa de Artesanías every half hour (US 80¢), or take a taxi for about US$10.

SAN MARTÍN TICA|ATE
Hwy. 175, 26 kilometers (16 miles) south of Oaxaca City

Oaxaca's most famous *alebrije* town is usually visited as part of a day trip to Ocotlán. Some 120 families are involved, each with their own designs and styles. Dozens of welcoming workshops are within a stone's throw of the plaza, waiting for visitors. But the best time to visit is during the week of Day of the Dead, when the **Fería de Alebrijes** (www.feriadela lebrije.org.mx) takes over town with more than 300 booths, food, music, and events.

There are too many artisans to list, but the subtly painted figures of **Jacobo and María Angeles** (951-524-9047; www.tilcajete.org; Calle Olvido 9, San Martín Tilcajete), which are exhibited in the Smithsonian and other museums, deserve special mention. Other important carvers include the Angeles, Fuentes, Ojeda, Ortega, and Vázquez families.

LA UNIÓN TE|ALAPAM
25 kilometers (16 miles) northwest of Oaxaca City

Well off the beaten path, the third and least commercial of the major *alebrije* towns offers a scenic excuse to explore rural Oaxaca. (Many mountainbike tours begin out here.) The specialty is "primitive *alebrijes*," a bit rougher around the edges and less precisely painted, but just as expressive and eye-catching. They also usually feature natural dyes. The most collected creations come from the Santiago, Lopez, Perez, and Santos families, but several other artists have workshops and homes scattered around the countryside.

Before painting, alebrijes *need to bake in the sun for several weeks.*

Amate Paintings

If you eat at the markets or on the Zócalo, you'll be offered bright, detailed, naïve paintings, usually of village life, on *amate,* a thick, rough paper made from tree bark. Traditionally painted in the neighboring state of Guerrero, this inexpensive, durable souvenir is now sold across Southern Mexico. Paintings range from absolutely exquisite to downright sloppy, and are priced accordingly. At least check a few out while you're waiting for your food to arrive. Salespeople appreciate the chance to show off their work even if you don't plan to buy, and they can be quite pretty.

Basketry

Perhaps the most ancient *artesanía,* baskets are produced throughout the state from palm, reeds, or *carriz,* similar to bamboo, as well as colorful and durable synthetics. Most woven goods sold in Oaxaca City, including hats, bags, and baskets, are made in the Mixteca and can be found more cheaply in the markets of basket-producing regions such as Huajuapan, Sol de Vega, and Coixtlihuaca.

Several towns of the Central Valleys also specialize in woven palm products, including tortilla holders, *petates* (mats), brooms, bags, baskets, and colorful purses. These include Albarradas (18 kilometers/11 miles southeast of Mitla); San Juan Guelavia (5 kilometers/ 3 miles south of Teotitlán), where the famous Towers of Fire fireworks displays are constructed; San José El Mogote (Hwy. 190, 18 kilometers/11 miles north of Oaxaca); and Animas Trujano (Hwy. 175, 10 kilometers/6 miles south of Oaxaca). In Oaxaca City, baskets are produced in the neighborhoods of Santa Cruz Papalutla, San Juan Guelavía, and Magdelena Teitipac, southeast of town.

Juchitán, along the palm-shaded shores of the Isthmus of Tehuantepec, is known for its hats, mats, and baskets, most characteristically the *tenat,* a sort of soft, square-bottomed basket that can be made watertight.

Ceramics

The Central Valleys have been exporting their unusually graceful pottery, made with distinctive gray clay, since at least 500 B.C. Despite the obvious difficulties with transport, ceramics from San Bartolo Coyotepec are found throughout the old Olmec and Aztec Empires. Today's tougher pieces will also be fine in your luggage or the mail; have the store or artists package it for you.

While pottery is still made throughout the state, the most popular styles hail from the Central Valleys. Santa María Atzompa is best known for its rich green glazed pieces; large, terracotta figurative pieces called *muñecas,* or dolls; and brightly colored glazed pots. San Bartolo Coyotepec is best known for its lustrous black pottery, while Ocotlán's Aguilar sisters make brightly painted red-clay figures, collected all over the world.

Several museums display ceramics past and present. Pre-Columbian pieces are exhibited at Santo Domingo and Museo Rudolfo Morales in Oaxaca City, while almost all of the small-town community museums feature ancient ceramics. The State Museum in San Bartolo Coyotepec is a great place to see flawless examples of contemporary pottery.

Santa María Atzompa

6 kilometers (4 miles) from Oaxaca

Oaxaca's most important ceramic production village is more of a neighborhood these days, rapidly being engulfed by Oaxaca City, just as when Monte Albán expanded into the neighborhood some 15 centuries ago. Now, as then, Atzompa is a ceramics center, best known for its striking *loza verde*, a safe, emerald-green glaze made with copper oxide. It's primarily used for utilitarian pieces, such as cooking pots, fruit bowls, and salsa dishes. The founder of the Potters' Union, **Mario Enríquez López** (951-512-7483; Independencia 510), produces some of the finest.

Serious collectors, however, come for the large, figurative, terracotta *muñecas* pioneered by artist Teodora Blanco, who was "discovered" by collector John D. Rockefeller. Today, her descendents have kept the tradition alive, usually portraying women—mothers, mermaids, angels, virgins—emblazoned with *pastillaje,* a thick relief of flowers, vines, animals, and other adornment, sometimes given a red wash or glaze to accent the texture. While the **Blanco Family** (Luis and María 951-512-7942, Libertad 502; Ima 951-558-0286, Juárez 302; Leticia, Juárez 109) continue to make very beautiful pieces, **Angélica Vásquez Cruz** (951-558-9061; Independencia 137) is considered the current master of the art, with very complex and detailed pieces of almost *retablo*-style beauty.

Colored glazes, most from Monterrey, are used on pieces made for both display and utilitarian purpose. **Dolores and Regino Porras** (951-169-9311; Hidalgo 502 and Libertad 619) began working with colored glazes in the early 1960s, and still make some of the best.

Incidentally, Atzompa is also the original home of the ch-ch-ch-Chia Pet. Traditionally a Semana Santa decoration, partially green-glazed animals are sown with *ch'a* seeds, a nutritious Aztec-era snack, then watered to create that thick green. You can find authentic Chia Pets, as well as the stunning ceramics created by more than 100 area families, at the **Artisan's Market** (Casa del Artesanos) on the way into town.

San Bartolo Coyotepec

Hwy. 175, 12 kilometers (8 miles) south of Oaxaca

San Bartolo Coyotepec's distinctive gray ceramics have been found as far away as Tehuantepec, Veracruz, and Guatemala. Today, the town is known for a luminous black pottery with a depth of sheen achieved by rubbing the greenware with a quartz stone.

The process, called *negro brillante,* "shiny black," was pioneered by potter Doña Rosa Real Mateo. You can visit her landmark 1952 workshop, **Doña Rosa Alfareria** (951-551-0011; Calle Juárez 24), where her family carries on the tradition; her son, Don Valente Nieto, gets raves.

Don't miss MEAPO, the State Museum. Check out the coveted work of artist **Carlomagno Pedro Martínez** (951-551-0034; Guerrero 1), who produces eerie and amazing scenes from folklore and modern life, using skeletons, devils, and other Oaxacan characters.

Ocotlán de Morelos

The famed, figurative terracotta pottery of Ocotlán, brightly colored like its beautiful Dominican church, is the work of the **Aguilar sisters** (951-571-0334), whose homes (unmissable thanks to the ceramics out front) are on the south side of Hwy. 175. Stop by to see Guillermina, Irene, Josefina, and Concepción Aguilar, as well as their numerous grandchildren, at work. Cheerful *muñecas,* colorful trees of life, and other motifs were passed down by their parents.

Clothing and Textiles

Each of the 16 Oaxacan ethnicities makes their own traditional clothing, still worn by many women on a day-to-day basis. You can purchase top-notch stuff in Oaxaca, or head out into the hinterlands in search of the perfect *huipil.*

Visitors are usually immediately attracted to the rich floral embroidered black velvet *trajes* (outfits) of the Isthmus of Tehuantepec, patterned after Asian designs. The Triqui women's distinctive full-length, red-striped, wool *huipil* is another eye-catching item, more often purchased as a wall hanging than a warm dress.

Dozens of towns make their own traditional *huipiles,* a long dress or shirt without a distinct waist, often embroidered with animals and other designs, or bedecked with ribbons. Among the finest are those from San Pedro de Amusgos, often carefully embroidered. The famous, painstakingly embroidered muslin "wedding dress" *huipiles* are sewn in San Juan Chilateca, San Pedro Martir, and most famously, San Antonino Castillo Velasco, all located on Hwy. 175 south of Ocotlán. Only those from San Antonio feature a row of very-difficult-to-sew little people hidden within the design, and the words *Hazme si puede,* "Make me if you can."

Also keep an eye out for woolen capes (*quechquémitl*), and *enredos,* or wrap skirts, often imported from Chiapas or Guatemala. Women of the Mixtec Coast make similar skirts, called *pozahuancos* and dyed purple with snails, and red with cochineal. They're often worn topless.

Oaxaca City

Adolfina, Xicotencatl (951-514-6618; 418 Rayón, Centro) Traditional clothing, including dresses from the Isthmus and men's *guayabera* shirts, are excellent quality.

The lush floral embroidery of the Isthmus was probably originally inspired by flowered Chinese shawls brought here with the railroad.

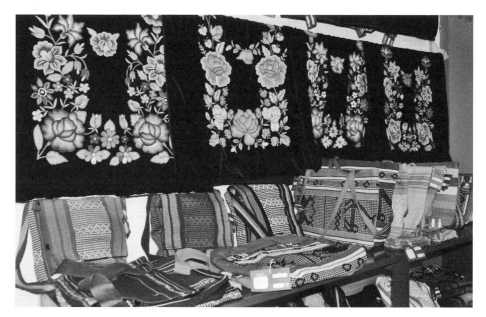

Arte Textil Indígena (951-501-0552; Macedonia Alcalá 403-2) This high-end boutique sells top-quality indigenous fabrics and clothing; there's another branch in San Miguel Allende.

Arte Textil Tusuchya (951-509-4669; Cinco de Mayo 217) This weaving collective produces more modern designs using traditional fabrics.

Los Baules de Juana Cata (Alcalá 403, Plaza Comercial Casa Vieja) A top-notch spot for traditional clothing, particularly natural-dyed *rebozos* and *huipiles.*

Boutique Raiz·es (951-514-7216; García Vigil 304; open 9 AM–8 PM Mon.–Sat.) Hidden in Plaza Etnias, this upscale boutique offers the best of Mexican designer Pineda Covalin (www.pinedacovalin.com), who is known for combining haute couture with traditional culture. The store also sells similarly stylish shoes handmade in Matamoros.

Codice Design (951-516-9691; Alcalá 302, Centro) This store sells bright Mayan designs and fabrics from Guatemala and the Yucatán. Clothing, bags, pillows, and beaded jewelry are all very high quality.

Étnico Textiles (951-516-0734; textilostipicos@hotmail.com; Allende 113, Centro) A kaleidoscope of Technicolor Mayan fabrics and quality Oaxacan fabrics at prices to match. There's another location at Gurrion 104, Centro.

✪ **Federico** (951-514-4996; Matamoros 307, Centro) This fabulous shop specializes in antique tapestries, *tapetes,* jewelry, and clothing, from Oaxaca State, the Philippines, Iran, Romania, Pakistan, Goa, and more.

✪ **Malacate** (951-516-8633; Gurrión 110, Centro) Designer Silvia Suárez works with traditional artists to recast traditional fabrics and designs, such as those from the Isthmus, into more modern silhouettes.

Tienda Q (951-514-8880; tienda_q@prodigy.net.mx; Manuel Bravo 109, Centro) Associated with Galería Quetzalli, this cool store has *dosa* cloths, *coyuchi* bedding, linen *guayabera,* designer shawls, and other artistic crafts.

CENTRAL VALLEYS

Guillermo Brena Cooperativa (951-518-0371; www.cooperativabrena.com; El Tule, Libertad 50, 14 kilometers/9 miles east of Oaxaca City) The four-pedal loom weavers' cooperative is geared for industrial orders, and offers tours with advance reservations.

Mitla (Hwy. 190, 46 kilometers/29 miles east of Oaxaca) A major cloth production center, here huge, modern pedal looms transform mainly hand-dyed cotton cloth into *rebozos* (shawls), tightly woven tablecloths, napkins, mantles, drapes, bedspreads, and more.

SANTO TOMÁS JALIEZA

(Hwy. 175, 25 kilometers/16 miles south of Oaxaca City) Famed for its five-century-old tradition of *taller de cintura,* or waist looms, this tidy market always features several local women demonstrating this fascinating art. The weaver ties one end of scores of cotton strands to her belt, the other to a pole. The art dates to about 900 B.C., and was exported from Oaxaca throughout Mesoamerica.

Oaxaca's first weavings were done on waist looms, still used today at the Santo Tomas Jalietza market.

CORN HUSK DOLLS

Better known as *totomoxtle*, this relatively new (for Oaxaca) art form uses corn husks to depict local folks, for instance, or the dance *trajes* of the Guelaguetza, often accented with dried flowers. The finest are displayed alongside the radish sculptures on December 23, when the Zócalo hosts *Noche de los Rabanos.* Most of the husks come from the Ocotlán Valley, and many are dyed using natural ingredients.

FINE ART GALLERIES

While other towns focus on *alebrijes* or black pottery, Oaxaca City's specialty is fine art. There are more than 20,000 registered artists in town, displaying their work on every blank surface in the city. Even more artists, from around the country and all over the world, take advantage of the art-savvy crowds, and exhibit their work at one of the city's galleries. These are just a few.

Arte Biulú (Avenida Juárez 503; closed Mon. and Tues.) In addition to great art, the gallery also offers live jazz, free of charge, Saturdays at 5 PM.

Arte de Oaxaca (951-514-0910; www.artedeoaxaca.com; Murgia 105 between Alcalá and Cinco de Mayo) Artist and philanthropist Rodolfo Morales founded this gallery to promote young artists, and hung a permanent collection of his own work to bring in the crowds.

BiuArte Mexicano (Alcalá 407, Plaza Santo Domingo) This important gallery showcases fine art done in the Oaxacan craft tradition, including truly outstanding ceramics, paintings, *alebrijes,* and textiles, much of it from the Mixtec Coast.

Blackbox (www.la-blackbox.com; Cinco de Mayo 412, between Abasolo and Constitución) Somewhere between art and craft is innovative Blackbox, which offers what you might call cutting-edge *artesanías.*

Galería Arte Azul (951-514-0475; www.arteazulgaleria.blogspot.com; Calle Abasolo 313) A beautiful whitewashed Colonial surrounding a pretty patio provides a premium place where local painters, whose work is usually more colorful and figurative, can display their wares.

Galería Indigo (951-514-3889; www.galeriaindigo.com; Allende 104, Centro) The shop offers high-quality contemporary paintings from all over Mexico, and other interesting contemporary and traditional objects from around the world.

Galería Quetzalli (951-514-0030, 951-514-2606; Constitución 104-1) This small gallery carries the big names, including local son and philanthropist Francisco Toledo. It's right behind Santo Domingo. There's another location at Murgía 400.

Tierra Quemada (951-514-6688; www.tierraquemada.com; Labastida 115-2 Plaza las Vírgenes) The "Scorched Earth" gallery specializes in cutting-edge ceramics.

HOJALATA (TIN WORK)

This classic Mexican art form dating to the 1600s uses flat sheets of tin, cut and hammered into different forms, and often painted with colorful lacquer. Oaxaca's most prolific work-shops are in the Xochimilco district of Oaxaca City.

Cost and quality vary widely, ranging from US$1 Christmas tree ornaments colored with automobile paint to elaborate sculptural pieces, such as trees of life and candelabras, worth hundreds. Note that all tin crafts must be checked as luggage on planes.

JEWELRY

Oaxaca has been a jewelry lovers' paradise for thousands of years, with an indigenous tradition of beautiful jade pieces, *cera perdida,* or lost wax, gold work, emulating pieces discovered at Monte Albán. Spanish-influenced work is also popular, such as the delicate filigree jewelry, and large "Mitla crosses." Mitla is a production town for filigree and other jewelry, often sold at the market outside the ruins. These stores are all in Oaxaca City.

Ambar de Chiapas (951-514-8577; joseambar@hotmail.com; García Vigil 212, Centro) This wonderful store sells the high-quality amber Chiapas is famous for, as well as the region's bright fabrics and weavings.

Casa Vieja (951-514-2019; www.danielespinosa.com; Alcalá 403-5) The fine jeweler next to Los Danzantes sells Daniel Espinosa designs, including lots of chunky silver. pieces.

✪ **Delfino García Esperanza** (951-514-6880; Vega 305, Centro) This friendly and very traditional filigree jeweler does it the old-fashioned way, and was even commissioned by Princess Letizia of Spain to create jewelry for her wedding. His pieces are also sold at the Casa de las Artesanías on Matamoros.

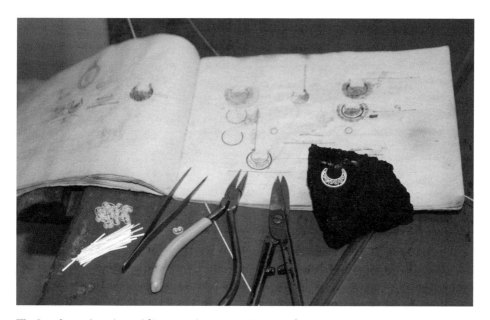

Watch as Oaxaca's traditional filigree jewelry is painstakingly crafted at Monte Albán jewelers.

Plata de Oaxaca y Atigüedades (951-516-3935; Abasolo 107, Centro) Specializes in fine antiques, primarily jewelry, but also clothing and artwork.

✪ **Oro de Monte Albán** (951-514-3813; www.orodemontealban.com; Gurrión and Alcalá, next to Santo Domingo) Upscale chain specializes in reproductions of cast-gold jewelry recovered from Monte Albán. There are several locations, including one at Monte Albán Archaeological Park, but this location has a small workshop where you can ask for a brief tour and demonstration, usually in Spanish only.

Que Tenga Buena Mano (951-184-8515; artesaniasbuenamano@yahoo.com.mx; Constitución 108) Right across from Santo Domingo, this local landmark specializes in filigree jewelry made by the owner's family, and also sells antique jewelry, *milagros,* and hammered tin *hojalata* pieces.

El Palacio de las Gemas (951-514-4603; Morelos 800, corner of Alcalá) Uncut gems and semi-precious stones are here just waiting to be set, as well as finished pieces ranging from inexpensive to astronomical.

Taller del Orfebre (951-514-4388; Alcalá 205-A and 206-D, Centro) Facing off across the busy pedestrian street, the husband-and-wife team of Antonio and Judith Roque operate two shops specializing in Oaxacan jewelry: gold and silver filigree, *milagros,* Zapotec and Mixtec designs, Spanish Colonial designs, and at the 205-A location, more creative, contemporary work.

El Copal (951-516-6512; Allende 113, corner of García Vigil) The store sells beautiful jewelry from the silver capital of the Americas, Tlaxco de Alarcón.

MEZCAL

The best place to by mezcal is at a roadside factory outlet; there are dozens between Oaxaca and Santiago Matatlán, the self-proclaimed, and uncontested, "Mezcal Capital of the World." But there are dozens, more likely hundreds, of varieties available in Oaxaca Centro.

Casa Chagoya (951-553-8251; kilometer 29, Hwy. 190) Good mezcal and great tours are on offer at one of the oldest distilleries in the region. Free tastings, of course.

Del Maguey (www.mezcal.com) Arguably the best mezcal available (and definitely the best packaging), Del Maguey offers several award-winning, single-village liquors, such as the Tobala, made with wild *maguey*, or the very limited run of *Pechuga*, triple-distilled with chicken breast, almonds, wild plums, apples, and mango.

Matatlán Mezcaleria (951-516-6974; www.matatlanmezcaleria.com; J.P. García 300, Centro) This boutique-style downtown Mezcal shop sells Alvaro Carrillo, El Rey Zapoteco, Mayordomo, Matateco, Mistique, Amigo, El Señorio, and other brands of mezcal.

Mezcal's flavor is affected by many things, including the distilling process. Using a copper still, like this 400-year-old beauty displayed at Santo Domingo, has long been considered one of the best methods.

Mezcal Benevá (951-514-7005; www.mezcalbeneva.com; Colón 518-A, Centro) Try this much-lauded mezcal at the maker's downtown Oaxaca shop, or visit the factory (Continental-Istmo Tours goes there) at kilometer 42 on the Oaxaca-Istmo Hwy., near Mitla.

Scorpion Mezcal (914-921-6988; www.scorpionmezcal.com) The award-winning artisanal mezcal made in small batches sets itself apart by adding a scorpion, rather than a boring old worm, to the mix. Arrange tours in advance.

NATURAL DYES

Tapetes are dyed using either natural or artificial colors, a difference that will be immediately obvious after you've seen a few examples side by side. Chemical dyes are usually more brightly colored, while the soft, muted tones of pricey natural dyes, favored by collectors, usually raise the price of similar rugs by about 30 percent.

The most famous and expensive Oaxacan dye, upon which the state's fortunes were built during the early Colonial era, is cochineal (carmine), made from the dried, ground-up bodies of a tiny insect, *grana cochinilla,* that lives in the paddles of prickly pear cactus. By using lime juice, calcium, and other catalysts, artisans can modify the rich, long-lasting red to a spectrum of pinks, orange, and violets.

Most other dyes, with the exception of purple (derived from a snail harvested on the Mixtec Coast) come from plants: mosses or alfalfa for green, marigolds or pomegranate skins for yellows, nuts for brown, *añil* (indigo) for blue, and black from a plant called the *huizache.* Almost any large workshop in Teotitlán or Santa Ana can give you a demonstration, or check out one of these special tours.

Natural Dyes Workshop (951-515-3376, 951-121-9386; www.duubee.blogspot.com; oaxacaventura@yahoo.com.mx; Calle Pajaritos 213, Jalatlaco; classes US$95, 10 AM–6 PM daily) Master weaver Roman Gutiérrez Ruíz offers daily classes on natural dyes, using *cochinilla* (red), *pericón* (yellow) and *añil* (indigo blue).

Tlapanochestli Rancho La Nopalera (951-551-0030; www.aztecacolor.com; Santa María Coyotepec, kilometer 10.5 Carretera; open 9:30 AM–5 PM; US$1) This exhibition-oriented dye factory and lab shows how *cochinilla* is farmed, harvested, dried, and used. It offers several tours and three-day workshops.

El Tono de Cochinilla (951-166-6172; www.eltonodelacochinilla.com; Teotitlán) *Tapete* workshop specializes in *cochinilla,* offering basic demonstrations and the chance to pluck one of the little ladies off a cactus paddle yourself. Go ahead, send her to a red end.

OTHER HANDICRAFTS

There's really no end to the types of handicrafts available in Oaxaca State, but here are a few shops you can explore in search of something completely different.

OAXACA CITY

Arte y Vidrio de Oaxaca Galeria (951-514-5640; www.arteyvidriodeoaxaca.com; Valdivieso 116, Centro) This shop has beautiful hand-blown glass, some functional, all sculptural.

Artesanías Taly (951-516-5695; Cinco de Mayo 409) Angela Garcia has been offering a fine selection of textiles, masks, *alebrijes,* jewelry, and traditional clothing, much of it antique, since 1965.

Jarcieria El Arte Oaxaqueño (951-516-1581; Mina 317, corner of JP Garcia) Long-standing folk art specialty shop close to the Mercado de Artesanías offers a great selection of local handicrafts.

✪ **La Mano Mágica** (951-516-4275; www.lamanomagica.com; Alcala 203, Centro) This absolutely spectacular shop showcases the very finest examples of Oaxacan crafts. It's a great place to explore even if you can't afford anything, just to know what a really good *tapete, alebrije,* or black ceramic pot is supposed to look like. It also offers weaving and other demonstrations, as well as a cooking school and several tours in and around Teotitlán.

CENTRAL VALLEYS

Each town in the Valley (and state) has its specialty. For instance, the wooden beaters used to make hot chocolate are created in San Bartolome Quialana (6 kilometers/4 miles south

Skeletons are a favorite in souvenir shops.

of Tlacolula), while *metates,* or grinding stones, are made at San Sebastian Teitipac (24 kilometers/15 miles southeast of Oaxaca City). *Velas,* the spectacularly decorated ceremonial candles blooming with delicate wax flowers, are a specialty of Teotitlán. And that's just for starters.

Arcano 13 Boutique Esoterica (951-168-7328; Gonzalez Ortega, Xoxocotlán) Jorge Cedillo offers everything from love potions to tarot card readings.

Ayuuk (951-518-1000; Santa María El Tule, Cristobal 1) Though more famed for its tree, El Tule offers this neat shop with local ceramics, *huipiles,* carvings, and other handicrafts.

Armando Lozano (San Bartolo Coyotepec, Calle Juárez near Doña Rosa Alfareria) In a town better known for its black pottery, Lozano produces beautiful brass jewelry.

Oaxaca Paper Factory and Center for the Arts (951-521-2829; papeloaxaca@hotmail .com; Francisco Madero, Barrio Vista Hermosa, San Agustín Etla) This small town in the Etla Valley is home to a community-based manufacturing collective founded by local artists and Finnish paper experts. Tour the factory, take part in a workshop, or just check out the gift shop, packed with all-natural paper products impregnated with local plants, sparkling mica, and natural dyes.

TAPETES

Oaxaca's renowned wool weavings, called *tapetes,* are mainly produced in Teotitlán and Santa Ana del Valle, both of which have excellent community museums describing the art form's history and technique. Dozens of workshops and showrooms are within walking distance of each. More adventurous *tapete* lovers could visit the nearby, but much-less-touristed weaving villages of San Miguel del Valle (14 kilometers/9 miles northeast of Tlacolula), with humble lodging, and Villa Diaz Ordaz (10 kilometers/6 miles north of Tlacolula). No matter where you go, bring a tape measure so you'll get the rug size you want.

The popular Tule-Mitla day trip offered by most tour operators usually stops at a rug workshop in Teotitlán, where you'll enjoy a fascinating demonstration that begins with from raw wool from the chilly Alta Mixteca highlands, where the sheep are woollier. After the uncombed *churro* wool is washed with a traditional herbal disinfectant, it is carded and spun by hand using *ruecas*, pine spinning wheels. Traditionally, women prepare and dye the thread (see Natural Dyes, earlier), while men do the actual weaving on large, standing pedal looms very similar to those brought by the Spanish in the 1500s.

If you visit on your own, almost any large workshop will be willing to give you the same tour—and because your guide won't be charging the artist a 40 percent commission, you'll get a better deal. Workshops and tour operators can also arrange classes and homestays; some folks stay for weeks and really learn to weave and dye.

Most, however, just come to shop. Compare prices and quality, and learn to spot the difference between brighter, less expensive chemical dyes, and subtler natural hues. It's a bit harder for newbies to tell the difference between pure wool and blends, but give that a try as well. There are around 300 *tapete*-producing families in the region, half of them in Teotitlán. Top-quality rugs can be pricey, but are generally much less expensive than Navajo rugs, with which they are often compared. The Santa Ana market seemed to have the best prices on good-quality (if not museum-quality) rugs.

OAXACA CITY

The best spot in the city to find good prices on very nice *tapetes* is **Jardín Labastida**, a small plaza close to Santo Domingo. All of the artisan markets also carry huge selections

Sheep in the mountains of the Mixteca produce soft, durable wool perfect for tapetes.

of *tapetes*. The really top-notch *tapetes* (worth admiring, at least) are displayed at galleries including **La Mano Mágica** (Alcalá 203), where you can watch them being woven, and specialty shops including:

Arte y Tradicion (Ollin; 951-516-3552, García Vigil 406 between Matamoros and M. Bravo) This store sells beautiful tapetes, Gobelin-technique tapestries, and interesting, often abstract art.

Rugs/Tapetes Laadi (951-524-4071; Aldama 18, Centro) The well-respected Mendoza family of Teotitlán sells their fine wares at this shop.

Tapetes de Teotitlán (951-516-1675; teotitlantours@hotmail.com; Alcala 402, Centro) Luis Martínez Jiménez and his family sell rugs in Oaxaca, but can arrange three-hour weaving and dyeing demonstrations in Teotitlán. The cost for up to six people is US$60.

TEOTITLÁN DEL VALLE

There are more that 150 weaving families operating in Teotitlán, many of whom are listed on Oaxaca Wiki (www.oaxaca.wikispaces.com/teotitlanweavers).

Arriero Zapotec Rugs (951-524-4355; www.arrierorugs.com; Constitución 12) Company founder Pantaleon Ruiz Martinez has a great Web site—and free shipping.

Casa Santiago (951-524-4154; www.artesaniascasasantiago.com; Avenida Juárez 70 Teotitlán del Valle) This shop has turned out some of Teotitlán's top rugs for 50 years, and offers demonstrations as well.

Centro de Arte Textil Zapoteco Bii Daüü (951-524-4452; www.biidauu.com.mx; Iturbide 19) The grass roots weaving collective of some 30 local artisans produces top-quality pieces, including purses, shawls, and blankets, using mostly natural dyes, and offers the usual demonstrations. The cooperative also offers classes and workshops, organic farming, and homestays.

Constantino López Martinez (951-524-4426; Calle Rayón 19) This top-notch rug weaver can do custom designs, or you can just drop in to see the cool adobe workshop. He also sells his fine work in Oaxaca City, at García Vigil 304, Centro.

Cooperativa de Artesanos (951-524-4092, 951-124-1947; viridiana_loom56@hotmail .com, gaspar_chavez@hotmail.com; Juárez kilometer 2.5) This well-organized cooperative offers all the dying and weaving tours, as well as classes, workshops, and special events.

Indigo Rugs (951-166-6210; indigorugs@yahoo.com; Carretera Teotitlán kilometer 2.5) Specializing in natural indigo dyes, the company provides transportation from Oaxaca City and complimentary demonstrations and tours. It also has a *temazcal* onsite.

Isaac Vasquéz García (951-524-4122; Hidalgo 30) The patriarch of the respected Vasquéz clan uses only traditional methods for weaving his award-winning tapetes. His daughter **Alda** (951-524-4132; vasqueztapetes@yahoo.mx; Juárez 119) is one of the few female weavers in this still very traditional world.

9

Transportation

Oaxaca State enjoys solid transportation infrastructure, including three international airports in Oaxaca City and the Pacific Coast resort towns of Huatulco and Puerto Escondido. Well-maintained federal highways radiate out from Oaxaca City, connecting it to other major state towns, including (clockwise from 12 o'clock) Tuxtepec, Tehuantepec, Pochutla and the Puerto Ángel Beaches, Puerto Escondido, Tlaxiaco, and Huajuapan. A much faster toll road, Hwy. 135, connects Oaxaca City with Mexico City in five hours.

Clean, comfortable first-class buses, with air conditioning, television, and bathrooms, connect those major cities; normally, it's best to get tickets at least a day in advance. Second-class buses and shuttle vans, without all those frills, serve the smaller towns (as well as the larger cities, where they are cheaper and generally take longer to travel the same distance).

Some of the smaller pueblos are only served by buses and/or shuttle vans a few times

Bicycles are a great way to get around rural Oaxaca, but are perhaps best left to professionals in the city center.

Though unpaved, many important secondary roads are well maintained and passable by normal cars most of the year.

weekly. However, many have regular service in covered trucks (*camionetas*) and *colectivo* taxis from nearby towns, but these rarely have set schedules, and instead generally leave when they have enough passengers to pay for the trip. Of course, it's possible to hire private taxis (*particulares*) almost anywhere, at press time running about US$20 per hour for up to four people.

You can also rent a car in Oaxaca City and other major towns, which is relatively expensive (around US$50 per day for the smallest car, even more for a four-wheel-drive). But all the roads covered in this book, though perhaps unpaved, are passable to regular cars, at least in dry season. Gas is also inexpensive compared to the United States and Europe.

Athletic types can also rent bicycles, not covered in this chapter (check the Activities sections of the destination chapters for listings). Local transport is also covered in the Getting Around section of each destination chapter.

Air

For information about the two international airports on the Pacific Coast—Huatulco and Puerto Escondido—please see that chapter.

Mexico City
Aeropuerto Internacional de la Ciudad de Mexico Benito Juárez (MEX; 552-482-2424; www.aicm.com.mx) The vast majority of international travelers will fly into Mexico City, where they will get either a plane or bus to Oaxaca. The airport is served by direct flights from more than 100 destinations worldwide, which brought more than 26 million people

through the airport in 2008. The sprawling airport is larger than many Oaxaqueño cities, with scores of restaurants and shops, and five-star hotels in both terminals. Domestic flights make regular connections to Oaxaca City, Huatulco, and Puerto Escondido.

While there is a bus station at the international airport, it does not offer direct service to Oaxaca. It does, however, offer first-class Estrella Roja buses every half hour to Puebla (US$17; www.estrellaroja.com.mx); make sure the bus goes to the Central de Autobuses Puebla (CAPU) station in Puebla, where you can catch Autobuses Unidos (AU) buses into Oaxaca City (US$12).

To get a direct bus from Mexico City to Oaxaca, you'll need to get a cab, about US$15, to the Terminal de Autobuses de Oriente (TAPO) bus station across town. Autobuses del Oriente (ADO) (www.adogl.com.mx) has buses to Oaxaca City (US$26) almost hourly, with continuing service to Huatulco (US$32) and Puerto Escondido (US$30).

Oaxaca City

Xoxocotlán International Airport (OAX) On a much more human scale, this tiny airport has one waiting room, one restaurant, and a couple of shops selling chocolate, mole, and mezcal. It is served by several charter and regular airlines, including:

Aerocalifornia (951-514-8570; Morelos 1207, Centro)

AeroMexico (951-516-1066; www.aeromexico.com; Hidalgo 513, corner of 20 de Noviembre)

Aerotucán (951-501-0530; 800-640-4148; www.aerotucan.com.mx; Alcalá 201, Centro) The local carrier offers inexpensive daily flights between Oaxaca City (951-501-0530, 951-501-0532; Alacalá 201, Centro) and both Huatulco (958-587-2427; Boulevard Chahué 164, Plaza Camelinas), which has offices in La Crucecita, and Puerto Escondido (954-582-3461; Hwy. 200, at the airport).

Aerovega (951-516-2777 Oaxaca City, 958-582-0151 Puerto Escondido; aerovega@prodigy.net, aerovegaoax@hotmail.com; Alameda de Léon 1-H) This small, local carrier offers four flights daily between Oaxaca City and Puerto Escondido. Make reservations at the Monte Albán Hotel in Oaxaca City (Alameda de León 1, Centro).

Aviacsa (951-518-4555 Centro, 951-511-5039 airport; 800-006-2200; Pino Sáurez 604, Centro; www.aviacsa.com)

A Volar (1-800-021-7000, 1-800-300-0700)

Continental Express (951-503-3414, 1-800-900-5000; www.continental.com; Airport)

Líneas Aéreas Azteca (951-501-0190; 1-800-229-8322; Murgia 301, corner of Reforma, Centro)

Mexicana (951-516-8414 Oaxaca City; 1-800-801-2010; www.mexicana.com; Fiallo 102, corner of Independencia, Centro Oaxaca; closed Sun.) Some flights are branded as Mexicana Click (www.clickmx.com); there's another office at the Oaxaca Airport (951-511-5229).

Mexicana Click (951-511-5766, 800-122-5425; www.clickmx.com; Airport)
There are three car rental companies at the airport (see car rentals, below), but these charge an extra airport service fee. It's usually better to rent from their in-town locations.

The airport is served by special shuttle vans providing inexpensive door-to-door transport into town. Tell the drivers (who flag you down after your plane arrives) where you are going, and they charge a set fee, around US$7, depending on your destination.

Public Bus

Mexico has an excellent network of bus companies, and **Different World** (www.different world.com/mexico/buses.htm) offers English-language descriptions of several of the nationwide carriers, as well as links to their Web sites. Also check out **Bamba Experience** (800-462-2622, Mexico; 555-584-4401; www.bambaexperience.com), a hop-on, hop-off bus company geared to backpackers, with service to Oaxaca City and the beach communities.

There are two main bus stations in Oaxaca City, the shiny new first-class bus station, just north of Parque El Llano; and the grungy but friendly second-class bus station, usually called Centro de Abastos, close to Mercado Abastos. There are also dozens of smaller companies that run buses to specific destinations from stations all over town. No matter which bus you take, keep an eye on your belongings; if someone tries to distract you (say, trying to speak to you through the window, or spilling something on you), that's a red flag reminding you to stay alert and keep your valuables close.

First-Class Bus Station (951-513-0529; Calz. Niños Héroes de Chapultepec 1036, at Calle Emilio Carranza) The sleek modern bus station rivals the international airport for comfort and style, and is complete with gift shop (last chance for mole and chocolate!), left luggage, convenience store, coffee shop, and climate-controlled sitting area close to the orderly ticketing and loading areas.

To reserve bus tickets online, or just check schedules and costs, log onto **Ticket Bus** (800-702-8000; www.ticketbus.com.mx), which has information and tickets for most first-class lines including ADO, OCC, UNO, AV, Sur, and Cuenca. If you'd rather buy tickets in person, you can do it directly at the bus station, or drop by Oaxaca's **Ticket Bus Office** (951-516-3820; 20 de Noviembre 103-D; open 9 AM–12:30 PM and 3 PM–9:30 PM daily). There's another Ticketbus kiosk (Avenida Universidad) at Mall Plaza del Sol, next to Scotiabank; use your bank card as you would at an ATM.

ADO (Autobuses del Oriente; 800-702-8000 Mexico, 1-800-950-0287 U.S.; 951-515-1248 Oaxaca City; www.ado.com.mx). The premier bus line of Southern Mexico and the Yucatán connects destinations all over Oaxaca, including Tehuantepec, Juchitán (971-711-1022; Calle Prologación 16 de Septiembre 68), Salina Cruz (971-714-1441; Calle 1 de Mayo 23), Huatulco (958-587-0261; Calles Gardenias Ocotillo), Pochutla, and Puerto Escondido.

AU (Autobuses Unidos; www.superbussesmex.galeon.com/amigos1389306.html) AU provides service to Oaxaca City, the Mitla Route, and Veracruz.

Estrella Blanca (800-507-5500 toll free Mexico; 555-729-0807 Mexico City; www.estrellablanca.com.mx) Estrella runs first and regular-class buses between Mexico City and the Pacific Coast Hwy. 200, stopping in Pinotepa Nacional, Puerto Escondido, Pochutla and Huatulco. There are offices in Puerto Escondido (954-582-0427; corner of Avenida Hidalgo and Avenida Oaxaca) and Huatulco (958-587-0680; Avenida Carpenteros, Lot 6, Sector 5).

Oaxaca Pacifico (951-514-0806, 951-514-5277; Oaxaca City, Armenta y López # 721) Bus lines connect most major towns on the Oaxaca beaches and Oaxaca City (US$8-13), with direct service to Mexico City (US$35) from Huatulco, Pochutla, and Puerto Escondido.

OCC (Ómnibus Crístobal Colón; 951-515-1214; www.occbus.com.mx) Now owned by ADO, OCC runs throughout Southern Mexico and Oaxaca with stops in Salina Cruz, Huatulco, Pochutla, Puerto Escondido, and Pinotepa Nacional.

UNO (800-702-8000 Mexico, 1-800-950-0287 U.S.; www.uno.com.mx) The nationwide line sells tickets in Huatulco (958-587-0261; corner of Calle Gardenias and Ocotillo, colonia Centro) and has service to Oaxaca City (951-515-1214; Calzada Chapultepec 1036).

Second-Class Bus Station (Centro de Abastos; 951-516-1218; Prolongación de Trujano at the Periférico) The dusty cement half-moon of Centro de Abastos is about what you'd expect, sort of scroungy with vendors, chairs, and frightening toilets.

Al Istmo (951-516-1674) Salina Cruz (three times daily; US$10), Tuxtepec (9 AM daily; US$19), Puerto Escondido (twice daily; US$13)

Autobuses Estrella del Valle (951-516-5429; autovalle@avantel.net) The coastal carrier serves Huatulco (10 PM daily; US$11), Puerto Escondido (five times daily; US$9), Pochutla (Puerto Ángel; 11:15 PM daily; US$8) and others.

Autobuses Estrella Roja del Sureste (951-516-0694) The line runs buses to Puerto Escondido (seven times daily; US$11), Pinotepa Nacional (three times daily; US$15), and other coastal cities.

Autobuses Oaxaca Cooperativa Tetzapotlán (951-516-1550) Buses leave for Zaachila (US 50¢) and Cuilapan (US 50¢) every half hour or so.

Cooperativa la Solteca (951-514-3881) The company runs buses and shuttles to Puerto Escondido (three times daily), with two continuing onto Pinotepa Nacional.

HPSA The line serves Mexico City (four times daily; US$20), Salina Cruz, Tehuantepec, Tlaxiaco, Putla, Pinotepa, Tonalá, Tapachula, Noxchitlán, Huajuapan, Matamoros, and more.

Sociedad Cooperativa Benito Juárez (951-516-5768) Buses run to Guelatao and Ixtlán (seven times daily; US$2.50), and Valle Nacional (9:30 AM daily; US$8) with continuing service to Tuxtepec (US$10).

Sociedad Cooperative Flecha del Zempoaltépetl (951-516-6342) Buses serve Ixtlán, Cuajimoloyas, and nearby towns in the Sierra Juarez several times daily.

Sociedad Cooperativa Fletes y Pasajes (951-514-3068, 951-516-2270; 1-800-375-0023 information) Buses go to Mexico City (11 times daily), Tuxtla Gutierrez (seven times daily; US$22), Tapachula (five times daily; US$22), Tonalá (five times daily; 8 hours; US$19). Buses leave every half hour to Tehuantepec (US$9.50) and Juchitán (US$10.50), on the Isthmus of Tehuantepec.

Valle del Norte The company runs shuttles between Teotitlán del Valle and Oaxaca throughout the day. Yellow-and-maroon colored buses depart for El Tule every 10 minutes.

Other Buses

Dozens of small companies run buses from Oaxaca City to specific locations around the state. This is by no means an exhaustive list.

Atlantida (La Noria 110) Service to Pochutla.

Autobús Comunitario de Benito Juárez Lachatao (Niño Perdido 306, Colonia Santa María Ixcotel) Runs vans to the Pueblos Mancomunados.

Autobuses Sur (951-514-9003; Periférico 606) Buses to Noxchitlán (every 30 minutes; US$2), Tlaxiaco (six times daily; US$3.50), Huajuapan (10 times daily, US$5.50).

Autotransportes Añasa (Bustamante 606, two blocks south of Iglesia San Francisco) Regular service to Zaachila.

Autoturismo Farias Costa Alegre (951-516-9666; Periférico) Buses to Mazatlán, Nayarit, Sinaloa, Jalisco, and Tijuana.

Chiguano (951-102-2971; Heroés de Chapultepec, Reforma) Seven shuttle buses daily to Tuxtepec (5 hours; US$17) and six to Valle Nacional (US$14), stopping in Ixtlán (US$5).

Colectivos to San Martín Tilcajete (Calle M Arista 107; US$1) Run every 45 minutes or so from Oaxaca City, about five blocks south of the Zócalo, to "el mero centro" de San Martín.

Costa de Oro (951-501-2018; 800-614-0421; Periférico) Nationwide carrier runs buses to Ensenada, Guadalajara, Mazatlá, Tecate, and Tijuana, among other destinations.

Eclipse 70 (Bustamante 622, Centro) Service to Pochutla, where you can get *camionetas* to Puerto Ángel.

Halcones (Bustamante 606-B) Direct buses to San Bartolo Coyotepec and Zimatlán.

San José del Pacifico Beach Shuttles (Hwy. 175 south, halfway between Oaxaca City and Pochutla) If you plan to spend an evening in the cool mountains between Oaxaca City and Puerto Ángel, note that shuttles run nine times daily from La Montaña Restaurant, right on the highway, to Pochutla (Puerto Ángel Beaches; US$6) and Oaxaca City (US$6).

Servicio Express (Arista 116, Centro) Vans to Pochutla and Puerto Escondido.

Servicios Turisticos de Huajuapan (951-501-2195; Valerio Trujano 420-A) Shuttle buses run several times daily to their offices in Huajuapan (953-530-5204; Nuyoo 31, Centro) and Juxtlahuaca (953-554-0813; Díaz and Allende).

Tierra del Sol (951-128-4230; Periférico) The other budget national carrier is conveniently located next to Costa de Oro, and serves most of the same destinations.

Transportadora Excelencia (951-516-3578; Ordaz 304, Centro) Runs minivans to Tlaxiaco.

Transportes de Tlaxiaco (951-516-4030; Trujano 505) Buses to Tlaxiaco.

Transportes Oaxaca Pacifico (Armenta y Lopez 121, Centro) Buses to Ocotlán.

Transportes Turísticos de Noxchitlán (951-514-1525; Galeana 222, Centro) Shuttle vans make regular trips to Noxchitlán.

TAXIS

Taxis are normally hired as *particulares,* that is, with one passenger or group paying for the entire car. Taxi drivers will often try to take slight advantage of tourists by charging a few pesos more than they would a local passenger. To avoid this, ask at your hotel or any other business what the approximate fare should be to your destination. Settle the fare with your driver *before* getting into the car.

You can hail a cab on the street, have someone call one for you (Taxi Express, 951-518-7479, is one reliable company in Oaxaca City), or walk to a taxi stand; any local can point the way. There is an extra fee after 10 PM.

While official taxis are generally very safe, let the driver know (especially at night) that you've made a point to learn his name and look directly at his face. I like to look at his ID, smile, and say something like, "Arturo Gonzalez, I've always loved the name Arturo." If someone can see you off, making obvious note of the taxi number, that's also helpful.

COLECTIVO TAXIS

Colectivo, or shared, taxis are a very common form of transportation, and not just to tiny towns with limited bus service. In the sprawling resort town of Bahías de Huatulco, which as yet has no regular shuttle bus service (it's theoretically in the works), the main form of transportation is collective taxis, running US$2 per person throughout most of the complex.

Basically, you're paying for a seat in the cab, which you then share with strangers. The *colectivos* generally leave from specific places in town; ask any hotel clerk or shop keeper to point the way. In Oaxaca City, *colectivos* have several specific stands, many surrounding Centro de Abastos.

Colectivos leave for Etla Valley and other northern areas from the corner of Trujano and the Periférico, just to the right of the bus station as you're leaving, and serve Villa de Etla, Barrio Atzompa, and San José de Mogote. *Colectivo* taxis leave from the 600 block of Miel-Teran for San Pedro and San Pablo Ayutla, Taessa, and Tamazulapam.

To go east, head to the corner of Victoria and Cinco de Febrero, south of the Periférico, to catch cabs to Tule, Teotitlán, and Mitla (where you can catch another *colectivo* to Hierve el Agua). If you're closer to the first-class bus station, you can flag down *colectivos* heading east just past the baseball stadium. Southbound *colectivos* headed to Ocotlán, Zaachila, and elsewhere, wait at the corner of the Periférico Sur.

CAMIONETAS

Camionetas, or covered trucks, are not for the faint of heart. In general, you'll use these as transport from a bus stop on the highway to a small town, most likely with an ecotourism project. The Puerto Ángel beaches are also conveniently connected with covered trucks. There is usually bench seating on either side of the truck bed, and locals will often help you on and off. Like *colectivos, camionetas* generally leave when they're full, rather than according to a specific schedule.

BOATS AND FERRIES

Oaxaca has several spots where you'll have the chance to use boat transportation, if you so desire. Most famously, many of the Bahías de Huatulco's bays and beaches are inaccessible by car, so you must hire a boat to take you for a ride or tour. Boat taxis also ply the more accessible beaches. For instance, you could take a *colectivo* taxi from La Crucecita to Playa la Entrega, then catch a boat back to Santa Cruz. You'll also need to hire a boat to reach certain remote lodges, including Bahía de Luna Hotel, near Puerto Ángel, and Isla Soyaltepec, in the Papaloapan. There's a cheap ferry that crosses the river in Tuxtepec; you might want to enjoy that ride just for fun.

DRIVING

Oaxaca has an excellent road system, with a smoothly paved and well-maintained network of federal highways connecting most major sites and towns. The excellent toll road 135 runs north to Mexico City via Puebla, connecting Oaxaca to the capital in just under six hours. Your rental car odometer, all local addresses, and all distances use kilometers, which work out to about .62 miles. I've included miles to help U.S. readers better envision distances, but it's easier to just accustom yourself to thinking in kilometers. For destinations off major highways, directions will sometimes be given as "make a left at kilometer 50 on Hwy. 101 from Oaxaca." Thus, 50 kilometers (31 miles) from Oaxaca on Hwy 101—kilometers are usually well marked on major roads—you can start looking for the sign to your destination.

Many secondary roads are unpaved, but usually graded and maintain well enough for normal, two-wheel-drive cars, in dry season at least. Some of the coastal roads accessing

Remember, you're sharing the road. So please, "Drive with care."

smaller, less-touristed beaches may require a four-wheel drive, in rainy season at least. If you aren't sure, ask a local if you'll be able to pass. A bigger concern, particularly if you've rented a small car, are speed bumps, usually (but not always) signed as *tope* or *redactor*. There is no standard size for speed bumps, and some of them can snap your axle or scrape off your undercarriage if you aren't careful. Pay attention.

Gas
Mexico is a petroleum-producing country, and all gas is pumped, refined, and sold by Pemex, the national oil company. While Mexicans will often complain that Pemex is corrupt and overpriced, visitors from almost anywhere else in the world, other than perhaps Saudi Arabia or Iran, will be pleasantly surprised by the low prices.

Parking
In smaller towns, parking is rarely a problem. Oaxaca City, on the other hand, as well as cities such as Huajuapan and Tuxtepec, are a bit more challenging. If you've rented a car, you'll probably need to either find a hotel with a lot, or pay for overnight parking. Hotels, particularly in the budget category, will often jam as many cars as possible into small interior lots, which can mean early morning wake-up knocks if your car is blocking someone else's. You can leave the car keys at the desk if you'd rather sleep in.

Though crime is rarely a problem in Oaxaca, never leave valuables visible in the car overnight, even in a guarded parking lot.

Rental Cars
For some reason, renting a car in Oaxaca is a longer and more complicated (and expensive) process than anywhere I've ever rented, including most of Central America. Be sure to allow an hour or more to make reservations, pick up the car, and return it, when your vehicle will be thoroughly examined for even the smallest scuff marks. For which you are liable.

You must be at least 25 years old to rent from most reputable agencies. You'll also need a credit card and driver's license from your home country. Mandatory insurance and a 15 percent value-added tax conspire to swell the original low quote.

All that said, if you want to see Oaxaca State and don't have time for the bus, this is the very best way to do it. There are three rental car agencies in the Oaxaca Airport, which charge a small extra fee, and several in the city center:

Alamo (951-51-4853; 800-002-5266 Mexico; alamo.oaxaca@hotmail; Calle Cinco de Mayo 203) Professional and friendly.

Europecar Downtown (951-143-8340 airport; 951-516-9305 Oaxaca City; Plazuela Labastida 104–A, between Cinco de Mayo, Murgia, and Alcalá; open 8 AM–8 PM daily) The cheapest for a reason—there's no parking lot, and returning the vehicle requires finding a parking spot in the busiest part of town.

Hertz Airport (951-106-5859; 951-159-9784; 1-800-709-5000; www.avasamexico.com) Hertz also rents cars with chauffeurs.

Only Renta de Autos (951-501-0816, 951-508-2575) This local operation quotes higher prices, but rents more cheaply.

Yes Rent-A-Car (951-514-5653; 800-667-6968; yes.mexico@hotmail.com; Calle 5 Mayo 315) A small, local operation.

Several tour companies also rent cars and shuttle vans with a driver and/or guide, including **Continental-Istmo Tours** (951-516-9625; www.continentalistmotours.com; Alcalá 201, Centro); **Monte Alban Tours** (951-520-0444; www.montealbantours.com; Alcalá 206F, Centro); and **Turísticos Marfils** (951-516-8138; turisticosmarfil@hotmail.com; Acalá 407).

10

Planning Your Trip

Oaxaca's wonders and (for the most part) solid tourist infrastructure make spontaneous travel easy, particularly if you're based in the hubs of Oaxaca City or one of the Pacific Coast resort towns, Bahías de Huatulco and Puerto Escondido. But if you're only here for a short visit, or if you're visiting during the peak holidays, it's worth taking the time to plan ahead.

Itineraries

These are only suggested itineraries, just to give you an idea of possible options. But keep in mind that Oaxaca is the sort of place that unveils her loveliest features with time; the more you spend in one place, in many ways, the more you will find.

One Week

With only a week, it's probably best to choose between the beach and Oaxaca City. Restless souls who enjoy wandering more than relaxing could certainly do both, however, though I'd recommend taking the 30-minute plane trip, rather than the 7- to 8-hour bus ride.

While it's good to leave a little leeway, plans and preparation help guarantee wonderful a vacation. (Nayarit culture, 200 a.d.–750 a.d., is displayed at the Rodolfo Morales Museum.)

Oaxaca City in a Week: Begin with breakfast on the Zócalo, watching Oaxaca swirl by, before hitting the Museum of Culture and Santo Domingo. Context! Browse Plaza Labastida, to take a look at the handicrafts, then it's time for a real Oaxacan *comida,* perhaps at La Olla or Danzantes. After a relaxing wander around town, it's an evening of music on the Zócalo, and who knows what else: Fireworks? Dancing? Love? The next morning, or afternoon (midday's not so good for photos), grab a shuttle bus to Monte Albán Archaeological Park. Spend another day or two exploring the city, making sure at some

> **Oaxaca Statistics**
> Area: 95,364 square kilometers (59,258 square miles) Oaxaca State
> Altitude of Oaxaca City: 1,550 meters (5,080 feet)
> Highest point: Cerro Nube Flan, 3,750 meters (12,303 feet)
> Population: 3,506,821 Oaxaca State; 383,600 Oaxaca City
> Days of sunshine per year: 311
> Number of bird species: 711 (two endemics)
> Number of chiles: 150 (60 endemics)
> Number of ethnic groups: Nine (arguably many more)
> Number of languages: 17 (Spanish and 16 indigenous languages)
> Number of archaeological sites: 7,000
> Lucky number: Seven: seven regions, seven moles, and seven years until *maguey* is ready to become mezcal.
> Year Oaxaca City and Monte Albán became UNESCO World Heritage Sites: 1987
> Year Oaxaca City and Monte Albán became cities: 1532 A.D. and 500 B.C., respectively.

point to: (1) have hot chocolate at the market; (2) visit the Rodolfo Morales museum; and (3) take in Basílica Soledad, and perhaps a *nieve*, Oaxacan ice cream, at Jardín Socrates.

Then it's time to get out of town, to the Central Valleys. Book a day trip or take a local bus to Mitla, visit the handicrafts pueblos, or (depending on the day of the week) a *tanguis*, or traditional market, perhaps in Zaachila or Ocotlán. If you're up for an overnight eco-adventure, book a trip to the Pueblos Mancomunados or rent a car and spend the night at Apoala Valley, both covered in the Northern Oaxaca chapter. Make your last night in town special with a gourmet traditional dinner at Casa Oaxaca, or perhaps one of the market stalls, using the money you save on mole and chocolate to take back home.

A Week at the Beach: You could certainly choose just one beach town and relax all week long, or make it a road trip! (Buses or taxis are probably a better bet than car rental, unless you plan to return.) Why not begin in Huatulco, with a boat trip to the nine beautiful bays, complete with snorkeling and perhaps swimming with dolphins. After a day of lying around at the beach, choose another adventure: Diving? Swimming beneath the Magic Waterfalls? Visiting the cool coffee plantations of the Sierra Sur? Or do it all!

Then hit the road, for the Puerto Ángel beaches, with wonderful ecotourism cabins and Playa Ventanilla, nude bathing at Zipolite, or nicer lodging at San Agustinillo or Mazunte, close to the Mexican Sea Turtle Center. Be sure to make it to your final destination, Puerto Escondido, before sunset, to watch the sun sink into the sea (a rarity on this south-facing coast) behind the Mexican Pipeline, one of the world's best beach breaks.

Two Weeks

Now you're talking, if you want to combine a beach vacation with a week in Oaxaca City. Stay busy with the recommendations above, or enjoy a more leisurely trip by choosing one beach town as your base. Adventurous culture lovers could also plan to spend some time exploring the Isthmus of Tehuantepec, or the Costa Mixteca and Pinotepa Nacional. Or consider one of these add-ons, if you'd rather head for the mountains:

Mixteca Route (5–15 days) If you've only got a day or two in the Mixteca, you can stay in

Online Resources

Mexico jumped on the information superhighway early, and today has an excellent online presence, including many Web sites in English and other languages (though smaller Oaxacan communities general have Web sites only in Spanish and assorted indigenous tongues). I've listed useful resources at the beginning of each chapter, but here are a few good general Web sites to get you started.

Anadiario (www.adiario-oaxaca.com.mx) This Spanish-language weekly covers protests, insurrections, and police violence, in addition to the usual news, sports, and entertainment.

Ciclo Literario (www.cicloliterario.com.mx) El Imparcial publishes this monthly literary magazine.

Imparcial (www.imparcialenlinea.com) The online version of "Oaxaca's best daily" the site lets you access the Tehuantepec edition as well.

Inside Mexico (www.inside-mexico.com) Excellent selection of books and videos highlighting Mexico's rich cultures.

Maps of Mexico (www.maps-of-mexico.com) Map junkies will love the detailed map of Oaxaca State.

MEXonline (www.mexonline.com) The site contains thousands of pages of travel information.

The News (www.thenews.com.mx) Mexico's best English-language news source is this newspaper, available everywhere for US$1.

Noticias (www.noticias-oax.com.mx) The paper of record has this online version.

Oaxaca Radio Stations Station listings and links to listen to radio from all over Oaxaca State are available at www. radiostationworld.com/Locations/Mexico/radio_Web sites.asp?m=oa~.

Palo Alto College (www.accd.edu/pac/lrc/oaxaca.htm) This remarkable portal links to academic and popular Oaxaca-related sites, and includes lots of information about the Day of the Dead, the 2006 uprising, and various archaeological sites in English.

People's Guide to Mexico (www.peoplesguide.com) The authors of the independent travel classic also operate this expansive travel guide, with information, advice, and links to help you make the most of any Mexico vacation.

Visit Mexico (www.visitmexico.com) The official tourism Web site offers introductory information in several languages.

Modern communications, from cell phones to WiFi, are becoming faster and more widely available around Oaxaca State.

Apoala Valley and perhaps drop by a couple of the Dominican churches. Or do the entire loop, stopping to appreciate all the Spanish monuments, fascinating archaeological sites, and wonderful community museum. Don't miss an overnight in the bustling town of Huajuapan and/or magnificent Tonalá Canyon, which has cute ecotourism cabins nearby.

Papaloapan River Valley (3–7 days) If you like your tropics lush and humid, as opposed to arid and wide open, head across the Sierra Juárez to the moist, green Papaloapan. If time is short, just spend a night or two in one of the wonderful ecotourism projects surrounding Valle Nacional. Or indulge your sense of adventure with a trek to Tuxtepec, or perhaps an overnight (or several) on Isla Soyaltepec. Make it a loop (this is best done in a rental car) by continuing west to the cloud forests surrounding Huautla, then south on Hwy. 131 back into and through the sunny desert.

One Month

Lucky you! But, while you technically have time to see almost everything in the book, you could take a little more time out to enjoy the sunshine. Consider spending a week taking Spanish classes in Oaxaca City or by the beach, or a weaving and dyeing workshop in Teotitlán. There are so many options, so enjoy!

Climate

Oaxaca, *Tierra del Sol,* or Land of the Sun, is a year-round destination. Oaxaca City's mild climate ranges from highs around 25 degrees Celsius /77 degrees Fahrenheit during the peak winter holiday period, while the hottest months, March through May, see average highs of 30 degrees Celsius/86 Fahrenheit; up to 34 degrees Celsius/93 degrees Fahrenheit in the Central Valley; and 36 degrees Celsius/96 degrees Fahrenheit on the Pacific Coast. The highest temperature ever recorded in the City of Oaxaca was 40.2 degrees Celsius/104.5 degrees Fahrenheit, and the lowest was 2 degrees Celsius/35.6 degrees Fahrenheit.

The rainy season, with hot, muggy weather and lush, green vistas, usually runs from June through October, with August and September the rainiest months. Rain usually arrives in the afternoon and lasts only a couple of cool, refreshing hours. The sun is more likely to prove a problem, as Oaxaca enjoys about 311 days of sunshine per year—at this altitude, almost guaranteed to toast the average European complexion to a fine ruby red. Bring sunscreen (but note that sunscreen is banned at beaches with coral formations, as it causes bleaching of corals) and a wide-brimmed hat; great woven-palm hats can be found for less than US$3 at many markets.

During dry season, when humidity hovers around 15 percent, be aware that you are losing water without registering much perspiration (it's evaporating immediately). Altitude, sunshine, and dehydration can conspire to make you light-headed or worse, so pay attention to your own water intake and particularly that of children; consider carrying fruits and juices to keep them hydrated.

It can get cool at night in Oaxaca City, and temperatures can drop to almost freezing in the surrounding mountains. Bring a light jacket and long pants, and even warmer clothes if you plan to visit the Pueblos Mancomunados or other mountain towns in the high Sierra, particularly between October and February.

High and Low Season

Peak travel periods in Oaxaca include Semana Santa (Easter Week), Guelaguetza (July), Day of the Dead (late October and early November), and the Christmas and New Year's holidays. If you plan to visit during one of these events (highly recommended), it's wise to make hotel reservations in advance, particularly for upscale accommodations. (You can almost always find budget rooms at the last minute.) First-class buses also sell out during these periods; make yours a few days in advance. With the Guelaguetza in particular, it's worth securing events tickets months in advance. Prices rise 10–15 percent during peak travel periods.

Lodging

There is an enormous range of lodging in Oaxaca City, which offers more than 200 hotels and thousands of rooms, ranging from five-star luxury hotels to basic budget backpacker digs. A smattering of B&Bs around the city and Central Valleys adds a personal touch.

The major beach resort towns also offer every level of accommodation, with most of the five-star and all-inclusive resorts concentrated in Bahías de Huatulco, but there are excellent hotels (as well as palm-thatched shacks and other budget options) at both the Puerto Ángel Beaches and Puerto Escondido.

Outside of these tourist meccas, however, hotel options begin to thin. Major cities such as Tuxtepec and Huajuapan have very comfortable four-star hotels, but most towns offer fairly basic accommodations, with top hotels reaching perhaps three stars, with cable TV, hot-water private bath, and good beds, but few other frills.

An excellent option, if you're up for it, are the many basic nature lodges that have been opened by indigenous villages throughout the state, mainly in the Sierra Juárez and Papaloapan, in Northern Oaxaca. These "ecotourism projects" (as they are rather unpoetically referred to) are always in stunning settings, and generally include private hot showers and, at higher elevations, fireplaces, as well as access to basic meals, guided hikes, horseback rides, and other options. Be aware that management at these wonderful and recommended places can be spotty. If you don't have reservations, try to show up early in the day, just in case it takes a while to find the manager and keys.

Be aware that *autohotels*, or *motor hotels*, usually located on the outskirts of town, with cheesy names like "Jardín Eden" and special garages that allow you to hide your car, are for discreet couples, and generally rent rooms in three-hour increments.

All hotels are subject to an 18 percent tax, which may be waived, partially or in full, if you pay cash. (Often this is described as a 10 percent discount for cash.)

Restaurants and Food Purveyors

Oaxacan cuisine is considered one of the world's finest, served at fabulous fine-dining restaurants and humble market stalls, almost all of them excellent. Mexicans dine a bit later than you may be used to, with breakfast starting around 8 AM, and the big meal of the day, *comida*, served between 2 PM and 6 PM, generally offered as a multi-course meal or buffet. Dinner is often a light snack, taken around 8 PM.

A Special Note About Tap Water and Food Safety

Oaxaca's tap water is not safe to drink, and long-timers recommend even brushing your teeth with bottled water, which is cheap and plentiful. Most hotels provide purified water, either free or for sale.

In Oaxaca City and the major beach resorts, food at markets and street stalls is usually safe to eat, washed and prepared with purified water. Some people say to avoid even the wonderful options at Mercado Benito Juárez, but these warnings are years out of date, as these *comedors* now use strict (or stricter) standards than many restaurants, where the kitchen is hidden. Don't deny yourself.

Outside the tourist areas, however, play it safe. Avoid eating raw, unpeeled fruits and vegetable from street stands, and use your best judgment when it comes to market *comedors*. Fully cooked foods are almost always safe to eat.

If you purchase your own fruits and vegetables, peel, cook, or wash them with an iodine-based water neutralizer, widely available in the produce section of any grocery store for about US$3. A popular brand is Biodyne. To use, fill a bowl or sink with purified or tap water. Add about five drops of solution per liter and let everything soak at least 10 minutes. You can even use the drops in an emergency to make tap water safe to drink, if there's no way to boil it. Add 10 drops per liter and allow the water to sit for at least 10 minutes.

SHOWERS AND BATHROOMS

First, and most important, Oaxaca does not have enough water. Please take short showers and otherwise conserve water. If other tourists at your hotel choose to waste water, it may run out; the hotel can order another tanker full, but that will take time. Please note that

When exploring the Oaxaca countryside, smart travelers always pack a bit of toilet tissue, just in case.

while many budget hotels have told me that they offer "24-hour hot water," some were probably stretching the truth. In general, cheaper hotels offer water from about 7 AM till 10 AM, and again in the evening. You can always ask the front desk to turn on the water heater just for you.

Most toilets, except (perhaps) in the very nicest hotels, are accompanied by a small wastebasket, where you are expected to throw dirty toilet paper. You'll get used to it. And, as unhygienic as this may seem, the other option is backing up the centuries-old sewage system, which was not designed for paper. If you forget, don't worry—a bit of paper will probably flush through OK. Probably. If not, let hotel management know what happened, as this will make it easier for them to fix the problem before mopping and cleaning your bathroom.

In very basic bathrooms, such as at markets and very cheap hotels, you may find toilets without flush handles, and huge plastic barrels of water with a bucket nearby. Don't stress! After using the toilet, simply fill the bucket with water, lift the toilet seat (if there is one), and pour the water into the bowl from about chest high. Repeat as needed. And *voila!* Now you're living (well, flushing) like a local.

PRACTICAL MATTERS

Visas and Entry Requirements

Citizens of Canada and the United States need passports to enter Mexico. You will be granted an automatic 90- or 180-day tourist visa if you are a citizen of Australia, Canada, Costa Rica, France, Germany, Great Britain, Ireland, Israel, Italy, the United States, and most other EU-member countries; Mexonline (www.mexonline.com/visa.htm) has a complete list. Citizens of other countries must first visit a Mexican Embassy to request a tourist visa.

When you arrive, you will be issued a Mexican Tourist Card (FMT) that you must present when leaving the country, or you will be fined $42—and could theoretically be detained in country until a replacement is printed.

Work and student visas must be arranged well in advance from your country of residence through the National Immigration Institute (www.inm.gob.mx). Solo parents traveling with children should carry a letter of permission to travel from the other parent; this is rarely checked, but if it is you could be detained for hours while authorities try to contact the other parent.

Embassies and Consulates

Most embassies are in Mexico City, but a few countries do have representation in Oaxaca. For a complete list of embassies and consulates in Mexico, check Embassies Abroad (www.embassiesabroad.com/embassies-in/Mexico).

U.S. Consulate (951-514-3054, 951-514-2853, emergency 951-547-1185; conagent@prodigy.net.mx; Alcalá 407, Centro; open 9 am–4 PM) Get to the consulate, on the second floor of Plaza Santo Domingo (across from Santo Domingo) early or prepare to wait in line.

Canadian Consulate (951 513 3777; Pino Suárez 700 Local 11-B; Multiplaza Brena Centro)

France (951-514-1900; Guerrero 105, Centro)

Great Britain and **Germany** (951-516-7280; Alcalá 407, Plaza Santo Domingo)

Emergency numbers

General Emergency Number: 066 (Oaxaca); 080 (Mexico City)
Green Angels (Highway Tourist Assistance): 915-516-9597
Center for Tourist Protection: 951-514-2155
Federal Police: 951-518-7870, 951-518-7871 (Oaxaca); 555-684-2142 (Mexico City)
Fire Department: 951-516-2231
Telephone Number Information: 040
Tourist Information: 078; 800-987-8240
Red Cross: 951-516-4455

CRIME

Oaxaca has happily avoided much of the drug- and gang-related crime that plagues the border states and Central Mexico, perhaps because federal troops stationed here since the 2006 uprising have convinced violent drug cartels to go elsewhere. Marijuana is grown in Oaxaca, and is smoked openly in some of the beach communities; just because locals get away with it doesn't mean that you can. Psilocybin, or hallucinogenic, mushrooms are also used by shamans and healers; this is culturally acceptable but technically illegal.

While there are armed muggings, particularly on unlit beaches and the walk to El Fortín in Oaxaca City, most crime is nonviolent. Pickpockets ply the crowds on the Zócalo and fiestas, so keep an eye on your belongings. Also avoid leaving valuables unattended at the beach. Scam artists abound, particularly on the Oaxaca City Zócalo. While most Oaxaqueños you'll meet on the plaza are genuinely cool people, just be wary if a new friend latches onto you all of a sudden.

MONEY

Mexico uses the peso as its monetary unit, symbolized with the "$" sign. Prices in US dollars are written "US$," and pesos "M$," throughout this book, to avoid confusion.

Please note: The peso was fluctuating wildly during the time of research (late 2008 and early 2009, as the global economic crisis hit), ranging between 10 and 15 pesos to the dollar. For simplicity's sake, I've calculated costs at 10 pesos to the dollar, which means prices quoted in the book may be slightly higher than on the ground.

Cash

Coins are denominated in M$1, M$2, M$5, M$10, and M$20 pesos. Bills, which are different sizes and colors, are M$20, M$50, M$100, M$200, M$500, and M$1000. Large bills can be difficult to change, particularly in rural areas.

While there are *cambios,* or currency exchange booths, close to the Zócalo, you usually get the best rates from ATMs, which are widely available and work on both the Visa/Plus and MasterCard systems. Both the Canadian dollar and euro can be changed in Oaxaca City, so there's no reason to change them to dollars before you leave, then into pesos once you're here; that costs you money. You can also order pesos before your trip from www .travelex.com.

ATMs

ATMs are available in most major towns throughout the state, usually within two blocks of the central plaza. Ask for a *cajero automatico*.

Inconveniently, many of the Central Valleys' artisan towns do not have ATMs, and many artists only accept cash. Shop prepared. There are cash machines in Tule, Ocotlán, and Mitla.

On the Pacific Coast, you can find ATMs in Tehuantepec, Juchitán, Salina Cruz, Huatulco, Pochutla, Puerto Escondido, and elsewhere. In Northern Oaxaca, there are ATMs in Huajuapan, Noxchitlán, Tlaxiaco, Tuxtepec, and elsewhere.

Contact your bank before the trip to inquire about maximum withdrawals and any possible partnership they might have with Scotiabank, HSBC, or a Mexican bank. Withdrawal fees can be as high as US$6, but some banks allowed me to withdraw from my U.S.-based bank for free. If you have a four-digit pin number (call your credit card company before you leave home), you can also withdraw cash with your Visa or MasterCard. Making cash-back debit card purchases at grocery stores is another way to avoid fees.

Credit Cards

Visa and MasterCard are widely accepted in Oaxaca City and the beach resorts, but American Express cards can only be used at a very few businesses, usually upscale hotels and fine-dining restaurants. Discover and Diners' Club are also sometimes accepted.

Outside the popular tourist areas, except for high-end hotels in larger cities such as Huajuapan and Tuxtepec, credit cards are rarely accepted. Adventurers should keep cash on hand. Credit cards are always accepted by Pemex gas stations.

Before you leave home, contact your credit card companies. Let them know the dates of your trip, find out which offers the best exchange rate, and ask if they offer free supplemental insurance coverage if you rent a car. Make sure you have their *international* toll-free number.

PayPal

This handy international online service is becoming popular throughout Mexico and Latin America, particularly with smaller hotels that need paid reservations, but can't afford stiff credit card charges. Basically, it allows you to pay using credit cards, your bank account, or other sources, in some cases without a transaction fee. Check out PayPal (www.paypal.com) to learn more.

Travelers Checks

Unless you're feeling nostalgic, there's little reason to bring travelers checks to Oaxaca. ATMs, credit cards, and other services have rendered them obsolete. They are, however, still accepted at a few hotels and stores, usually for a small fee.

SPECIAL NEEDS TRAVELERS

While Oaxaca City and other colonial towns remain challenging for wheelchair users and other people with disabilities, with help you can get almost anywhere. Ask any private tour outfit about renting wheelchair-friendly vehicles, or organizing wheelchair tours. **MPG**

Wheelchair Tours (958-100-4517; info@mpgtours.com; Andador Cacaluta 93 Fracc, Residencial San Agustín) offers tours of the Pacific Coast communities, including zip-line canopy tours and other activities.

TAXES AND TIPPING

Mexico is a tipping country, and unless service is just atrocious, you should tip at least 10 percent at inexpensive eateries, 15 percent or more at nicer restaurants. This may already be included with your bill, so check. Tour guides merit a tip for good service; I always leave a few coins for hotel cleaning staff as well. There is no need to tip taxi drivers, unless service is outstanding.

MAIL

Sending packages through the regular mail system is inconvenient and, according to online complaints, unreliable. You must go to a stationery store to have packages wrapped in plain paper, which is inexpensive but sort of a hassle. Many stores will ship your purchases home for you, but may charge a small, hidden service fee. There are several private shipping companies that are your best bet.

Main Post Office (Zócalo, corner of Independencia and Alameda Park; open 9 AM–7 PM Mon.–Fri., 9 AM–1 PM Sat) This is worth visiting just for the architecture.

AREEM (951-514-0337; Independencia 500, Centro)

Monte Albán, 2500 years old, is now wheelchair accessible, well ahead of Oaxaca City.

Mail Boxes Etc. (951-144-7961; www.mbelatam.com; Universidad 200-B, Fracc. Nuestra Señora) The company ships art and anything else using FedEx, UPS, DHL, Multipack and others. Credit cards accepted.

Multipack (951-515-1414; Cinco de Mayo, Jalatlaco) Good prices.

Pakmail (951-516-8196; García Virgil 504 between Allende and Alcalá; open 9 AM–7 PM Mon.–Fri., 9 AM–2 PM Sat.) The company provides DHL, UPS, Aeroflash, Estafeta, and other private mail services.

TELEPHONES

Public phones are plentiful and convenient for making calls. Some phones accept coins (M$1, M$2 or M$5) while others require Ladatel calling cards, widely available at many shops and newsstands in M$20, M$50, and M$100 increments. Many Mexican businesses have toll-free 800 numbers; to use them, dial 91-800 plus the rest of the number. To dial a U.S. toll free number, dial 95-880 plus the number.

Note that while I've punctuated phone numbers in US style (e.g., 951-555-1234), they are written in a variety of different ways, such as 951 55 51 234, or 5 12 34, etc.

Many Internet cafés offer international telephone calls at much cheaper rates, or will let you use Skype; many also send faxes. The telegraph office is located downtown, at Avenida Indepencia 600, at the corner of Calle 20 de Noviembre.

Many U.S.-based and international phone services work in Mexico, including AT&T. However, you could be charged up to US$1 per minute.

Suggested Reading

ARCHAEOLOGY

Balkansky, Andrew K.; Stiver Walsh, Laura R.; Pluckhahn, Thomas J.; Chamblee, John F.; Kowalewski, Stephen A. (ed.). *Origins of the Nuu: Archaeology in the Mixteca Alta, Mexico.* 2009. US$65.00. This study of the Mixteca, using its famous codices and new archaeological discoveries, aims to elucidate.

Blanton, Richard E.; Feinman, Gary M.; Kowalewski, Stephen A.; Nicholas, Linda A. *Ancient Oaxaca.* 1999. US$24.99. This academic survey of pre-Hispanic Oaxaca is accessible to laypeople.

Blomster, Jeffrey P (ed.). *After Monte Alban: Transformation and Negotiation in Oaxaca, Mexico.* 2008. US$65. The collection of essays discusses the fall of Monte Albán and Oaxaca's subsequent political restructuring, and how it affected day-to-day life in the pueblos.

Flannery, Kent V., and Marcus, Joyce (eds.). *The Cloud People: Divergent Evolution of the Zapotec and Mixtec Civilizations.* 2003. US$43.50. The definitive study of pre-Hispanic Oaxaca.

Nuttall, Zelia (ed.), and Miller, Arthur G. *The Codex Nuttall.* 1975. US$22.95. The original edition, published at least 700 years ago and currently in the British Library, has been faithfully copied in 88 full-color plates chronicling Mixtec politics from 838 A.D. to 1330 A.D., including the story of Lord Eight Deer Tiger Claw, whose military triumphs—finally uniting the Mixteca Alta, Baja, and Costa—were overshadowed by his tragically Shakespearean home life.

Pohl, John, and Mcbride, Angus (illus.). *Aztec, Mixtec and Zapotec Armies.* 1991. US$17.75. From the 1450s until the Spanish arrived, Oaxaca's Zapotec and Mixtec people were at war with, and later partially occupied by, the Aztec army. Detailed illustrations, descriptions of weapons and strategies, and other information make this a must for military history buffs. The "Men-At-Arms" series has several books about Mexico.

Winter, Marcus. *Oaxaca: The Archaeological Record.* 2004. US$8. This great little book describes the history, culture, art, and technology of pre-Hispanic Oaxaca, and includes detailed, hand-drawn maps of the sites themselves (and a foldout map to sites within the state, but that could use more detail).

ARTESANÍAS

Barbash, Shepard, and Ragan, Vicki (photographer). *Changing Dreams: A Generation of Oaxaca's Woodcarvers.* 2007. US$39.95. Ten years after the success of their ground-breaking book *Magic in the Trees,* below, Barbash and Ragan return, to find the alebrijes market glutted and many artists struggling to survive. Evocative black and white photos.

Barbash, Shepard, and Ragan, Vicki (photographer). *Oaxacan Woodcarving: The Magic in the Trees.* 1993. US$19.95. The book has great photos and a focus on a few area *alebrije* artists; it's fascinating to see how much the art form has evolved since this book was researched.

Chibnik, Michael. *Crafting Tradition: The Making and Marketing of Oaxacan Wood Carvings.* 2003. $22.95. An academic look at the history, economics, and "how-to" of *alebrijes,* Chibnik focuses on how local, grass roots initiatives to build a handicrafts market, combined with talent, skill, and hard work, have created a thriving and beautiful indus- try where so many foreign NGOs have failed.

Fischgrund Stanton, Andra, and Phillips, Jaye R. (photographer). *Zapotec Weavers of Teotitlán.* 1999. US$29.95. An intimate look at the lives of Zapotec weavers, and how their world changed in recent decades, is interwoven with wonderful color photographs that offer insight and information into how the rugs were made.

✪ Rothstein, Arden Aibel, and Rothstein, Anya Leah. *Mexican Folk Art: From Oaxacan Artist Families.* 2007. US$39.95. Indispensible to serious *artesanía* shoppers and fascinating for almost anyone, this beautiful coffee-table book includes interviews and photos of the Central Valleys' top artisans, detailed descriptions of different crafts, and maps of 13 small *artesanía* towns, with workshops marked.

Wasserspring, Lois, and Ragan, Vicki (photographer). *Oaxacan Ceramics: Traditional Folk Art by Oaxacan Women.* 2000. US$18.95. Excellent photos illustrate some of the work of Atzompa's top potters, Teodora Blanco's *muñecas* and Dolores Porras' colorful glazed ceramics, plus brightly painted pieces from the Aguilar sisters.

CHILDREN'S BOOKS

Arquette, Kerry; Zocchi, Andrea; and Vigil, Jerry. *Day of the Dead Crafts: More than 24 Projects that Celebrate Dia de los Muertos.* 2008. US$19.99. The book gives step-by-step instructions on how to make simple Day of the Dead folk art, with cool photos and information.

Miller, Nancy B. *The Wondrous Toy Workshop; Hanni's Inspiring Life and Her Toys Anyone Can Make.* 2008. $15.95. After being diagnosed with muscular dystrophy, toymaker and col- lector Hanni Sager came to Oaxaca to teach disabled children to make their own beauti- ful toys. This is her story, and a how-to guide, with instructions for making 12 simple and fun toys.

Stein, R. Conrad. *The Story of Mexico: Benito Juárez and the French Intervention.* 2007. US$28.95. The book tells the story of Benito Juárez and his fight against the French occupation, aimed at tweens.

Weill, Cynthia; Jiménez, Moisés (illus.); and Jiménez, Armando (illus.); Basseches, K.B. (photographer). *ABeCedarios: Mexican Folk Art ABCs in English and Spanish.* 2008. US$14.95. This bilingual alphabet book is illustrated with awesome *alebrijes.*

CULTURE

Britton, Scott A. *Zapotec-English/English-Zapotec (Isthmus) Concise Dictionary.* 2004. US$14.95. There are dozens of English-Spanish dictionaries and phrase books (and I recommend that adventurous travelers bring one of each). But only Britton can prepare you for your trip into the Tehuantepec hinterlands.

DeMott, Tom. *Into the Hearts of the Amazons: In Search of a Modern Matriarchy.* 2006.

US$26.95. The women of the Isthmus of Tehuantepec have a reputation throughout the country as strong, economically and politically powerful—even, perhaps, a matriarchy. But a closer look reveals that this isn't a matriarchy, it's almost equality.

Holo, Selma Reuben. *Oaxaca at the Crossroads: Managing Memory, Negotiating Change.* 2004. US$39.95. This study of Oaxaca's culture of museums, from tiny *museos comunitarios* in the hinterlands to the world-class collection atop Monte Albán, offers real insight into the workings of the Oaxacan cultural community.

Flores Magon, Ricardo; Bufe, Chaz (ed.); and Verter, Mitchell Cowen (ed). *Dreams of Freedom : A Ricardo Flores Magon Reader.* 2005. US$19.95. If you've ever owned a Che Guevara T-shirt, consider this collection of incendiary writings from Oaxaca's own revolutionary journalist.

Nevaer, Louis E.V. *Protest Graffiti Mexico: Oaxaca.* 2009. US$27.95. Art and politics meet on the street, and during the 2006 protests, that meant the walls of Oaxaca. From stylized scrawls to magnificent murals, Nevaer recorded this transient work, still there beneath layers of tourist-friendly paint.

Perry, Richard D. *Exploring Colonial Oaxaca: The Art and Architecture.* 2006. $29.50. Churchaholics, and you know who you are (I'm one too), will enjoy and appreciate their trek even more with this heartfelt guide, complete with wonderfully detailed drawings and color photos, to the major Catholic churches of Oaxaca, the Central Valleys, and Mixteca.

Stephen, Lynn. *Transborder Lives: Indigenous Oaxacans in Mexico, California, and Oregon.* 2007. US$24.95. Many Oaxacans, particularly those from the parched Mixteca, work in the United States illegally for a few years, almost as a rite of passage. Stephen studies this lifestyle from an academic perspective, offering insights into the private lives of the folks playing a high-stakes game of border roulette to better their communities.

Stephen, Lynn. *Zapotec Women: Gender, Class, and Ethnicity in Globalized Oaxaca.* 2005. US$24.95. The 1991 classic look at Teotitlán's traditional gender roles and the rise of women's artisan cooperatives was completely updated in 2005.

Wasson, R. Gordon. *María Sabina and Her Mushroom Velada (Ethno-Mycological Studies).* 1974. Out of print. Though there are several other books and CDs recording the spiritual wisdom of María Sabina, this out-of-print scholarly study, with cassette recordings of the mushroom ceremonies, is the definitive publication.

FICTION

Barba, Les. *Life Imitating Death: Making Dollars and Sense in Chiapas.* 2003. The Artful Codger Press. $10. This fast-paced thriller set in Oaxaca and Chiapas weaves the author's observations of Southern Mexico's social fabric, including the indigenous issues that presaged the Chiapas rebellion, into a novel with mystery, romance, hard-boiled characters, and chase scenes.

Resau, Laura. *Red Glass.* 2007. US$15.99. A six-year-old boy, the sole survivor of a botched illegal border crossing into the U.S., is discovered with Sophie's stepfather's business card in his pocket. As the tale unfolds, it takes Sophie through the Mixteca, where author Laura Resau worked for several years, and beyond, on a harrowing trip that touches on the human reality of immigration.

Food and Drink

Martinez, Zarela. *The Food and Life of Oaxaca: Traditional Recipes from Mexico's Heart.* 1997. Authentic, sometimes labor-intensive recipes are spiced with slices of real Oaxacan life.

Sanchez López, Alberto. *Oaxaca: Tierra de Maguey y Mezcal.* 2005. US$10. It's worth looking for *Oaxaca: Land of Maguey and Mezcal* for anyone interested in learning more about the distilling process and economics of mezcal, Oaxaca's signature drink. Most of the book is in Spanish, but there's a 50-page English-language summary at the end (which is really all you need), as well as an interesting DVD.

Trilling, Susana. *My Search for the Seventh Mole.* 1996. US$8. This slim volume about the quest for the seventh mole includes more than a dozen classic regional recipes, each introduced with the tale of its discovery.

✪ Trilling, Susana. *Seasons of My Heart: A Culinary Journey Through Oaxaca, Mexico.* 1999. US$25.50. The beautifully written cookbook includes recipes, stories, and photos from the seven regions of Oaxaca and Oaxaca City.

History

Cook, Lorena Maria. *Organizing Dissent: Unions, the State, and the Democratic Teachers' Movement in Mexico.* 1995. US$27.00. This rather academic history of Oaxaca's unusually outspoken teachers' union has new relevance after the violent protests of 2006.

Greenfield, Amy Butler. *A Perfect Red: Empire, Espionage, and the Quest for the Color of Desire.* US$26.95. 2005. The fast-paced tale of a red that no European had ever seen, and of conspiracies to bring down a Spanish monopoly on *cochineal,* carmine, produced on the cacti of the Oaxacan countryside.

McNamara, Patrick J. *Sons of the Sierra: Juárez, Díaz, and the People of Ixtlán, Oaxaca, 1855-1920.* 2007. US$24.95. Two of Mexico's most powerful presidents came from the mountains now known as the Sierra Juárez: reformer Benito Juárez and dictator Porfirio Díaz. A painstakingly researched tale of two men of Ixtlán in the chaotic period after the Mexican-American War.

Overmyer-Velazquez, Mark. *Visions of the Emerald City: Modernity, Tradition, and the Formation of Porfirian Oaxaca, Mexico.* 2006. US$22.95. Controversial local son and Mexican dictator Porfirio Díaz (1876-1911) made Oaxacan development a focus of his administration. How Oaxaca would develop, however, was a course Oaxaqueños would decide for themselves.

Photography

Albro, Ward S., and Defibaugh, Denis (photographer). *The Day of the Dead /Dia De Los Muertos.* 2007. US$39.95. This full-color coffee table book has amazing shots and insightful text covering the Day of the Dead.

Jaffe, Mathew and Haden, Judith Cooper. *Oaxaca: The Spirit of Mexico.* 2002. US$59.88. Vivid narration and outstanding photography capture endless facets of Oaxaca's city life.

Mendoza, Mary Jane Gagnier, and Mendoza, Ariel (photographer). *Oaxaca Celebration: Family, Food, and Fiestas in Teotitlian.* 2005. US$24.95. More than 100 photos of Día de los Muertos, Semana Santa, and other celebrations in Teotitlán

Travelogues

⊗ Sacks, Oliver. *Oaxaca Journal.* 2005. US$10.95. Neurologist, amateur botanist, and off-beat essayist Oliver Sacks went on a fern-hunting expedition to Oaxaca, and found so much more.

Lawrence, D. H. *Mornings in Mexico.* 1927. US$24.95. Classic essays from a great writer, who was actually in Oaxaca to work on another manuscript. Ahem. The "Marketplace" essay is worth the price of admission.

Outdoors

Beletsky, Les. *Tropical Mexico: The Ecotravellers' Wildlife Guide.* 1999. US$65. One of the best wildlife-spotting guides available for Southern Mexico (well, birders have more choices), this 512-page tome specifically discusses Oaxacan species, including mammals, amphibians, reptiles, birds, and amphibians.

Beletsky, Les; Barrett, Priscilla (illus.); Beadle, David (illus.); and Dennis, David (illus.). *Travellers' Wildlife Guides Southern Mexico: The Cancun Region, Yucatan Peninsula, Oaxaca, Chiapas, and Tabasco.* 2006. US$27.95. This hefty wildlife spotting guide includes all sorts of area animals.

Edwards, Ernest Preston, and Butler, Edward Murrell (illus.). *A Field Guide to the Birds of Mexico and Adjacent Areas: Belize, Guatemala, and El Salvador.* 1998. US$22.95. A classic guide with the 850 most common bird species in the region.

Forcey, John M. *Birds & Birding in Oaxaca.* 1998. US$10. The locally published birding book covering local birding sites (San Felipe del Agua, Yagül) is available at Amate Books in Oaxaca City.

Howell, Steve N. G., and Webb, Sophie. *A Guide to the Birds of Mexico and Northern Central America.* 1995. US$49.95. This serious field guide has 1,010 pages and 1,070 species, with illustrations and information.

Van Perlo, Ber. *Birds of Mexico and Central America.* 2006. US$29.95. Some 1,500 species are described and illustrated in a more portable 336 pages.

General Index

Lodging by Price

Inexpensive ($)   Up to US$50
Moderate ($$)   US$50 to US$100
Expensive ($$$)   US$100 to US$200
Very Expensive ($$$$) US$200 and up

City of Oaxaca

Inexpensive
Hotel Florida, 55
Hotel Posada del Tía, 55
Oaxaca Learning Center, 55

Inexpensive to Moderate
Casa Arnel, 55
Casa Azucenas, 55
Posada Catarina, 55
Posada del Centro, 55

Moderate
Casa de las Bugambilias, 52–53
Casa de los Abuelos, 45–46
Casa de los Frailes, 46
Casa Pereyra, 47
Hospederia La Reja, 46
Hostal Casa del Sótano, 48
Hotel Cazomalli, 48–49
Hotel Las Mariposas, 54
Hotel Los Olivos and Spa, 50–51
Hotel Monte Albán, 51–52
La Casa de los Sabores, 53
Oaxaca Bed & Breakfast Ollin, 54

Moderate to Expensive
Casa Colonial, 52
Casa los Cantaros, 54
Encanto Jalatlaco, 54
Estancia de Valencia, 53
Hotel Angel Inn, 56
Hotel Marqués del Valle, 51
La Casa de Mis Recuerdos, 53
La Catrina de Acalá, 47

Expensive
Casa Conzatti Hotel, 45
Casa de los Milagros, 53
Casa de Sierra Azul, 46
Fiesta Inn, 47–48
Hostal los Pilares, 48
Suites Regente, 56

Expensive to Very Expensive
Casa Antigua, 44–45
Casa de Siete Balcones, 46–47
Hotel de la Parra Oaxaca, 49

Very Expensive
Casa Cid de León, 45
El Camino Real Oaxaca, 43–44
Hostal las Cúpulas, 54, 56
Hotel Hacienda and Spa Los Laureles, 49–50
La Casa de Adobe, 54
Posada Casa Oaxaca, 52

Central Valleys

Inexpensive
Cabinas Guacamaya, 107
El Rincón de San Agustín Etla, 107
Hotel and Restaurant Mitla, 107–8
Hotel El Angel, 108
Hotel Restaurant Guish Bac, 108
Hotel Restaurant Regis, 108
Hotel Rey David, 104–5
La Calenda, 108
Las Granadas Bed & Breakfast, 106
Posada El Niño, 108
Restaurant y Hotel El Pacifico, 108
San Miguel El Valle y El Carriza, 107
Tourist Yu'u Santa Ana del Valle, 107
Villa de Etla, 107
Zapotec Hotel and Restaurant, 108

Moderate
Cabañas Puesto del Sol, 108
Casa Linda, 105
Hotel Don Cenobio, 104

Moderate to Expensive
Casa Raab, 105–6
Casa Sagrada, 105

Pacific Coast

Inexpensive
Cabañas Playa Cangrejo, 154
Finca Cafetalera El Refugio, 179
Finca El Pacifico, 180
Finca Monte Carlo, 180
Hotel Carmona, 155
Hotel Fatima, 149
Hotel La Cabaña, 148
Hotel Las Gaviotas, 155
Hotel Montserrat, 147
Hotel Tucán, 149
Huatulco Trailer Park, 147
La Escobilla, 152
La Ventanilla, 153
Lachiguiri, 152
Mexico Lindo y Que Rico, 147
Rancho El Sagrado, 181
Presidencia de San Ysidro Roguia, 120
Santa Ana, 152–53
Santiago Jocotepec, 153
Villa Mozart y Macondo, 149

Inexpensive to Moderate
Barlovento Hotel, 149
Hostal Frida, 149
Hotel Altagracia, 154
Hotel Flamboyant, 147
Hotel Ines, 149
Hotel María Mixteca, 147
Hotel Oasis, 142
Hotel Puesta del Sol, 148–49
Hotel Vinisa, 154
Shambhala, 149–50

Dining by Price

Inexpensive ($)	Up to US$5
Moderate ($$)	US$5 to US$10
Expensive ($$$)	$10 to $20
Very Expensive ($$$$)	US$20 or more

City of Oaxaca

Inexpensive
Casa de Tio Güero, 59–60
Verde Aceituna, 51

Inexpensive to Moderate
Escapularío, 60

Moderate
El Bicho Pobre, 58
El Retablo Restaurant, 56
La Olla, 61
Las Quince Letras, 61–62

Moderate to Expensive
Casa de la Abuela, 64
Como Agua pa' Chocolate, 64
Hostal los Pilares, 48
La Hierba Santa, 61
Los Pacos, 61
Restaurant Catedral, 62
Restaurante los Danzantes, 62
Terranova, 64
1254 Marco Polo, 58
Yu Ne Nisa, 63
Zandunga, 63

Expensive
Casa Antigua, 45
El Asador Vasco, 64
La Toscana, 63
Temple Restaurant and Bar, 62

Expensive to Very Expensive
El Che, 60
Trastévere, 63

Very Expensive
Casa Oaxaca, 60
La Biznaga, 58–59
La Catrina de Acalá, 47
Los Cypreses, 50

Central Valleys

Inexpensive
Hotel Restaurant Guish Bac, 108
La Calenda, 108
Restaurant Familiar Los Alebrijes, 109
Restaurant La Montaña, 112
Restaurant Rayita del Sol, 112

Inexpensive to Moderate
Azucena Zapoteca, 111
Caldo de Piedra, 110
La Taberna de los Duendes, 111–12

Moderate to Expensive
Cabañas Puesto del Sol, 108
El Patio, 110
Hacienda San Agustín, 111
Hacienda Santa Martha de Barcéna, 111
La Capilla de Zaachila, 109
La Perla, 110
Monte Albán, 125
Restaurant El Descanso, 110
Restaurant Tlamanalli, 110–11

Pacific Coast

Inexpensive
Isla del Gallo Restaurante, 176
Restaurante Roca Blanca, 174

Inexpensive to Moderate
Las Margaritas, 161
Restaurant Almendres, 142
Rollo Chino, 159
Shambhala, 149

Moderate
Cabañas Punta Placer, 147
El Alquimista, 146
La Calenda, 159–60
La Galera, 160
Terra Cotta Restaurant and Café, 143

Moderate to Expensive
El Grillo Marinero Restaurant-Bar, 158
La Dolce Vita, 160
La Torre, 161–62
Restaurant Bar Doña Celia Lobster House, 158
Restaurant Casa Grande, 156–57
Restaurant Scarú, 157
Restaurant Viña del Mar, 157
Santa Fe Restaurant, 150

Moderate to Very Expensive
Sabor a Mar, 161

Expensive
El Sabor de Oaxaca, 159
Guadua, 160–61
L'Echalote, 144

Expensive to Very Expensive
Il Giardino de Papa, 158
La Bohéme, 157–58
Las Cúpulas Bar, 145
Las Tugas Cozhína, 150–51
Restaurant Onix, 158–59

Very Expensive
Azul Profundo, 143
Chez Binni, 143

Dining by Cuisine

City of Oaxaca

Argentine Steak
El Che, 60

Asian
Casablanca, 63
Super Oriental y Cafetéria Nagomi, 64
Sushi Express Kin Su, 64
Sushi Itto, 64

Bakeries
CentroBamby Pan, 64
La Carmelita, 64
La Pasión, 65
Pan & Co., 64–65
Pandería Fidel, 65

Cafés
Arabia Café, 65
Café Brújula, 65
Café del Teatro Macedonio Alcal, 65–66
Café La Antigua, 66
Café Royal, 66
Café-Bakery La Visconia, 65
Como Agua pa' Chocolate, 64
Italian Coffee Company, 65

Fast Food
Itanoní: Flowering of Corn, 68
La Antequera, 67
La Gran Torta, 67–68
Mall Plaza del Valle, 68
Tacos Alvaro, 68

International
Casa Antigua, 45
Los Cypreses, 50

Istmeño
Zandunga, 63

Italian
La Toscana, 63
Trastévere, 63

Latin Fusion
Temple Restaurant and Bar, 62

Mexican Fusion
La Biznaga, 58–59

Oaxacan
Casa Antigua, 45
Casa de la Abuela, 64
Casa de Tio Güero, 59–60
El Asador Vasco, 64
El Bicho Pobre, 58
El Retablo Restaurant, 56
Escapularío, 60
Hostal los Pilares, 48
La Casa de Adobe, 54
La Catrina de Acal, 47
La Hierba Santa, 61
La Olla, 61
Las Quince Letras, 61–62
Los Cypreses, 50
Los Pacos, 61

Restaurant Catedral, 62
Terranova, 64

Oaxacan, Contemporary
Restaurante los Danzantes, 62

Oaxacan, Gourmet
Casa Oaxaca, 60

Pizza
Casa de Maria Lombardo, 66
El Sagrario, 66
Pizza La Rustica, 66
Vieja Lira, 66

Seafood
1254 Marco Polo, 58

Spanish Basque
El Asador Vasco, 64

Vegetarian
Casa de Tio Güero, 59–60
Flor de Loto, 68
Manantial, 68
Naturel, 68
100% Natural, 68
Trigo y Miel, 68
Verde Aceituna, 51, 68

Central Valley

Barbecue
La Calenda, 108

Cafés
Café Express, 112
El Valle Café, 112
Sacred Bean Café, 112

International
La Taberna de los Duendes, 111–12

Oaxacan
Azucena Zapoteca, 111
Cabañas Puesto del Sol, 108
Caldo de Piedra, 110
El Patio, 110
La Capilla de Zaachila, 109
La Perla, 110
Restaurant El Descanso, 110
Restaurant Familiar Los Alebrijes, 109
Restaurant La Montaña, 112
Restaurant Rayita del Sol, 112
Restaurant Tlamanalli, 110–11

Oaxacan, Buffet
Hacienda San Agustín, 111
Hacienda Santa Martha de Barcéna, 111

Seafood
La Perla, 110

Steak
La Caballeriza, 111